Cannibal Translation

FLASHPOINTS

The FlashPoints series is devoted to books that consider literature beyond strictly national and disciplinary frameworks and that are distinguished both by their historical grounding and by their theoretical and conceptual strength. Our books engage theory without losing touch with history and work historically without falling into uncritical positivism. FlashPoints aims for a broad audience within the humanities and the social sciences concerned with moments of cultural emergence and transformation. In a Benjaminian mode, FlashPoints is interested in how literature contributes to forming new constellations of culture and history and in how such formations function critically and politically in the present. Series titles are available online at http://escholarship.org/uc/flashpoints.

A complete list of titles begins on page 321.

Cannibal Translation

Literary Reciprocity in Contemporary Latin America

Isabel C. Gómez

NORTHWESTERN UNIVERSITY PRESS | EVANSTON, ILLINOIS

Northwestern University Press
www.nupress.northwestern.edu

Printed in the United States of America

10 9 8 7 6 5 4 3 2 1

Library of Congress Cataloging-in-Publication Data

Names: Gómez, Isabel C., author.
Title: Cannibal translation : literary reciprocity in contemporary Latin America / Isabel C Gómez.
Other titles: FlashPoints (Evanston, Ill.)
Description: Evanston, Illinois : Northwestern University Press, 2023. | Series: Flashpoints | Includes bibliographical references and index.
Identifiers: LCCN 2023002096 | ISBN 9780810145955 (paperback) | ISBN 9780810145962 (cloth) | ISBN 9780810145979 (ebook)
Subjects: LCSH: Latin American literature—Translations—History and criticism. | Translating and interpreting—Philosophy.
Classification: LCC PQ7081 .G5676 2023 | DDC 860.998—dc23/eng/20230124
LC record available at https://lccn.loc.gov/2023002096

Contents

Illustrations

Thirteen Theses on Cannibal Translation

1. Cannibal translation devours texts, norms, and taboos.
2. Digesting and recombining sources foreign and local, cannibal translation allows all elements to remain visible, in process, held in common, unassimilated.
3. Nobody owns cannibal translations: signed collectively, they resist resolving into private property.
4. Responding to a history of the Eurocentric gaze demonizing Latin American culture, Latin American thinkers reclaim the figure of the cannibal as self-defining and creative.
5. Regions in the wake of colonialism include multilingual histories; cannibal translation does not recognize languages as stable or contained by national borders.
6. The so-called original was never stable either; cannibal translation shows its process, presents works as unfinished, partial, messy, open.
7. Cannibal translators cannot be invisible; they operate from a position, a vector, a hunger.
8. Absent a muse of translation, cannibal translators find their muse in other translators.

9. "Translation," from *translatio* (to carry across), is often too limited and unidirectional; cannibal translations go by other labels to emphasize reciprocity, a return.
10. Centered on the creative act, cannibal translation still draws from critical work to be thickly descriptive, supported and informed by linguistic histories and language politics.
11. Cannibal translations demand to be read *as translations*: readers can never passively forget the translator's mediation; they may even think the author is a heteronym.
12. Although it might share qualities with its source text, a cannibal translation will also unmake or betray those qualities, putting genre or authorship into question.
13. Cannibal translation is loving, expresses admiration, attention, and care.

Acknowledgments

Scholarly writing, like literary translation, can never be a solo act. So many friends, interlocutors, and family members have nourished me as I developed this project.

I am incredibly grateful to all my intellectual mentors for their guidance, feedback, and conversation over the years: Efraín Kristal for introducing me to translation studies; José Luiz Passos for sparking my fascination with Brazilian poetry; Barbara Fuchs for her encouragement to pursue literary theory; Suzanne Jill Levine for drawing attention to translation practice as a site of critical intervention; Anna More for bringing me into sorjuanista scholarship which has given me new research directions; Jorge Marturano, Benjamin Moser, Christopher Mott, and Maarten van Delden for their courses at UCLA which inspired ideas for this project; Michelle Clayton, who nurtured my interest in poetry and helped me place this book with the FlashPoints series; Agnes Lugo-Ortiz, who guided my first forays in literary research as an undergraduate; Sandra Bermann, for getting me involved in the International Comparative Literature Association, a space where I could share work in progress with interlocutors from across the world; Esther Allen, for appreciating my interest in the detailed work of translators; and the late, great Michael Heim, who taught me what translation practice could mean within a scholarly life.

This book owes much to Augusto de Campos: for his expansive and creative translation praxis, which has been my muse in the writing, for showing me his personal archives during a visit to São Paulo, and for generously granting me permission to reproduce many of his concrete poems and translations.

Sincerest thanks go to all the libraries and archives I had the opportunity to visit during the process, and everyone who made my work there possible: the Biblioteca Ayacucho publishing house and all those who welcomed me there: executive director Luis Edgar Páez and editors Elizabeth Coronado, Shirley Fernández, and Daniel Pérez Astros; citations from letters held in the archive at the Biblioteca Ayacucho are included with permission; Jessica Gordon-Burroughs, who introduced me to the archival materials held in their collection and invited me to travel to Caracas with her; the Casa das Rosas in São Paulo and everyone who helped me make the most of my time there: Maria José Coelho, Júlio Mendonça, and Marcelo Tápia; citations from the Haroldo de Campos Collection are included with permission; the Fondo de Cultura Económica in Mexico City, María Antonieta Hernández Rojas for facilitating my visit to the publishing house archives, and Heriberto Sánchez for all his help obtaining permissions for citing from FCE publications; the Houghton Library Special Collections at Harvard University where I consulted the E. E. Cummings Papers to better understand the translation praxis of his many translators; the Carmen Balcells Literary Agency and Cristina Pacheco, widow of José Emilio Pacheco, for permission to cite his poems and his approximations; and Adriana Varejão for kindly allowing me to feature her artwork on the cover and Laura Dias Leite, studio manager at the artist's ateliê in Rio de Janeiro, for her assistance.

I feel so fortunate that my research has benefited from generous material and institutional support: from the American Council of Learned Societies through a fall 2019 fellowship, from the American Comparative Literature Association through the Helen Tartar First Book Subvention Award, and from the International Comparative Literature Association through the ECARE First Book Subvention Prize. To bring the project to fruition, I deeply appreciate the work of everyone at Northwestern University Press and the FlashPoints Series, especially my editor, Faith Wilson Stein, series editor, Susan Gillman for your belief in my project, my two anonymous readers for your generative feedback, copy editor Christi Stanworth, and the whole production team for creating this book object even with the challenges inherent in presenting visual poetry in three different languages.

My *colegas* in the Latin American and Iberian Studies Department gave me the warmest welcome to New England, and I appreciate Nayelli

Castro-Ramírez, María Cisterna-Gold, Reyes Coll-Tellechea, Susana Domingo-Amestoy, Peggy Fitzgerald, Susan Gauss, Nino Kebadze, and Diego Mansilla for making our department a place where our teaching and research can thrive together. Many other people at UMass Boston have also supported my writing process, and my gratitude goes to Sari Edelstein and Aaron Lecklider for creating space for my work in the Center for Humanities, Culture, and Society; the Mellon Grant Faculty Advisory Board (FAB), especially our leaders, Betsy Klimasmith and Bonnie Miller, for their tireless advocacy for the humanities on our campus; María Carvajal Regidor and Florianne (Bo) Jimenez for starting the Faculty of Color Writing Group; Brian Halley for his kind help preparing my book proposal; Alex Mueller for his mentorship through the Junior Faculty Research Seminar as well as my whole cohort and other participants in the Junior Faculty Writing Group for workshopping early portions of my manuscript. And my heartfelt thanks to all the UMass Boston students I have been privileged to work with, especially those in the Translation Studies Track: you always had such great questions about my research, and you always reminded me of how exciting it is to be writing a book.

My process was greatly enriched by many opportunities to share research in progress, and I thank those who made that possible: Leah Middlebrook and the Poetry, Poetics, and Myth Speaker Series at the University of Oregon; the Tepoztlán Summer Institute 2017 cohort; Ellen Elias-Bursać and Mark Schafer with the Boston Literary Translators Group; Marlene Hansen Esplin and Emron Esplin for their generous invitation to visit the Translation Studies Working Group at Brigham Young University in 2019; Héctor Zavala and the UNAM-Boston network; Patrícia Lino and the UCLA Center for Brazilian Studies; Youngmin Kim for including me in the Symposium on the Ethics of Translation in World Literature with the Korea East-West Comparative Literature Association; and Joseph Ford for inviting me to deliver a Convocation Seminar through the London Intercollegiate Network for Comparative Studies.

Many brilliant friends shared space with me as I worked on this project. I deeply appreciate my book-writing *comadres* Maia Gil'Adí, Renee Hudson, and Natali Valdez, with whom I spent many rewarding days of parallel laptop time followed by delicious meals. I cannot thank enough everyone who lovingly read pieces of this book in draft form, especially Kristal Bivona, Ricardo A. Wilson II, Nayelli Castro-Ramírez, Daniel Cooper, Jenny Marie Forsythe, Roanne Kantor, Rebecca Kosick, Janet

Hendrickson, Corine Tachtiris, and Luigi Patruno—your gracious feedback and *ánimo* helped me refine my ideas and keep pursuing the best way to express them.

My practice of cowriting started in graduate school with the Revolutionary Women, a writing group at UCLA composed of women of color pursuing doctorates in the humanities; thanks to Juliann Anesi, Carolina Beltrán, Andretta Lyle, Kimberly Mack, Marilu Medrado, Yvette Martínez-Vu, Erica Onugha, Sandra Ruiz, Ester Trujillo, Brandy Underwood, and Joyce Pualani Warren for cheering me on from the start; and in remembrance of our departed member Mariana Grajales: we miss you, *querida*. I learned the perfect combination of writing and cooking together from the Interdisciplinary Humanities Graduate Student Writing Retreat Group: my fellow organizers Jenny Marie Forsythe and Roni Hirsch (also known as Noodle Group) and members Shir Alon, Nasia Anam, Gelare Khoshgozaran, and Lilith Mahmud. I feel so lucky we were able to do so much writing together in beautiful natural settings thanks to our host, the University of California Natural Reserve System (UCNRS), which let us stay at the La Kretz Field Station in Malibu, the Sedgwick Reserve in Santa Ynez, the Sweeney Granite Mountains Research Center in the Mohave Desert, the Landels-Hill Big Creek Reserve in Big Sur, and the James San Jacinto Mountains Reserve in Idyllwild. During pandemic, my habit of writing in company expanded to include online spaces: I am so grateful to Charles Petersen for starting a remote writing group in 2020, and to all the Chronophages, especially other regulars Brian Goodman, Erin Hutchinson, Daniel Immerwahr, Cecilia Weddell, and Amy Zanoni—we devoured many hours together in writerly solidarity, and I could not have finished without the supportive coworking space and the jumping-jacks. My sincere gratitude goes out to all my other friends and collaborators on projects large and small, everyone not already mentioned with whom I have shared study spaces, after-library hangs, yoga classes, sparkling conversations, poetry readings, dance parties, pep talks, and more: Dani Álvarez-Gavela, Ione Barrows, Amber Bryant Williams, Tommy Connors, Zoë Cullen, Katrina Dodson, Magdalena Edwards, James Flynn, Heather Gillers, Audrey Harris, Bizzy Hemphill, Molly Hirschfeld, Ben Kain, Ana Paulina Lee, Katie Lennard, Anna Lewis, Dana Linda, Rebecca Lippman, Nicole Louie, Meagan Manas, Rose McCarron, Kevin McDonald, Jake Mensch, Pam Mensch, Erin Mizrahi, Ben Oviatt, Amanda Reilly Waldman, Daniel C. Remein, and Stephanie Wolahan.

I end by thanking my family, where my love of reading and writing began: my mother Diana, my father Greg, and my sister Angelina; the extended Gómez and Wyneken families; and in memory of my grandparents Phyllis Williams Gómez, Henry Enrique Galván Gómez, Martin L. Wyneken IV, and Cherise Brosz Wyneken, who gave me my middle name; I love you all so much.

Thank you, everyone.

Cannibal Translation

INTRODUCTION

Routes, Reading Practices, and Recipes for Cannibal Translation

"Cannibalism" as a cultural trope of art-making has a long critical legacy in Latin America, from the 1920s Brazilian avant-garde movement known as *modernismo* to its reactivation by Brazilian writers as a precursor for the 1950s concrete poetry movement. A touchstone for literary theory, Walter Benjamin imagined an adoringly anthropophagous scholar in "The Critic's Technique in Thirteen Theses" (1925–26), writing that "genuine polemics approach a book as lovingly as a cannibal spices a baby."[1] Framing a specifically Brazilian mode of dialogic creative production, Haroldo de Campos places this line from Benjamin as an epigraph to his essay "Anthropophagous Reason" (1981) and expands on the task of the cannibal critic to include anthologizing as another mode of transcultural digestion, claiming, "The cannibal was a 'polemicist' (from the Greek *polemos*, meaning 'struggle, combat'), but he was also an 'anthologist'—he devoured only the enemies he considered courageous, taking their marrow and protein to fortify and renew his own natural energies."[2] His brother and fellow founder of the Brazilian concrete poetry movement, Augusto de Campos, draws on the work of Oswald de Andrade, a Brazilian contemporary of Benjamin's, to insist that literary cannibalism is loving and destructive at once: he introduces his translation collection *Verso, reverso, controverso* (1978) by claiming "My way of loving the ancient poets is to translate them.

Or to swallow them, according to the Cannibalist Law of Oswald de Andrade: I'm only interested in what is not mine . . . the untranslated and the untranslatable."[3] For Haroldo, cannibalism patterns a polemic method to anthologize and theorize tradition; for Augusto, a translation practice.

Yet their artistic reclaiming of symbolic cannibalism practiced by Indigenous Brazilians only comes after centuries of colonial vilification. The "cannibal" as a figure of taboo, a human who eats other humans, has its linguistic roots in coloniality. The word *caníbales* first appeared in the diary of Cristóbal Colón on November 23, 1492; the term vacillated, yet stuck to both the region of the Caribbean and the Carib people, depicted as a threatening minority to be distinguished from a peaceful Arawak majority.[4] After repeated resignification by the Brazilian avant-garde and Latin American cultural critics seeking autochthonous epistemological roots, "cannibalism" came to mean a strategy of encounter based in self-determination. No longer a demonized other, the "cannibal" is now central to a range of cultural concerns in the American hemisphere. For example, in the face of the white supremacist *arielismo* of postindependence Latin American thinkers such as José Enrique Rodó, Cuban intellectual Roberto Fernández Retamar demoted the spirit Ariel and elevated the cannibal Caliban as the central Latin American identity position and producer of decolonial political thought in his essay "Caliban" (1971).[5] Creative experiment through the structuring device of cannibalism had vast repercussions in Brazil, as in the cultural movement of music and art known as Tropicália, inspired by 1960s counterculture and other popular forms in Brazil and the Caribbean.[6] For Zita Nunes, the figure of the cannibal and what she calls the "remainder" left behind to evidence the cannibal scene serves to understand the nonincorporation of Black citizens in Brazil and the United States.[7] In short, the cannibal trope has many cultural afterlives; this book examines the impact of the Brazilian-born concept of cannibal translation as it travels into Spanish and into a broader Latin American literary practice.

Drawing on an archive of translations and translation-process materials, *Cannibal Translation* illuminates understudied translation projects to demonstrate their critical, creative potential for engaging in cultural exchange based in reciprocity and nonassimilation. Although all are celebrated writers, the translations by Augusto and Haroldo de Campos, Rosario Castellanos, Clarice Lispector, Héctor Olea, José Emilio Pacheco, Octavio Paz, and Ángel Rama have not garnered equal attention.

These authors deploy alternative labels for their translations to emphasize the creative work involved: untranslation, version, transcreation, transspeaking, approximation, and porous prose. By paying attention to these terms that resist the normative pressure of translation, I show how Latin American poet-translators contend with the underexamined assumption that the concept of translation is translatable. This approach follows Robert J. C. Young, who reminds us of the multiplicity of translation concepts from different traditions, times, and places, and Maria Tymoczko, who links the hegemony of the English word "translation" with theorical and practical epistemicide erasing translation practices from outside dominant cultures.[8] I choose "cannibal translation" as an umbrella term to unite diverse translation practices, connecting them through the Brazilian tradition and providing grounds for comparison among different critical translation projects from Latin America. While these individual labels may be as disparate as their authors or source texts, I read them together to illuminate a pan–Latin American network that produces its own translation theories. Executed in Latin American varieties of Spanish and Portuguese, this cannibal translation archive destabilizes the idea of textual originals to invent practices that reject what Roman Jakobson calls "translation proper," between two languages.[9] The translators studied herein challenge the enduring conventions of "properness" in translation, which also tend to uphold false perceptions of languages as naturally discrete or cleanly divided along lines of nation or ethnicity.[10] By drawing on archival materials to emphasize the praxis and visibility of these cannibal translators and their creative strategies, I spotlight the routes traveled by this Brazilian translation theory and offer reading practices modeled on the loving dissection of cannibal translation, modes of apprehending and questioning the mediation, positionality, and political situatedness of literary works in translation.

CANNIBAL TRANSLATION ROUTES

In 1928, Brazilian poet Oswald de Andrade inaugurated the new literary journal *Revista de Antropofagia* with the explosive, celebratory "Cannibalist Manifesto." This key document of the avant-garde artistic movement known as Brazilian *modernismo* championed an independent Brazilian culture based not on imitation of European aesthetics but on creative digestion and recombination. With aphoristic aplomb,

Oswald's text devours, reverses, and reconfigures a series of Eurocentric cultural norms including conquest ("Those who came here weren't crusaders. They were fugitives from a civilization we are eating"); patriarchal settler colonialism ("in the matriarchy of Pindorama [an Indigenous Tupi name for the land now known as Brazil]"); Western historiography and temporality (he dates his manifesto "In Piratininga, in the 347th Year of the Swallowing of Bishop Sardinha"); normative language ("we never had grammars"); and the Cartesian mind/body split ("The spirit refuses to conceive of a spirit without a body").[11] The speaker repeatedly ridicules and devours received concepts and symbols of authority: "I asked a man what the Law was. He answered that it was the guarantee of the exercise of possibility. That man was named Balder Dash. I ate him."[12] Oswald drew from Tupi-Guarani cannibalism to metaphorically revalue their practice of incorporating worthily defeated enemies into one's own body, to view cannibalism as an honorable relationship with the other and use it as a guiding technique for Brazilian art-making.

The "Cannibalist Manifesto" by Oswald de Andrade marks only one of the three phases of Brazilian *modernismo*.[13] Yet decades later, the founders of the Brazilian concrete poetry movement, Augusto de Campos, Haroldo de Campos, and Décio Pignatari, elevated Oswald above all other Brazilian *modernistas*, naming him among their "Forerunners" in their own manifesto. The "Pilot Plan for Concrete Poetry" (1958) defines "verbivocovisual" poetics, in which "sound, visual form, [and] semantic charge" all work together.[14] Stylistically, they take from Oswald the condensed form of his poetry, what they call his "poemas-comprimidos" or his "pill-poems"; methodologically, they draw from Oswald's use of found-text citation and his inventive written projection of the orality of Brazilian Portuguese.[15] In his introduction to a 1975 reprinting of the *Revista de Antropofagia*, Augusto again claims Oswald's cannibalism revitalized Brazilian literature more than any other *modernista*.[16] Moreover, he asserts that the creative gesture of *antropofagia* finds full expression only beginning with his own generation of concrete poets.[17] Yet Augusto eventually laments that their best efforts did not salvage the savage energy of Oswald's "Cannibalist Manifesto"; in 2011, he quips that "cannibalism has been turned back into beef" at the hands of scholars and students rather than philosophers or poets.[18] But what about translators?

In *Cannibal Translation* I demonstrate that this literary practice still has teeth in Latin America, in the work of translator-poets who devour norms of translation the way Oswald's cannibal devours Balder Dash, the man who defines the law. After the introduction maps the intellectual history surrounding the "cannibal" and defines cannibal translation as a reciprocal translation praxis cultivated in Latin America, my chapters trace the routes of cannibal translation from Brazil through Mexico and into other Hispanophone spaces, analyzing how major writers connect, compete, conspire, and copy one another in a Latin Americanist translation zone.

The "Cannibalist Manifesto" by Oswald de Andrade has an unresolved tension at its heart: Is "cannibalism" a procedure specific to Brazilian identity formation or a broader strategy of decolonial art-making? Readers inside and outside Brazil largely understand the manifesto as a structuring device for the Brazilian nation, what Benedito Nunes calls a "triumph of our intellectual autonomy."[19] The new Brazilian intellectual devours the Portuguese colonizer and all European artistic traditions, then combines foreign materials with local qualities to form a national self. Though mutable, always incorporating new elements, this cannibal subject does anchor a national identity. Yet Sara Castro-Klarén's genealogical reading of Oswald's "Cannibalist Manifesto" demonstrates that the Indigenous Tupi structure of cannibalism refuses dialectical synthesis, opposes national identity formation, and refutes the modern notion of narcissistic incorporation. Instead, cannibalism is an operation of alteration, of becoming.[20] In excavating the cannibal translation practices of the Brazilian concrete poets and their collaborators in Spanish America, I land on the side of Castro-Klarén: the practice does not resolve into "being" Brazilian or "being" a translation; rather, it continues "becoming."[21] Cannibal translation emphasizes that translation is always becoming, never resolving into being, never wistfully looking back to any stable point of origin.

The internal inconsistency within the "Cannibalist Manifesto" is matched and echoed by the contested reception of "cannibal translation" as an adequate label for Haroldo de Campos's Brazilian translation theory or as a metaphor for decolonial translation writ large. Haroldo himself sets up this tension. His essays identify a counter-hegemonic tradition of Brazilian translation practice, reading the Brazilian literary canon backward through Oswald's "Cannibalist Manifesto" to locate cannibal translators in earlier times, including the Baroque or Romantic periods. Haroldo tracks a legacy of "anthropophagous reason" in Brazil, beginning with Gregório de Matos da Guerra (1636–96), whom he champions as "the first experimental cannibal in our poetry" for his assertive translation-qua-rewriting of Iberian Baroque sources.[22] In another essay he defends the work of Manuel Odorico Mendes (1799–1864) who translated the *Odyssey* creatively, inventing new compound words and interpolating phrases from the early modern Portuguese lyricist Luís Vaz de Camões (ca. 1524–80) into Homer's verses, gestures viewed as excessive by the scholarly reception.[23] While other critics such as Antonio Candido leave Matos or Mendes out of the Brazilian canon, and those like Sílvio Júlia disparage their efforts as derivative plagiarism, Haroldo ultimately celebrates both translators as precursors.

Yet although Haroldo is the one to identify the Brazilian countertradition of cannibal translation, his brother Augusto uses these ideas most explicitly in his translation practice, starting with the E. E. Cummings poems he presents in what he calls the new "jaguar language" of Brazilian Portuguese, as I will explicate in chapter 1. Haroldo himself never labels his works "cannibalistic"; instead, he develops another concept with his neologism *transcriação*, or "transcreation." He first defines creative translation in the early essay "Translation as Creation and Criticism" (1962), then coins the term "transcreation" itself in "Tradução, Ideologia e História" (1983), where he clarifies that he means transcreation to respond only to intratextual structures, a creative translation that preserves aesthetic information from the source text.[24] To be clear: "Transcreation does not mean free adaptation of the original but extreme fidelity. . . . Creativity here means being able to find solutions within the semiotic scope of the poem, and not outside it," as Thelma Médici Nóbrega and John Milton assert.[25] Acknowledging that other operations might add functional or transhistorical considerations reliant on extratextual factors, Haroldo often publishes transcreations in editorial packages with additional extraliterary material. As Odile Cisneros demonstrates, in the 1980s Haroldo began to transition from an intratextual vision of translation as transcreation into a more capacious and politicized category.[26] For example, in the case of *Transblanco* studied in chapter 2, Haroldo's transcreation of Octavio Paz's poem *Blanco* centers the collection, but the two poet-translators supplement the poem with additional context, letters, drafts, photos, ephemera, and discussions of the political turmoil of their two countries as well as Haroldo's translation choices. In short, for Haroldo, the strictly re-creative act of transcreation produces a remainder—as Zita Nunes describes the bones left behind evidencing the cannibal scene. She reads these "remainders" as the unincorporated Black body, excised from national identity-building projects in Brazil and the United States.[27] One of the potential gains offered by the broader textual archive I deem cannibal translation might be the simultaneous acknowledgment of the epistemological violence that produces the unassimilated remainder while finding spaces to make more visible the cultural fragments left in the wake of coloniality.

As I demonstrate, both Augusto and Haroldo's translation practices remained inspired by Oswald's cannibalism—for Augusto, within translations themselves, for Haroldo, through the editorial packaging of transcreations. Yet scholarly reception tends toward an ambivalence in exploring the wider implications and applications of these translation praxes.[28] Instead, cannibal translation serves as an attractive if contested theoretical framework for Brazilian translation theory, often related back to the Eurocentric translation studies field rather than investigated as a practice that circulated in Latin America. The cannibal translation concept-metaphor is attractive because it champions a decolonial positionality and enables the translator to invert power relations.[29] Yet it is contested because some critics perceive the cannibal trope as too limited to sufficiently sum up Haroldo's translation theories, too reliant on prior literary knowledge to account for the majority of translation practice, or too close to the settler-colonial Eurocentric gaze denigrating an Indigenous other. Marcelo Tápia insists that "anthropophagy is not sufficient as a label for Haroldo's theory of translation," and in his scholarship on Haroldo's work, other terms including "transcreation" and "plagiotropia" take precedence.[30] John Milton calls the translation program envisioned by the de Campos brothers an "authoritarianism of rupture" for the demands this approach makes on readers and translators alike to both know and break with literary tradition.[31] As the Brazilian cannibal translation concept moves into an English-language comparative literature readership, it indeed risks placing Brazil and Latin America yet again as a passive object of study vulnerable to mislabeling, as Gabriel Borowski argues.[32] Certainly, "Caliban" by Retamar began the process of resignifying "cannibal" as a label.[33] And Augusto consistently reaffirms cannibalism as a crucial aesthetic philosophy, "Taboo until yesterday, today totem."[34] Yet the cannibal trope does have a violent history in the Americas of demonizing the Indigenous body or framing the Black body in the Caribbean as an object of labor and consumption.[35] By elevating cannibal translation as practice, an art and knowledge-making procedure rooted in becoming rather than being, I go beyond inverting the label or placing Brazilian translation theories in dialogue with European translation studies. Where the discourse of conquest saw the cannibal as a figure of primitive barbarism, Tupi epistemology framed the cannibal act as creative, generative, a vital element, a hinge between destruction and production.

The original Oswaldian deployment of Tupi cannibalism emphasizes a loving devouring not just of radical alterity but also of the nearby other, the competing neighbor, the sacred enemy.[36] Translations between spaces in Latin America—and translation theories developed in Brazil or Spanish America—have been ignored in favor of analyses that continue to center French, German, and English as languages of theory.[37] As Augusto writes: "Oswald's grave sin really was having written in Portuguese. Had he written in English or French, who knows maybe even in Spanish, his cannibalism would already be enshrined in the constellation of ideas."[38] I focus on cannibal translation not as the end result of work by Oswald, Haroldo, or Augusto but rather to examine the ongoing process of circulating and deploying these Brazilian ideas about translation to enable an intra–Latin American, South-South mutual readership.

Cannibal translation holds together the aesthetic concerns and the political stakes of a creative, nonassimilationist translation practice. While my formulation of cannibal translation is rooted in the Brazilian tradition, I am most interested in the routes these practices of translation and readership travel through Spanish-speaking Latin America and back to Brazil in a reciprocal exchange, in which cannibal translation concepts get applied to Brazilian literatures as they are translated into Spanish. Where some elevate cannibal translation theoretically as a decolonial philosophy of translation, others reject the cannibal label for Brazilian translation theories as indicative of a Eurocentric fascination with Brazil as a demonized other. Instead of choosing either of these options, I reengage with cannibal translation as a set of reading practices, which become visible when you look at the travels of this Brazilian translation theory into Spanish America and back again.

CANNIBAL TRANSLATION READING PRACTICES

When Augusto laments that in contemporary Brazilian letters Oswald's cannibalism has turned back into beef, he mourns a readership attuned to that counter-hegemonic gesture. Answering this call, I argue that cannibal translation can provide nutritive translation and reading practices not just to Brazilian poetics but also more broadly to the universal canon, scholarly field, practical problem, and mode of reading that has come to be known as world literature.

Emerging in the nineteenth century, the concept of *Weltliteratur* framed the decline of national literature as the advent of a larger marketplace of ideas, where the world and not the nation is the proving ground for a literary product. In 1827, Johann Wolfgang von Goethe mused to Johann Peter Eckermann that "poetry is the universal possession of mankind. . . . The epoch of world literature is at hand, and everyone must strive to hasten its approach."[39] This statement marks a fitting beginning for a fertile but unstable category: Goethe introduces world literature (or is it poetry?) as already the collective property of a readership of all mankind (a Martin Luther–esque fellowship of all mankind), something that exists but must also be brought into being. Marx and Engels soon baked the term into their own confection, defining *Weltliteratur* as the opposite of "national one-sidedness," the choice reading material of the bourgeoisie who bring "a cosmopolitan character to production and consumption in every country."[40] Goethe's vision of world literature gained practical grounding in the Marxist material historical notion that world literature was not only a class of products but also constitutive of the literary market itself.

Contemporary scholars have reactivated world literature as a framework for literary modernity through the lens of rapid globalization, which promises stability and prosperity but also exacerbates conflict and inequality. World literature serves as an avatar for either experience of globalization, a comparative literature application of Emmanuel Wallerstein's world systems theory.[41] As major contributors to this revival of world literature, Franco Moretti and Pascale Casanova both tend to reinforce the relationship between structures of international capitalism and patterns of literary influence. For Moretti, the "problem" of apprehending world literature could be addressed by "distant reading," in which the comparatist mines literary scholarship from national traditions worldwide to unearth points of convergence without direct engagement with literary texts. He tests a "law of literary evolution," deducing that peripheral cultures produce modern novels "not as an autonomous development but as a compromise between a western formal influence (usually French or English) and local materials."[42] Casanova did not see *Weltliteratur* as overtaking national literatures; rather, she believed that the nation-state had co-opted the literary imaginary to such an extent that readers naturalized a conflation of nation, language, and literature. Her project revives the transnational dimension of literature, drawing on Pierre Bourdieu's concept of the cultural field to demonstrate the independence of a world literary sphere from the world economic sphere. Yet her ideas of literary value still operate along economic terms: a "bourse" of literary value consecrates individual works, and "Paris became the capital of the literary world," the established center of a "World Republic of Letters" that interacts through competition and power over literary production far and wide.[43] Cannibal translation reverses Moretti's recipe and challenges Casanova's notion of value. The local cannibal devours materials from abroad: not as a compromise but as nutritive marrow incorporated into the forms already established by the local body; not to consecrate the source text but to transgress, deauthorize, and experiment with it.

Translation plays a central role in creating and comprehending world literature—and I place *Cannibal Translation* alongside Emily Apter's *Against World Literature* as another critical encounter between translation studies and world literary studies. This intervention was necessary from the moment Casanova enlisted translation in the creation, accrual, and distribution of literary value.[44] While not untrue, this perspective only underlines translations taking place in one direction, toward the capital of the World Republic of Letters, into French and now into English. Yet this only tells one kind of story, and translation studies, despite many calls to the contrary, remains impacted by this limited frame.[45] David Damrosch developed a more ecumenical model in *What Is World Literature?*, in which a work can become world literature "first by being read *as* literature; second, by circulating out into a broader world beyond its linguistic and cultural point of origin"; adding third condition borrowed from Claudio Guillén, that the traveling work must also be "actively present within a literary system beyond that of its original culture."[46] This mode of defining world literature—as traveling works that contribute to a literary system outside their initial frame—might then be examined through "different geo-linguistic standpoints," as Sandra Bermann encourages.[47] In building cannibal translation from the Tupi epistemology of cannibalism as an enactment of becoming, I also echo Pheng Cheah's idea that world literature is less about finding worlds than about making and remaking them.[48]

Cannibal translation, then, could simply be a mode of producing world literature or ideas of the world from Latin American perspectives. Yes, and cannibal translation might also offer the framework of world literature another way of doing and reading translations, other than Casanova's extractive model of literary capital, and other than Apter's untranslatability. For Apter, both fields of world literature and translation studies had been charged with lofty intellectual and institutional goals, including extricating comparative literature from methodological Eurocentrism and saving the place of the humanities in the neoliberal university through the practical applicability (read: marketability) of global citizenship and translation skills.[49] Yet she aims her book as a corrective to both fields which, in relation, still reinforce capitalist models. Apter contends that world literature could voice a more convincing anticapitalist critique by challenging "what it means to 'have' a literature or to lay claim to aesthetic property. . . . Translation, seen as authorized plagiarism, emerges as a form of creative property that belongs fully to no one."[50] She proposes "untranslatability" as a critical framework to center the political and philosophical stakes of what cannot or must not be translated.

With *Cannibal Translation* I amplify Apter in my insistence that translation need not operate through property-driven mindsets of extraction or accumulation—but I do so from the perspective of Haroldo and Augusto de Campos's reactivation of Oswald de Andrade's cannibal. For Haroldo de Campos in 1981, the cannibal was Brazil's response to Goethe's *Weltliteratur*.[51] Reading what Haroldo calls "anthropophagous reason" into Latin American translation practices, I position the cannibal translator opposite Goethe's evangelical or Casanova's merchant, both of whom treat translation as an extension of power or a return on investment: the cannibal translator, by contrast, devours everything and declares, "I am only interested in what is not mine."[52]

Cannibal Translation offers another approach to reconfiguring the relationship between translation studies and world literature away from the model in which translation serves to accumulate value on a world literary market. Instead of untranslatability, cannibal translations insist on devouring anything while also emphasizing the fragmentary, mediated nature of translation. Translation into Latin American varieties of Spanish and Portuguese provokes these theoretical insights precisely because they are not languages of the Casanovan capital of literary consecration. Instead, they interact from a translation zone of shared colonial linguistic experience. *Cannibal Translation* tests the hypothesis that studying translation theory from Latin America and translation practices into and between Latin American languages allows us to see world literature as formed through reciprocity rather than extraction or imitation, as a practice of holding literary worlds in process and in common rather than stabilizing or assimilating them into national emblems or transnational products.

Chapter 1 begins this argument in a comparative mode: I draw on letters and drafts to show that the process of translating E. E. Cummings into Augusto's Brazilian Portuguese and Paz's Mexican Spanish allowed these two Latin American poet-translators—in their own, divergent ways, working independently in the late 1950s and early 1960s—to creatively, lovingly destroy and remake their source texts and to theorize their process while they did so. Their translations benefit from the greater distance they have from the author and from Casanova's center of literary value. Conversely, the French and German translators of Cummings inhabit all the norms of "translation proper"; they maintain a pose of invisible servility, and their respectful correspondence and polite translations reproduce Anglo-American literary modernism as an expression of and export by liberal capitalist democracy in a Cold War environment.

In chapter 2, I turn from this moment of parallelism to one of direct contact. When they begin their correspondence in 1968, Octavio Paz comments to Haroldo de Campos with a tone of shame and regret that he previously had only read the concrete poets in translation, that he "had to go through English to meet you."[53] While this initial quip affirms the gravitational pull of Casanova's capital of the World Republic of Letters, the mutual translation projects by Paz and Haroldo mark an effort to shape an intra–Latin American reading practice independent of any external center. Framing translation between Mexican Spanish and Brazilian Portuguese as unique and decolonial, Haroldo meditates on the productive challenge this translation pair poses, to avoid the most obvious translation choices, instead creatively renewing the source text, as in his transcreation of Paz's poem *Blanco* as *Branco*. Haroldo and Paz ultimately publish both versions in a larger heterogeneous collection titled *Transblanco* (1986), a volume I am calling a cannibal translation because it includes years of letters between Paz and Haroldo, arguments over poetics, discussions of translation choices, and commentary on the 1968 Tlatelolco Massacre of student protestors in Mexico City, as it impacted both poet-translators.

Chapter 3 focuses on two female writer-translators to demonstrate the necessity of reading translations from an intersectional perspective that accounts for translator identity positions. Rosario Castellanos and Clarice Lispector were both celebrated writers in Mexico and Brazil, yet due to prejudices around gender and mastery, their translations were dismissed as poorly executed or immature when they practice the same cannibal translation techniques as their male contemporaries. To contest this legacy, I draw on language philosopher Willard Van Orman Quine's principle of "indeterminacy of translation" in which a potentially infinite number of "translation manuals" produce equally logical translations, which nevertheless are entirely disparate from one another.[54] Quine's principle shifts the object of study away from comparative descriptive analysis, in which the target text is put to the test of the source text. Instead, observing the patterns in a translation and drawing on extratextual materials that contribute to a "translation manual" allows me to analyze the translation's achievements within those terms of engagement. In the cases of Castellanos's and Lispector's translations, I draw out patterns visible in their own "translation manuals" to contest the assumptions publishers and scholars brought to their translation work; what was dismissed as error, I elevate as choice.

In chapter 4, the language pair of Latin American Spanish and Brazilian Portuguese takes on broader aspirations of regional consolidation within the Biblioteca Ayacucho translation project. Editor Ángel Rama gives pride of place to Brazilian Portuguese as a source language for Latin American cultural studies in Spanish—and, more importantly, he imagines it as a future target language, when ideally one of his Brazilian interlocutors will execute a mirror project and translate his Biblioteca Ayacucho canon into Portuguese. Understanding the danger of accepting a Latin American canon formed under a "World Literature" rubric conceived by academics outside Latin America, Rama constructed a shared literary past to build regional unity. Rejecting the assumption that languages are discrete or independent and that translation is unidirectional, I read the Ayacucho publications as remaining in the "translation zone," in Apter's terminology, a space of border-crossing that resists state-sponsored or corporate standardization.[55] In Latin American translation zones, Indigenous and African languages enrich Portuguese and Spanish, but also carry in language the violent coloniality that produced these linguistic mixtures. Héctor Olea, the Ayacucho translator, draws on these histories to emphasize and proliferate "untranslatables" in his translation of Mário de Andrade's complex avant-garde work *Macunaíma*.[56] Cannibal translators often describe translation in multilingual, polyvocal terms: they see one another not on different sides of a language divide but working together against the coloniality of European language norms.[57] Their translations between Spanish and Portuguese within Latin America take on a sense of urgency as interventions against the history of colonial peripherality and mutual separation.

Paz, Haroldo, and Rama did have precursors in their efforts to translate across the linguistic divide between Brazilian and Spanish American cultural production. Yet the reciprocal approach they strive for was an innovation: most of their predecessors were figures like Alfonso Reyes,

Mexican ambassador to Brazil, whose translations aimed more to serve his own nation-building agenda within a postrevolutionary Mexico than what Rama will frame as cultural integration.[58] Although much recent Latin Americanist scholarship emphasizes the importance of dialogues between Brazil and Spanish America, translation itself appears marginal to these analyses, mentioned but then sidelined in favor of other cultural formulas.[59]

I end, in chapter 5, with an analysis of what I call cannibal translation anthologies by Augusto de Campos and José Emilio Pacheco. Published in the 1980s, these two poet-translators collect a broad canon of world literature while also calling into question that framework to explore and translate from fragmented incompleteness, from a pose of nonmastery in which the translator is a loving amateur and in which the source authors become a mask, a heteronym, a voice held in common and reactivated through their Latin American varieties of Spanish and Portuguese. In my reading, they find through cannibal translation practices another potential response to what Mariano Siskind calls "cosmopolitan desires." Siskind identifies in the late nineteenth-century *modernista* generation a participation in world literature discourses to redress the "traumatic experience of crippling marginality."[60] If Spanish American *modernista* writers of the 1890s crafted world literature discourses to express cosmopolitan desires in response to the trauma of peripherality, these two anthologies use cannibal translation techniques to perform a mode of making world literature from and including Latin America as incorporation without synthesis. Throughout the chapters, I identify the unique practices of cannibal translation, first as distinct from translation as consecration, then as a pan–Latin American project, and finally in chapter 5 as a way to read the world.

The prolific network of poet-translators illustrated herein works primarily with poetry and poetic prose; their interrogations and disruptions of genre and poetic tradition often inform the theoretical approaches I am uniting as cannibal translation. Joining other scholars in Latin American and decolonial studies who have leveled critiques of world *literature* frameworks which are in fact based only on the modern European *novel*, I engage with the way poetic production rather than narrative prose serves as a template for Latin American translation praxes for crafting world literature. Gayatri Spivak connects the imperialism that globalized the novel with the Anglocentric nationalism of treating scholars with linguistic knowledge as informants producing raw material for the comparatists.[61] For Efraín Kristal, focus on prose rather than poetry in world literature undervalues Latin America's role as exporter of poetic innovations.[62] Ignacio M. Sánchez Prado adds that "inequalities both in the translation of critical thinking and in the symbolic capital affecting languages other than English, German, and French can be even worse than those determining literary circulation itself."[63] In the light of these insights, *Cannibal Translation* seeks to make legible in English the critical thinking of Latin American literary translators working in Spanish and Portuguese and to elevate how their strategies of translation aimed against nationalist literary production and were grounded in poetry and not the modern novel, even to the extent of sometimes translating a prose text into poetry.

I contend that practices of reading world literature could also draw on concrete poetry rather than the global novel. As a Latin American genre of world literature, concrete poetry was itself "born out of translation," and cannibal translation was forged in the same theoretical crucible.[64] Siskind proposes that a more diverse range of genres of world literature could be identified, specifying magical realism as one genre of world literature from Latin America—yet it tends to be dehistoricized when transformed into global genre.[65] Instead, concrete poetry remains connected with a critical reading practice through cannibal translation, which centers qualities of opacity, untranslatability, heterogeneity, positionality, transgression, transformation—all qualities prized in Latin American literary history that do not always fare well in translation.[66] Routing a way into world literature through the translation praxes of Haroldo and Augusto de Campos, Octavio Paz, Rosario Castellanos, Clarice Lispector, Héctor Olea, Ángel Rama, and José Emilio Pacheco, paying attention to their labors to craft what I am calling cannibal translations in Latin American varieties of Spanish and Portuguese, challenges the Eurocentric framework that major literary genres or critical paradigms only originate in the center.[67]

Cannibal Translation's ethical stakes include amplifying translations into languages other than English; figuring Latin America as a producer of translation theories; and imagining translation as a mode of encountering difference relationally and reciprocally rather than through economic structures of extraction or consecration. As Sandra Bermann builds on Judith Butler's work to argue, when translation provides a counter-hegemonic alternative to the nation, it "makes an ethical demand on the reader" and "acts as a model for political and ethical *relationality*," in which translation "cannot be a simple assimilation of what is foreign into what is familiar; it must be an opening to the unfamiliar."[68] For Paul Ricoeur, translation "serves as a model for other forms of hospitality."[69] While engaging in what Paz will call the "carpentry" of translation and writing, my reading of their letters, archives, and paratexts proves that these poet-translators often imagine larger sociocultural and relational shifts can take place as a result of the particular choices they make, other ways of being together—and they invite their readers to participate in this destructive and constructive labor of love.

Although Damrosch has always framed world literature as a mode of reading,[70] I concur with Lawrence Venuti's challenge that "we are still in the process of learning how to read translations *as translations*."[71] If world literature presents readers with an appealing plated meal, seasoned according to the knowledge base and tastes of the target culture, cannibal translation shows readers how the sausage is made. Cannibal translation can offer the growing field of world literature a practice of reading translations as such, evoking productive suspicion and interest in the process as mediated, unfinished, and lovingly disruptive. Cannibal translations refuse readers the comfort of a finished "target text"—and they also call into question any fixed notion of textual originals, already decisively destabilized by Karen Emmerich's *Literary Translation and the Making of Originals*. Emmerich suggests that translations be regarded as "translingual editions," replacing the imagined stable original with contingent source texts, constructed by editors and translators, to emphasize the parity of mediation between all editions of a work.[72] The cannibal translations I study make this mediation visible, marking world literature made in Latin America as deowned and nonassimilated. Furthermore, I highlight the techniques translators use to present those qualities to readers: publishing materials from the process; producing multiple versions of the same translation; internally inconsistent translations that leave options open; paratexts that demonstrate the hypermediation of the translation, and more. I unfold cannibal translation as a mode of making world literature and a mode of reading world literature that figures literary forms as collective, held in process and in common.[73]

CANNIBAL TRANSLATION RECIPES

Cannibal Translation reads world literature with teeth, where readers can see the bite marks of the process, where translators never stay invisible. Each chapter illuminates strategies that cannibal translators use to challenge assumptions readers bring to translations. Toward this end, my readings are informed by archival material that highlights the unfinishable and mediated nature of translations. The archives of translators provide evidence of what Quine calls the "translator's manual" informing any translation. María Constanza Guzmán defines the "translator's archive" as an open material and cultural archive that includes but goes beyond genetic criticism focused on manuscript drafts. She advocates adding "translator sociographies," which would encompass personal archives, materials that speak to their self-conception as translators, and sociohistorical context, to enrich the analytical frame.[74] Translators are one of many "agents of translation," so I also look into the archives of publishing houses to demonstrate the negotiations between the distinct "translation manuals" held by individuals and the larger organization.[75] These methodological choices are informed not only by my interest in emphasizing the situated impact of translators but also by my objects of study: in cannibal translations, translators and editors often incorporate their process into a published (but never final) result.

By drawing from the archives of multiple translators, this book also addresses a gap in comparative analysis between major Latin American translation thinkers who translated the same authors in literary circles marked by collaboration, competition, and creative destruction. This approach necessarily leaves out several other crucial turns in Latin American literary translation studies, including the focus on individual translators or memoirs written by translators themselves, analysis of fictions of translation, or the role of translation in mass culture.[76] Walter Benjamin writes that "there is no muse of philosophy, nor is there one of translation. But . . . there is a philosophical genius that is characterized by a yearning for that language which manifests itself in translations."[77] Careful attention to their praxis demonstrates that in fact translators often find their muse in other translators. This book aims to draw attention to the pleasurable, generative, proliferating game of literary translation—and when that aesthetic game takes on stakes outside the literary. While each of the writers included merits greater attention to their translation projects, I put them in dialogue to focus on translation as an act of literary reciprocity. In the chapters that follow, I distill these cannibal translation recipes from the way poet-translators describe their process, their diverse labels and neologisms, archival material, and the translations themselves.

Intradução, *or Untranslation*

Augusto de Campos first coined the neologism *intradução*, which blends *introdução* (introduction) with *tradução* (translation) as a poetic title for a concrete poem. I translate his term as "untranslation" because the Portuguese prefix *in-* functions to negate, as in terms like *inábil* (unable) or *inacreditável* (unbelievable) or even *intraduzível* (untranslatable). Like Apter's "untranslatability," Augusto's "untranslations" paradoxically highlight the untranslatable while translating. They introduce but refuse to fully translate longer texts, instead hyperfragmenting the work and inviting readers to investigate what is missing. Augusto affixed the title "Intradução" to his version of a stanza of a longer poem by troubadour Bernart de Ventadorn, interspersing syllables from the source language, Provençal, together with Portuguese and distinguishing the two only by typeface. The two fonts, Old English and Computer, evoke the writing implements of their moments of composition: the former mimics the calligraphy of medieval manuscripts, and the latter references the emerging technology of personal computing and word processing (see fig. 1).

Dated both 1174 and 1974, Augusto's poem "Intradução" blends languages across centuries, and the cannibal translator holds authorship in common with the source author. Augusto's untranslations challenge legibility by mixing together source text and translation; in this case, the mash-up occurs on the level of letter. Readers face an interpretive chal-

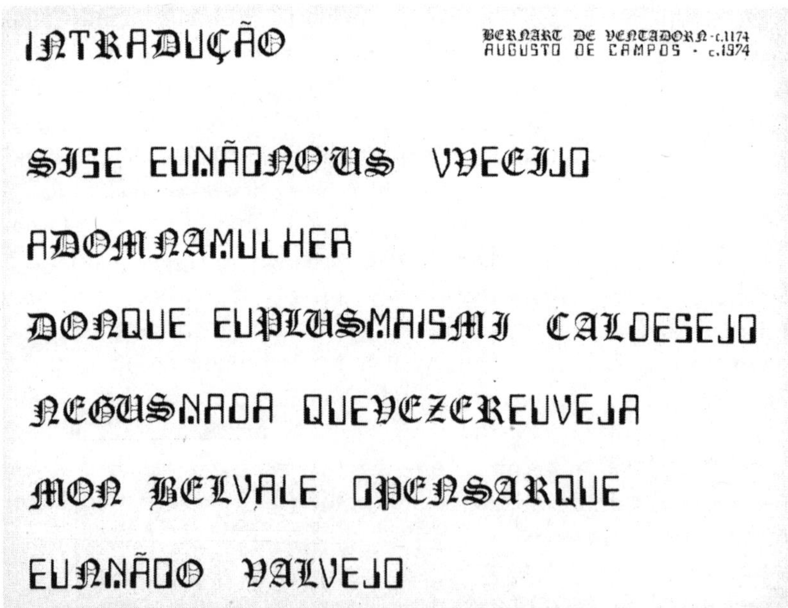

Fig. 1. Augusto de Campos, "Intradução" (1974), in *Verso reverso controverso* (1978). © Augusto de Campos.

lenge to puzzle through two fonts, two times, two languages rather than separate and discrete source and target texts. Also, Augusto salutes Ezra Pound while leaving his Anglocentric worldview behind. This same passage in Provençal features in Pound's "Canto XX," and Augusto could easily have inserted "Ezra Pound ca. 1924" between Ventadorn's name and his own. Instead, he excises Pound from the translation legacy. As I discuss in chapters 1 and 5, Augusto uses the untranslation term for complex translations that add visual elements to nonconcrete source poems.

Versión, *or Poetic Version*

While not a neologism, Octavio Paz consistently labeled his translations as "*versiones*," connecting his praxis with two references: the late nineteenth-century *modernista* tradition, in which *versiones* would nourish Latin American poetries from languages beyond the Spanish peninsular legacy; and the twentieth-century modernist Anglophone tradition of the "poetic version," which tended to eschew knowledge of the source language.[78] Pursuing a modernist translation practice in Spanish was a way to resist both peninsular Spain and local Latin American *modernistas* as poetic precursors. Translating T. S. Eliot, Ezra Pound, E. E. Cummings, and William Carlos Williams allowed Paz and other Latin American poets to perform being "modern" or "cosmopolitan."[79] By studying Paz's versions alongside paratextual material and letters, however, I show that Paz does more than imitate the Anglophone literary sphere. He also explores play, iterability, and nonauthority—as in the title of his translation collection, *Versiones y diversiones* (1974). Reading his work in the context of his contact with the Brazilian concrete poets, and the letters in which he praises multiple multilingual versions of his own poetic lines, allows me to emphasize cannibal translation elements in his *versiones*.

Transcriação, *or Transcreation*

Haroldo de Campos began to define a practice of creative translation in an early essay, "Translation as Creation and Criticism" (1962), where "every translation of a creative text will always be a 're-creation,' a parallel and autonomous, although reciprocal, translation."[80] Haroldo defines transcreation as an artistic translation that prioritizes aesthetic information over documentary or semantic information. The procedure claims translation as an art form and addresses the "untranslatability" of aesthetic information in a literary work, following the maxim Haroldo cites from *School of Translators* by his Brazilian predecessor Paulo Rónai: "Isn't the objective of all art something impossible? The poet expresses (or tries to express) what is inexpressible, the painter reproduces what is unreproducible, the sculptor molds what cannot be molded. It should not be surprising, then, that the translator seeks to translate what is untranslatable."[81] Largely operating inside the literary text, a "transcreation" does not have the reach of a cannibal translation, in which a crucial historicizing of language and translational politics also obtains.

Laboratório de textos, *or Laboratory of Texts*

Haroldo envisioned translation projects as ideally collective, polyvocal, transdisciplinary, and full of pedagogical potential. Although Ezra Pound features in his work as a major inspiration, much like Augusto's "untranslation," Haroldo's "laboratory of texts" highlights the Brazilian poet's departure from Pound's ethnocentric approach to the Chinese poetic tradition, which appropriated the ideogram without understanding the source language. Haroldo writes that problems such as Pound's "must be overcome through the project of a laboratory of texts, where the two contributions, that of the linguist and that of the artist, will complement each other and be integrated into a work of translation that is simultaneously competent as such and valid as art."[82] Chapter 2 exemplifies *Transblanco* as a transcreation embedded within a laboratory of texts, making the whole volume a cannibal translation.

Self-Reflexive Intersectional Translation

Neither Rosario Castellanos nor Clarice Lispector invents a term to describe their translation practices. Instead, reviewers of their work came up with translation labels that feminize, infantilize, and diminish translation projects executed by women: *traducir mocosuena* (to translate by sound, or to translate like a *mocosa* or a childish girl) and *traducción lunar* (a "lunar" translation predicated on fidelity and invisibility, as opposed to the masculinized "solar translation" that takes liberties to create and invent). Analysis of their translation work in chapter 3 reveals translation manuals that self-reflexively incorporate translator positionality along with other creative strategies. Given how their gender impacts the reception of their translations, I argue that we need to read cannibal translations with an awareness of race, gender, class, and other elements of translator positionality, or as intersectional translations.

Tradecir: *To Transspeak or Transsay*

Héctor Olea coins the verb *tradecir* to capture his interest in the orality of Latin American Spanish. To translate the sounds and oral idioms of Mário de Andrade's *Macunaíma*, he decides to "transspeak" this Brazilian modernist text working with a geographically vast corpus of Spanish American varieties. The neologism "transsay" also reflects his conviction that readers could hear meaning contextually even when semantic meaning is not present; trusting readers to complete for themselves the logical leap to understand idiomatic expressions through mood, context, or sound qualities. Translating *tradecir*, I want to keep two English-language options open. "Transsay" produces the same aural and visual off-rhyme with "translate" as *tradecir* does with the Spanish *traducir*. Yet the verb "to speak" evokes the communicative, dialogic impact of *decir*; to "transspeak," one needs an interlocutor. As I argue in chapter 4, this approach to his task shares underlying aims or political goals with what Kwame Anthony Appiah calls "thick translation," where the translator must add significant explanatory material within the text or paratexts in order to make up for a lack of knowledge of the source culture—and to overcome notions of cultural superiority in a decolonial context.[83] In the project Olea worked on with Biblioteca Ayacucho, he resisted Ángel Rama's desire to incorporate many footnotes, yet the project's resulting cannibal translations display multiple approaches to transspeaking a pan–Latin American Spanish that could incorporate Brazilian literatures and repair colonial divisions.

Aproximaciones, *or Approximations*

José Emilio Pacheco titles his 1986 anthology *Aproximaciones*: rather than hitting the "target language" as in standard translation parlance, Pacheco's "approximations" draw near the target but never reach it. Calling translation "the bloodstream of the body of poetry," he imagines his project as a collective act in which he participates in a long line of translators in Mexico, beginning with the Indigenous translators working from Nahuatl into Spanish; he claims that "the true author of these approximations is the Spanish language."[84] This nod to anonymity and to world literature as collective property of all readers might seem opposed to the performative hand of the translator present in his approximations, where he frequently magnifies his own interventions by importing Mexicanisms and altering poetic structures. In chapter 5, though, I demonstrate that along with his playful use of pseudotranslations (texts posing as translations that are his original compositions) as well as heteronyms (invented personas with biographies through which the author writes in other poetic voices), his translation anthology ultimately provokes suspicion and curiosity in readers, inviting them to work with the translator to understand what mask he is wearing.

Prosa porosa, *or "Porous Prose"*

Augusto de Campos borrows the term *prosa porosa* from the concept of "ventilated prose" coined by US architect Buckminster Fuller. But I prefer to back-translate his *prosa porosa* translation genre as "porous prose" for the organic image and alliterative label. In his translation anthology *O anticrítico* (1986), Augusto rejects the professionalized voice of the academic to instead craft "amateur criticism out of love, criticism through creative translation."[85] Analyzed in chapter 5 alongside Pacheco's anthology of approximations, Augusto's porous-prose collection exemplifies world literature from a Latin American geo-linguistic perspective. Mixing together poetic glosses with visually dynamic translations of fragments of world literature classics—including several Brazilian greats—Augusto blends creative translation with critical research into the translation tradition. Much like Pacheco's approximations, readers experience his anthology of world literature without ever losing sight of Augusto's mediating position.

* * *

Ideally, these recipes might prove generative: as a set of provocations for translators into any language; as questions for students or any reader to bring into reading a translation as a mediated creative act in its own right; or for scholars of these Latin American writers seeking to understand their translation work. Grouping them together under the rubric of "cannibal translation" illuminates the critical contributions of practices and theories in Brazilian Portuguese and in Latin American Spanish. As a set of translation practices that grew out of concrete poetry, a global literary genre that is always already in translation, cannibal translation offers a praxis of reading world literature that centers less on the object or its points of origin or reception and more on the creative energy generated through becoming, a reciprocal movement among languages.

CHAPTER 1

Unrequited Gifts and Perilous Translations

Writing from São Paulo in 1956, Augusto de Campos not only introduces himself to E. E. Cummings as a poet "compelled" to translate—he also introduces his language. Augusto adopts the triumphant discourse of the cannibal translator from the start, distinguishing his Brazilian Portuguese both from the European variety and from European translation norms.

> i have been "compelled" to translate
> into my old unused (portuguese)
> and now new (brazilian) jaguar language
> some of your most perilous poems.[1]

What does a "jaguar language" do but devour? Positioned as an apex predator, Augusto's Portuguese is the polar—equatorial?—opposite of "old unused (portuguese)." His "new (brazilian) jaguar language" is sleek, urgent, present-centric: a powerful yet dangerous New World tongue, a worthy vehicle with much to offer Cummings's "perilous poems." In turn, Augusto continues the Brazilian modernist project of remaking Brazilian Portuguese and recombining the political and aesthetic challenges of his source texts with local materials. The stakes of his incipient cannibal translation practice include resignifying the "jaguar," reversing European language values, framing translation as a reciprocal gift both "compelled" and voluntary, and putting tepid translation norms at "peril."

Augusto's bold opening gambit demonstrates the cannibal translator's interest in the creative, collaborative thinking generated in the space between their poetics and their languages. While the two poets correspond until 1960 when *10 poemas* is published, the translation theorization that underwrites Augusto's letters goes largely unreceived and unrequited by Cummings. I analyze their interaction as a form of nonreciprocity and nonmutuality, in which Cummings ignores Augusto's theorization of the translation process and instead attempts to maintain the hierarchy of author above translator.

In 1958, Octavio Paz initiates a similar exchange, sending Cummings six poems he had translated into Spanish "for himself and a few of his friends."[2] Paz's translations also remain invisible to the author—as do his translation strategies or the theories underpinning those strategies. Spanish was more accessible to Cummings than Portuguese was: he had traveled with John Dos Passos in Spain; his partner, Marion Morehouse, spoke Spanish. Yet Paz encounters an equally indifferent ear when sounding out a discourse of translation; like Augusto, he resists the dominant paradigm of translator fidelity, describing his translations as "more from love than respect."[3] These letters show a missed opportunity, a failure of reciprocity in translation. Yet they also show the Brazilian and Mexican translator-poets rejecting the translation norm in which respect for the author is paramount. Instead, they position their cannibal translations into Portuguese and Spanish as spaces to creatively meditate on the gains possible in translation.

The assertive, creative pose they strike as translators stands in stark contrast to the attitudes displayed by Cummings's translators based in Europe: D. Jon Grossman and Eva Hesse. Both take great pains to uphold his authoritative role, humbly asking him to weigh in on their interpretations of his source texts and their translations alike. In those author-translator relationships, Cummings gets to be the expert not only in his own American idiom but also in French and German, and notions of fidelity dominate the unspoken translation theory in operation.

Cummings largely ignores the theoretical framings of his two Latin American translators and remains primarily interested in the reprinting of his own poems in English. Yet I posit that the translation theories of Augusto and Paz have roots in these interactions, where their language was invisible and peripheral but therefore more able to resist the interventions of the living author and reject the norm of fidelity. Their unreciprocated gifts of translation theories find fertile ground a decade later, when Paz and Haroldo de Campos begin to collaborate, bemoaning the triangulation of their encounter through English and Cummings, the topic of chapter 2.

To emphasize through comparison the unique, reciprocal characteristics of later intra–Latin American translation collaborations, this opening chapter demonstrates the nonreciprocal "status quo" Cummings expects from literary translation, where authors from the global South translate authors from the global North, diffusion is unidirectional, and the hierarchy of author over translator—while challenged by the translators—was never relinquished by the author. To shed light on different translation strategies deployed from Latin America and from Europe, I build a corpus of material around the different translation processes used with the same Anglo-American modernist. The materials held in the E. E. Cummings Papers at Houghton Library at Harvard University and carefully organized in Augusto de Campos's personal papers tell rich, complex stories about the assumptions and values different translators working in the 1950s brought to bear on this poet's work.[4] Both Augusto and Paz approach Cummings with a tone that is markedly theoretical and places translation on equal footing with authorship, compared to his more voluminous yet hierarchical dialogue with the translators into French and German, D. Jon Grossman and Eva Hesse. For both US expatriate translators based in Europe, their work is subsumed within the soft-diplomacy goals of publication venues circulating Anglo-American modernism in the Cold War literary milieu. Their dialogue with Cummings, while often lively (and even, in the case of Grossman, personal) remains largely deferential to the author, who corrects their readings of his source texts and intervenes into their translation choices.

Conversely, the letters Augusto and Paz write to Cummings anticipate their incipient theories of creative translation. In the case of Augusto, the concept of *intradução*, or "untranslation," shines through his commentaries to Cummings on his translation praxis. He persistently describes and glosses his Portuguese translations, emphasizing how they refuse to leave the source text behind, how by publishing proofs from the translation process in bilingual facing-page collections, the target poems remain in process and in dialogue with their sources. His correspondence with Cummings in the late 1950s reveals "untranslation" as a long-standing element of Augusto's translation praxis, a decade before he coins the term *intradução*, using it as the title of his 1974 concrete poem translation of Provençal poet Ventadorn (recall fig. 1), and even longer before he would explicitly define the procedure in his 1984 essay "Intradução de cummings." Augusto's untranslations—first of Cummings, and eventually of many other poetic figures of world literature—begin by preserving or expanding visual elements of the source text over semantic meaning, and they feature the creative remainder of the translation process. Selective, fragmentary, and visually complex, untranslations do not assimilate source texts; rather, they restage them in relationship with his jaguar Brazilian Portuguese.

Paz's characterization of his translations as showing "more love than respect" anticipates the argument of his essay "Translation: Literature and Literalness" (1971). In this piece, Paz considers the irony that poets ought to be the best translators—but they are in fact often the worst, culprits of a loving crime in which they are too passionately cathected onto the source text to be able to resist using it to create a poem of their own, that the "love" a poet has for both the source poem and for his own poetic instrument (his own voice or his own language) might prevent him from making a translation that "respects" its source. In later cases, he will even produce multiple translations of the same text, correcting an initial translation that showed too much love for the creative possibilities in Spanish by providing a new version that demonstrates greater respect. Although he does not take this step with Cummings's poems, he does share with the author himself this underlying tension between love and respect that will mark his later translation practice.

The distinct positionalities of all four translators contribute to their translation tactics, yet they cannot entirely explain the divergence between what I am calling the cannibal translation approaches of Augusto and Paz and the more subservient and fidelity-focused translation attitudes of Grossman and Hesse. When both Augusto and Paz began translating Cummings in the late 1950s, they did so as established poets with different levels of cultural capital and access. Paz may not have won the Nobel Prize yet, but he already had a Guggenheim Fellowship (1943) under his belt, and his work had been translated by none less than William Carlos Williams.[5] Conversely, the concrete poets would not circulate widely in the United States or in English until a decade later in *An Anthology of Concrete Poetry*, edited by Emmet Williams (1967), and *Concrete Poetry: A World View*, edited by Mary Ellen Solt and Willis Barnstone (1968). Augusto wrote to Cummings without any prior introduction, while Grossman met him through a mutual Harvard friend before moving to Paris after World War II, where the two maintained a lively correspondence. Eva Hesse, a US doctoral student living in Munich, sought permission to translate Cummings formally through his publisher Brandt & Brandt, unlike the three male translators, who approached the poet directly.

Spanish, Portuguese, French, and German also hold different positions within the linguistic economy of these author-translator relationships. While Paz and Cummings may address one another as poetic equals, they also maintain the distance of each writing within his own language. Conversely, Augusto writes in English, yet he also delights in explaining what he can accomplish with Cummings's poetry in Portuguese. Paz recognizes that, for better or worse, Spanish represents for Cummings a language he has frequently heard and admired but never learned or understood. As the Mexican poet describes wryly, Cummings reminisced with him about traveling in Spain with John Dos Passos and marveling at the Spanish poets without comprehending a word of their conversation. Augusto's "Brazilian Portuguese" represents uncharted territory for the New Englander.[6] Instead of relying on any prior experience with his language, Augusto explains his choices by building comparisons for Cummings through Italian and French, Romance languages the poet did know. The Brazilian translator characterizes these translation achievements through a framework of worthy competition rather than subservience, providing examples to prove that wherever he may have "lost" a particular poetic element, he is able to "win" back a parallel stylistic flourish in Portuguese.[7] He also provides Cummings with English and French translations of select concrete poems from the *Noigandres* journal issues he sent him, to share the poetic project taking place in Brazil that relates to Cummings's work and to demonstrate the eager readership awaiting his "jaguar" translations.[8] The two European translators display no need to introduce French or German, yet neither do they make same effort as Augusto to place Cummings within the target culture's literary sphere. Instead, they aspire to improve Cummings's status within the larger panorama of Anglo-American modernism circulated in Europe, where he was overshadowed by T. S. Eliot.[9] Hesse and Grossman address Cummings as US expatriates with full ownership of English, not as native speakers of their target languages, like Augusto and Paz. This makes it all the more notable that they ask Cummings about his meaning in the source texts, deferential gestures that Augusto and Paz never make.

Cummings was perhaps the only modernist who could appeal to the divergent poetic projects of both Augusto and Paz. In their prolific translations, he was the only living poet they both work on, although both also translate the earlier precursor Stéphane Mallarmé. For Paz, Cummings represents a decidedly US reinvention of older verse forms. He portrays Cummings's lyric voice as a welterweight boxer, combative, yet light on its feet, dancing in agile staged combat with the Elizabethan legacy of English. For Augusto, Cummings confronts language itself, breaking decisively with normative English grammar, and landing all his punches, hard. Both translator-poets explore Spanish and Portuguese varieties that create a rupture with these colonial languages, and so translating Cummings matches their own poetics: he writes in a pointedly US English. Despite their nonreciprocal correspondence with the author, both take advantage of translating Cummings to develop their translation theories through his work; they alter his poems through translation to amplify elements they favor—and turn the volume down on others. The work of their cannibal translations stands out all the more against the different affective qualities and literary assumptions on display in the translations into French and German by Grossman and Hesse.

SOFT-DIPLOMACY TRANSLATION VERSUS CANNIBAL TRANSLATION

In his initial letter, Augusto auditions for the author, framing his skills as a translator using stylistic devices favored by Cummings, showing that he has digested elements of the poet's work to give them back in new form. Signing off with the bold portmanteau "SINCEREYOURSLY," all capitalized, he otherwise maintains the idiosyncratic all lowercase, which visually registers rejection of grammatical norms and projects an antiestablishment mood by eschewing the formality of capital letters.[10] He writes with casual, clever orality: "anyway these devoted translations would be sleeping in my drawers for some many moneyless years," and peppers sentences with parenthesis and extra spacing: "my old unused (portuguese) and now   new (brazilian) jaguar language."[11] Displaying his careful attention to Cummings's poetic game, the Brazilian poet-translator seeks recognition less as a stranger and more as a kindred spirit.

Augusto's letters are not simply flattering imitations; they craft a purposeful distinction between his homage and that of other translators. By deploying aspects of Cummings's poetics—typography, *mise-en-*

page, neologism, syntax shifts—within prose correspondence, Augusto signals that these are the particular stylistic devices that "compel" his choice to translate particular selections, the author's "most perilous poems." I connect his category of "perilous poems" with the destructive homage of cannibal translation, devouring the strength of those most challenging poems and pushing them further in a new language and a new poetic sphere.

Echoing the label of "perilous poems" in his reply, Cummings deploys the term to insist on approving proofs, although the translator had requested clemency given the expense of sending proofs from Brazil. The author writes: "you will continue to send me proofs of my own 10 poems (as reprinted in connection with your translations) until one proof satisfies me & I okay it. Thus & only thus may readers of your translations be able to appreciate the extraordinary problems presented by these verily 'perilous' poems."[12] Cummings asserts his privilege of final approval to maintain intact the presentation not of the translations but of his own poems.

When Augusto clarifies his adjective "perilous" as ironic, the term acquires a political dimension related to the qualities that evade translation. Insisting that his Portuguese translations serve a critical aesthetic purpose, he claims that the perilous vector of his translations traces an opposite approach to that of the French and German translators. Augusto writes:

> i do want to be sure my consciously ironical "perilous" dont [*sic*] make you figure i'm less conscious of the problems arisen by your poems. in this sense i think the choice of the 10 poems speaks by itself. i mean there is a qualitative difference between my anthology and say that of mrs. D. Jon Grossman & Alain Bosquet for profils 2. mine is not an occasional choice. . . . it implies a criticism, a direction, a vector.[13]

Augusto refers here to the French translations in *Profils* (1953), the French version of *Perspectives USA*, distinguishing between that translator's project and his own simply by observing the selections published. He may not have known how right he was, or the extent to which this other "vector" of translation into French instrumentalized Cummings's poetry, maintaining the author's primacy but neutralizing his creative and political interventions. The distance between the Cummings translations for *Profils* and Augusto's exemplifies the differences between translation in service of a world literature that upholds translation norms and a taboo-breaking cannibal translation in Latin America.

Founded by James Laughlin of New Directions and funded by the Ford Foundation, the literary journal *Perspectives USA* (1952–56) circulated in France, Germany, and Italy to improve European perceptions of US culture. Designed in a post–World War II milieu, the journal curated US modernism to supplement the lowbrow popular appeal of Hollywood and the aura of consumerism and utilitarianism projected by US military, industrial, and economic neoliberal domination. Although the parent organization, Intercultural Publications, refrained from including any commercial advertising or overtly political material in the journal, its board of directors included banking and industry figures, who were often in conflict with the advisory board, composed of New Critics and New York leftist intellectuals.[14]

Although Augusto correctly reads the translation vector traced by *Profils*, the archive inevitably shows a more complicated story. The translators, D. Jon Grossman and Alain Bosquet, did not have full authority over selection: in fact, the safer translation choices were the responsibility of volume editor Lionel Trilling; the French editor, Edouard Roditi; the journal editor, James Laughlin; and the larger editorial board of Intercultural Publications. Grossman, who had translated Cummings's poetry years earlier, did write to Roditi to advocate for the inclusion of an antiwar or an anticommunist poem.[15] He writes in high polyglot tenor: "again je gueule à tue-tête [I shout at the top of my lungs] that any selection from C'gs without an anti-war poem is playing C'gs false. (Or maybe an anti-Commie poem?)"[16] The translator's suggestion to include a more balanced selection was ultimately rejected, showing the degree of editorial control over how Cummings would be exported to Europe. It also shows an intriguing tension between Cummings's work and the carefully curated apolitical stance of the journal—which was never particularly believable to any sector of its readership. While translators Grossman and Hesse both comment that European readers mistrusted the literary journal because of its low cost and Americanized packaging, the second issue drew heavy fire from conservative US writers, who called Cummings out by name and accused the journal of communist sympathies.[17]

Although Grossman did want to present a more complete Cummings, he is aware of the limitations of the magazine's editorial perspective. On the typescript of "les communistes ont de beaux Yeux," he handwrites: "If you wd rather suppress this? In any case I am not offering it for magazine publication," flagging the political content to ask whether Cummings wishes it to circulate in France.[18] This poem does not appear in *Profils* (1953), nor did he include it in his collection *En traduction* (1960). This volume does include the "anti-commie" poem "kumrads die because they're told." But Grossman follows it with what can only be called an anti-American poem, "he does not have to feel because he thinks," about the character Smith, who cannot think, know, understand, but can drink, marry, and lie; the poem ends, "afraid;aggressive and: American."[19] Neither would have fit the bill for *Profils*. Yet he never published the poem in question, his translation of "the communists have fine Eyes." In short, although Grossman did translate a wider range than appeared in *Profils*, the political quietism of the journal influenced his process and which translations he ultimately included even in his own independent volume.

Uninterested in the "perilous" poems that Augusto translates for his Brazilian readers, *Perspectives USA* exported a curated modernism that divorced its formal qualities from the political contexts in which it originated.[20] Augusto's translations do the opposite: they enhance and expand on those formal qualities to show their inextricable links with the political gesture of freedom and destruction of past models. The translation archive illuminates this distinction: for Augusto, *Profils* defanged Cummings of his perilous aesthetic choices and of his antiwar, anti–United States, anticommunist, and antiassimilationist poems. Yet for the US milieu, he has not been defanged enough; and for the French and German translators, no European public was ever convinced by the journal's Cold War public relations attempts at image repair.

Regardless of this complex publication history, the translation processes of Grossman and Hesse represent an extreme adherence to the idea that the author is the best and final authority on his own work. For Grossman and Hesse, there was never a question of "winning" anything in a translation; the author's choices, decisions, and readings of his own work always prevail.

Writing the poet more than ninety letters between 1944 and 1962 and sending him at least three drafts, Grossman seemingly imagined Cummings himself as the intended reader of his French translations. Over numerous pages of detailed questions, he asks the author how he should be allowed to accommodate any lexical gaps, such as flora and fauna, or references to vividly known locations in the US cultural imaginary that would be meaningless in France. Grossman's wife, Anne-Marie, appears periodically to offer alternative translation choices. Some of his queries take on the voice of his "pedant," a translatorly alter ego, invented to express the part of himself obsessed with conservative precision and adherence to strict equivalence. When Grossman and his pedant disagree, the author gets called in to arbitrate.

Grossman maintains a striking combination of friendly joviality and consistent subservience when addressing Cummings. While he may express mock resentment—"a lot of help you are!" he pencils in—he consistently asks "please" for a word choice and "begs" for small alterations, which frequently Cummings rejects.[21] Grossman found it so important that Cummings approve all aspects of his translations that, in his initial drafts, he subtitles *En traduction* a "cotranslation." Cummings spurns this honorific with characteristic hyperindividualism: "no. The undersigned wasn't & isn't &, he sincerely trusts, won't be a co-anything: including translator. So delete 'avec l'auteur' subito, piacere."[22] The codedication to their respective wives, "For Marion / Pour Anne-Marie," does survive through all drafts and makes it into the final publication.

Grossman also offers his services to other translators—again, basing his authority on his knowledge of the choices the author would make and his own deference to those choices. Writing to the French editor Roditi, he forwards his translations along to the Italian translator Salvatore Quasimodo, as though they might serve as an ideal translation manual, legible as a set of rules approved by the author. "I'll be only too delighted to give what help I can: my Italian, God knows, is by no means anything to be proud of, but I may at times be able to be helpful. Same goes for your German translator. . . . please note, too, that C'gs is a horrible stickler for punctuation, etc. Where he writes &, he won't put up with an et français or a german und, etc."[23] Grossman's offer of help veils a command for other translators: any lawful translator would follow the author's precise instructions rather than playing along with his literary game—or, worse, trying to best him, as Augusto does.

Although Eva Hesse did not translate for *Perspektiven*, the German *Perspectives USA*, Augusto finds similar fault in her translation volume *Gedichte* (1958); he writes to Cummings, "just saw german cummings' poems which eva hesse sent to pignatari. her choice seems to me rather shy."[24] Again, the translation archive confirms his instinctive judgment based only on the publication. In her letters, Hesse approaches Cummings with great deference, naming the author as final arbiter of any of her translation choices. In her first letter to his publishers, she assures them that she "always made it a practice to submit copies of my translations of his work from time to time for approval."[25] In a letter to Marion Morehouse, she asks about Cummings's idiosyncratic use of the word "by" in the poem "anyone lived in a pretty how town," and the poet himself responds with a prescriptive guide, including an intralingual translation of alternative wordings:

> "more by more"—more & more ad infin.
> "where by now and tree by leaf"—always & at any instant
> "bird by snow and stir by still"—spring by winter (birth by death)[26]

Translating his poem into alternative English phrases, Cummings ensures that Hesse's German translation will proceed according to his intentions and asserts his own interpretation as the only one that matters. When Hesse translates his play *Santa Claus*, she asks permission to change a stage direction on behalf of a theater director, who "asks whether E.E.C. could possibly make a slight change . . . by deleting 'weeping' and giving the woman a stiffer upper lip. He thinks this opening would otherwise be very difficult to put over on the stage. I said I was not at all sure whether this might be possible, but would ask."[27] While the director might have simply made that change within their purview as an adaptor of a staged performance, inevitably different from the written script, Hesse demonstrates her commitment to a higher degree of fidelity and subservience as a translator of a text.

The story of Cummings in translation in Europe ultimately shows an adherence to the hierarchy of author—and publisher—over translator. As with Augusto, Cummings asks (or, rather, "demands") final proof approval from both Grossman and Hesse.[28] But with these two European languages, he also actively intervenes and corrects the translations. The archives show the many hands involved in crafting the E. E. Cummings presented to European readers—and how the translators were at the bottom of any decision-making tree. The *Profils* translations are credited to Grossman and Bosquet, but, as Grossman wrote to anyone who would listen, these translations were based on his drafts but included errors introduced by Bosquet, an imposition he resented to the utmost degree. Laughlin casually requests to his French collaborator from on high, in his Boston Brahmin tone, "Do be a good chap and work it out with him, won't you."[29] Unlike the translation efforts of Augusto or Paz, their work was never framed as part of a project to reinvent French or

German, nor did their translators "win" any points over Cummings, much less develop theories of translation through their practice. In fact, Hesse implies that her real work of literary criticism will begin when her work as translator ends, writing: "When I finish work on your poems, I plan to give up translation. I will then have translated all the American poetry that I think deserves to be translated. . . . I have always considered translation as properly belonging to the field of literary criticism, for one's choice of works to translate is essentially an act of criticism. It is my intention to turn to analytical criticism when I stop translating."[30] Hesse might relate translation and criticism—but in her practice, she evinces precisely the opposite position to Haroldo and Augusto, who insist that translation, creation, and criticism are reciprocal: inextricable and mutually reinforcing literary activities. For his part, Grossman attaches an epigraph to his translations from the earliest draft to the final published version that expresses his own reductive position on translation: "Un poème est ce que ne peut pas être traduit" (A poem is that which cannot be translated).[31]

TORTUOUS ORTHOGRAPHY: AUGUSTO DE CAMPOS AS CANNIBAL TRANSLATOR

Far from the quietist soft-diplomacy of the poems featured in *Profils*, or the polite choices of German translator Eva Hesse, Augusto translates those poems that give him the most chance to devour language and subject it to aggressive "tortography" that would violently reconfigure the relationship between the reader and the poem on the page. His cannibal translations of these untranslatable poems often expand on or create new visual or sonic echoes that extend the linguistic games of their source texts. Presented as facing-page parallels of their source texts, they allow readers to also witness these choices and expansions, sucking the marrow out of what elements are "won" through moving the works into Portuguese, what Augusto will eventually theorize as "untranslation." Finally, when he includes in his publication a page of proofs, showing the challenges and errors in the process, the translator's mediating hand, Augusto's presentation of Cummings in his Brazilian Portuguese stands far from the safer choices of the French and German translators.

When Augusto describes his "compulsion" to translate the "most perilous" poems, he echoes Walter Benjamin's assertion that works resistant to translation most attract the artistic eye of the translator.[32]

Yet this dramatic statement of attraction, imitation, and danger implied by his translation choices perhaps backfires—or, at least, the stakes of the cannibal translations are not perceived by the author. Cummings remains focused on the repair work to his original poetry made possible by their publication in Portuguese—disinterested in discussions about extending the perilous political vector of his poetry into Portuguese. As though to demonstrate the necessity of his oversight, he remarks: "Quite incidentally: despite the best efforts of myself, my wife & a Harcourt Brace professional proofreader, Poems 1923–1954 is full of errors."[33] For Cummings, the translation publication in Portuguese becomes an occasion to reinforce his authority, particularly within the most experimental vein of his work.

When Augusto chooses to translate *only* those poems that disintegrate words, he does some violence to Cummings's work by eliminating a significant portion of his output, rejecting the lyric and fixed form sonnets or ballads that Grossman, Hesse, and Paz all gravitate toward.[34] Even when he adds other, less "tortographic" poems in the subsequent *20 poemas* (1979) and *40 poem(a)s* (1984)—including some he calls the "greatest hits"—Augusto insists that even though they are apparently less experimental, these other selections *still* include a quality of "artistic disobedience" and "anarchic individualism."[35] In short, his choices continue to foreground the political and aesthetic rebellion within Cummings's work, the vector emphasized from the start.

Augusto frames his translation of Cummings within a context of bellicosity and the need to "upbraid" a stagnant humanity and shake them out of passive, deathlike habits with new approaches to language. In his introduction, titled "Olho e fôlego" ("Eye and Breath"), he draws from the semantic fields of violence and war to emphasize the value of his poetic innovation. Throughout this essay, Augusto chooses violent words and physicalized metaphors to describe Cummings's poetics.[36] Defending orthographic innovation against critics, he uplifts these poetic choices as serious interventions that only appear to be chaotic, arbitrary, or merely "epidermal." Augusto appreciates what he calls Cummings's "tortography" that tortures traditional orthography and typography, "disfiguring" the discursive order, a violent corrective to the deathlike "mortography" of his poetic tradition.[37] Paz describes Cummings with a similar attention to the bellicose, depicting him as a boxer, athletic despite his age. Yet he portrays the pugilistic stance of the Anglo-American modernist as an eternally young, almost clownish iconoclast: a welterweight, never a heavyweight. For Paz, Cummings projects the image of a mere balletic play-fighter, not a warrior; for Augusto, the punch of his poetry lands—and it is the translator's task to extend the reach of that punch.

Augusto takes pains to distinguish the language experiment in Cummings from that of other modernists, and especially from surrealists, who were "compromised to the teeth with conventional formal syntax."[38] Depicting the modernist poetic sphere as a battlefield, evoking World War I, which inaugurated the period, he describes *Tulips and Chimneys* (1923) exploding like "dynamite" on the poetic landscape and destroying "the tired architecture of traditional versification." Ignoring the fact that Cummings also works in fixed forms, for Augusto the poet achieves a "structural revolution" and nourishes this rebellious impulse in younger poets—and poets in other languages. Literary reciprocity implies a translation practice that imagines what comes after translation: for Augusto, the translations of Cummings into Portuguese will bear repercussions in this vector of poetry, now in his own language as well.

Augusto translates for the ear and the eye: his translation strategies follow the same logic that governs his translation selections. He tends to amplify, expand, and create visual or sonic echoes that call further attention to Cummings's tortured orthography, words disarticulated and arranged on the page to invite the freedom of confusion, surprise, and multiple readings. Where Cummings breaks words apart, achieving two or three within one, Augusto does the same, even if this requires alterations in spelling or meaning. His translations will even expand on this poetic strategy, finding more words within words than the source text could achieve. For example, the word "twilight" appears as a key image in several of the selected poems and receives careful reworking into Portuguese. The poem "twi-" opens with the two lines "twi- / is -Light bird"; Augusto's translation "crep- / úscu -Luz ave" alters the Portuguese word *crepúscular* to better approximate the emphasis Cummings places on the fading floating effects of light or *luz* at that time of day.[39] Yet for the poem "birds(" where the same word appears broken apart as "tw / iligH(/ t's"—in Augusto's version, "crep / uscuL(/ ar"— the translator's choice manages to create the word *ar* (air), which emphasizes the vastness of twilight air under the bird's wings and echoes with the same word placed a few lines above.[40] In both cases, Augusto must change elements of his source to preserve the poetic device Cummings uses to divide words up into fragments that signify in multiple ways.

A second strategy focuses on visual economy and maintaining the balance of letters and lines as they are laid out on the page. Augusto avoids the expanded word count that can occur when translating English into Romance languages—a tendency on display in the translations by Paz and by Grossman. The number of letters in each line, their proportions, often takes precedence over a direct semantic translation—a change in word order or transposition from one part of speech to another can occur, to maintain proportionality or minimalism in the number of letters used. For example, in the poem "un," he alters both word order and part of speech. The poem by Cummings can be glossed together to read as "under fog's touchings fingerings whichs turn into whos people become un" and was translated into "ao toque dos dedos da névoa quês viram quems gente se torna a."[41] The two words "touchings" and "fingerings" become the singular image *toque dos dedos* (touch of fingers) in Augusto's translation, allowing him to create a poem as spare and direct as its source. Transposition, or shifting from one part of speech to another, can be free (driven by a translator's choice) or obligatory (based on differences in grammar in different languages). Because grammatical shift was an important poetic device in Cummings, Augusto uses the same flexibility and freedom of syntactical transposition as a translation device. Augusto's translations attend to the number and proportion of letters: their visual qualities, the shapes they make on the page.

Augusto also amplifies these poetic elements when possible, expanding beyond the source text to emphasize Cummings's tortured typography. In some cases, this allows him to produce a poem even more attuned to the ear. For example, in the poem "(fea" the Portuguese version of the opening lines "(fea / therr / ain"—in Augusto's translation, "(plu / mas plu / viais"—maintain the weight of letters and syllables; while he loses the double *r*, his version gains the alliteration of the repeated *plu* for visual and sound-based effects, the sound of rain plinking down.[42] He also achieves the word *mas* (more) through his placement of the line break; the textured plurality of both feathers and soft raindrops are echoed more times in the Portuguese with his *plu-mas*. Choosing *pluviais* for "rain" rather than the more common option available in Portuguese, *chuva*, demonstrates the translation strategy that Augusto will deploy to maintain and even expand the visual and sonic effects. The process Augusto went through with eight rounds of proofs—ostensibly to perfect the English—also gave him opportunities to observe and become attuned to these possibilities.

The eight sets of proofs in Augusto's papers confirm that this careful process played a role in the precision of his translations, as the repeated editing allowed him to identify every opportunity available within Portuguese keep his translations as attuned to the eye and ear as possible—

sometimes achieving a rhyme or visual echo where there was none in the source text. The love poem "i will be" or "eu estarei" conflates the body of the beloved with an ecstatic, fascinating cityscape, and contains the lines "mYveRylitTle // street" which in Portuguese becomes "minhAmíniMa // rua."[43] In the first three proofs, the line appears as "minHamuIpeqUena // rua," a more direct translation for "my very little," which also reduces the word *muita* into *mui*.[44] The drafts never included any direct translations without creative accommodations, but Augusto ultimately opted to shift *mui pequena* or "very little" into *mínima* or "minimal" to create a beautiful series of triangle shapes made by the repeated *A*'s and *M*'s on the page in a visually compelling pattern. This line evokes the tripping up and down of stairs, or perhaps the iconic sidewalks in Rio de Janeiro made of black and white tiles arranged in hypnotic waves: either way, the visual enhancement justifies the verbal shift. Looking and sounding more fluid, this line is also an example of his strategy of expansion or invention when he cannot directly transfer the word-within-word play. The Cummings poem builds up three lines, like a staircase, or tripping over a curb:

oh
        ver
                mYveRylitTle

street[45]

sô
        bre
                minhAmíniMa

rua[46]

In Augusto's translation, the wordplay of "oh / ver" transforms into "sô / bre," which pulls the word *sô* (alone) out of *sobre* (over). The "oh," read as a sigh of solitude or desire, introduced into the word "over" by Cummings's additional *h*, comes through in the added diacritical mark by Augusto, indicating the feeling of aloneness of the poetic speaker.

In the final lines of this translation, Augusto also adds a moment of erotic clarity. In the Cummings poem, the final phrase "at twilight soon & there's a moon" is presented as

at twi li ght
s(oon & there's
a m oo
)n.[47]

Augusto's version back-translates as "at twilight nude and there's a moon" and reads:

ao crep úsc ulo
n(ua e háu
m a lu
)a.[48]

The Brazilian translator introduces the more explicit "nude" into this already sexy poem, allowing him to retain the final ring of the consonant rhyme of "soon"/"moon" with *nua/lua.* Where the source poem perhaps left the erotic, voyeuristic moment in suspension, with the long break, deferring the object of "there's a . . ." and allowing the imagination to fill in the details, the translation fills in the indeterminacy. Yet the translation did defer feminizing the figure described until this final moment. Where the Cummings poem represents the female figure present in the poem immediately with the first line that arranges itself into "I will be moving in the street of her body," Augusto defers using any gendered language until this moment. His version begins "eu estarei Andando na Rua de seu corpo," and the final *nua* must be associated with the person *chegando* because the other noun, *crepusculo*, is masculine. To borrow from Augusto's own vocabulary, he may have "lost" the indeterminate moment at the end of the poem, but he "won" a deferral of the gender of the described beloved toward—or through—whom the poetic speaker is moving.

In the case of Cummings's poem "o pr," Augusto's strategy of amplification works to great effect, expanding the poem's critique of political positivism and the US ideology of progress. The key letter *o*, which begins the English version and then is removed from the first word or syllable in subsequent lines, is also the Portuguese word for the definite article "the." In the source text, the missing *o* taken out of the word "progress" becomes merely the absence of the ball, which the president is throwing in a game of baseball. The hypercapitalized "The" takes precedence over the capitalization of the title "President," which does not appear as capitalized until the last of eight iterations, building up one word at a time to the phrase "The President Of The)United States // Of America" (see fig. 2).[49]

However, in Augusto's Portuguese version, everywhere Cummings's emphatically capitalized "The" becomes a repetition of the letter *O*—the same letter which had been absented from the earlier sections of the poem. All the missing *o*'s are displaced, violently scattershot over the page of the second half of the poem. Instead of the capital *T*'s in "The President" of the source text, the singular capital *O*'s, as in "O presidente," become the balls being thrown, the bullets being shot, the eyes

o pr
gress verily thou art m
mentous superc
lossal hyperpr
digious etc i kn
w & if you d

n't why g
to yonder s
called newsreel s
called theatre & with your
wn eyes beh

ld The
(The president The
president of The president
of the The)president of

the(united The president of the
united states The president of the united
states of The President Of The)United States

Of America unde negant redire quemquam supp
sedly thr
w
i
n
g
a
b
aseball

Fig. 2. E. E. Cummings, "o pr," in *NO THANKS* (1935). © E. E. Cummings 1935, © 1963, 1991 by the Trustees for the E. E. Cummings Trust, © 1978 by George James Firmage.

beholding, contemplating the spectacle, the emptiness, the null void, the absolute zero of the supposed grandeur of "progresso" (see fig. 3).[50]

Augusto himself highlights the translation strategy of displacement and compensation in his letter to Cummings analyzing his translations and demonstrating to the author the value of these strategies to re-create

ó pr
gresso és em verdade m
mentoso superc
lossal hiperpr
digioso etc t
dos sabem e se v

cê nã
sabe ora pr
cure os assim chamad
s cinemas assim chamad
s teatros e com seus pr
prios olhos c

ntemple O
(O presidente O
presidente d O presidente
dos O)presidente d

os(estados O presidente dos
estados unidos O presidente dos estados
unidos da O Presidente Dos)Estados Unidos

Da América unde negant redire quemquam sup
stamente j

g
a
n
d
o
u
ma bola

Fig. 3. E. E. Cummings, "ó pr," translation by Augusto de Campos, in *10 poemas* (1960). © Augusto de Campos.

and even enhance his work in Portuguese. Unlike the translators into French and German, who never contest the conventions that the author knows his own work best and that translations will produce primarily losses, Augusto instead insists on the capacity of Portuguese to re-create Cummings's work, and on his ability as reader and poet to see everything the author could—and perhaps more. Continuing the performance of the initial letter where he has absorbed and adopted elements of Cummings's poetry, Augusto identifies some of his translation choices as creating a balance of "losses" and "wins." For example, discussing his translation of "birds(" he writes: "(you lost the nn, you might say (meaning ness/now). to which i can reply: but i won the aa (agora/alma)."[51] Augusto points out how his strategy of transposition allows him to preserve the source poem's alliterative moments.

Drawing attention to the translational wins and losses on both sides of the language divide, Augusto places the translation and its source as equals, competing on a level playing field. He describes moments of alliteration and visual echoes that his translation "lost," but points out others he "won." The bellicose yet diplomatic phrasing of his musing "you lost . . . you might say . . . to which I can reply: but I won" reinforces my argument of a foreclosure of real exchange between translator and author. In this moment, Augusto claims both sides of a conversation. Containing Cummings's discourse within his own, he flags certain poetic choices, anticipates the author's potential concerns that these choices have been "lost in translation," and reassures him that, in fact, the Portuguese translation has provided an adequate compensation. The cannibal translator wholly devours the author's role: first by taking the words out of his mouth, and then by claiming the right to talk back.

Cummings does not respond in kind—in fact, his response does precisely the opposite. Instead of reading or engaging with the insights Augusto tries to give him from the Portuguese, he takes the opportunity to correct Augusto's English citations of his own text—made casually, in the course of a letter—insisting on seeing all proofs through the process. Hand-correcting and sending back pages of Augusto's own letter to him is tantamount to sending back a gift.[52] Where Augusto shared these early examples to demonstrate the reciprocal exchange of wins and losses between Portuguese and English, Cummings only saw the necessity to assert his privilege and expertise over the English, fundamentally ignoring the translations themselves.

BRIDGES TO BRAZILIAN PORTUGUESE AND UNREQUITED TRANSLATION DIALOGUE

Augusto builds a bridge from English to Portuguese for Cummings, perhaps to engage him in conversation around translation poetics, mapping pathways through French and Italian to exhibit his attention to detail by referencing other Romance languages that Cummings knows—and perhaps holds in higher regard. Readers can witness the poet's knowledge of both French and Italian as these are linguistic resources he draws on to create multilingual moments or scenarios in his poems.[53] Augusto translates one of his most Italianate poems, "Memorabilia," which conjures the sights and sounds of an embodied experience as tourist in Venice. In the same commentary on "birds(" he demonstrates how he re-created in Portuguese the splitting apart of one word into two: where the words "using twilight's vastness" is laid out on the page to read "U /)sing" to introduce the word "sing." Augusto's solution is "encantam crepuscular vastidão [enchanting twilight vastness]" which he explains saying "i rearrange into encantam (=enchant) which gives also cantam (=sing), these verbs functioning like the french chanter/enchanter."[54] He explains several other verbs by giving their French equivalents (*se tornam* is glossed as *se changent*, *são* as *sont*), pointing out why these choices preserve the sounds or echoes of other words present in the source text.

In an earlier letter, Augusto had already initiated these attempts to demonstrate the creative fertility of his Portuguese language and the concrete poetry movement's translation strategies so that Cummings could understand, when he sent a copy of *Noigandres* 2 along with a sheaf of typescript translations of poems by Haroldo de Campos, Ronaldo Azeredo, and himself into French and English.[55] In the case of his English translation of "semi di zucca" by Haroldo, he includes a page of commentary, connecting the poetic concerns of the Brazilian concrete poets and Cummings. Here, Augusto demonstrates his translation prowess with formally experimental pieces: showing his facility in the opposite direction, from Portuguese to English, he proves his potential as a translator of Cummings into Portuguese. Providing bullet points to interpret and pronounce key words in Portuguese, he wants his reader to see, hear, and understand the source text, the translation, and the movement between them. The underlining in Augusto's typescript pages appear to add emphasis to the Portuguese:

translation is literal: it needs some explanations to become more intelligible:

só—means, in portuguese, only and alone at the same time. pronounce as saw.
sun(alt(lone(ry—echoes the preceding call. "ss" of the words sal (salt), só (alone), sêco (dry) cut off.
parenthesis: typographical device for waves of sound. eco = echo. the whole, in portuguese sol al ó eco sounds as an echo, a deformated [*sic*] echo, a parody of solilóquio = soliloquy.[56]

Augusto's reference to the use of parenthesis as a visual representation of a sound effect recalls his interest in Cummings's punctuation that draws from similar devices. From the start, he performs translation as an expression of their shared poetic tools and an expansion of Cummings's reach into Portuguese. His dense translation commentary shows not only his skill as a translator but also his gesture of reciprocity, a repayment of the debt the concrete poets owe Cummings, a return gift both voluntary and compelled.

Reading this correspondence as a part of the translator's archive testifies to the nature of Augusto's translation approach as a reciprocated gift. He has cannibalized the author's aesthetic even in the letters he sends, absorbing Cummings before the fact, describing his Brazilian language as "jaguar" and his translations as superseding their originals in some moments. In this way, Augusto shows translation to be a pathway forward for the elements of Cummings's work that had been rejected by the aesthetically and politically neutralizing versions by other translators working under the compromised publication norms of European translation venues impacted by the cultural Cold War. His cannibal translation choices and strategies expand, give back, and propel forward the perilous vector of this poetry that operates on the poetic unit of the letter. Augusto's commentary on his own translations show their generative potential through this reciprocal balance of loss and gain, in which his translation strategies of emphasis, transposition, and expansion not only reply to any concerns of loss in translation before the fact; they also demonstrate a form of reading that seeks to give back to the text by translating and rewriting it.

In his elegant limited-edition *10 poemas* (1960), Augusto includes a facsimile page of proofs hand-corrected by Cummings, subverting the author's authority, and circulating a version of the poem the author rejected with this detailed correction. Augusto here usurps the right to determine what a translation may include. His cannibal translation of Cummings includes the process, the errors, the attention to detail, all the surplus and remainder get included as a part of the presentation of the poems (see fig. 4).

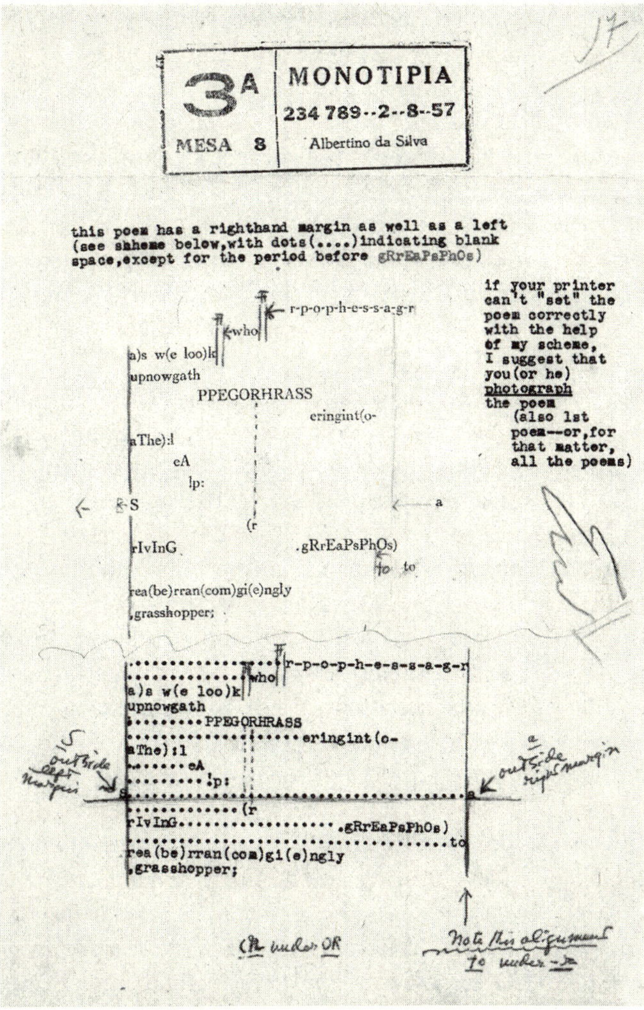

Fig. 4. E. E. Cummings, "r-p-o-p-h-e-s-s-a-g-r," page proof hand-corrected by the author, in *10 poemas* (1960). © Augusto de Campos.

I read this gesture of publishing a page of corrected proofs, a page that literally includes the "hand" of the author, as an example of a cannibal translator's refusal to submit to the author's authority. Including these corrections, Augusto draws attention to the process through which translations reconstruct a poem. Although this corrected proof page might appear to cede responsibility, or give the author all the power over his text, it ultimately demonstrates to readers that Cummings was primarily interested in preserving the integrity of the "spatial architecture" in English and largely reliant on his translator.[57] Compare this to Grossman, who embraced the author's primacy so much that he wanted to name Cummings as a cotranslator on the cover of his book. Instead, Augusto subsumes the author, devouring and displacing his authority. Cummings appears relegated to the endpapers, and only in English, therefore in need of the translator's voice in Portuguese to frame and explain this page of proofs. In fact, the two never discuss the inclusion of this proof page in their correspondence, and Augusto confirms that he never sought permission from Cummings to publish his hand-corrected proofs.[58]

These proofs show translation as another stage in the larger editorial challenge posed by Cummings's poems, what Karen Emmerich defines as a "translingual edition." Augusto includes more pages from this initial process in each subsequent publication: the most recent 2012 edition ends with eleven facsimile pages of proofs and letters.[59] Although the creativity of these translations may never have been fully perceived by Cummings, the energy generated between the two writers continues to have reverberations for Augusto and other translators, even now, over fifty years after the first edition.

The readers impacted by Augusto's translation praxis would include other Latin American translators into Spanish and Portuguese—but another delighted reader was the French-language translator D. Jon Grossman. Writing to Augusto from Rome in 1967, Grossman praises *10 poemas* for their exploitation of possibilities in Portuguese: "I've spent many hours envying you a language that permits you [so much . . .] and even has an 'O' for the definite article! The language serves you well, but you have taken advantage of nearly everything it contained."[60] Although overall his praise is unmitigated, he does question a few choices, asking "why 'cristais' for 'glassworks'?"[61] Augusto does alter this lexical choice in subsequent editions of this poem, though he does not take Grossman's suggestion, *vitrificação*, and instead chooses *vidrios*. The page of proofs included in the final publication pulls back the veil to show the process and invites contributions from translator-readers like Grossman. Augusto's translations are an open work, a "translingual edition" that continues becoming, always incomplete.

This page of corrections also demonstrates a moment of cocreation of visual poetry, where multiple forms of aesthetic information coexist and interact to produce meaning. It includes typed instructions, handwritten corrections, information about spacing conveyed through dots and dashes, and a little sketch of a hand with a finger pointing emphatically to the suggestion, or perhaps admonishing order, typed up by Cummings: "if your printer can't 'set' the poems correctly with the help of my schema, I suggest that you (or he) photograph the poem (also 1st poem—or, for that matter, all the poems)."[62] The image of the hand, pointing, and the suggestion that poems might just as easily be photographed speak to the concrete poet's larger project of seeing poetry in a field that includes the plastic arts, where the verbal draws on vocal and visual elements, and where multiple sign systems construct meaning across the open field of the page, unconfined by traditional lineation or divisions between image and word. As both Augusto and Haroldo de Campos will theorize in later essays, this performative disruption of authority exemplifies the Brazilian translation style, which Augusto anticipates here by including the corrected page. Yet the gift of these translation strategies remains unseen by the author, despite the multiple efforts Augusto makes to draw him into the opportunities possible in his "jaguar language" to creatively expand on Cummings's works through translation.

Including this page of proofs and the visual qualities of Cummings's corrections also enact the translation practice of "untranslation," or *intradução*, that Augusto would apply to other source texts. Untranslations include visual elements, although they only sometimes take visual poems as source texts. Remaining in process and in confrontation with their sources, refusing to fully translate, or intermingling source and translation as in the poem "Intradução" discussed in my introduction, the source text remains inside the untranslation, devoured but not absorbed.[63] If cannibal translations perform their own taboo nature, the untranslations by Augusto refuse to stand alone, to do what a translation "should" do; instead, the two versions talk to one another, remain in process, in relationship—becoming, not being.

To be fair, Cummings warmly received the homage of Augusto's translations, and he did express gratitude for the opportunity to see his work anew. The author sent postcards reading "Congratulations!" and "Merci mille fois OK HAPPY NEW YEAR" to give final approval for *10 poemas*.[64] Curiously enough, Cummings did draft a more effusive thank-you letter—but either he never sent it to Augusto or it never arrived, because only the E. E. Cummings Papers contain this warmly ebullient reaction, full of exclamation and emphasis in red typescript: "'10 poemas' arrived today—*bravissimo*! It's by far the *handsomest* opus this nonhero has glimpsed in *decades*; but he *truly* can't tell when I've felt so extraordinarily *cheered*! *Please accept our very deepest morethangratitude*—et *BONNE CHANCE*!" (see fig. 5).[65]

Despite this sweet, superlative "morethangratitude," the letters exchanged make it clear that Cummings never fully received the gifts of the translation strategies Augusto took such pains to lay bare to him, and never fully absorbed the theoretical implications of the process described by his Brazilian correspondent. Far from engaging in any original composition or translation himself using these strategies, as will occur between Latin American translators studied in this book, Cummings persisted in an English-centric view of his work even in translation. What does manifest is the Brazilian translator's effort to make these discussions and translation challenges visible and legible to readers by including a piece of the process in his publication.

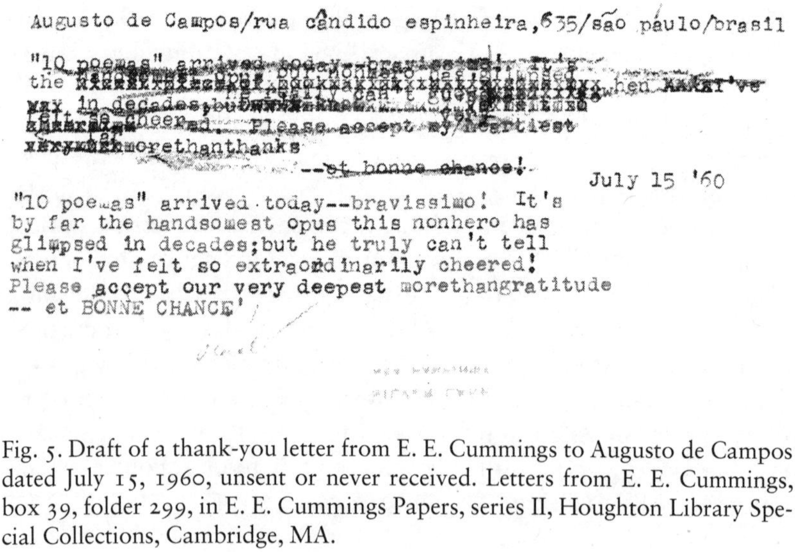
Augusto de Campos/rua cândido espinheira,635/são paulo/brasil

July 15 '60

"10 poemas" arrived today--bravissimo! It's by far the handsomest opus this nonhero has glimpsed in decades;but he truly can't tell when I've felt so extraordinarily cheered! Please accept our very deepest morethangratitude -- et BONNE CHANCE'

Fig. 5. Draft of a thank-you letter from E. E. Cummings to Augusto de Campos dated July 15, 1960, unsent or never received. Letters from E. E. Cummings, box 39, folder 299, in E. E. Cummings Papers, series II, Houghton Library Special Collections, Cambridge, MA.

MORE LOVE THAN RESPECT IN OCTAVIO PAZ'S VERSIONS

Where Augusto chooses to translates the most "perilous" selections from Cummings, Paz instead elevates the Anglo-American modernist's reinvention of early modern fixed forms through syntax shifting and other innovations within set metrical rules. While Paz's selections may appear to be closer to the safer, more politically toothless preferences of Grossman and Hesse, his correspondence with the author and the paratextual frames he gives to his versions paint a more ambivalent picture. Read in the context of the subtle critique Paz levels at Cummings's nonapprehension of the Spanish language and his subsequent exoticizing gaze on its poetry, his versions emerge as a measured rejection of some of the elements he identifies as central to the poet's oeuvre alongside an experiment in Spanish with accentual-syllabic verse form.

Paz approaches Cummings through personal correspondence and stages his translations as a continued conversation between friends, yet the language barrier forecloses their closeness. The two poets had met in the Cummings home in 1956; as in the exchanges with Grossman, they reminisce on previous social occasions and include greetings to their respective wives.[66] Unlike the other three translators, Paz never characterizes his translations as destined for a public audience, describing them as casual, meant to circulate among a small group of intimates.[67] Cummings never demands to review proofs as he did with Augusto, Grossman, and Hesse; instead, he merely expresses shame that he cannot appreciate Paz's work because he does not read Spanish. Unlike the other three translators, Paz remains on his own side of the language divide: he writes in Spanish, Cummings replies in English, which naturally conditions their discussion. Paz alludes to the fact that Cummings's "charming wife" will likely translate his letter: "Since she knows Spanish, I imagine she will be the one who will translate this letter (my English is too poor)."[68] The Cummings Papers demonstrate the incredible contribution Marion Morehouse made to the poet's public life, correspondence, scheduling, and other practical matters. She also corresponded with Grossman and Hesse, responding and answering questions when Cummings had not yet taken the time, and so it was not an unusual assumption for Paz to think of her as the primary recipient of his letters. The writerly exchange of gifts in the form of poetry and translations, while it may appear reciprocal at first, takes on a different quality when Paz depicts the language attitudes of Cummings. In a missed encounter between their two languages, Cummings can literally "see" the Spanish language as spoken with gestural emphasis and can appreciate the way it sounds, yet he fails to grasp, or even attempt to perceive, its meaning.

While Cummings cannot understand the Spanish translations Paz sends him, he insists on the value of an extrasemantic apprehension based entirely on sound or sight. He expresses regret that "my shameful ignorance of Spanish forbids me to appraise [your translations] but which all my eyes and ears greatly enjoy."[69] For Cummings, the pleasure he takes in the Spanish translations can be merely visual and sonic. In a later essay, Paz would describe Cummings indulging in the same form of appreciation without understanding in personal interactions with Spanish poets. During the 1956 visit Paz made to the poet's New York home, Cummings reminisced about a trip to Spain with novelist John Dos Passos, where despite his "shameful ignorance of Spanish" he found himself thoroughly enchanted by the Spanish poets the two encountered. Paz paraphrases Cummings's comment, explaining that despite the language barrier, Cummings perceived something valuable: "While Dos Passos sustained long conversations with them in Spanish, 'I meanwhile examined them, alternating between fear and laughter. It didn't matter that I didn't understand what they said: I got enough from their physical presence, their gestures, the sound of their voices.'"[70] The ambivalence of this description Paz gives of Cummings, blithely claiming that the mere sound and image of their incomprehensible Spanish speech-acts give him access to perceptions beyond the semantic, echoes his own ambivalence about translation as executed by poets. Cummings, an exemplary "bad" poet-translator, cannot understand the Spanish poets, yet the sounds of their voices charm him, and he imagines this is sufficient to enable him to comprehend something. In the translation theory Paz will develop, poets who translate may only ever see, hear, or write, what their own poetic instrument invents for them, an imagined poetic projection.

In light of this attention paid to what is merely "visible" or "audible" rather than fully apprehensible in poetry as it moves between languages, I assert that when Paz characterizes his translation as coming "more from love than respect," he is not merely giving a rhetorical flourish. Although the Brazilian and Mexican translators both engage in a discourse of humility, lowering expectations for their translations, Paz expresses the stakes of his translation choices differently. Paz writes: "I approached their originals with respect and love. More the latter than the former. I don't know if my translations could be literally faithful; at least I have tried to be faithful to the spirit if not the letter."[71] Paz still gives some credence the category of "faithful," which is no longer operative at all for Augusto. Yet unlike the fidelity-focused translators Grossman and Hesse, Paz creates a tension between "respectful" or "faithful" translations and his own, which come from love but are faithful only to the spirit of the poems. Concepts of "love" and "respect" could be aligned—but for Paz, when it comes to the objectivity or selflessness he envisions a translator should adopt, the two affective states work against one another, and this letter to Cummings from 1958 demonstrates that his translation practice is mapping out this tension he will later theorize.

Before that, in "e. e. cummings: Seis poemas y un recuerdo," first published in *Puertas al campo* (1966), he represents this tension between "love" and "respect" once more as it connects to the language divide between himself and Cummings. With a nostalgic tone of fond but frank backward glance, Paz couples praise with measured critique and mild condescension, subtly undercutting Cummings, much like the reception he received, when the Anglo-American poet neglected to fully apprehend Spanish or examine his exoticizing and othering of Paz and Mexico. Given that Cummings was sixty-two and Paz forty-two when they met in Greenwich Village in 1956, when Paz describes Cummings as childish, feisty, almost clown-like, his tone strikes a surprising note of tolerant disdain mixed with admiration for an older man who seems younger. From his first encounter as a reader in 1944 to their last interaction one year before his death in 1962, Paz saw Cummings as pugilistic and minimalist, perfectly fit and streamlined. Yet he also describes a man who fails to see—or who does not bother to understand—the people in front of him. In Paz's retelling, Cummings exoticizes the Spanish poets he remembers meeting, imagining they are "made from the same substance of the earth and air of Spain," and representing their Spanish as almost prelinguistic, comprehensible through "their outbursts or gestures, their silences, their exclamations" rather than through their language.[72] Cummings also fails to hear when Paz pushes back against his fetishization of both Spain and Mexico as more "authentic" than the United States. When Paz insists that Mexico has made great strides lately, Paz remembers him replying "'Better not to make progress . . .'"[73] The nonreciprocal relationship observable in the letters between Cummings and Paz—while not as extreme as in the case of Augusto—filters through in this essay.

Paz's ambivalence extends from the interpersonal to the poetic, where he references Cummings's critics who disparage his experimental qualities as "extravagancies." Calling into question this term while not precisely rejecting it, he instead praises these qualities for following their own logic: "None of the so-called 'extravagancies' of cummings is arbitrary: typography, punctuation, wordplay, syntax that tends to transform nouns, adjectives, and even pronouns into verbs—it is a game. And like all games, it obeys a strict logic."[74] The praise grows fainter when he agrees with detractors that Cummings "repeats himself," though he takes pains to soften this judgment: "If there is no evolution in his work, neither is there any decline."[75] Overall, Paz paints him as a prolific and innovative poet who never changed his writing style—or matured his persona—beyond his first youthful contributions.

In spite of this measured defense, Paz translates poems decidedly bare of these "extravagancies," and instead cannibalizes Cummings to experiment with a style of accentual-syllabic verse in Spanish. Although Paz—like Augusto—selects poems ranging from 1926 to 1950, they are largely written in strict accentual-syllabic verse forms and contain none of the political force of "o pr" or the raw eroticism of "i will be," focusing instead on abstract representations of love and the human experience. Of the four qualities he praises in the poetic "game" Cummings plays—typography, punctuation, wordplay, unusual syntax—Paz's Spanish translations only preserve the final quality of shifting syntax. For example, the title line of "love is more thicker than forget" uses the verb "to forget" as a noun and attributes the physical quality of thickness to this verb-made-noun. The German translator Eva Hesse, critiqued by Augusto for her "shy" choices, also translated this poem—which does in fact pose some challenges. In the typescript Paz sent Cummings in 1958, he chooses the verb form *amar* as a translation for "love"; in his first version, "amar es más espeso que olvidar," the line starts and ends with matching verbs, as in "to love is more thick than to forget."[76] Although he maintains this choice in the first publication of this poem in *Puertas al campo* (1966), by the time the selection is recollected in *Traducción: Literatura y literalidad* (1973), and in all subsequent publications, he changes it to "Amor es más espeso que olvidar," emphasizing the noun form of the word "love," which then increases the weight of the use of *olvidar* as a parallel, emphasizing the noun-like qualities of the verb. With this edit, Paz gets closer to the source, as a "good translator" ought to, pointing readers to pay attention to the non-normative syntactical relationship between words in Cummings's poetry.

Paz's translation strategies do little to amplify Cummings, as Augusto strives to—in fact his choices tend to reduce, domesticate, or erase entirely certain moments of strangeness in the source poems. Instead, he explores accentual-syllabic verse in Spanish through translations that mimic some of the metrical qualities of the English source texts. Preferring the *líricos isabelinos* (Elizabethan lyrics), Paz translates selections that combine Cummings's minimalist tendencies with fixed forms to produce brief but evocative sonnets or other short metrical poems.[77] However, within these verse forms, he does not make translation choices that preserve the minimalism he prizes in Cummings. Whereas Augusto would change even semantic meaning to better preserve an economy of syllables or letters, the shape or quantity of words on the page, Paz instead imports his own key words and eliminates "extravagancies." For example, in the love poem "in spite of everything," Paz lengthens lines and domesticates punctuation, orthography, and spacing of words on the page. The following lines feature what Augusto called Cummings's "tortography":

> i turn,and(stooping
> through the morning)kiss
> this pillow,dear[78]

Cummings visually conveys the intimacy and proximity of the speaker, also speeding up time in this precious encounter with the everyday object associated with the beloved by eliminating the spaces around parentheses and commas, making every second of this morning more fleeting. In his version, Paz normalizes the typography:

> me vuelvo y (parado
> en mitad de la mañana) beso
> esa almohada, amor mío[79]

His translation also interpolates a subtle reference to the opening lines of Dante's *Inferno* in which the speaker stops in the middle of the road of life, translating "stooping / through the morning" as "parado / en mitad de la mañana" or "stopped / in the middle of the morning." While Paz could have inadvertently mistaken "stooping" for "stopping," I prefer to consider it a deliberate choice, an opportunity to write Dante into Cummings in his Spanish version. By normalizing spacing on the page and setting off this echo of a classic poet of world literature, Paz's version of Cummings hews more closely to the poetic tradition than its source.

In the same poem, Paz introduces an element of his own writerly voice when he chooses the word *Destino* as a translation for "Doom": the opening lines "in spite of everything / which breathes and moves, since Doom"[80] in his version read as "A pesar de todo / lo que respira y se mueve, pues el Destino."[81] This word choice fits Paz's recurring poetic figure of love as an endless cycle on the wheel of "Destiny" rather than love as always encoding its own end, in the more melancholic framing found in Cummings. Other choices available to him in Spanish could better approximate the darker tone or the single-syllable landing on "Doom" at end of the poetic line. Paz could have chosen *sino* or *azar* if he wanted to maintain a shorter line but still indicate inevitability and predetermination achieved with *Destino*. Or he could have better approximated the negative connotations of the source: *ruina*, *desastre*, *derrota*, or even *muerte* would have gotten him closer. The word *fin* (end) could have preserved both syllabic number and meaning, yet Paz's translation strategies do not appear focused on either diction transference or an economy of syllable or letter.

While he may morph the semantic field of his source text to best overlap with his own key words, Paz does tend to preserve the metrical qualities of Cummings's poems, especially when they update the Elizabethan tradition. For example, "love is more thicker than forget" has a strict rhyme scheme and four-line stanzas that follow what is known as the common meter (tetrameter followed by trimeter) or are all in iambic trimeter. In his version, Paz achieves lines that approach iambic meter in Spanish; echoing the source, his first stanza includes iambic pentameter and tetrameter lines. He bends the syllabic verse form of the Spanish *silva*—an early modern poetic form that mixes lines of seven and eleven syllables—into accentual-syllabic verse, where accent or emphasis stands out more than syllable count or line length. In the first stanza of Paz's translation, he opens with a line with four accented syllables, followed by three, four, and three, mimicking the singsong common meter of the source text:

> Amor es más espeso que olvidar
> más tenue que recordar
> más raro que una ola mojada
> más frecuente que caer[82]
>
> love is more thicker than forget
> more thinner than recall

more seldom than a wave is wet
more frequent than to fail[83]

Paz creates a new accentual-syllabic verse form in Spanish through this approximation of existing forms in English. His tetrameter verses, lines 1 and 3, include ten syllables, unusual in Spanish versification, mixed with the more traditional seven-syllable lines 2 and 4.

However, his translation method of preserving meter does not prioritize the invention of neologism or the bending of syntax. The second stanza also reproduces Cummings metrically, with a Spanish version all in iambic trimeter, yet the wordplay infringing on English norms does not receive the same attention from Paz as it did in Augusto's translation work. For example, the lines "it is most mad and moonly / and less it shall unbe" become "es más loco y lunar / y menos no será," a translation that beautifully transposes the sonic characteristics of meter and alliteration, while eliminating the inventive bending of English presented by "moonly" and "unbe." Back-translated into English, the version by Paz would be "it is more mad and lunar / and less it shall not be." The full stanza reads:

es más loco y lunar
y menos no será
que todo el mar que sólo
es más profundo que el mar[84]

it is most mad and moonly
and less it shall unbe
than all the sea which only
is deeper than the sea[85]

Read aloud, the Paz translation smoothly reproduces the musical sonority and repetition of Cummings in English. Yet his grammatically correct *no será* (shall not be) does not reproduce the strangeness of Cummings's "shall unbe." Furthermore, "lunar" was also available in English, but Cummings instead invented "moonly," avoiding the formal register conveyed by the collocations of "lunar" associated with forms of measurement (lunar calendar), scientific precision (lunar eclipse), or mystical attunement to the universe (lunar cycle). Paz instead draws straight from those semantic families, which fit with his poetic interests. Paz makes the same choice a stanza later, where he translates "it is most sane and sunly" as "es más solar y soleado" (it is more solar and sunny), eliminating the invented adverb "sunly" and removing "sane" to instead amplify the sunniness of the image.[86] Where Cummings builds verbal connections between love, thickness, thinness, madness, and sanity, Paz in Spanish translation eliminates sanity as the other side of the coin.

Rather than reading these choices as born of necessity or mere lack of attention, I contend that Paz's versions consistently show an effort to smooth Cummings's wordplay out into a musically fluid and fluent Spanish. Paz's translation strategies focus on preserving their clarity while he experiments with metrical syllabic verse in Spanish and draws out diction that echoes his own poems. In short, he uses the Cummings poems as "points of departure" to create poems of his own and to expand what is possible in his own language—precisely what he claims, in a later essay, poets who translate will almost inevitably do, even though they ought not—poets who, like him, operate from "love" rather than "respect."

Compared to Augusto, on the playing field of Cummings's poetry, Paz emerges as a reluctant cannibal translator. In his essay "Translation: Literature and Literalness," Paz presents the challenge of translation as poetic self-discipline and denial of one's own literary impulses:

> In theory, only poets should translate poetry; in practice, poets are rarely good translators. They almost invariably use the foreign poem as a point of departure toward their own. A good translator moves in the opposite direction: his intended destination is a poem analogous although not identical to the original poem. He moves away from the poem only to follow it more closely. . . . The reason many poets are unable to translate poetry is not purely psychological, although egotism has a part in it, but functional.[87]

Paz here defines the task of the translator precisely as the challenge to have the self-knowledge, humility, and respect to function as a "good translator" rather than making an original poem from the starting point of another's work. Yet the habitus of the poet makes the functional distinction between translation and creation difficult to maintain. Rather than placing translation on a continuum with creation, he prizes the translator's capacity to maintain those boundaries.

Contradicting this theoretical assertion, when Paz introduces his collected translations *Versiones y diversiones* (1974), he reverses the values of his earlier essay while echoing some of its language. He emphasizes the personal work he does as a translator, driven by desire and chance encounters with other poets and executed through his own practical skills of poem-making. Like building a house, a poet-translator knows the materials needed and works with them in his own way. He writes that his versions are born out of "passion and chance."

> Passion and chance—but also labor of carpentry, bricklaying, watchmaking, gardening, electricity, plumbing—in a word, verbal industry. . . . So I ask that you not judge this book as a work of literary investigation. For the same reason I have not included the original texts: from poems in other languages, I wanted to make poems in my own.[88]

In these closing lines, Paz echoes and reverses the argument in his translation essay. Framing his versions as poems in "his language"—while not going so far as to claim them as his own poems—he does not wish readers to compare them to their source texts. As a translator, Paz expands his *parole*, his personal use of the Spanish language, the expression of his individual lexicon, not just the abstract *langue* of Spanish.

Paz's reversals of his own theoretical claims extend to the visual; in his essay on translation, he claims that "when translating, a translator knows the poem should reproduce the one he has before his eyes."[89] This essay—and in fact Paz's letter to Cummings—may prompt us to ask why Paz made so little effort to reproduce certain elements of the poems "before his eyes." Paz perceived yet discarded the very same tortographic elements he describes—and halfheartedly defends—in his essay on Cummings. Why so little respect? Paz, more of a cannibal translator than he claims, sees but refuses to reproduce analogous effects—much like Cummings, who saw and heard the Spanish poets but never bothered to understand them.

Paz does show awareness that he sometimes translates against his own principles. In the second edition of *Versiones y diversiones*, published in 1978, he demonstrates enduring concern with his own lack of objectivity as a translator. In his introduction to the second edition, he points out changes he made to his translations of sonnets by the French Romanticist Gérard de Nerval. Characterizing these changes as necessary if reluctant retractions, Paz ultimately highlights how his initial versions of Nerval included lines that echoed the early modern Spanish lyricist Luis de Góngora and the Latin American fin de siècle *modernista* Rubén Darío—but needed to be edited because the "Hispanic brio" of his versions strayed too far from the source.[90] Yet these retractions, so limited and performative, reveal Paz as the cannibal translator who wants others to translate him with a bit less love and a bit more respect—but who tends to serve his own poetic voice as a translator of other poets, devouring their work within his own language.

In his early letter to Cummings, Paz interrogates this tension with the author himself, the difference between "love" and "respect" when it comes to appreciating the work of another poet in another language. Although Cummings also displays a lack of "respect" in his loving but impressionistic, uncomprehending gaze toward poets and poetry in Spanish, he nevertheless fails to engage in the reflective self-interrogation that Paz invites—and in fact practices, by writing his translation paratexts that prevaricate between oppositional concepts: love versus respect, good poets versus good translators.

INTRA–LATIN AMERICAN TRANSLATION THINKING

Only one poem by Cummings—"l(a" or "(a leaf falls)"—claims the privilege of a translation by both Augusto and Paz. Letters stretch down the page, two at a time, visually tracing one moment of falling and slowing down the reading process with line breaks that challenge apprehension, extending the embodied experience of being alone.[91]

s (u	l(a
na	le
ho	af
ja	fa
ca	ll
e)	s)
o	one
l	l
edad[92]	iness[93]

First published in *95 Poems* (1958), the last collection printed during the poet's lifetime, "l(a" was unavailable to them during their initial encounters with Cummings, yet both add it to subsequent editions of their translations. "l(a" fits with both of their translation priorities: the perilous, "tortographic" characteristics Augusto pursues and Paz's disrespectful appropriation of a foreign poem to match it with his own poetic vocabulary. This poem represents a symbolic meeting point between the two Latin American translators.

Stringing the lines together, the Spanish "s (una hoja cae) oledad" directly reproduces the English "l(a leaf falls)oneliness"—although one could argue that *soledad* (solitude) may not be the only Spanish option available to translate "loneliness." Despite other options, such as *el estar sólo*, *aislamiento*, or *desamparo*, only *soledad* relates so closely to Paz's own literary vocabulary. Echoing in a minimalist vein his treatment of solitude as a key concept for Mexican identity in *El laberinto de la soledad* (1950), this poem stands alone in his Cummings translations for including the atomization of words that attracts Augusto. Not only does he repeat the single letter "l" alone on one line, marking the downward trajectory of the leaf; he also finds a word-within-a-word to transpose this element from his source text. Cummings drew "one" out of "loneliness": standing out on the third to final line as the only legible word among a waterfall of mere letters, the word "one" emphasizes the singularity shared by the falling leaf and the human experience of loneliness. Paz's version, built on his own key term, *soledad*, also achieves the word *edad* (age) in the final line, introducing temporality, duration, and human frailty experienced through the aging process as reflected by seasonal changes. I read this translation as a resolution of the tension Paz traces between a poet-translator's love or desire to write a poem in his own voice based on another author's work and the respect or objectivity needed to be a "good translator" and create a poem analogous to the original. It both draws on Paz's poetic vocabulary while also carefully reproducing the visual qualities of the source text. The publication record shows that Paz likely translated the poem between 1971 and 1973.[94] Since Paz and Haroldo met in Cambridge, Massachusetts, in 1972, it is possible that Paz translated "l(a" only after his dialogue with the Brazilian concrete poets and after he wrote his own concrete poems, *Topoemas* (1968), discussed in chapter 2.

Augusto's expanded edition of Cummings titled *40 poem(a)s* (1986) features his Portuguese version of the same poem on the cover in full color. Maintaining the identical strict economy of letters as the source text, he translates “a leaf” as 1 *folha* with the numeral 1 rather than spelling out the indefinite article *uma* to preserve the number of letters in each line. Augusto’s untranslation expands on the poem’s existing visual elements by adding an ornate plant-like typeface that evokes the organic curlicues of a fiddle-head fern and by using two shades of green ink to further conjure up images of the falling leaf, changing colors with the season (see fig. 6).

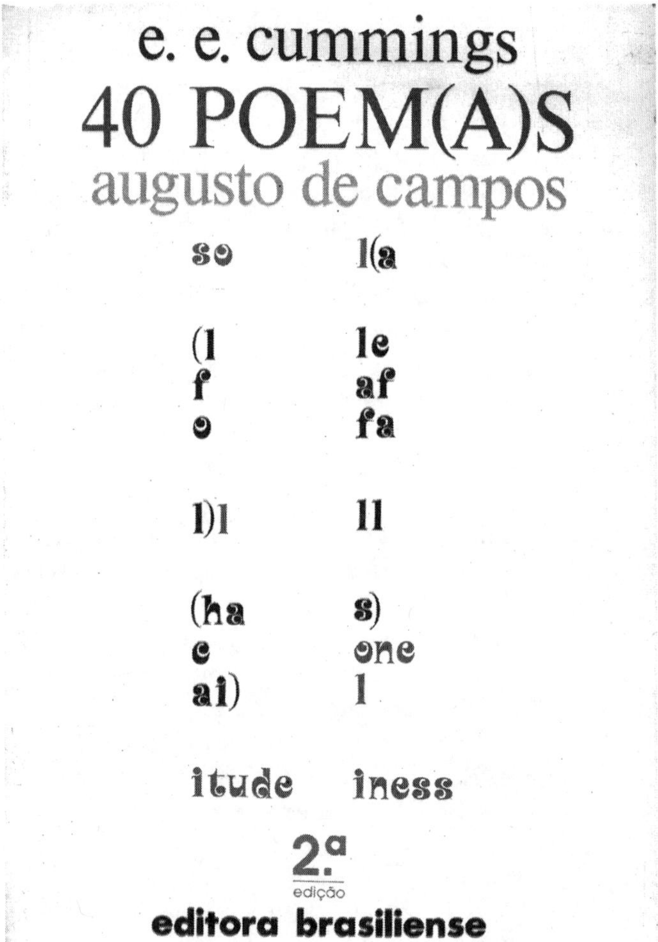

Fig. 6. E. E. Cummings, “so l(a,” translated by Augusto de Campos, on the cover of *40 poem(a)s* (1984). © Augusto de Campos.

Reading the first lines of the two versions from left to right, across as "so l(a," blends the two languages together to achieve the Portuguese word *sola*, "alone." Yet the narrow poem in fact appears far less lonely as a matched pair; from Cummings "loneliness" articulated in "l(a," Augusto drew out the musical notes of the solfege scale, two voices singing "so" and "la," playing counterpoint off one another. This untranslation ultimately lets the Portuguese version remain in productive tension with the English source, which receives the same artistic treatment with additional visual qualities of font and color.[95] The bilingual *mise-en-page* does not defer to the source text by providing the "authoritative" original—in fact, the translation appears first. Instead, it gives readers the chance to observe his changes and choices—the cannibal translator wants the work to be visible. While Augusto would not name this procedure "untranslation" until creating this piece, I argue that the letters he wrote to Cummings decades earlier reveal the seeds of this concept.

This poem—which always stands apart from their other Cummings translations—serves as a key and a bridge between Paz and Augusto.[96] The one shared source text represents a brief convergence between both poets' different translation strategies. As this chapter has shown, the cannibal translations by Augusto and Paz represent not only the lack of reciprocity Cummings shows to his Latin American translators but also the distance between the translation thinkers in Brazil and in Mexico—the sociocultural distance that meant their encounter took place first through the mediation of Cummings and through English. Yet it also shows these two translators to be ahead of their time in the late 1950s, striking out where more normative translators would not dare, developing translation theories through their practices of translation, and working all the more to articulate them because they remained so invisible to the author.

CHAPTER 2

Belated Encounters between Latin American Translators

Before they met in person in 1972, even before they began a lively correspondence in 1968, Octavio Paz and Haroldo de Campos shared the vision that poetry should reinvent language, and that translation was one means to that end. Both poet-translators are drawn to procedures of destruction and accumulation, exploding normative language and putting the fragments back together in new ways. Performing these aesthetic concerns, Haroldo chose to translate the following section of "Trabajos de poeta," a long prose poem by Paz, a moment that features the cannibalistic dream of a language with teeth: "A language that cuts off your breath. Rough, rude, cutting. An army of swords. A language of exacting steel blades, of sharpened lightening, of angles and razor edges, tireless, shining, methodical, daggers. A guillotine language. A gnashing denture that makes a paste out of Iyouhimherusthem."[1] The image of a language that "makes a paste out of Iyouhimherusthem" captures the tension of cannibal translation: at once defiant and destructive, cumulative and constructive.

Paz and Haroldo favor a definition of translation and poetry in which "he is no poet, he who was never tempted to destroy language or create another, he who has never experienced the fascination of non-meaning."[2] Both writers take some distance from politically engaged literature, which they view as problematically presuming an uncontested representation of social reality, or even worse, dictating condescendingly to readers. Yet they also agree that poetry can metalinguistically rehearse greater political freedoms. Both poets liberate language from compulsory meaning-making by breaking it down and aggregating the pieces in new ways—a process that can occur within one language, and even more so through translation.

This chapter analyzes the complex "translationship" between Octavio Paz and Haroldo de Campos, which began with letters hashing out differences of opinion and resulted in mutual translation publications. Their correspondence during the social turmoil of 1968, with Brazil enduring a military dictatorship and Mexico's government violently repressing student protestors, reflects their shared experiences of frustration and their investment in translation to redress historical non-communication between their two Latin American literary traditions. The cannibal translation practices they use show the importance of intra–Latin American literary exchange, in which translation serves as a form of decolonial cultural repair, both acknowledging and correcting what Paz calls a "shameful" lack of communication between their circles.

I borrow the term "translationship" from Magdalena Edwards, who coins it to describe the connection between poets Elizabeth Bishop and Octavio Paz, who translated one another's work in ways that left marks on their own poetry and treated one another as "absolute accomplices in the creative sense."[3] The translationship Paz enjoyed with Haroldo takes on an additional quality of political positionality, which is reflected in the collection *Transblanco* (1986). As discussed in my introduction, for Haroldo, a "transcreation" entails the strict intratextual creative reconstruction of the literary work. While his transcreation of Paz's poem "Blanco" as "Branco" is the core of the publication *Transblanco*, the whole volume exemplifies my corpus of cannibal translation because it supplements the transcreation with a significant remainder of additional material. By including correspondence from 1968 to 1983 between the two authors, readers get privileged access to details that historicize the work, discussions between author and translator on word choice, and interpersonal elements of their translationship. Contrary to the author-translator relationship both Paz and Augusto had with Cummings, where the translation theories born out of practice were not interesting or visible to the author, I posit that the translationship between Paz and Haroldo flourished because of their shared interest in theorizing the act of translating as a mutually enriching project. Their letters evince disagreement, collegial sparring over ideas, and the tensions between them remain visible in the publication, rather than smoothed out or resolved into just one target language. Instead, matters of translation between Latin American poetic languages determine, mediate, and enhance their creative output. Rather than letting a translation—or even a transcreation—stand alone in place of a source text, they explore a voracious heterogeneity in which many elements of the lives they lived during the process of translating show up through the publication.

My analysis of this translationship draws on the published volume *Transblanco*, other unpublished ephemera, and their reciprocal publications in Brazilian news media and Mexican literary journals. Other studies examining *Transblanco* as a part of comparative analysis on the work of Paz and Haroldo tend to focus either outside the translation on the place of this correspondence in mutual poetic influence or inside the translation to reveal the extent to which they adhere to their own translation theories as practicing translators.[4] By incorporating additional elements of the translator's archive, I can illuminate the reciprocal nature of their translationship and their dialogue on the role of poetic translation in their political moment.

For example, the Haroldo de Campos library, held at the Casa das Rosas archive in São Paulo, provides vast evidence of the Brazilian translator's lifelong reading practice of creating detailed personal indexes inside the back covers of his books. In the case of Paz, he tracks themes and cross-references different works by Paz, tracing his analysis of the Mexican poet through poetry, essays, and even putting Paz's concepts in dialogue with other translation theorists that both poets studied, including Walter Benjamin and Roman Jakobson. Haroldo's marginalia evidences the importance of Paz in his teaching and writing, but the physical volumes also register long-term literary friendship. Knowing that Haroldo would take interest, Paz mailed him a copy of his *Veinte poemas* translation of William Carlos Williams, with the following inscription: "A Haroldo y Carmen, con un inmenso abrazo-arco-puente desde México a São Paulo" (To Haroldo and Carmen, with an immense embrace-arching-bridge from Mexico to São Paulo).[5] One of many affectionate greetings, the archival record testifies to the two writers thinking together, bridging Mexican Spanish and Brazilian Portuguese.

Political realities of the late 1960s deepen their commitment to a horizontal translation exchange. Despite their shared rejection of transparently political poetry, after the state-sponsored violence against student protestors in October 1968 when Paz resigned as Mexico's ambassador to India, he asked Haroldo to place a poem in Brazilian newspapers for reasons that went beyond the literary. Only one of the two Brazilian media outlets framed the poem as Paz requested, as a statement against the Mexican government—which may be unsurprising, given the military dictatorship that had been ruling Brazil since the 1964 coup. Yet the Portuguese translation of "México: Olimpiada de 1968" interpellated and reflected citizens living under any regime exerting social control such that the army could strike against its own citizens. This episode shows mutual interest in translation strategies that preserve aesthetic qualities and expand solidarity across languages of Latin America.

After this first publication in 1968, the two translator-poets continue to respond to and circulate one another's work. Paz first composed his *Topoemas* (1968) in homage to both the visual style of the Brazilian concrete poets and their discursive explanations; soon afterward he edited a special dossier on Brazilian concrete poetry in *Plural* (1972) and an early segment of Haroldo's *Galáxias* along with an interview in *Vuelta* (1978). Haroldo translated poems by Paz in *Constelação* (1972), essays in *Signos em rotação* (1972), and finally *Transblanco* (1986). In each case, their editing and translation strategies emphasize the proximity between Spanish and Portuguese, the necessity to translate between them in a reciprocal way, and the use of cannibal translation techniques to imagine pan–Latin American solidarity in the face of mutual historical isolation. The fact of the prior triangulation through English and the belatedness of their encounter produces shame and rage, as Paz will describe it, at being isolated from fellow Latin Americans with parallel poetic concerns and a shared investment in repair—affective states that conditioned their translationship.

THE HAROLDO DE CAMPOS AND OCTAVIO PAZ TRANSLATIONSHIP THROUGH *TRANSBLANCO*

The letters included in *Transblanco* show Haroldo and Paz crafting a more horizontal translationship than Cummings allowed with any of his translators, and they depict their translations and correspondence as necessary to redress a prior lack.[6] Paz had expressed his conviction in two essays from 1967 that the avant-garde of that decade thrived in Brazil, not in Spanish America.[7] Yet he also admits his "lamentable ignorance": he had only read the Brazilian concrete poets in translation until Haroldo wrote and sent him the recent issues of *Noigandres*:

> Unfortunately, my knowledge of the Brazilian movement is imperfect. It's a shame, but that's the way it is: I had to go through English to meet you. I'll tell you an anecdote to illustrate the situation: in 1959, talking to Cummings in New York (I had translated some of his poems years before), he enthusiastically mentioned a group of young Brazilian poets to me: four years later, when I finally found out more about the concrete poetry movement, I was able to identify the poets that Cummings had vaguely alluded to.[8]

Paz knows Haroldo will be only too familiar with their "situation": failing to reach readers elsewhere in Latin America except perhaps when routed through the cultural centers of Paris, Barcelona, and increasingly the United States. Paz's "shame" at his "lamentable ignorance" underwrites the urgency of their communication on an affective and political level. The belatedness of their encounter exemplifies the divide between the literary spheres of Brazil and Spanish America and the unique pathway they represented for one another in fulfilling what Mariano Siskind calls the "cosmopolitan desires" expressed through Latin American approaches to literary world building. Yet in addition to making up for this lack, the mutuality of their position allows for a generative spirit of worthy competition, in which their disagreements also underwrite their collaboration.

Paz alludes to isolation that goes beyond the cultural: his material conditions, despite access to political and cultural capital, also tempers his poetic circulation. He reciprocates Haroldo's gifts with a limited, out-of-print edition of his poetry collection *Viento entero* published in Delhi—but he sends the only copy he has, which is somewhat used and beat-up, as he apologizes in his letter.[9] This episode illustrates a paradox both writers inhabit: despite their elite roles in state-sponsored positions—Paz as Mexican ambassador to India, Haroldo as a professor at the University of São Paulo (USP)—they still have limited resources that challenge and circumscribe their literary circulation. Paz draws on a mutual understanding that books fare poorly in the climates they write from—both politically and physically. The humid climate in Brazil makes Haroldo more likely to understand why a book arriving from Delhi, even if it is fairly new, might look like it has been hardworn for years. Without dwelling on these material realities, their acknowledged limitations can go unspoken, assured of a mutual empathy, a shared embodied experience.

Transblanco exhibits sparks of rivalry and differences of poetic opinion alongside assumed mutual understanding of conditions for Latin American poets. Annotated by Haroldo, his perspective mediates the entire exchange, and he adds bibliographic references, turning the letters into a fully sourced essay in two voices.[10] From Haroldo's paratexts, the reader learns that when Paz and the concrete poets worked through similar poetic questions, the younger Brazilians sometimes arrived before the older Mexican poet, as when Augusto translates the complex "Sonnet en yx" by Mallarmé a year before Paz completes his own version.[11] Nevertheless, the larger affective stance is mutual frustration that they were not in contact sooner. When Haroldo translates selections from *Libertad bajo palabra* (1960) into Portuguese, instead of just pride or excitement, Paz expresses rage about having been the one to write these first prose poems in Spanish. "I confide this to you without modesty and with a bit of rage (rage eliminates modesty). You will understand: I am Spanish American and I live in a world of closed-off people."[12] Paz resents being the first to experiment in Spanish with poetic forms common to international modernism, a symptom of his isolation as a Spanish American poet. This sense of belatedness or segregation recalls philosopher Peter Sloterdijk's description of the rage provoked by being denied the capacity to give and receive honorably, being left out of reciprocal exchange.[13] While Paz does betray problematic elitism, looking down on the people around him as limited or closed-minded, he appears certain that Haroldo will understand this rage at being first.

Yet Paz and Haroldo disagree about the nature of his poetic innovation in *Libertad bajo palabra*. For Paz, this collection initiates the prose poem in Spanish; conversely, Haroldo favors its move away from discursive metaphor and toward metalinguistic poetry. Roughly speaking, a "metaphoric-discursive" poem creates meaning with words linked together in a creative but logical chain reliant on a reader's knowledge of a language; a "metalinguistic" poem would disrupt the stability of words, downplaying semantics to create meaning visually or sonically. For Haroldo, these categories are far apart and index the rupture concrete poetry makes from the lyric poetic tradition. For Paz, these poetic modes are mutually constitutive and trace long-standing tensions and continuities within universal poetry. This debate conditions the cannibal translation tactics they use when responding to one another's work.

In his first letter to Paz, Haroldo identifies "something more unique, the short, stripped-down, 'metalinguistic' poems, alongside the poetry from the metaphoric and rhetorical-discursive tradition characteristic of Spanish and Spanish American expression."[14] Taking issue with what he calls Haroldo's "disdainful tone," Paz insists in his reply that all Western poetry, including Brazilian concrete poetry, comes from the same metaphoric-discursive tradition.[15] He writes: "The elimination of discourse, moreover, does not save you from discourse: the proof is that your poems are almost always accompanied by an explanation, each commentary a grenade of intellectual dynamite. . . . The concrete poem is sustained or prolonged in a discourse (explanation of the poem, translation of the ideogram)."[16] In this retort, Paz refers to the Brazilian poet's contribution to *An Anthology of Concrete Poetry*, edited by Emmet Williams (1967). Whereas most poets in this international collection leave their work uncommented, to be read visually rather than semantically, or provide a simple word-for-word key at most, Haroldo writes complex and sometimes extensive explanations for his own poems and those of Ronaldo Azeredo, Augusto de Campos, José Lino Grünewald, and Décio Pignatari.[17] As Paz flags, these discursive "translations of the ideogram" rarely stop at providing the necessary to "explain" the poems; instead, they often clarify their political commitment. For example, in his note to his own poem "Servidão de passagem," Haroldo describes the "linguistic and existential play between *poesia pura* (pure poetry) and *poesia para* (committed poetry, poetry with a social purpose, poetry *for*)."[18] For another piece by José Lino Grünewald, which plays on the words *petróleo*, *preto*, and *nosso* ("petroleum," "black," and "ours"), Haroldo contextualizes the piece as "a placard-poem, with a political commitment to the campaign for maintaining Brazilian oil under Brazilian control."[19] These explanations provide background information about Brazil that might not be widely available, incorporating international readers into multiple levels of discourse, both poetic and political. By praising these discursive explanations as "intellectual grenades" that "translate the ideogram," Paz calls into question the concrete poets' definition of their own project.[20]

This debate represents the hinge between their two perspectives on how literary language can impact the political sphere. Paz innovates in dialectic continuity with tradition, whereas Haroldo breaks with the past and works with shattered elements of a once-familiar language. Where Paz and Augusto were not able to engage Cummings in a metacommentary on the translation process, Haroldo addresses Paz with respectful provocation and Paz responds in kind, deepening their translationship and conditioning the way they accommodate one another's perspective.

When Haroldo asks Paz about translating the poem "Las palabras" from *Libertad bajo palabra* for an article by Celso Lafer, their discussion about this poem demonstrates their unfolding translationship. Paz grows to trust and accept Haroldo's elevation of his metalinguistic works above other styles, and the Brazilian translator shares insights born from his examinations of multiple versions in other languages, searching for translation choices that avoid the most obvious options in the transfer from Spanish into Portuguese. While he does ask the author a few questions about diction, giving Paz the opportunity to identify some of his word choices as "Mexicanisms," Haroldo's general tone could not be further from the shy queries of those who translated Cummings's poems into German and French. Instead, he assertively describes the bold choices he makes to achieve an effective transcreation in Portuguese.[21]

For example, Haroldo explains an important translation shift from the imperative to infinitive verbal tense, which he claims sounds better in Portuguese.[22] Marked by a spirit of destructive creativity, the poem "Las palabras" exacts revenge on words themselves and on those who have subjected the poetic speaker to discursive violence. Every line of the poem begins with a verb—in Paz's Spanish, an imperative command; in Haroldo's Portuguese, an infinitive verb, often modified to contract with a pronoun. These aggressive, increasingly violent verbs describe an action to be performed on words themselves. The Spanish by Paz speaks through informal, second-person directives—"you, go do all these terrible things to words"—while Haroldo's impersonal infinitive verbs can be read as a recipe, how one might treat the indirect and direct objects *las palabras* (words) identified in the title.

> Dales la vuelta,
> cógelas del rabo[23]
>
> Girar em torno delas,
> virá-las pela cauda[24]
>
> Flip them over, [Spanish] / Circle around them, [Portuguese]
> catch them by the tail

The translation into Portuguese, in addition to taking some grammatical distance from the "words" subjected to such aggressive treatment, also crafts an opening line at greater remove. I have translated Haroldo's version as "circle around them," which differs from Paz's "flip them over," where physical contact has already been made with the words, from the very first line.

Rhythmically, too, Haroldo's Portuguese backs away one or two steps. In Paz's Spanish, each line begins on an accented syllable, the slap falls right away. Lines that read in Spanish "sécalas, / cápalas, / písalas," (dry them, / skin them, / stomp them,) become in Portuguese the slightly softer "secá-las, / capá-las, / cobrí-las," with the emphasis falling on the second syllable. Continuing the pattern, and increasing the gustatory semantic field, the commands continue:

> dales azúcar en la boca a las rejegas,
> ínflalas, globos, pínchalas,
> sórbeles sangre y tuétanos[25]

> dar-lhes açúcar na boca, às renitentes,
> inflá-las, globos, furá-las,
> chupar-lhes sangue e medula[26]

> feed them sugar, stuff their stubborn mouths,
> blow them up, balloons, prick them,
> suck their blood and marrow

Words, in this poem, are eating and being eaten; words are being force-fed sugar, but they are also being sucked dry. The extended digestive metaphor for poetry and language, the instruction to "suck the blood and marrow" out of words, to "whip, twist the neck, pluck the feathers, gut, and drag" words, all fit within the cannibal trope of creative destruction. The power to animalize resides with the poetic speaker and any writer listening who decides to reclaim power over language.

The final lines of the poem, however, include another onlooker, a "them" who once used words against the poet, who now takes the agency, twisting them back, whipping them into a new shape, reclaiming them cannibal translation style. Haroldo's choice to transform Paz's imperative commands into infinitive verbs especially impacts the final lines of "Las palabras," where Haroldo's Portuguese translation opens to a more fertile set of interpretations than the Spanish source text.

> hazlas, poeta,
> haz que se traguen todas sus palabras.[27]

fazer, poeta,
fazer com que engulam todas as suas palavras.[28]

make it happen, poet,
make them swallow all the words.

Paz's penultimate line "hazlas, poeta," an informal, singular command, dictates one interpretation of the final phrase: "haz que se traguen todas sus palabras," rather than "tus palabras," must mean "make them swallow all their words." In Haroldo's translation, the infinitive does not specify the poet interlocutor on any level of formality, so "fazer com que engulam todas as suas palavras" could be making the unnamed "them" swallow all of their own words or all of the poet's words.

These phrases of subjugation also signify as remembered insults, now turned back against the words themselves, or against those who have used them in this dehumanizing way. This poem urges poets to acts of creative violence against language and against those who have used language against them, deploying a cannibalistic, digestive metaphor of how to remake language. Furthermore, the transfer between Spanish and Portuguese—published as a facing-page bilingual edition, with the differences on display—doubles the poetic space, expanding the site of language experiment and creativity. Haroldo's transcreation doubles the message of creative devouring of the source text—because the translator poet has, indeed, stripped the words of the poem down and made them his own, to be swallowed, again. The metapoetic poem has become a metapoetic translation.

Reading this translation through the letters marks Haroldo's work as a cannibal translation, in which their disagreement remains present, unresolved, and sets more translation and writing into motion. Selecting metalinguistic poems above all others for his collection *Constelação*, Haroldo divides this aspect of his Mexican interlocutor's work from a significant portion of his Spanish American generation's poetic production—specifically, the influences of surrealism and politically committed poetry. In much the same way that Augusto elevates Cummings's "tortographic" vector above his lyric verse, Haroldo surgically removes Paz's more surrealistic work and establishes a parallel between Brazilian concrete poetics and Paz's metalinguistic poems. While he is specifically aiming at Pablo Neruda—the premier Latin American surrealist and a mentor of Paz's—for his politically engaged poetry that had become increasingly populist, he also rejects broad swaths of Paz's work as embedded in this *vanguardista* tradition.

If Haroldo transcreates Paz so as to manifest his poems as more metalinguistic than the author might recognize, Paz in turn experiments with concrete poetry to show that this poetics might invert discourse but still relies on it. When he asks for Haroldo's thoughts about his *Topoemas*, in contrast to the previous sense of "rage" at having to be the first to experiment in prose poetry in Spanish, he conveys instead the impression of happy simultaneity, kismet: "Nearly all my recent attempts bring me closer to you . . . And in the last few days I finished four concrete poems. Your letter could not have been more timely! You'll soon see how I've taken advantage of the lesson of concrete poetry."[29] While he does present his concrete poems as the first of their kind in Spanish, in this case, being the first does not provoke rage.[30] Their mutual translationship allows Paz to turn this "lesson in concrete poetry" into a chance to demonstrate a lesson of his own: that these counter-discursive poems still benefit from discursive explanations.

Reading them through this correspondence, Paz's *Topoemas* respond to an international tradition of concrete poetry in which translation is centered and in which explanatory notes, typography, place-specificity, and play with space on the page work together to create meaning that can be read in multiple languages at once.[31] Paz proudly offers them as an homage to the Brazilian poets of Noigandres and claims them as the first of their kind in Spanish, while also humbly downplaying them as clumsy. He writes to Haroldo: "I never thought to finish so quickly: in one week I projected (literally) six concrete poems onto the page. I call them Topoemas. The letters, the proportions—in short, the execution, is imperfect. Please excuse their manual clumsiness and tell me how my attempt seems to you."[32] This description of his writing process as quick, almost involuntary, throwing ink onto the page, indicates a state of urgency, intensity, creating a physical metaphor for his incorporation of the "lesson" he received from Haroldo, something outside his control. The projector mechanically projects a film, a series of visual images, onto the screen—so too did Paz "project (literally)" his concrete poems onto the blank page. Far from the lyric poetic voice of an individual shaping language at his whim, Paz here is not the subject composing his poems but, rather, their object: their projector, not their writer. In a letter to another Brazilian collaborator Celso Lafer, Paz repeats the same unusual choice of verb: "Soon you will receive some 'Topoemas' (*topos* + poems) that I *projected* (it would not be exact to say I *wrote*) a few months ago and which are an homage to Haroldo and Augusto de Campos, Pignatari and the rest of the Brazilian poets."[33] His description of composing concrete poems approaches an exercise in automatic writing, even though Paz largely rejected surrealist techniques of automatic and unconscious writing.[34] Paz disavows authority over the poems, distancing them from his own writing under his control—almost as he would as a translator—and describing them as at the limit of the "poetic function."[35] Given his defense of the metaphoric surrealist tradition, this depiction of concrete poetry as a form of unconscious projection appears to be another link between the concrete tradition and the rest of Spanish American vanguardism, framing the former less as rupture than as a new adaptation, a reconfiguration.

Yet Paz's initiation of concrete poetics in Spanish American poetry does not remain in this automatic, projected state. He adds an extensive "Comentario final" to "translate the ideograms," just as he insisted in his letters to Haroldo that discursive explanations enhance the Brazilian concrete poems included in the Williams anthology. Giving pride of place to the Brazilian poets, Paz echoes his debate with Haroldo, calling his "Topoemas" "spatial poetry, as opposed to temporal, discursive poetry. Device against discourse."[36]

In addition, Paz may have drawn the formula for his title "Topoemas = topos + poemas" from Haroldo's place-centric concrete poem "Topogramas." Originally written in Spanish, not Portuguese, "Topogramas" consists of three columns, identical architectural figures on the page that list complex associative sounds and images to evoke the three inimitable Iberian cities of Sevilla, Córdoba, and Granada.[37] Much like Haroldo's piece, each of the six "Topoemas" by Paz creates a sign (*grama*) for particular places (*topoi*) or relationships between places.[38] Drawn from the Greek *topos* for "place" and *grama* for "written character, letter, that which is drawn" (from the verb "to scratch, scrape, graze"), Haroldo's concept links the production of a concrete poem with the relationship between a specific place and the sign for that place. Paz particularly explores this relationship in the concrete poem "Palma del viajero," which draws on the iconic image of a palm tree to evoke a tropical location, perhaps an island in the Caribbean, as witnessed through the eyes of a tourist, a traveler (see fig. 7).

First in the series of "Topoemas," this image figures as a Latin American or Caribbean aesthetic, a Mexican *tropicália* even, with the palm tree evoking the place itself along with the foreign gaze projected onto

Fig. 7. Octavio Paz, "Palma del viajero," in *Topoemas* (1968).

that place by a leisure- and pleasure-seeking tourist. The word *palma* (palm) arches above the vertical *del*, together forming the leafy umbrella and sturdy trunk of an idyllic palm tree, resting atop a wavy line, which could be a beach, a wave, an island on the page. As an imaginative space, the "island" also represents a traveler's fantasy of escape, privacy, alterity. The smaller word *viajero* attaches itself to the bottom of the trunk, either a small boat arriving at the palm tree island, or a resting traveler, enjoying some shade beneath the umbrella of the palm leaves.

Yet in his commentary, his discursive translation of this ideogram, Paz complicates the image to associate this particular species of palm tree with his own travels to India and the global, multilingual history of European colonization. "*Palma del viajero* (Ravenala madagascariensis): 'A tree whose leaves are arranged in a peculiar fanlike shape. The sheathing leaf-bases form receptacles in which considerable quantities of water are stored and hence the name.' (Guide to the Royal Botanical Gardens of Paradeniya, Kandy)."[39] In this explanatory note, we experience several reversals. The more singular, anonymous tourist-traveler *viajero*, resting alone under the palm tree, transforms into the numerous British English settler-colonizers in Kandy, Sri Lanka (née Ceylon), where they took over a royal garden that local rulers had cultivated for centuries, appropriating that horticultural legacy into the Royal Botanical Gardens maintained under the aegis of the British Crown. Yet the tree itself has also traveled: the *palma del viajero* actually takes its name from Madagascar, an early site of Portuguese maritime navigation. Furthermore, this genus of palm tree negates the image of a luxury tourist traveler. Instead, this palm serves as a water receptacle, evoking the traveler in trouble, the shipwrecked or lost explorer so desperate for fresh water he will drink water collected in crevices of plants. In a reversal common to Latin American literature, the imagined dream of a New World paradise becomes the nightmare of shipwreck. The poem could not "signify" in the same way without the connection to a particular "topos," because of the extent to which the palm tree is symbolically associated with the imaginary of paradise islands projected onto the Caribbean.

Through his letters with Haroldo, we understand Paz's *Topoemas* as grounded in his interpretation of the Brazilian praxis of this form, in which the discursive explanations are paramount. By framing his experiment with concrete poetry as homage to the Brazilian concrete poets, he ties this art form to a relationship with place, a reclaiming and redevouring of the material around him, while also acknowledging the generations of prior consumption, construction, and colonization that have gone before. For Haroldo, concrete poetry represents an ideal bridge between the two languages of Latin American poetic world, and he reports to Paz that other Spanish American poets are also incorporating concrete elements into their work: mentioning his correspondence with Julio Cortázar and Nicanor Parra, he paraphrases Parra's exclamation that "'I think I'll end up a concrete poet!'"[40] Paz may be the first, but he will not be alone.

When Paz publishes a dossier on concrete poetry in his journal *Plural* (May 1972), the discursive "translations of the ideogram" again are foregrounded. In some cases, the expansion is a matter of degree, as with "Cristal" (1958) by Haroldo: in the English anthology by Williams, he simply names the poem's procedure "poetic crystallography";

in the Spanish dossier for *Plural* he adds several sentences to explain how to read—and perhaps reproduce—that procedure.[41] In the case of Augusto's poem "cidade" (1963), the single-word source text relies on a maximalized minimalism, structured as one long horizontal line, punctuated with the three final trilingual phonemes, "-cidade / -cité / -city," a sideways skyscraper of words crowding together and difficult to decipher, describing and performing urban life (see fig. 8).

atrocaducapacaustiduplielastifeliferofugahistoriloqualubrimendimultipliorganiperiodiplastipubliraparecipro rustisagasimplitenaveloveravivaunivoracidade
city
cité

augusto de campos (1963)

Fig. 8. Augusto de Campos, "cidade" (1963), in *Viva Vaia: Poesia, 1949–1979*. © Augusto de Campos.

In the version printed for Mexican readers of *Plural*, the discursive explanation in Spanish supersedes—and nearly overwhelms—the long single line of the poem positioned below. This extensive gloss emphasizes the poem's precondition as multilingual (Portuguese, English, and French), drawing on the ambiguous overlap between the word *cidade* (city) and the suffix *-cidade* (-city), as in *atrocidade* (atrocity), *historicidade* (historicity), and more (see fig. 9).

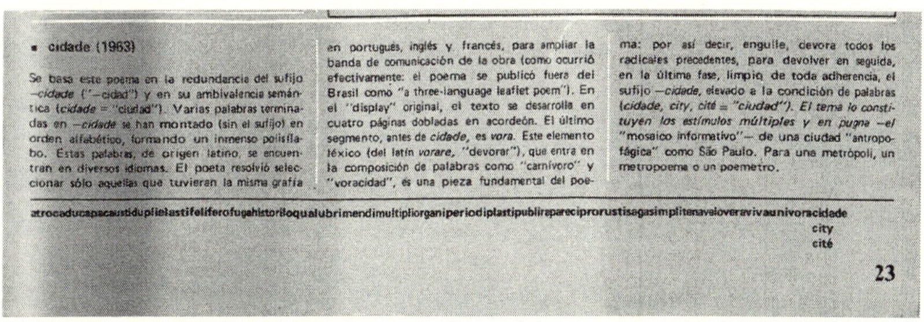

▪ cidade (1963)

Se basa este poema en la redundancia del sufijo *–cidade* ("–cidad") y en su ambivalencia semántica (*cidade* = "ciudad"). Varias palabras terminadas en *–cidade* se han montado (sin el sufijo) en orden alfabético, formando un inmenso polisílabo. Estas palabras, de origen latino, se encuentran en diversos idiomas. El poeta resolvió seleccionar sólo aquellas que tuvieran la misma grafía en portugués, inglés y francés, para ampliar la banda de comunicación de la obra (como ocurrió efectivamente: el poema se publicó fuera del Brasil como "a three-language leaflet poem"). En el "display" original, el texto se desarrolla en cuatro páginas dobladas en acordeón. El último segmento, antes de *cidade*, es *vora*. Este elemento léxico (del latín *vorare*, "devorar"), que entra en la composición de palabras como "carnívoro" y "voracidad", es una pieza fundamental del poema: por así decir, engulle, devora todos los radicales precedentes, para devolver en seguida, en la última fase, limpio de toda adherencia, el sufijo *–cidade*, elevado a la condición de palabras (*cidade, city, cité = "ciudad"). El tema lo constituyen los estímulos múltiples y en pugna –el* "mosaico informativo"– de una ciudad "antropofágica" como São Paulo. Para una metrópoli, un metropoema o un poemetro.

atrocaducapacaustiduplielastifeliferofugahistoriloqualubrimendimultipliorganiperiodiplastipubliraparecipro rustisagasimplitenaveloveravivaunivoracidade
city
cité

23

Fig. 9. Augusto de Campos, "cidade" (1963), in the Mexican literary journal *Plural* (May 1972). © Augusto de Campos.

Landing in the realm of cannibal poetics, the explanation ends by analyzing why the final word placed in combination with the city, after so many options, must be *voracidade* (voracity).

> The final segment, before *cidade*, is *vora*. This lexical element (from Latin *vorare*, "devour"), which enters into the composition of words like "carnivorous" and "voracious," is a fundamental piece of the poem: it engulfs or devours, so to speak, the preceding root-words, to immediately give back, clean of all attributes, the suffix -cidade elevated to the condition of words (cidade, city, cité = ciudad). The theme is made up of the multiple and competing stimuli—the "informative mosaic"—of an "anthropophagic" city like São Paulo. For a metropolis, a metropoem, or a poemeter.[42]

Of course, this gloss also emphasizes the fact that unlike with other Latinate languages, such as English and French, the Spanish word for "city" is unfortunately not cognate with a suffix. Contrary to the vision of easy translation or mutual understanding between Spanish and Portuguese, this poem instead paints Spanish as further away from Portuguese than English or French.

As read through the correspondence between Haroldo and Paz, this careful effort to place Brazilian concrete poetics for a Spanish American readership, within both a sociopolitical context and a poetic tradition, takes on the higher stakes of cannibal translation in which the Spanish versions become an occasion to expand on the discursive translations of the ideograms of the poem. Reading their published translations in the context of the translationship unfolding in their letters, we can witness how their reciprocal exchange allows Paz and Haroldo to each reshape and rewrite one another's works and ideas. When Octavio writes to Haroldo from Paris on March 10, 1969, his life is still in a state of upheaval after leaving his ambassadorial post in New Delhi, and though Paz lacks the time to write a full letter, he adds a postscript praising Haroldo's translation of "Las palabras." Paz writes: "The most important thing (for me)—your translation is splendid."[43] Translation mediates their relationship and remains paramount, even in times of turmoil.

TLATELOLCO MASSACRE 1968 WITNESSED FROM DELHI, SÃO PAULO, AND NEW YORK

On October 2, 1968, the Mexican army opened fire on a mass protest in the Tlatelolco neighborhood of Mexico City. Despite hundreds of deaths and thousands of injuries among the protestors, the state covered up the event, cleaning blood off the streets by the next morning and wildly underreporting casualties in state-controlled media. Throughout the summer of 1968, largely peaceful protests like this one had grown to include hundreds of thousands of citizens demanding greater access to resources, education, and public policy decision-making. Initially the Mexican government had tolerated this pluralistic movement, but when it threatened to embarrass them at their Olympic Games, the crackdown now known as the Tlatelolco Massacre cleared the streets, tarnishing the international reputation of the host nation and damaging Mexican democracy.[44]

As Paz writes to Haroldo on October 9, 1968, he can no longer serve this government, so he resigns from his long-held post in the Mexican foreign service. This letter cements the political stakes of their translationship, as Paz asks Haroldo to translate for the Brazilian press an enclosed poem and open letter addressed to the Olympic Organizing Committee denouncing these crimes committed by the Mexican state against the people. Publishing Paz's open letter in the two major Brazilian newspapers ensured for the first time that their solidarity found public expression "not, only, for literary reasons" as Paz writes to Haroldo.[45] The prior letter collected in *Transblanco*, when Paz sends Haroldo his newly drafted *Topoemas*, had been typewritten on official Embajada de México letterhead.[46] By contrast, this handwritten correspondence on blank, unlined paper marks the poet's new independence from his official capacity as a state representative.

The poem and open letter, circulated in the global press, refer to a history of imperial and colonial violence in Mexico and express shame and rage as affective strategies writers draw on for taking action in the face of oppression.[47] But Haroldo's translation expands the poetic voice of Paz's protest poem, "México: Olimpiada de 1968," to include *any* citizenry threatened by its own oppressive government. This first translation publication—while less overtly experimental than the others Haroldo would translate for *Constelação* and *Transblanco*—anticipates the metalinguistic translation strategies Haroldo would choose. While the resulting news bulletins in Brazil obscure more than illuminate the political import of Paz's poem and open letter—perhaps a reflection of the military dictatorship's increasing censorship in Brazil at the time—a shared discourse of collective resistance against state oppression still shines through. Thematizing shame as a collective national rage that prepares a people to strike for social change, the poem itself breaks through official discourse around the Tlatelolco Massacre, enacting the two poets' shared belief in the literary as a realm independent from but relevant to the political. Furthermore, the poem shares the metalinguistic style of "Las palabras," which fascinates the Brazilian translator. By staging its own scene of writing, the self-referential quality also allows this poem to resist the censoring frame of the Brazilian press.

Paz was the most prominent Mexican writer to condemn this event by resigning his post as ambassador to India—yet this first public statement is oblique. Neither the poem nor the open letter condemns the Mexican state directly—instead, adopting a formal yet cordial bureaucratic tone, the statement refers to "recent events" that motivated him to ultimately accept an invitation to write a poem commemorating the Olympics although he had previously declined to participate in cultural events around the games. Paz had practical reasons for not openly condemning the state until he could leave India: the legal framework governing his public service had no mechanism for him to resign—he needed to request that the Mexican State Department put him in a new status of *disponibilidad*, or, in other words, make him "available" to be hired elsewhere.[48] The state-aligned press then claimed that he had been fired for disloyalty, occasioning his insistence that "I was not fired, I quit" in an independent paper, the *Excélsior*, later that month.[49] The political and personal nature of this transformative act—and the poet's relationship to any political agenda over the course of his life—continues to provoke debate. He had followed and supported the protest movement closely from his ambassadorial post in New Delhi, the students marched carrying placards with some of his Spanish Civil War poetry, and he was the only government official to resign. Taken as a figurehead of the resistance, Paz's daughter and ex-wife Helena Paz Garro and Elena Garro critiqued him in the Mexican official press for using his platform to support the student movement, "accusing him, along with other intellectuals, of having turned the Mexican youth into 'real terrorists.'"[50] Yet he continued to situate himself with sociological, writerly distance rather than taking up any role as an active mouthpiece, let alone as a leader.[51] Eventually, those who embraced him after his reisgnation as a leftist hero—a position he never claimed for himself—would grow disillusioned with his posture of remaining outside the fray of active resistance.[52]

The bureaucratic euphemism of "availability" led to others: Paz refers repeatedly to "recent events" without naming them and encodes the killing of protestors within metaphors of pre-Columbian human sacrifice. In several of the personal letters Paz wrote from Delhi to inform friends and literary collaborators of his resignation, he draws the same parallel between the current Mexican state and both Spanish colonization and pre-Columbian ritual sacrifice as forms of state control.[53] To Haroldo he writes, "After the events that occurred in Mexico and the sudden (but not unexpected) return of the bloodthirsty gods and their priests, I decided to retire from the Embassy."[54] Refraining from naming culprits, Paz instead figures them as reincarnations of past tyrants and Aztec priests of human sacrifice. Writing to James Laughlin, editor of his English translations published by New Directions, he shares: "After the huge Aztec ritual on October 2 in the so-called Plaza of the Three Cultures, I decided that the only decent thing I could do would be to cut off all connection to Huitzilopochtli and his high priest."[55] To his friend and collaborator Charles Tomlinson, the British poet and translator, he writes: "The old gods roam free once more, and our President has transformed into the High Priest of Huitzilopochtli. I've decided not to continue on as a representative of the Great Moctezuma (the first, famous for the numerous victims he sacrificed in the teocalli)."[56] Here, Paz comes closest to naming and blaming one individual, President Gustavo Díaz Ordaz of Mexico. To Haroldo in particular he writes about his hopes for the impact of his actions: "I hope the poets who were planning to participate (Montale, Neruda, Graves, Yevtushenko, Elytis, Nicolás Guillén and others I do not remember) have now withdrawn. Hopefully my letter and poem will be published in Brazil—and not only for literary reasons."[57] Paz enumerates his contemporaries who share his political convictions and might want to retract their participation in Mexico's Olympics.

Unlike the intense images of these personal letters, Paz's open letter grounds itself entirely in the language of diplomacy, and in his voice as longtime cultural attaché, Paz formally accepts an invitation to write a poem "exalting the Spirit of the Olympics" which he had previously declined:

> I did not feel that I was the person best suited to participate in this international meeting and even less to write a poem

> on that subject. Nevertheless, the recent course of events has changed my mind. I have just written a short poem commemorating these Olympic games. I am sending it to you, attached to this letter, with the request that you would be so kind as to send it to those poets who do attend the Colloquium.[58]

Strikingly formal, this open letter resides squarely in the sphere of officialdom: impeccably polite, Paz makes one last show of his privilege as a diplomat to circulate the poem that does just the opposite of celebrating Mexico's entrance to modernity on the international stage as represented through the Olympics.

In contrast with the dry bureaucrat-speak of the open letter, the poem itself makes the most direct political statement. Incorporating the same images of pre-Columbian sacrifice from Paz's personal letters, the circular poem denounces the complicity of a whole culture in the cruel act of killing vulnerable bodies so that a powerful state may remain in control. "México: Olimpiada de 1968" begins and ends with the word *limpidez* translated as "clarity" in Mark Strand's English version published the same year.[59] Opening by creating a parallel between the abstract quality of "clarity" with the clear, white, untouched newness of a blank piece of paper, the poem immediately questions and ultimately negates any potential "blank slate" onto which a writer—or a national culture—could ever project itself.

> La limpidez
> (quizá valga la pena
> escribirlo sobre la limpieza
> de esta hoja)
> no es límpida:[60]
>
> A limpidez
> (Vale a pena talvez
> Deixá-lo escrito sobre o limpo
> Desta página)
> Não é límpida:[61]
>
> Clarity
> (Maybe it's worth
> Writing it down on this clear
> White paper)
> Is not clear:[62]

These first five lines link together "clarity" as the concept, the quality, and the lack of that attribute in the writing process, no matter how clean and white the paper might be. Interrupted by a cautiously hopeful parenthetical, that perhaps "writing it down" would be worth it, the first and fifth lines together read as "la limpidez . . . no es límpida" (clarity . . . is not clear), setting the poem up for further reversals and negations, begging the question of what *limpidez*, or clarity, can ever be. Much like the letter Paz wrote to Haroldo to tell him of his resignation from his ambassadorship, for the first time on a blank sheet of paper rather than official Embassy of Mexico letterhead, the blankness of the page does not undo the prior crime of complicity with state-sponsored violence. To produce clarity, then, requires writing, but along with the awareness that much has already gone before, that the clean whiteness of the blank page is an illusion, a constructed distraction from the historical record, which is already filled with a palimpsest of prior acts. Haroldo's translation subtly elevates the value of writing down the violent events of 1968 in two ways. First, he changes the verbal structure: where Paz and Strand's versions say *escribirlo* (writing it down), Haroldo chooses *deixá-lo escrito* (leaving it written), a construction that emphasizes the record, the trace, implying not just the writer's choice to put events down onto paper, but also the reader, who will find the written record left behind. Second, he delays by just a moment the undercutting of the potential value of this act by translating the opening phrase as "a limpidez / vale a pena talvez" (clarity / matters, maybe), contrasting with the more immediate introduction of doubt in Paz's Spanish, where "clarity / perhaps matters." In Haroldo's transcreation, leaving a written record of the attempt to seek clarity does matter, even while it might be undermined or necessarily problematized.

Replacing the image of the blank sheet of paper with an utter lack of clarity, an oozing mess of bodily fluids, the poem continues, vividly illustrating the claim from the prior line that "it isn't clear" (*no es límpida*):

> es una rabia
> (amarilla y negra
> acumulación de bilis en español)
> extendida sobre la página.[63]

> É uma raiva
> (Amarelo e negro
> Acúmulo de bile em espanhol)
> Estendida sobre o papel.[64]

It is a madness
(A yellow and black
Concentration of bile in Spanish)
Stretched over the page.[65]

The page, *la página*, or *o papel* (the paper) receives the almost-automatic projection of an emotional state, a *rabia* or rage, a translation I prefer to Strand's choice, "madness." Parenthetically redefined as almost putrid excrescence, unwanted bodily fluids or "yellow and black bile," this "rage" has been accumulating, concentrating, a buildup of bile and anger, both personal and collective. These lines echo in a more politically urgent key Paz's description of his *Topoemas*, which he described in letters as "projected onto the page." The physicality of the poem, rendering the textures and colors of the writing process "stretched / over the page," which further down will be characterized as "stained / before having said anything," reflects the physical violence that took place in the plaza, where bodies were "stretched" across the pavement "stained" with blood. The emotional reaction to the massacre precipitates the writing process, spurs it forward, and transforms it into language. Imagining the Spanish words of the poem as a pustule of black and yellow bile, bursting onto the page, implies that this wound has been festering for a long time, and in fact has a direct connection with the Spanish, the colonial past of Mexico. This inclusion of the linguistic legacy of Spanish colonization draws out one of the three cultures present in Tlatelolco Square, also known as the Plaza de las Tres Culturas, where Aztec, Spanish, and modernist Mexican architecture frame the public space. If the poem, hoping to bear witness on a clean sheet of paper, instead finds itself writing over *una rabia* or *uma raiva* (a rage), the accumulation of colonial violence beginning with the Spanish language represents one of the elements of this yellow and black bile. The Portuguese and English translations could have chosen to replace the mention of Spanish by naming their own colonial languages—but that gesture of transcreation might have gone one step too far in rewriting the specific event of the Mexican Olympics of 1968 into other national legacies of modern state power reiterating colonial violence by quashing a peaceful citizen-led social movement with military force.

The poem's central lines—italicized, as though citing a motto, slogan, Bible verse, or other form of received wisdom—also connect collective societal shame and rage with preparation for action. Shame becomes a potential tool, a catalyst for taking a leap forward—just as in their letters the two poets figure the shame of their prior situation of being triangulated through English as a motivator to translate between Spanish and Portuguese and forge a direct, reciprocal literary relationship.

La vergüenza es ira
vuelta contra uno mismo:
si
una nación entera se avergüenza
es león que se agazapa
para saltar.[66]

A vergonha é ira
Voltada contra nós mesmos:
Se
Uma nação inteira se envergonha
É leão que se encolhe
Para o salto.[67]

Shame is anger
Turned against oneself:
If
A whole country feels shame
It is a lion crouched
Ready to leap.[68]

Reading this poem both backward and forward, Paz places the national shame of the Tlatelolco Massacre into a larger historical dialectic process in which the oppressed gather strength and self-knowledge to leap forward. If the "body politic" has been a fertile metaphor for nation-state, naturalizing brutal divisions of power between "head" and "hands" or the "Crown" and "labor," this poem imagines a different social organization. The "lion crouched / ready to leap" is the embodied though unplanned, ashamed, disorganized, unincorporated part of the national body; it has been made the victim of a "nation turned against itself" but is now ready to act. The single word *si* (if), set as a line of its own and justified to the right rather than the left margin of the poem, visually marks a logical hinge between the two halves of an equation, both introducing the conditional mood of the statement and sidelining that conditionality. Paz's poem asks "if" the whole nation feels shame; yet the spatial organization undermines that indeterminacy, landing on the result of the condition of national shame: the country *is* a lion, "crouched / ready to leap." Paz frequently designs poems with circular structures, such as his long poem *Piedra del sol*, which begins and ends with the same six lines; "México: Olimpiada de 1968" begins and ends with "La limpidez," inviting a circular or reversed reading.[69] These central italicized lines can be roughly scanned backward as "*Una nación entera se avergüenza si vuelta contra uno mismo*" (*A whole nation becomes ashamed when it turns against itself*). The circular reading expresses both the individual, who experiences shame as anger turned inward, and a collective, a whole nation that experiences shame when it turns against itself. As I will analyze further in the context of the newspaper publications of Paz's open letter and poem, Haroldo's translation alters the poem to place this shame on a broader public by introducing the first-person plural. His version reads: "*a vergonha e ira / voltada contra nós mesmos*" (*shame is rage / turned against ourselves*) rather than the first-person singular in the Paz source text and Strand's translation, "*shame is anger / turned against oneself*." In his transcreation, Haroldo amplifies the poem's circular logic that links the individual writer and the collective, the moment of composition and the experience of reading, historical trauma and present-day responsibility to put an end to cycles of violence, all with this small but significant shift to categorize the sense of shame as a social rather than personal experience.

Buried in parenthesis once again, the following stanza redoubles the question of collective culpability by shining a light on those tasked with the physical labor of the cover-up: city employees, state workers, regular citizens doing their jobs who wind up in service of a state-sponsored crackdown on peaceful protestors, which they did not commit and may not support. Framed within the polite screen of a parenthetical clause, the "yellow and black bile" already marring the page is now joined by the red hue of "blood" staining the streets and the blank paper:

(Los empleados
municipales lavan la sangre
en la Plaza de los Sacrificios.)[70]

(Os funcionários
Da limpeza pública lavam o sangue
Na Praça dos Sacrifícios.)[71]

(City
Employees wash away blood
In the Plaza de los Sacrificios.)[72]

Strand's translation here, beginning with the word "city" set apart from "employees," highlights the urban landscape of the massacre, making the city itself a central figure in the poem. Naming a specific site in Mexico City, but with an alternative title, Paz reiterates the connection in his letters between the contemporary loss of life in the modern Plaza de las Tres Culturas and the history of ritual human sacrifice in the ancient Plaza de los Sacrificios. Furthermore, it references two historical moments: the pre-Columbian Aztec human sacrifice and the Spanish Inquisitorial policies enforcing *limpieza de sangre* (blood purity) used to sort people into a strict religious and racialized hierarchy during the colonial period. Connecting these municipal workers, public sanitation employees of the city, with both the present-day dead bodies of the protestors and the historical human sacrifices to what Paz called in his letters the "old gods," the poem begs several questions: Who are the new gods? And how are they being served by the deaths of student protestors and the swift cleanup after the fact?

Paz ends the poem by putting the "stain" of state-sponsored violence back onto the page. Repositioning, reexamining that stain (*mancha*), the disappeared bodies cleared from the streets themselves become the only source of *limpidez* (clarity), rather than the falsified *limpieza* of the cleanup—or, rather, the cover-up. The final lines combine a directive to bear witness with the continued doubt that anything worthwhile can be said:

Mira ahora,
                    manchada
antes de haber dicho algo
que valga la pena,
                    la limpidez.[73]

Vê-la agora,
                    Manchada
Antes de ter dito algo
Que valha a pena,
                    A limpidez.[74]

Look at this,
                    Stained
Before having said anything
Worthwhile,
                    Clarity.[75]

The exhortations *Mira hora* and *Vé-lo agora* in Spanish and Portuguese would be more literally translated as "Look now" or "Look at this now" rather than Strand's "Look at this," which eliminates the urgency of "now" in the source text. The poem demands the reader participate in the search for clarity, to take on the challenge of finding something worthwhile to say or do about this loss of life. Because Mexico City cleaned itself up so quickly, the poem seeks to redistribute and recirculate the bloodstains, to ask a wider public within and outside Mexico to "look now." The poem "México: Olimpiada de 1968" directs the reader's gaze away from the Olympic Games and the celebration of the modern nation-state's new gods of neoliberal capitalist triumph and instead toward the repetition of violent oppression and its cover-up.

Paz sends these pieces to Haroldo to be published in Brazil, "not, only, for literary reasons."[76] Yet the Brazilian newspapers present the oblique open letter too literally, framing this protest poem as though it represents genuine if belated support of the Mexican Olympics. The unattributed article published on November 16, 1968 in the *Jornal do Brasil* completely overwrites his gesture of protest, calling Paz "The Olympic Poet" below the mild headline "Octavio Paz Writes Poetry about Mexico."[77] Although his open letter appears in full, the framing paragraphs reverse his meaning, stating that after initially refusing the invitation, he agrees to write a poem for the Olympics. By presenting his sardonic letter at face value with no mention of the protests, their violent suppression, or Paz's abdication of the post of ambassador, the poem itself appears apropos of nothing.

The *Folha de São Paulo* gives a more balanced view with the headline "Olympic Poet Writes Protest Poetry." While still co-opting Paz on behalf of the state, *Folha* at least conveys that his poem was written in protest, not celebration. The unattributed article also describes the student protestors clashing with police and highlights Paz's resignation from the ambassadorship. Unlike the Rio newspaper, the São Paulo periodical offers some context for these Olympic Games, which opened after "a series of tumultuous events that involved police and students in violent confrontations."[78] However, Paz's last-minute acceptance of the invitation to write a poem is still taken literally, and the hope Paz expressed to Haroldo, that other poets invited to attend will also decline, does not appear anywhere in the Brazilian press. Instead, Paz is described as the obvious choice of Mexican poet to preside over the Encuentro Mundial de Poetas, a nod to the Greek tradition, in which athletic competition was accompanied by poetic contest.

Despite this erasure of the open letter's ironic tone, the article connects Paz's protest poem with the Black US Olympic athletes who staged their own protest under the spotlight of the athletic games.

> The gesture of the poet Octavio Paz, although it may be isolated within Mexican letters, may further complicate the already troubled climate of the current Olympics. The expulsion of the Black athletes from the USA from Mexico City is now aligned with the rebellion of the official poet from the Olympic celebrations. Octavio Paz . . . raised his voice in a song of protest against a celebration with ultimately peaceful intentions, a celebration which, nevertheless, cannot be immune to the climate of violence and injustice of our times.[79]

Ironically, the Brazilian paper asserts that Paz's poem is "isolated within Mexican letters" even while it circulates outside Mexico and uses the first-person plural in the final line; by naming the "climate of violence and injustice of our times," the article identifies an atmosphere shared by Mexican citizens and Brazilian readers under a repressive dictatorship.

However, placing this article in the newspaper's illustrated weekend supplement *Folha Ilustrada*, at the bottom of a full-page spread situating the Olympic Games in Mexico City, undermines this shared experience and neutralizes the critique encoded within the analysis of Paz's poem and gesture of resignation. Under the headline "México, Mistérios e Encantos," the feature by Vladir Dupont falls into breathless stereotyping and advertises Mexico with largely touristic and folkloric images.[80] Undercutting any proximity between the two nations with an ethnographic gaze that emphasizes distance between Mexico and Brazil, the full-page spread presents picturesque, regionalist tropes and depicts a citizenry excited to celebrate the Olympics. This classic travel chronicle shows the relationship between Brazil and Mexico as mediated by the United States both through the images propagated by the Hollywood film industry and as an overbearing power broker in the geopolitical landscape of the Western Hemisphere. The piece begins by rehearsing common Hollywood images projected onto the cultural and racial origins of Mexico ("the Aztec riddle") and ends with an imagined conversation between an arriving Brazilian visitor and a Mexican customs agent. The agent quips that Brazil might be even more tightly controlled if they also shared a border with the US, concluding with the comment "With a neighbor like that, who wouldn't put a lock on the back door?"[81] This article stages the triangulation of Mexico and Brazil through a conversation about the "bad neighbor" of the United States—not a surprising label in the late 1960s, when "good neighbor" foreign policy had long since disintegrated into Cold War interventionism. The full page of the *Folha Ilustrada* represents Mexico as a fascinating oddity, doubly afflicted by the "open wound" of Spanish colonization and the defensive posture necessitated by their aggressive neocolonial neighbor to the north. Dupont cites Paz in *El laberinto de la soledad* describing the "Mexican character" as a blend of extremes: "stone-faced" stoicism punctuated with periodic cathartic release embodied by popular culture comedian Cantinflas, violent and humorous. Expanding on the stereotypical local color of the text, the four illustrations place Octavio Paz, the "Olympic Poet," amid picturesque *charros* showing off their lasso skills and mariachis hailing tourists in sombreros.

Yet the shared political oppression expressed at the end of this article *does* stand out when compared to the *New York Review of Books* presentation of the same texts, which opened the issue dated November 7, 1968, with the translation by Mark Strand headlined "The Shame of the Olympics" and a note describing the "recent uprisings in Mexico City." The *Los Angeles Times* prints the same poem in Eliot Weinberger's translation on October 14, 1990, when the Mexican poet won the Nobel Prize for Literature, under the title "Paz in Fury: 1968."[82] While both publications may emphasize in their headlines the "shame" and "fury" expressed through Paz's poem, they do nothing to link this Mexican protest poem to the national shame or turmoil also occurring in the US at that time—a parallel the Brazilian press did draw.

While the Brazilian headlines may repeat the erasing, cleansing gesture of the state cover-up by calling Paz the "Olympic Poet," the poem itself identifies its real target: any government perpetrating violence against its citizens and then requiring public workers to clean blood off the streets—literally or metaphorically. The poem figures the staining of the public square and the conscience of the country as a staining of the page on which the poem is composed: "escribirlo sobre la limpieza / de esta hoja" (writing it down on this clear / white paper) refers to the paper as though it were touched by poet and reader alike. Furthermore, the metapoetic emphasis on the relationship between *limpieza/limpidez* and the *sangre* being cleaned stands out in comparison to Pablo Neruda's own vehement poem rejecting the rise of twentieth-century fascism, "Explico algunas cosas." From *España en el corazón* (1937), a collection published in response to the Spanish Civil War, the lyric ends with the repeated exhortation to "Venid a ver la sangre por las calles" (Come and look at the blood in the streets).[83] Whereas Neruda's poem figures the poet's role as calling for witness to violence, Paz figures the act of writing as registering both the violence and its cover-up, its conditions of possibility. And the Brazilian translation, again, performs both the historical cleansing role of translation while sharing a rejection of that cleansing—that cover-up—of a violent moment in the history of the present.

Translated and framed by the *Folha de São Paulo* in the broader context of "the climate of violence and injustice of our times," the forward leap envisioned in the poem certainly interpellates more than just Mexican citizens; it extends to also include the Brazilian readers. Yet the Portuguese translation published there and in the *Jornal do Brasil* does not fully exploit that possible expansion of the poem's implied readership. The newspaper translations are not attributed, but they are not the same as the translation by Haroldo published later in *Transblanco* and cited above. Two translation choices conflict with the strategies Haroldo and Paz both favor in the transcreation of *Blanco*. Comparing the two Portuguese versions shows the distance between Haroldo and other Brazilian translators. The first discrepancy again spotlights the "we" claimed by the article in *Folha*. The translation published in the Brazilian newspapers fails to take the same opportunity within the poem, translating Paz's line "*La vergüenza es ira / vuelta contra uno mismo*" more directly as "*A vergonha é uma ira / que se volta contra mim mesmo*."[84] Strand made a similar choice in English, with "*Shame is anger / turned against oneself*." In his own version of this key line, "*A vergonha é ira / Voltada contra nós mesmos*," Haroldo changes the impersonal singular of Paz's work to a larger collective, where "*Shame is anger / turned against ourselves*."[85] His protest does not remain isolated within Mexican letters but extends to other poets and readers in other countries, anyone also experiencing the shame and anger at a national government that has turned against its own people.

The version in *Transblanco* by Haroldo also extends the wordplay of Paz, where he juxtaposes two words: *limpidez* (clarity), the concept that begins and ends the lyric, and *limpieza* (cleanliness, purification, clearness), which is both proposed and negated throughout the piece. Haroldo's translation takes an opportunity to insert an additional iteration of this keyword when he renders "(Los empleados / municipales lavan la sangre / En la Plaza de los Sacrificios)" as "(Os funcionários /

Da limpeza pública lavam o sangue / Na Praça dos Sacrifícios.)"[86] We can contrast this with the more direct translation published in the *Jornal do Brasil*: "(Os empregados municipais / lavam o sangue / na Praça dos Sacrifícios)." In his translation of *Blanco*, just as with this translation of the protest poem, we will see Haroldo consistently emphasize or expand on the aesthetic qualities of the source provided by Paz.

Collected in *Ladera este* (1969), Paz added another title, "Intermitencias del Oeste (3)," or "Interruptions from the West (3)," to connect this piece with a series of four lyrical departures that contrast with the Eastern mood of this volume largely set in India. These four poems break in with "Western" concerns, and center on frustrated, failed, and compromised revolutions. "Intermitencias del Oeste (1) and (2)" bear the subtitles "Canción rusa" and "Canción mexicana," and both refer directly to historical events related to the Russian Revolution and the Mexican Revolution as failing to fulfill promises made in past generations. The third and fourth poems subtitled "México: Olimpiada de 1968" and "Paris: Les aveugles lucides" ("Paris: The lucid blind") give a sense of the potentially dangerous opportunity for transformation represented by the uprisings and student movements exploding in cities all over the world in 1968.[87] Haroldo's translation participates in the same expansion of Paz's poetic gesture as these other three intertexts.

Despite the aforementioned sociological distance Paz maintained from political activism, his critique of the Mexican state did have serious personal and professional consequences. Carlos Fuentes wrote him to commiserate about the censorship both writers experienced, saying he felt they were "living in Mussolini's Italy or Hitler's Germany" because, although their new works reached publication, journals and newspapers had been rejecting review articles about these books, which denied them a larger readership.[88] In the light of these challenging circumstances, and in the face of their shared aversion to politically committed poetry, Haroldo's support stands out. When Haroldo responds to Paz, he refers to the open letter and poem published in two Brazilian newspapers and expresses his admiration: "What a beautiful demonstration of proud coherence, your resignation from the post of ambassador! Double the joy when you can admire, in the same person, both the poet and the man."[89] This exchange confirms their political compatibility, prefigured but not confirmed by their aesthetic debates. Haroldo did not need his poetic admirations to include the personal or political; his admiration for Pound never ceased, nor did he ever absolve Pound for his fascism. By contrast, he does comment on the unique joy of his integrated esteem for Paz, particularly in this moment of crisis and increased state control occurring in both countries.

There is no way to know how many Brazilians read this protest poem in 1968. Regardless, the cultural translation at work in the Brazilian press triangulates the Latin American experience through the United States while also performing a shared political reality. In the midst of increasing violence perpetrated by their nations against the people, the literary sphere may provide a place for anger to be placed on the page and mobilized rather than turned inward. Finally, the changes that Haroldo makes put into practice the opportunity a translation between Spanish and Portuguese can represent for achieving latent qualities in a source text that are not yet fully realized. While the headlines in English might have made the "shame" written into Paz's poem more apparent, it is all located elsewhere, outside the political body of the United States. In the Brazilian newspapers, there is less clarity in framing the event, yet there is the construction of a "we," a collective experience. Not only does translation between Latin American spaces reveal the shared experiences of writers working in oppressive states; this case exemplifies translation between Spanish and Portuguese as a strategy of resistance.

PRACTICING A LATIN AMERICA–CENTERED LABORATORY OF TEXTS

Haroldo's translations of Paz, read through this broader context provided through the collection *Transblanco*, exhibit what he calls the *carinho micrológico* (microscopic care) necessary for an intra–Latin American translation praxis. He writes that "all this is merely testimony of the microscopic care I gave to the transcreation of your grand resplendent poem into my Brazilian and Camões-esque Portuguese tongue, and the happiness it gives me to see it sing in my language."[90] Their correspondence explores the unique relationship between Spanish and Portuguese, as languages that are somehow both "closer" to one another than to other languages but also kept farther apart in Latin America, tied to a similar geopolitical trajectory, yet also historically isolated from one another. Their proximity produces, as Haroldo demonstrates, the need to avoid "easy" transfer and the opportunity to expand on, renew, affirm, improve a poem through cannibal translation between these two languages in which the process remains a part of the published work in a reciprocal relationship between translation and explanation, between poetry's metaliterary and discursive elements.

The portion of *Transblanco* focused on the poem "Blanco" / "Branco" exhibits three main elements of cannibal translation: a "transcreation" approach in which the translator values the aesthetic information of a poem and will therefore intervene and make changes to best reflect its potential; reference to translations into other languages as a part of the corpus used to inform the translation in a "laboratory of texts"; and a self-conscious attention to the process, awareness that letters and paratexts will be part of the final publication. When Paz describes the "shame" implied by the *necessity* to read Brazilian poets in English or French because he cannot otherwise access their books, reading in translation is a sign of those poets' marginality. Yet for Haroldo, referring to other translations increases the power and value of his own transcreation into Portuguese—his belatedness or peripheral positionality becomes an *opportunity*, a choice to devour more, cannibalizing not only the poem itself but also the creative labor that others have done to understand and translate that work. The "laboratory of texts" approach consistently drives poetic insight in their exchange.[91] For Haroldo, looking at French, Italian, or English translations of Paz's "Blanco" gives him alternative solutions; observing other options helps solidify his own choices. He consumes and destroys other translations along with the source text, drawing other translators into his discussions with Paz and supplementing his own instincts in the transcreation process with their versions.

Paz emphasizes these explanations in his appraisal of Haroldo as a translator. Just as he praises and emulates the explanatory paratexts added to Brazilian concrete poems, he cherishes Haroldo's explanations and arguments about translation, and in fact, about poetry itself. The final complete letter included in *Transblanco* dated May 7, 1981, closes with an appreciation of their shared values of the physical, auditory element of poetry, which Haroldo has carried into his translation. Paz writes that he was amazed by Haroldo's letter "not only for the felicitous solutions you found for every problem but also for the way you explain the reasons behind the solutions"—in short, Paz perceives and appreciates how this cannibal translation explores and exposes its own operations.[92] Paz reiterates the relationship between geographical transfer and metalinguistic transformation in a later letter, cited in Haroldo's introduction: "I'm delighted at your wordplay in the title: 'Transblanco' evokes, at the same time, the geographic (trans-Siberian, trans-Pacific) and the physical or metaphysical (translucent, transfinite)."[93] Proliferating further meanings for the title, Paz recognizes *Transblanco* not only as a translation of his poem but also as a system of poetic translation between Spanish and Portuguese, potentially repeatable and expandable.

This letter again demonstrates how their conversation about translation becomes a conversation about poetics, and how the explanation—of a concrete poem, of a translation choice—emerges as a valuable element of cannibal translation praxis between these two thinkers and their two Latin American languages. Haroldo comments on the challenges and opportunities involved in translating between Spanish and Portuguese:

> In a translation like this one, between languages so proximate and apparently in such solidarity, as Spanish and Portuguese, the obsessive avatars of that same practice nevertheless open themselves up to an assault at any moment by the pervasiveness of chance differences. The microscopic inter-punctuation of these divergences propels the translator passionately beyond the resigned ambivalence of the servile translation, falsely "innocuous," monologically-literal; the dialogical-transgressive vocation of any translation that proposes itself as a response to a radical text must enter into its game also by the root—rooting itself in it and uprooting itself in the same movement of loving duplicity.[94]

Articulating the core challenge of intra–Latin American translation, the two languages are "so proximate and apparently in solidarity" the translator is in danger of falling into a "servile translation" that is only allegedly "innocuous." The word "solidarity" politicizes the stakes of his transcreation praxis, where passive solidarity is not enough, it must be worked at through language. Echoing Paz's distinction between the respect of a "good translator" and the love he brings to his translations of Cummings, Haroldo works from "loving duplicity." He resists the mere faithful in order to "root" his translation in the same game of language—which is itself an uprooting—in order to enact translation as a "dialogical-transgressive vocation." Haroldo identifies this reciprocal, cannibal process as uniquely important in translations between these two languages because they are deceptively similar; but we might expand the frame to include any translation that proposes itself as radical, in both senses: "from the root" and "politically invested." Haroldo here posits, as with his poetry in the example above of "Cristal," that there is necessary linguistic play between a *traducción pura* and a *traducción para* of a committed, radical translation, marked by "loving duplicity." If the transcreation of "Blanco" as "Branco" is a *traducción pura*, then the whole volume *Transblanco*, with all the explanation, context, argument, is a cannibal translation, a *traducción para*, a translation *for* the act of solidarity joining Brazilian and Spanish American poetic traditions.[95]

Because of the translationship between them, Paz apprehends and acknowledges what Cummings never could—that Haroldo has changed his poem, making it better, using the nature of Portuguese to exploit possibilities latent in his Spanish but not fully realizable. Paz praises Haroldo's work in no uncertain terms, writing, "I am truly moved. Not only is it very faithful, but even more, sometimes the Portuguese text is better and more concise than the Spanish. You succeeded in re-creating not just the meaning of the poem but also its movement."[96] Paz makes eighteen specific line-notes, and half of them praise the choices Haroldo has made, pointing out moments in which he sees that the Portuguese translation improves on his poem.

Author and translator work together to appreciate and theorize around the "wins" of the translation process, achievements that include eliminating articles to sharpen lines, shifting verb tenses, adding words, and more. For example, Paz's line "ánima entre las sensaciones" (soul between sensations) becomes "alma animando sensações" (soul animating sensation), which prompts Paz to comment: "Another win. *Soul animating sensations* is full of animist resonances, which is what I wanted. Thank you."[97] Another shift recalls the choice to import word resonances that we observed in "Olimpiada" with *limpieza*, where the line "Un pulso, un insistir" (a pulse, an insistence) becomes more simply "Pulso, impulso" (pulse, impulse) in Haroldo's transcreation.[98] In another case, Paz highlights the choice to expand on internal consonant alliteration when "inminencia de violencias violetas" becomes "iminência de violências violáceas." Many of Haroldo's changes expand the sonic qualities of Paz's poem.

In several places, Haroldo's translation choices map onto the process Paz went through to write and revise his poem; their reciprocal conversation illuminates this act of retracing poetic steps. For example, when Haroldo adds a word to the erotic line "Tremor / terra, desventras, / explodem tuas sementes," Paz comments that "in the final version, I eliminated the word 'tremor,' but it doesn't displease me to see it reappear, at least not in Portuguese."[99] In addition, Paz expresses disappointment in a few cases that he cannot back-translate into Spanish the version Haroldo has found in Portuguese: "Unfortunately, I can't retranslate your version to Spanish without breaking the rhythm."[100] These final comments display their mutual conception of the translation as another version of the work, one that is in relationship with the ongoing unfolding of the poem in any language, which, perhaps, moves it further into a realization of the work's possibilities. There is also a conviction that the translator and the writer, in the best of cases, will go through a similar process of consideration and selection. For example, Haroldo translates the tricky line "aire son nada / son" as "aire som nada / som" (air sound silence / sound). Paz affirms his choice of which homonym to draw out in translation, commenting that in Spanish the word *son* means both the present third-person plural of the verb "to be" and the word "sound."[101] These comments not only praise the precision of Haroldo's translation, and by extension, his reading of the source poem, they also express a sense of what was possible for him in Portuguese that was not possible for Paz in Spanish, dwelling on the subtle differences between their two languages that were felicitously exploited by an expert. The idea of a word "reappearing" in the Portuguese version that had been cut out of the most recent Spanish version is an elegant performance of the Benjaminian concept of the fragments of a work in all languages fitting together to approach "pure language."[102] As careful readers of Walter Benjamin's translation theory, they share the conviction that all versions of a literary text participate in the work, "making both the original and the translation recognizable as fragments of a greater language, just as fragments are part of a vessel."[103] Their mutual attention to these varied fractals of micromoments speaks to their joint perspective that the poem arrives through these choices, which have been negotiated and renegotiated in between multiple languages and by multiple poets.

This sense of negotiation, weighing choices and options, comes through even more clearly in the responses Haroldo gives to those moments when Paz expressed doubt. Other than two simple corrections to spacing and line breaks, Paz disagrees in five instances with Haroldo's lexical choices, and the translator only accepts Paz's correction in one case.[104] In the other four cases, Haroldo draws on range of different translation concepts and strategies to justify his choices: explaining the different tonal and formal registers of particular words in each language; referring to translations into other languages to justify his own choice; or developing an internal argument for why the choice responds to the source text through meter, sound, or even visual resonance with other words in the translation. For example, to defend his translation of "Silencio / sello / centello" (silence / stamp / I sparkle) as "Silêncio / selo / centelha" (silence / seal / spark), losing the first-person verb "I sparkle," Haroldo uses several of these strategies at once.[105] He describes the verb as far more awkward in Portuguese, defends the sonic effects of his choice, and cites from the translations into French and English by Claude Esteban and Eliot Weinberger respectively. No longer using English and French in the conversation between Spanish and Portuguese as a step of necessary triangulation, Haroldo instead presents these other options to Paz "fr.: Silence / sceau / scintillement; ingl.: Silence / seal / dazzle," using them to demonstrate that all the translators had to change the third word and that the other translations are further away metrically and sonically from his Portuguese solution.[106] The relationship between Spanish and Portuguese is proven to be more sensitive, more proximate through these comparative moments. Haroldo ends with a comment that the wordplay of the Spanish *son* reminds him of other contemporary Brazilian poets who work with sound, the poet João Cabral de Melo Neto and the musician João Gilberto, other works in Portuguese that test the limit of meaning, sound, and silence in ways similar to *Blanco* by Paz.[107] He also continues to distinguish the Brazilian language from Portuguese, as Augusto did in his translations of Cummings. For Haroldo, the language is "Brazilian and Camões-esque" after the Portuguese poet Luis de Camões renowned for his global Lusophone poetic explorations; for Augusto, the language is "Brazilian and jaguar-like." Both have made the language their own: locally relevant, capacious, and generative as a target language for translation.

Haroldo describes his transcreation of "Blanco" as the "nucleus" of this book, the "point of convergence" that draws together many other questions of poetry and poetics.[108] I understand the whole volume *Transblanco* as a cannibal translation: remaining in dialogue with the source text; including the debates and negotiations of a mutual translationship between them; and demonstrating to readers the labor of the translation process, the political context, and the stakes of translating between Latin American languages. Although Paz may have lamented that he could not back-translate into Spanish some of Haroldo's "microscopic" poetic insights, the larger frame of *Transblanco* was indeed reciprocally translated back into Spanish. In another instance of the ever-extending afterlife of the work and of their generative translationship, Paz's editor at the Fondo de Cultura Económica Enrico Mario Santí published a beautiful boxed set titled *Archivo Blanco* (1995).[109]

Santí's art-book edition includes the poem in the fan-folded scroll format designed by the author along with a volume of extensive supplementary materials, including facsimile versions of annotated drafts and letters Paz exchanged with editors and colleagues Emir Rodríguez Monegal and Julio Ortega; his English translators Charles Tomlinson and Eliot Weinberger; his French translator Claude Esteban; and the later phase of correspondence with Haroldo from 1978 to 1981. All this material makes available in Spanish the translation-centered discussions between the author and those who translated his work into three languages. Haroldo's personal library held at the Casa das Rosas archive includes a copy gifted from Santí dated April 9, 1995, with a touching inscription that gives the Brazilian translator pride of place as "el verdadero padre de este libro" (the true father of this book).[110]

THE CANNIBAL TRANSLATOR AND TRANSLATION VISIBILITY

After the nonreciprocal translation correspondence with Cummings, the translationship Paz and Haroldo enjoy allows them to recognize one another as poet-translators, along with their perspective, methodology, and the mutual exchange of ideas, disagreements, debates during the process. This vision of the cannibal translator—selective, historical, political, aesthetic—is centered and included in the frame, both conceptually and literally in the images included in at the end of the collection *Transblanco* (see fig. 10).

The two images feature a snapshot of Octavio Paz and Haroldo de Campos taken by the latter's wife, Carmen de Arruda Campos, in Cambridge, Massachusetts, where Paz was delivering the Charles Eliot Norton Lectures at Harvard University in 1972. Underneath the original is a photo montage by Gil Hungria, where their two faces appear reframed within the eyeglasses of a graphic cartoon of Haroldo, capturing the perspective of the cannibal translator. I see this artistic vision of the translator's gaze as a framework to understand other cannibal translations produced with the same degree of self-awareness, mutuality, aggression, reciprocity, and situatedness.

The photograph shows the two poets seated together and appears to be candid: neither is posed, and both seem absorbed in discussion. Paz looks mildly surprised midspeech, bright-eyed and leaning slightly forward as though making a point; Haroldo adopts a relaxed posture,

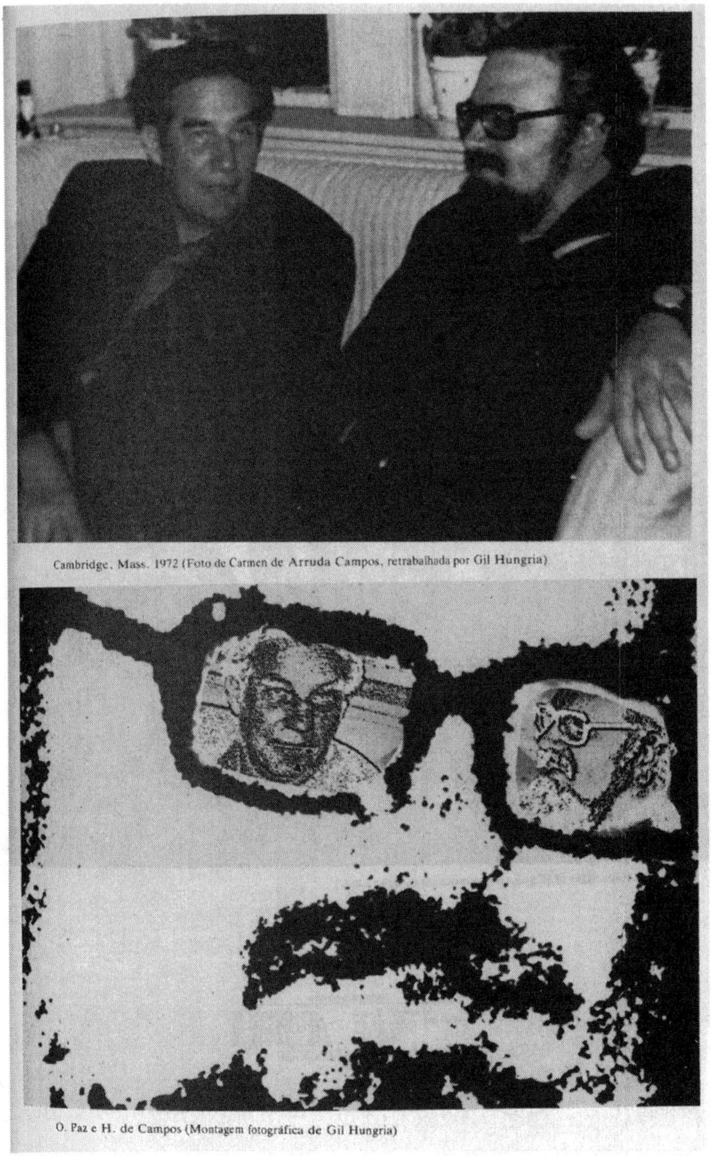

Fig. 10. Photograph of Octavio Paz and Haroldo de Campos taken by Carmen de Arruda Campos in Cambridge, Massachusetts (1972). Photo montage by Gil Hungria for *Transblanco* (1986).

smiling, his arm draped across the couch, perhaps even with his eyes closed, listening. Even his heavy facial hair and dark-rimmed glasses cannot obscure his engaged delight at their conversation.

Underneath the original, a photo montage by video and visual artist Gil Hungria shows the same two faces, but the two poets look out from beneath a larger image of a face with glasses and a mustache. Logically, I read this larger face as Haroldo again—although the stylized graphic could also represent his brother Augusto, given that both brothers wore thick-framed glasses and mustaches at this point in their lives.[111] A fitting image to end the collection *Transblanco*, the montage reframes the entire scene within Haroldo's gaze, placing him as the intermediary for both sides of the literary conversation, and, indeed, of the entire collection: although it took place in Spanish and Portuguese, it has all been translated into Portuguese. The book is framed by Haroldo's vision of Spanish American poetry—which, as he expressed at the outset, he saw as too metaphorical and insufficiently aware of Brazilian contributions to world poetry or to Latin American poetics. The gifts he and Paz exchanged with one another (books, publication opportunities, translations) were ways of correcting this past, but that past also remains visible, processed but unforgotten.

Cannibal translation produces a hypervisible frame, one that includes the translator's gaze, along with the other's gaze into the translator's culture. The translationship between Paz and Haroldo, precisely because it incorporates elements of competition and disagreement, was centered around mutuality and reciprocity rather than extraction, unidirectional movement, or assimilation. Yet who has the privilege and authority to take charge of the frame, to engage in the destructive, creative homage of cannibal translation? Women were largely absent from this literary circle, except as wives receiving cordial greetings, or in this case as photographer. The masculine privilege of inventive translation praxis will be challenged in the next chapter, where two prominent women writers contest their position and their exclusion from this network.

CHAPTER 3

Intersectional Translation, Gendered Authority, and Biographical Positionality

In no less eminent a publication than the literary journal *Plural*, edited at the time by Octavio Paz, an anonymous, poison pen reviewer cruelly dismisses Mexican writer Rosario Castellanos (1925–74), accusing her of translating based on sound rather than meaning. Claiming that she should never have even tried her hand at the French Nobel Prize–winning poet Saint-John Perse (1887–1975), the author takes her Spanish phrases out of context to comment sarcastically and dissect "only *some* of most ridiculous" moments in her translation.[1] The scathing review ends by labeling her method *traducir mocosuena* or *traducir como suena*, providing the following authoritative dictionary definition drawn from the *Real Academia Española*: "*mocosuena*, adv. m. fam. Atendiendo más al sonido que a la significación de las voces: *traducir mocosuena*" (*mocosuena*, adverb. masculine. familiar. Attending more to sound than to the meaning of words: *to translate sike it lounds*).[2] Of course, the spoonerism *mocosuena* itself sounds like another deprecating word: *mocosa*, from *mocos* (snot); literally, a *mocosa* is a snot-nosed little girl. While it can be a diminutive term of endearment, *mocosa* always evokes an immature, perhaps whiny or spoiled, picture of childishness that could not be further from the image of the brash, unafraid feminist author Castellanos cultivated through her writing.

Brazilian author Clarice Lispector (1920–77) also drew critique for translating based on sound rather than meaning. Even her publisher Álvaro Pacheco attributed the fact that she chose "'words translated by deduction, or by the closest sound to a Brazilian word,'" to careless rapidity; because she worked as a translator during a time of great financial need, critics regard her choices as unconscious, careless, the unfortunate and accidental consequences of working at a fast pace inspired by material insecurity.[3] Yet, as the prior chapters demonstrated regarding Augusto's translations of Cummings or Haroldo's translations of Paz, attention to nonsemantic aesthetic qualities—including sound—was a prized technique when deployed by these male translators. Clearly, gender can impact the reception of the translation strategies I am calling cannibal translation. Male translators could perform creative destruction, visibility, and intervention into the target language because their privilege of assumed intellectual mastery allowed these modes to be perceived as choices rather than errors. When Castellanos and Lispector make the same choices, critics assumed they are merely translating badly—what other translators claim as creative selection or craft reads as their failure of skill. Cannibal translation aesthetically and politically resists full assimilation—but it also demands a reading practice that disaggregates translator and author and reflects on the translator's positionality.

Castellanos and Lispector both play with this assumption of their failures as "faithful translators," evincing self-awareness that their literary work enters a field that draws on gendered hierarchies to place production over reproduction.[4] They write about adopting paradoxically oppositional poses as both authors and translators, at once the submissive, servile scribe and the aggressive usurper. Read in this context, their translations exhibit qualities of autobiography and self-reflexivity informed by their gendered and racialized positions. I read Castellanos and Lispector as translating from an intersectional awareness of their positionality: they self-consciously occupy a marginalized gender position in literary cultures centered on men, which intersects with their centralized racial position as educated white women within racialized hierarchies based on suppression of Indigenous, Afro-Mexican, and Afro-Brazilian voices. To take their translation work seriously as a part of their writerly craft involves reading from this intersectional awareness they evince in their translations and writing about translation.[5]

Feminist translation studies has only recently incorporated intersectionality as an important framework to ensure that feminist translation theories do not reproduce other inequalities.[6] Kimberlé Crenshaw first defined intersectionality in the specific context of Black women seeking legal recourse for their experiences of discrimination, who then faced challenges to their lawsuits because as Black women the grounds for their cases often fell outside the categories of Blackness and womanhood already defined in discrimination case law.[7] As a heuristic device, the broadening field of intersectionality studies takes both identity and structural contexts as fields onto which intersectionality can be deployed and where "intersectionality helps reveal how power works in diffuse and differentiated ways through the creation and deployment of overlapping identity categories."[8] Castellanos and Lispector anticipated this interest in multiple inequalities, and to fully apprehend the creativity of their translation work, it must be read in the context of their feminized identity as authors and their awareness of class, language, racial, and ethnic differences; for Castellanos, based in her critiques of the colonial history of Mexican Spanish; for Lispector, tied to her identity as a Jewish woman from a family of immigrants.

Neither translator invented a term for her own creative translation practice, as did the other translators included in this book. To contest and challenge *Plural*'s insulting label of *traducir mocosuena*, I propose "self-reflexive intersectional translation" as a potential mode of reading marginalized translators. The heuristic of intersectionality asks readers to notice when the procedures of cannibal translation are received as failures rather than choices based on the identity positions of translators, and how readers can reframe this reception. When Haroldo recovers the translation practices of Brazilian translators Gregório de Matos or Odorico Mendes, he redefines what had previously been labeled plagiarisms or failures as creative acts, or, as Augusto puts it, the taboo of translation becomes its totem.[9] Yet the reception of Castellanos and Lispector's translation work shows that this reversal of translation values did not benefit women translators equally. In the face of this exclusion, I emphasize the ways their translations performatively reject the neutrality of the translator's position, going against Paz's ideal of a "good translator" who can erase the self, replacing the concept of "objective" translation with self-reflexive intersectional translation.

Both writers achieved critical acclaim during their lifetimes, which were tragically cut short midcareer.[10] Yet their translation work was widely rejected at the time and largely ignored by subsequent scholarship; excluded from the translation circles of Paz and the de Campos brothers, neither enjoyed the status of poet-translator. When they subvert norms of "straight" or "faithful" translation in much the same ways as celebrated male translators, their choices are rebuffed as unconscious, erring, or immature. To instead take their translation manuals seriously, I read them through the lens of cannibal translation. Castellanos describes translation as anything but an objective, self-erasing version of a source text, rejecting Paz's theories. She defines her use of Spanish as intersectional, determined by her position as a female author writing in a language that has reinforced social hierarchies and forced linguistic assimilation of Indigenous populations. Castellanos's translations of Emily Dickinson draw the nineteenth-century poet's metaphysical speakers down to earth, where the physical body experiences pain that in the source poems was only a metaphorical wound. Like Castellanos in Mexico, Lispector's translations are disregarded as mere trade or even the work of other people. Despite these gendered dismissals, her translations of Poe—published as versions for children, now in their fourteenth edition—disarticulate the masculine narrative voice in Poe, erasing his signature authoritative tone to import her own informal narrators. In Lispector's translations, Edgar Allan Poe's domineering, logical, historian-narrators become haphazard, oral storytellers who forget important details and leave out elements of the story, echoing the narrators of Clarice's own fictions and her own narration of her writerly pose.

For Castellanos and Lispector, a self-reflexive intersectional translation practice provides a space to rehearse their public images as singular female literary celebrities, capturing authority in the face of critique. Their translation strategies indicate the widespread impact of cannibal translation practices in Latin America in the 1960s and 1970s, even when they were dismissed as bad, incomplete, or facile translations. Ultimately, these case studies substantiate the importance of cannibal translation as a reading practice. Only by taking their translation activity seriously rather than dismissing it as failure or noncreative work can we appreciate it as a radical tool to challenge literary authority and to include positions of gender, race, class, and identity traditionally excluded from the privilege of literary experiment.

ROSARIO CASTELLANOS: REJECTING THE OBJECTIVE TRANSLATOR

Studying Rosario Castellanos as a self-reflexive intersectional translator provides a new pathway into understanding her complex gender performance as a writer and public intellectual. Scholarship on Castellanos's vast work in poetry, fiction, essay, and *crónica* explores her lifelong interventions into the limitations women and Indigenous people faced in Mexican society.[11] She wrote a weekly newspaper column at the *Excélsior* in which she introduced her Mexican readership to international feminist movements and a wide range of female authors in Spanish and other languages, always writing from a self-reflexive examination of her own position in an unapologetically casual, accessible register.[12] Yet her legacy within the Mexican canon as "one of the boys," as Emily Hind puts it, reinscribes the gendered limitations Castellanos worked against. Hind positions Castellanos within a tradition of Mexican female authors dating back to Sor Juana Inés de la Cruz (1648–95), a brilliant writer and Hieronymite nun who gained prominence as an exceptional, singular woman, celebrated despite her gender in a literary sphere framed as masculine. For Hind, what she calls the "Sor Juana archetype" allows Mexican women to be intellectuals—but only if they also adopt a posture of self-abnegating, asexual, life of service to their genderless intellectual gifts.[13] Castellanos needed to actively embrace her female identity within her writing to resist the "Sor Juana" archetype that clung to her and to the singularity of her position. Writing with painful self-awareness of the fact that many generations of women were not welcome as writers, or even fully human subjects, translation becomes a powerful tool for Castellanos to combat writerly shame and subvert power dynamics keeping women submissive to men or translators submissive to authors. In her literary arsenal, cannibal translation takes on the capacity to carve out space for women writers and translators while acknowledging the challenges they face.

The treatment Rosario Castellanos received in the pages of *Plural* that called her translations *mocosuena* symbolizes a larger pattern of gendered intellectual labor division at that premier Mexican literary journal.[14] Even after her tragic death in 1974, Castellanos was never free of gendered dismissals of her work. An obituary published in *Plural* describes her with shocking disdain and back-handed compliments as "a serious person despite being young, open in spite of her Catholicism, and an undeniable talent despite being a woman."[15] Under the editorial leadership of Octavio Paz from 1971 to 1976, this monthly publication curated Mexico's participation in Latin American and world literature, and translation was always central to the project.[16] Although prominent women writers and translators were featured, they played supportive roles to male intellectuals. In two different interviews, the celebrated Mexican journalist Elena Poniatowska remembers the "machista" treatment of Castellanos and her translations, also alleging that her own participation in *Plural* was more amicable, but only under the unspoken condition that she play a "docile" role in "service" to male intellectuals.[17] Poniatowska reflects: "I devoted myself to interviewing them for a long time; that always seemed right to them. I was very docile, I still am. I wrote the interviews and articles they asked me for, I was truly at their service. . . . They never said to me 'why don't you write an article yourself.'"[18] Examining the translations published in *Plural* by other authors shows the "docility" that Poniatowska describes as an expectation for female contributors, one that Castellanos failed to maintain. For example, while the journal frequently published world poetry in translations by Paz, José Emilio Pacheco, Antonio Alatorre, and Tomás Segovia, the major female contributing translator, Ulalume González de León, primarily translated articles and prose literary texts.[19]

The exception to this typical gendered distribution of translation labor proves the rule: when González de León publishes a translated poem, she does so only as a supplement to a male translator's more creative translation. In a letter to the editor Octavio Paz, she writes that Cristobal Serra's translations of Edward Lear published in the prior issue of *Plural* strayed too far from the source, and she offers her own "versión *lunar*" to compare to the "versión *solar*" by the male translator. "I think Serra *re-created* Lear: in my opinion, he let himself be seduced by picturesque, rich-sounding words (very Spanish), which have their own charm but do not reflect the nostalgic, melancholic tone of the original. Do you think *Plural* readers would be interested to compare a solar version (Serra's) with a lunar version (my own)?"[20] Leaving aside comparative questions of the manner in which her translation differs from Serra's, I emphasize her frame for Paz's eyes: she promises a "lunar translation," less of a "re-creation," more disciplined and less "seduced" by her own language, less "picturesque" than the "very Spanish" re-creation by Serra. In other words, she presents her translation manual as more aligned with Paz's concept for the "good translator" who will not fall in love, will not be "seduced" by the possibilities in his own language. Echoing Paz's editing of his versions of French Romantic poet Nerval to shift away from the inadvertent influence of the Spanish Baroque, González de León persists in this paradoxical stance that a translation into Spanish should somehow avoid being "too Spanish." Her "lunar" mode of translation obeys the "good translator" discipline that Paz did not always adhere to himself—but which the *Plural* editorial board apparently expected of women translators and mocked Castellanos for failing to maintain.

Rather than performing this pose of docility, for Castellanos, poetry in translation represents a powerful tool for intervening into the patriarchal nature of language. Instead of Paz's model of a self-repressive poet-translator, Castellanos's translator figure takes a stance at once aggressive and submissive, but always fundamentally exploring her own writerly needs. In the essay "Translating Claudel" (1973), Castellanos draws on gendered and racialized vocabularies of docility and servility to champion a complex vision of translation that takes into consideration who the translator is and what the translator needs. Working with metaphors of servitude, she sees the translator as containing revolutionary potential, the subjugated figure ready to rise up and dethrone the author: "Only a servant betrays, and he only betrays the one he obeys, to whom he submits. And the translator is an ambitious subject who fundamentally aspires to usurp."[21] Yet this act of usurpation takes place in the wake of submission, from within an embodied, almost eroticized position of obedience and consensual power exchange. Castellanos envisions translation as a break from her own confusion through submitting to another's voice; I cite the Spanish here because the feminine article of *la mano* conveniently evokes a female translator:

> La mano es dócil al dictado de una forma no sólo viable sino viva y se ejercita en seguir los lineamientos seguros y conclusos del autor hasta llegar, con él, a la feliz culminación y al cumplimiento total.[22]
>
> (The hand becomes docile under the dictation of a viable and enlivening structure, following the author's sure and conclusive guidelines until reaching, with him, happy culmination and total fulfillment.)

While this passage echoes the "docility" Poniatowska describes, Castellanos's docile translator goes a step further, reaching an erotic fulfillment distinct from the self-effacement of González de León's "lunar translation." Instead, the translator takes advantage of the source text and finds freedom and pleasure in submission. The prototypical masculinity of the author figure emphasizes the gendered nature of this power imbalance, but the feminized hand of this translator works from a posture of considered, chosen docility—submission with consent and self-awareness.

Yet Castellanos's submissive translator also "penetrates" the persona of the author: dressing up in his clothing, "copying his gestures, his tone, going beyond what his public image offers to exhibit and penetrate his intimate space."[23] Finally, Castellanos posits that writers will translate precisely what they cannot write themselves, either out of limitation or shame. In translation, she and other writers encounter "what we wish we could have discovered, formulated, invented; that which corresponds quite accurately to the demands of our temperament, to the aims of our work, to the needs—shameful or explicit—of our self-expression."[24] This last phrase connects the "needs" of writers to their choices as translators. Her formulation links contradictory positions: the desire to have been the one to write something and the potential shame for wanting to express oneself that way. Translating allows her to write in a way she needs to but cannot—or may be ashamed to even try. In an unresolved paradoxical move, Castellanos defines translation as a performative mirror that can show writers both what they would have liked to achieve and what they might be ashamed to have written themselves but nevertheless are drawn to translate.

In each of these images of the translator—the usurper, the submissive, the mimic, the self-expressive performer, the shadow-side explorer—the translator's own realities, drives, and desires are central. Yet the stakes of this individual experience are heightened based on the social, racial, and gendered position of the translator. From the very title of her essay collection, in *Mujer que sabe latín . . .* (1973), the question of access to the language of knowledge production operates as contrary to a feminine identity. Referencing the proverb "Mujer que sabe latín no tiene marido ni buen fin" (The woman who knows Latin has no husband and comes to no good), the title caustically centers the question of whether the category of woman and intellectual are able to overlap in Mexico. Castellanos defines her intersectional experience with Spanish in the essay "Divagación sobre el idioma" (1969), where language poses a problem for her as both a female writer (*escritora*) and a Mexican: the Spanish language "was created for a people profoundly different from ours, with other ancestors, temperaments, circumstances, projects, expressive needs."[25] Describing the brutal, normalizing force of Spanish in Mexico, she historicizes the cultural capital associated with hypereloquence from the colonial Baroque to the contemporary performance of rhetorical skill as a structuring element in racialized power divisions. She indicts the Catholic Church, state bureaucracies, and lyric poetry alike for maintaining a racialized hierarchy of language, in which "what mattered most was to signal at first sight, to prove to any stranger the rank you occupied in society; skin color said a lot but not everything—

you needed to add demonstrations of pure faith and total dominance of the means of oral expression."[26] In short, the Spanish language in Mexico always served to indicate social rank, and it excluded women and Indigenous people. For Castellanos, the only way for language to contribute to decolonizing Mexican culture would be to emphasize the dialogic and relational value of the language—as cannibal translation aims. Equality among all interlocutors are intentions, not preconditions: language liberates when used carefully between "those who consider and treat one another as equals" and those "who desire one another to be free."[27] For Castellanos, to question who has the license, the agency with language to enter the public sphere represents a crucial task for translators. The Mexican literary sphere needs to recognize its pre-Hispanic Indigenous cultural base and incorporate writing from a female perspective: her mode of cannibal translation, which I call self-reflexive intersectional translation, can accomplish both goals and break new ground for those who have been historically excluded from authorship: Indigenous and female voices.

BEYOND THE SOR JUANA ARCHETYPE: CASTELLANOS CANNIBALIZES DICKINSON

The self-reflexivity and intersectionality of Castellanos's writing has been explored through her fiction, her essays, and her poetry.[28] Yet she has not been studied as a critical, creative translator—perhaps because of the harsher criticism her translations received. Using the particular case study of Castellanos's work on Emily Dickinson, I read her into the corpus of cannibal translation. Dickinson serves as one of several problematic avatars of female writers in Castellanos's pantheon; with the Amherst poet as much as other Hispanophone models like Santa Teresa or Sor Juana, Castellanos finds that inhabiting these archetypes costs too much, asks her to give up too much of her embodied and gendered life experience. Translating Dickinson, Castellanos explores the place of a woman writer in public, devouring the metaphysical and indeterminate poetry of her nineteenth-century source texts to put them into motion and on the street: materially grounded, female, and related to the bureaucratic and social world in addition to the spiritual world.

Castellanos's Dickinson translations were first published in her weekly column in the newspaper *Excélsior* embedded in the essay "Emily Dickinson: Una mujer singular" (1964).[29] This essay both insists on the unique qualities of Dickinson's drive to write and also imagines other writers like her, then and now. In addition, Castellanos emphasizes elements of Dickinson's biography—her unusual education for a woman of her time, her spiritual rebelliousness, her unsuccessful romances—that match her own. She finds in the works she translates a space to explore what she could have written herself, rejecting the norm of "single"-ness, the singularity of women writers, reanimating the archetype and exploding it from within. Castellanos inhabits the Emily Dickinson archetype to write these translations, but she betrays it by taking it into the public square, the pages of the newspaper, inviting other women readers to take note and become writers themselves.

Introducing Dickinson, Castellanos speaks to her readers with the assumption of a shared vocation, invoking them as other women who want to be writers. Speaking with a powerful "we," she observes that "we who were born in this century found much cleared ground, open pathways. But those who preceded us had to achieve some degree of heroism for their vocation to be realized in adverse circumstances."[30] While this essay presents Dickinson's biography as a model—or counter-model—for other women writers, it also expresses frustration at the confinement or limitations reified by always reading a woman's works through her gender. Castellanos makes a similar argument in "Otra vez Sor Juana," rejecting Ludwig Pflandel's psychoanalytic analysis of Sor Juana and protesting that reading women's lives through the lens of their gender creates a trap for female intellectuals, framing their work in reference to a limited set of female biographical tropes (whore, mother, Madonna, monster, madwoman). Castellanos reminds us that Sor Juana figured her femininity as a "hypothesis" rather than a conclusion or explanation.[31] Castellanos both critiques the hyperfocus on gender as conditioning the authorial position of the woman while also emphasizing the gendered framework into which her precursors were carving out new terrain. Translating a female author like Emily Dickinson puts her in the position to both entertain and negate autobiographical interpretations of her work.

For example, when analyzing Dickinson's poem "My life closed twice" in her essay "Una mujer singular," Castellanos gives her reader the biographical reading of this work as referring to Dickinson's two frustrated romances but also questions that interpretation, asking, "Are these the episodes to which one of her most celebrated poems refers?"[32] She then gives her translation, as though it answers the question. Through her Dickinson translation, she both introduces and troubles the poem's autobiographical interpretation:

Dos veces antes se cerró mi vida
y yo permanecí para mirar
si la Inmortalidad, sin velos, me guardaba
algún evento más;
concebido tan grande, ay, tan sin esperanza
como la doble llave de mi encierro.
La despedida es lo único que sabemos del cielo.
Y no necesitamos nada más del infierno.[33]

My life closed twice before it's close;
It yet remains to see
If Immortality unveil
A third event to me,

So huge, so hopeless to conceive
As these that twice befell.
Parting is all we know of heaven,
And all we need of hell.[34]

In her gloss on Dickinson, she both accepts and problematizes the persistent conflation of the biographical self of a female author with her works. Yet in translation, Castellanos meshes her own biography with that of Dickinson, leaving as an open question whether her poems can be sufficiently explained by her life. Castellanos adds the captivating image of the *doble llave*, which makes her translation seem even more imprisoned. Doors with old lock mechanisms sometimes can be locked twice for a deadbolt lock; the sound they make will echo with more finality than a regular, single lock. She also reuses the word *cerró* as *encierro* to give the same sense of repeated death and closing off that the poem speaks of. Whereas the source poem has this repetition in the first line, Castellanos delays the second appearance of enclosure, again to increase the sense of claustrophobic, depressive entrapment. She also activates the alternative meaning of *velo* (wake) when she renders the "unveiling" as *sin velos* rather than *develar* or *revelar*.[35] Inserting the exclamation *ay* in the middle of the poem, Castellanos amplifies the poignancy of a source text that had tempered its own emotionality. The pain contained in Castellanos's line "concebido tan grande, ay, tan sin esperanza" conveys the translator's pain of her own *doble llave*—her two miscarriages before giving birth to her son Gabriel. She also reorders the phrase to place more emphasis on *concebido*, which in Spanish as in English shares the meaning of an abstract and a biological conception.

Reading autobiographical information from the translator into their work may seem counterintuitive. However, in her essay "Translating Claudel," Castellanos did acknowledge the reality that writers are drawn to translate works they relate to. Her essay shows a suspicion of biographical interpretation, yet as a translator, she uses Dickinson to express the pain of two major losses that made her doubt the possibility of a third event to measure up.

Castellanos places her two miscarriages among many experiences that accustomed her to solitude, writing in one of her *Excélsior* columns: "I was an only child . . . abandoned during my adolescence. . . . I remained single until the age of thirty-three when I contracted a marriage that was strictly monogamous on my side and totally polygamous on the other. I had three children, the first two of whom two died; when I received my divorce papers I was already in Tel Aviv."[36] In fact, she frequently describes them not as miscarriages at all but as the deaths of her first two children; she dedicates her poetry collection *Lívida luz* (1960) "A la memoria de mi hija" (To the memory of my daughter). Unlike other selections in *Materia memorable* that express the speaker's proximity to death, this poem instead focuses on the feelings of confinement, waiting, uncertainty that come *in between* brushes with death. She can write from the place after the two miscarriages that put her in touch with death twice, but before conceiving for the third time and bearing her son. The greater emotionality of the *ay* and the greater physicality of the pacing of Castellanos's self-reflexive and intersectional translation, read autobiographically, insist that the female embodied experience itself produces these literary and philosophical insights, experiences that are not singular but shared by many.

In addition to the translations, Castellanos also incorporates Dickinson's voice and persona into several of her own poems in *Materia memorable*. In "Meditación en el umbral," Dickinson figures along with a pantheon of other female precursors, avatars for building a female writerly life, pushing Castellanos's poetic speaker across a threshold and over the brink, into the unknown. From the first line, "No, no es la solución," the speaker rejects all prior models of female writers seeking independence. She recalls Santa Teresa de Ávila and Sor Juana, both of whom chose the self-enclosure of the convent to be able to access greater intellectual freedom. While Santa Teresa appears free to roam outdoors in the "páramos de Ávila,"[37] she is also depicted as mentally cloistered, waiting passively for the "angel with the dart" before she "tightened her veil / to begin to act." The speaker also rejects the alternative form of the cloister available to nineteenth-century female authors—that is, chaste confinement within the family home:

> No concluir las leyes geométricas, contando
> las vigas de la celda de castigo
> como lo hizo Sor Juana. No es la solución
> escribir, mientras llegan las visitas,
> en la sala de estar de la familia Austen
> ni encerrarse en el ático
> de alguna residencia de la Nueva Inglaterra
> y soñar, con la Biblia de los Dickinson
> debajo de una almohada de soltera.[38]
>
> Nor to deduce geometric laws by counting
> the beams of one's solitary confinement cell
> like Sor Juana did. It's not a solution
> to write, while company arrives,
> in the Austen family living room
> or to shut oneself up in the attic
> of some New England house
> and dream, with the Dickinson's family Bible
> under a spinster pillow.[39]

The confinement of these lines, Sor Juana counting the beams of her cell, Austen's time interrupted and circumscribed by others, Dickinson shut in and buried, uses embodied language to express the restricted range of movement for these accomplished authors—even when they chose alternatives to the family-life norms of their day.

Subsequent stanzas jump further back into history and religious parable to uncover other precursors, modeled after Sor Juana's own pantheon of female intellectuals from myth and history, collected to support her claim to the right of intellectual freedom in "La Respuesta." All of these women become shorthand for the way history, the Catholic faith, and the literary world have reduced them to a one-dimensional stereotype, history representing the lives of women only as cautionary tales. The poem ends by positing but not confirming that there must be another way "to be human and free."[40] The *umbral*, the "threshold" or "brink" of the title, indicates the desire to surpass the limits of these models: the speaker must plunge into an unknown where these social codes can be rejected, but what replaces them is not yet visible. In the atmosphere of physical enclosure and architectural density of this poem, Castellanos stages the authorial position of women as breaking free within a written language that has constructed them as objects of speech rather than speakers, circumscribed by fictional, historical, and religious narrative scripts.

Castellanos cannibalizes the voice and the persona of Emily Dickinson, alongside other female writers in this poem, to speak truths about herself—about her two miscarriages, about her loss of faith in both Catholicism and social world of Mexico—within a register unlike the brash, bold, sarcasm of her essays. Why does she need another writer's voice? As she says in "Translating Claudel," submitting to the hand of an author makes this self-revelation more pleasurable—and more possible, with the author's work pushing beyond the threshold of her own shame at wanting to write these words.

Several other poems in *Materia memorable* can be read as Castellanos dressing her poetic speaker up in an Emily Dickinson disguise and cannibalizing her voice, images, and vocabulary. In "Canción," the opening line, "Yo conocí una paloma" (I met a dove), could easily introduce a Dickinson poem. Growing harsher and more violent, the poem ends with two lines that depict the same painful limbo between life and death expressed in "Dos veces antes se cerró mi vida."

Yo conocí una paloma
con las dos alas cortadas;
andaba torpe, sin cielo,
en la tierra, desterrada.

La tenía en mi regazo
y no supe darle nada
Ni amor, ni piedad, ni el nudo
que pudiera estrangularla.[41]

(I met a dove
with both wings cut;
limping along, skyless,
on earth, banished.

I had her in my lap
and had nothing to give
No love, no mercy, nor even the knot
that could have strangled her.)

The formal simplicity of this poem and the speaker's pity for the bird's plight echo Dickinson, who frequently uses images of communion or identification with birds, flowers, and bees. The play on words in the line "en la tierra, desterrada" also draws on a Dickinson trope, of the human soul as suffering exile on earth, banished from heaven.

Images of being left behind with the fear of life run through *Materia memorable* and perhaps culminate in Dickinson's poem "'Tis not that Dying hurts us so," which Castellanos translates as "Morir no hiere tanto." The poem frames the human condition as the life of an unnatural, foolish bird, unable or unwilling to obey the instinct to migrate. The speaker cannot depart to warmer climes and instead remains, trembling and beholden, waiting for the benevolent hand of a kind stranger or a natural death.

'Tis not that Dying hurts us so -
'Tis Living - hurts us more -
But Dying - is a different way -
A kind behind the Door -

The Southern Custom - of the Bird -
That ere the Frosts are due -
Accepts a better Latitude -
We - are the Birds - that stay.

The Shiverers round Farmer's doors -
For whose reluctant Crumb -
We stipulate - till pitying Snows
Persuade our Feathers Home[42]

The "hurt" in Dickinson's first line is amplified by Castellanos: she physicalizes the experience of psychic pain by choosing *herir* (wound) rather than "hurt," again grounding and physicalizing the metaphysical experiences of Dickinson into her own embodied translations. Her version also eliminates the "Farmer," who appears to grudgingly provide a "Crumb."

Morir no hiere tanto.
Nos hiere más vivir.
Un modo diferente, una forma escondida
tras la puerta, es morir.

Los pájaros del sur tienen costumbre
—cuando la escarcha está a punto de caer—
de emigrar hacia climas más benévolos.
Nosotros no sabemos sino permanecer.

Temblorosos rondamos en torno de las granjas
buscando la migaja que alguno ha de arrojar.
Tal es el pacto. La piadosa nieve
persuade a nuestras plumas de volver a su hogar.[43]

Instead of Dickinson's benevolent although reluctant or unreliable Farmer, the birds here have an even less certain source for compassion; "buscando la migaja que alguno ha de arrojar," their *alguno* (someone) may not arrive. Castellanos also chooses a more active verb: not merely "surrounding," the birds are actively "looking"; they cannot just wait passively.

Dickinson's poem presents a spiritual condition of abandonment; in the Castellanos translation, the abandonment is also social. Her choice to translate the verb "stipulate" loosely allows her to associate the existential uncertainty of life with the bureaucratic uncertainty of people living in an unfeeling system within a neglectful state. She translates "We stipulate" as a full sentence: "Tal es el pacto" (Such is the agreement). As Maureen Ahern highlights, Castellanos frequently writes literary works that draw from the language of nonliterary genres: newspapers, bureaucratic forms, official reports, or questionnaires.[44] Reading Castellanos through Dickinson, we see that her bureaucratic language is often paired with the vocabulary of religion. If the *pacto* in the Castellanos version is a spiritual covenant with the divine, it is also a legalistic contract with the state.

Cannibalizing Dickinson, Castellanos's poem "Nota roja" echoes her translation "Morir no hiere tanto," with the line "Es tan fácil morir, basta tan poco." Instead of the bucolic migrating birds of the Amherst poet, Castellanos borrows images from newspaper coverage of urban violence and murder; for the dead body depicted, death came easily and quickly. The title, "Nota roja," refers to sensationalistic news reporting on local crime or street violence, which often included a graphic photo.

The poem begins with a description of the newspaper's front-page image of a dead body, and how it impacts readers who remain to walk the streets of the same city; as in the Dickinson poem, the living are left behind to tremble.

> Es tan fácil morir, basta tan poco.
> Un golpe a medianoche, por la espalda,
> y aquí está ya el cadáver
> puesto entre las mandíbulas de un público antropófago.
> . . . .
> Pero este cuerpo abierto en canal, esta entraña derramada en el
> suelo
> hacen subir la fiebre
> de cada Abel que mira su alrededor, temblando.[45]
>
> (It's so easy to die, it takes so little
> A blow at midnight, in the back,
> and now here lies the corpse already
> served up for the jaws of a cannibal public
> . . . .
> But this open body in the canal, these entrails spilled on the
> ground,
> raise the temperature
> of every Abel watching his back, trembling.)

The readership for this "Nota roja," the disembodied "jaws of a cannibal public," consumes the violent image, yet devouring the pain of others is the false "crumb" that never satiates the hunger of the shivering birds. The poem ends with another echo of Dickinson: the living are left *temblando*, just as she translated "Shiverers" as *temblorosos*. In the New England setting of Dickinson's "'Tis not that Dying," they tremble from cold; in the warmer climes of Castellanos, they tremble from paranoia, from danger always around the corner. In both poems, the simple finality of death makes the problem of how, where, and why to live seem all the more daunting, shiver-inducing. Naming the living after the biblical fratricide victim Abel, Castellanos again connects the lack of state protections to a lack of divine mercy. The failure to fulfill a social contract promising security to the public, in the final stanza of the poem, maps onto a larger betrayal experienced by the faithful.

Castellanos expands the emotionality of Dickinson by increasing the physicality and impact of what remains indeterminate in the source text. Translating Dickinson autobiographically, as a technique to embody the other, to write precisely what she is unable to say or write herself, her translations of Dickinson show that this embodiment always occurs with an awareness of the historical and cultural position she occupies as an *escritora mexicana* working in a language that has historically excluded her voice. Whereas Octavio Paz airs and processes with Haroldo de Campos the shame at needing to travel through the hegemonic languages of English and French to meet the Brazilian poet, or his rage being the first to experiment with new modes of prose poetry in Spanish, Castellanos's poetry performs shame and rage that respond to the social placement of female writers and the treatment of their work, either dismissed as trivial or celebrated only on the condition of their "singular" ability to occupy the categories both of woman and of intellectual. Devouring elements of her source texts to speak through their mask, to reanimate them within her own context, her self-reflexive, intersectional translations show the importance of understanding cannibal translation as a reading practice invested in challenging readers to value her creative contributions not *despite* their female embodiment but *because* of them.

CLARICE LISPECTOR AND TRANSLATION AS AUTHORIAL SELF-FASHIONING

In the case of acclaimed Brazilian author Clarice Lispector, her translations have been consistently dismissed as trade and not craft. Both her contemporaries and current criticism question her capacity to act as a creative translator; this reception contributes to making her choices and skills as a translator invisible despite their success on the publishing market and despite her deployment of similar cannibal translation techniques as her literary peers.

In the past ten years, Lispector's work has enjoyed renewed critical attention and careful retranslation.[46] One of her most active champions, Benjamin Moser, authored the first English-language biography of Lispector, *Why This World* (2009). Following this successful publication, Moser persuaded New Directions to publish a carefully produced series of retranslations of her novels and short stories under his editorship.[47] Yet even this critically acclaimed translation project into English has been beset with questions of gendered power dynamics indexing questions of translator authority and mastery. As Magdalena Edwards claims in her widely circulated essay documenting her experience translating Clarice Lispector under Moser's editorial aegis, his treatment of women translators and biographers exhibited a pattern of dismissive behavior. In fact, the process of translating *The Chandelier* (New Directions, 2017) resulted in adding Moser's name as cotranslator, after the fact and due to his claims that he would need to "rewrite the whole thing from scratch."[48] Moser is not the only critic to dismiss Lispector's translations; much like Castellanos, her translation work merits an intersectional framework of analysis to appreciate its complex and self-reflexive stylistics.

Even in the context of this resurgent interest in Lispector's work aligned with questions of translation, her own translations have received scant and wary critical attention—although her translations of stories by Poe have remained in print since the first edition in 1974.[49] Because these translations were presented as adaptations for a juvenile readership, the care with which she reconstructed these stories in Portuguese has not been fully appreciated. Her translations actively intervene into Poe's work to fit within her own literary output. As a cannibal translator, she reconstructs the frames of his stories by adding epigraphs, often drawn from his philosophical writings; she creates different narrative voices that craft an oral storytelling mood in an informal Portuguese rather than the faux-historical tone Poe's narrators sometimes adopt; and she reverses the relationship between readers and Poe's characters by avoiding the distancing effects on which Poe relied, instead crafting her translated characters within recognizably Brazilian voices or racialized character types. Like the translator as usurper described by Castellanos, Lispector builds on Poe's material and pares away excess—yet this was seen not as literary art but as necessary labor at best or unskilled laziness at worst.

Lispector's biographical record and other material—both present and absent—in her translator's archive contribute to the exclusion of her translation work from her creative output. Severino J. Albuquerque explores the ambiguous provenance of Lispector's translations as connected with her financial situation, a form of literary labor she took on for money, along with writing for women's magazines and ghostwriting for celebrities. He writes that "it is widely accepted that Clarice agreed to add her by-then famous name to a number of translations done by others. It is not clear, however, precisely which of the several translations attributed to Clarice are her own work and which are not. In an existence such as Clarice's, so defined by ambiguity and evasiveness, it is almost fitting that this authorial uncertainty would surround her translation."[50] As Fernando Arenas describes, to resist being pigeonholed as a literary subordinate to any author or movement, she would contradict herself when responding to questions about her reading or influences.[51] Her works have grown in acclaim, but interest in her translation work has not kept up.

Lispector translated actively during a time of great economic instability in the 1970s, as Moser says, "to try to make ends meet."[52] Her biographer dismisses her translations for three reasons: they were not done with great care, she translated primarily to earn money, and it was rumored that Lispector did not translate the works attributed to her hand. Lispector's translations provoke curious ambivalence in what is otherwise an opinionated and decided literary biography. This ambivalence attaches to both the selection of works to translate and the execution of the translations. Moser acknowledges both that she translated whatever she was assigned for money and that she did have a choice in some cases, allowing her to translate works that she connected with, both personally and aesthetically. In the case of *Burning Lights*, the Yiddish memoir of Marc Chagall's first wife, Bella Chagall, Moser imagines her biographical identification with another woman from the same Central European Jewish background.[53] Moreover, he remarks on how frequently she translated works connected to her own interests even in the case of the trade fiction: "Many of them deal with the same themes of crime, sin, and violence that so often appear in her own work. There were the Poe stories and *Dorian Gray*, there were two novels by Agatha Christie, and there was Anne Rice's *Interview with the Vampire*."[54] Moser evaluates her translations but bases his conclusions on letters in the publisher's archive at Artenova—communications between Lispector, her editor Álvaro Pacheco, and his assistant Anna Maria da Silva Telles Watson—more than on the translations themselves.[55]

> Her work as a translator was not distinguished, and she seems to have thrown her translations together in off hours. "I work quickly, intuitively," she said. "Sometimes I check the dictionary, sometimes not." This lassitude was partly inspired by the pittance she was paid. Álvaro Pacheco, who paid translation by the page, remembered the pathetic spectacle of Brazil's greatest writer coming to his office with a few pages at a time. This did not encourage her to do her best. In 1976, one of Pacheco's assistants chastised her translation

> of a French book. Among its faults were "entire sentences omitted," "words translated by deduction, or by the closest sound to a Brazilian word," "modification of the meaning of words and even reversal of the sentence's meaning." She concluded haughtily, "I think that you have been assisted in this translation by someone who did not take the work very seriously."[56]

As with Castellanos, when a woman translates based on sound it is perceived as laziness or ignorance, although the same gesture in male translators is praised as artistic craft. Furthermore, to draw on "intuition" as a guide for writing or translation practice need not be judged or discarded. Clarice herself claimed and celebrated her instinctive process and famously rejected the idea of herself as a professional writer or an intellectual: "In her crônica 'Intelectual? Não' ('Intellectual? No'), Lispector writes: 'To be an intellectual is to use your intelligence first and foremost, which I do not do: I use my intuition, my instinct.'"[57] When applied to translation, the concept of using intuition goes against the authoritative, objective image of translator as disciplined expert, fully in control. These letters provide invaluable information about Lispector's translation work and how it was evaluated by those involved in its publication. Yet unless we closely read the translations themselves, we risk downplaying elements of her translation manual, or the set of consistent stylistic choices that can be distilled from her translations, as ineffectual or unconscious when they were active choices at work. In other words, the same mistrust that characterized the reception of her own writing, dismissing it as instinct or magic, may have affected the reception of her translation work. Rather than excising them from her literary oeuvre because they participated in the market economy of the publishing industry, or because of gender norms that deny female translators the privilege of using experimental techniques, what becomes visible when we take her translations seriously?

The critical analysis of her versions of Poe tends to frame her work as simplified, or even "spontaneous" adaptations for the children's book market—in short, never as art or as creative translation.[58] Élida Paulina Ferreira and Karin Hallana Santos Silva come the closest to appreciating the artfulness of Lispector's translations, questioning the distinction between translation and adaptation by comparing two Portuguese translations of Poe's collection *Tales of the Grotesque and Arabesque* (1840), by Lispector and by Breno Silveira. Their analysis finds many points in which both translation and adaptation make similar shifts from the source text, which include removing sections of Poe's text without noting the change; altering the age of a character to match the age of majority in the target culture of Brazil; adding material or condensing paragraphs without remark; using simpler syntax than Poe's; and adding or modifying adverbs or adjectives that clarify but also interpret.[59] The authors conclude that differences between adaptations and translations may have more to do with the publisher's desired marketing strategy than with any observable aspect of the text.[60] This comparative analysis concludes by reverting to a market-oriented perspective, in which the classification of "adaptation" responds primarily to the cultural capital Lispector brings to Poe's work as a famous writer. Yet her fame as a writer does not outweigh the gendered dismissal of her translation work; these investigations do not search for literary or theoretical qualities of her translations, perhaps because her situation of financial need made her translations seem less valuable as a part of her artistic production. In the following section, I analyze her translations to demonstrate the careful aesthetic choices that cannibalize Poe's stories to exhibit her own sensibilities.

POE IN BRAZIL: LISPECTOR'S INFORMAL TRANSLATION MANUAL

Titled *Historias extraordinárias de Allan Poe: Textos selecionados e reescritos por Clarice Lispector*, the Brazilian author's collection of Poe translations includes her name and draws its title from Charles Baudelaire's renowned French translations of the US storyteller's work.[61] Lispector's translation manual, as described negatively by her publisher and ambivalently by the author herself, includes operating on intuition; omitting full sentences freely and without note; translating based on sound; changing or even reversing meaning; and translating works that match her own favored themes. Her versions of Poe bear out some of these qualities, and I define her not as a haphazard trade-press translator but, rather, as an artist practicing self-reflexive intersectional translation. In this light, her translation strategies also include taking the liberty to add a new frame to a story; reducing details or elements of otherness to make Poe's curiosities seem more uncannily familiar; using unmarked language where the source was marked by an accent; and drawing on Brazilian literary orality to create a casual storytelling mood.

One of Clarice's most frequent interventions comes through the addition of epigraphs that frame the story in a new way and usually draw from another text by Poe: his metaphysical essay "Matter, Spirit, and Divine Will," lyric poems such as "Eureka" or "Al-Aaraf," or additional stories not included in her translation collection.[62] Far from simplifying her task, these epigraphs evidence her deep readings into Poe's work and Baudelaire's translations of Poe, as she draws from both the English and the French versions.[63] In her translation of "Metzengerstein," she adds an epigraph drawing from an outside source that echoes a similar addition by Baudelaire. Poe's tale weaves mysterious circumstances around the final demise of two families in conflict for generations, where a wild and powerful horse arrives after the destruction by fire of the Berlifitzing estate and appears to take revenge on the surviving heir to Château Metzengerstein, perhaps moved by the spirit of their dead paterfamilias through "metempsychosis": the departed soul's transfiguration into a new living body. While Poe begins his tale by stating that it concerns a Hungarian community in a time when people held "a settled although hidden belief in the doctrines of Metempsychosis," he immediately refuses to define this "superstition," instead referring to it as a more extreme version of a notion he explains in French: "'The soul' . . . (I give the words of an acute and intelligent Parisian) '*ne demeure qu'une seule fois dans un corps sensible: au reste—un cheval, un chien, un homme même, n'est que la ressemblance peu tangible de ces animaux*."[64] Where Poe dissembles, Lispector opens with a clear definition in an added epigraph.[65] "Metempsychosis: theory of the transmigration of the soul from one body to another. Passage of the soul from one body to another. Doctrine according to which the thinking immortal soul can animate successive different bodies. Our lives would be a series of metempsychoses."[66] Unlike Poe's oblique gloss on metempsychosis, which allowed his story to center around the damage caused by family competition, unchecked access to resources, and intergenerational violence, Lispector instead centers the story around the idea of a soul transforming through multiple bodies, emphasizing the universality of this doctrine and the endurance of the concept itself through different cultures.

In this case, she alters the frame in accordance with her reading of Baudelaire's version. The French poet-translator, who appears to have shared her frustration with Poe's evasive treatment of the topic, took the liberty of adding a footnote to point out the bizarre and incomplete nature of Poe's citation in French. He also claimed for himself the opportunity to correct it: "I do not know who wrote this strange and obscure text; however, I allowed myself to rectify it slightly, adapting it to the moral sense of the story. Poe sometimes quotes incorrectly from memory. Besides, the meaning seems to me closest to the opinion attributed to Father Kircher—that animals are locked up spirits—C.B."[67] Whereas Baudelaire flags his alterations, adding footnotes with his own initials to Poe's texts and making changes based on his authority as a French speaker, replacing the fictional "Parisian" in Poe's story, Lispector never signals her additions. In spite of the previously mentioned scholarly consensus that Lispector signed translations that were not her own, I assert that the addition of this extensive epigraph on metempsychosis, a subject that matches with her own interests, supports the claim that Lispector did author these Portuguese versions based on careful readings of Poe in English and in French translation by Baudelaire.

Lispector frequently transforms Poe's narrative frames to match her own style—and, in the case of his story "The Devil in the Belfry," to invite an interpretation within the Brazilian cultural moment. Depicting a highly rigid and regimented society threatened by the arrival of a foreigner, her story transforms Poe's imaginary and foreignized space to draw it closer to Brazil and replaces the invading bizarre stranger with an internal "menace" recognizable to Brazilian readers: the impoverished, insignificant, Afro-Brazilian migrant to the cities from the Northeast. Poe's story depicts the order-obsessed residents of the town of Vondervotteimittiss, who "have adopted these three important resolutions: 'That it is wrong to alter the good old course of things;' 'That there is nothing tolerable out of Vondervotteimittiss;' and 'That we will stick by our clocks and our cabbages.'"[68] When a stranger arrives on the horizon, the citizens are amazed and fascinated by his foreign appearance, and then appalled by his out-of-step movements as he dances up to the top of their beloved clock tower, the center of their society, and the clock strikes "thirteen" hours for the first time. His tale ends with an appeal to the "lovers of correct time" to banish this disruptive element.[69] Lispector's Brazilian Portuguese version transforms Poe's story by eliminating his construction of Germanic character types, doubly distanced from the reader by a historically obsessive narrator; replacing the narrator's historical pose with a casual oral register; and creating common ground between the characters, the narrator, and the readers themselves by signaling that this imaginary town could be located in Brazil itself. The outside element that disturbs the order of this town is not depicted with the same foreign qualities or air of self-satisfaction; her invader is small, poor, broken—the subaltern other of the Brazilian class system, a legacy of race-based slavery, rather than the exotic foreigner of Poe's story.

In her translation "O Diabo no campanário" (1975), Lispector reverses the narrative frame entirely: Poe's aspiring historian-narrator who authorizes himself with research becomes Lispector's forgetful storyteller speaking in a casual, lackadaisical style. Poe's story dramatizes xenophobia, and the narrator shares the townspeople's obsession with time and order, displaying from the start a conviction that the value of the town rests on its preservation in its original state. Poe's story begins with multiple paragraphs of faux historiography, while also performing the uncertainty of all of his information. After the narrator self-authorizes as a trustworthy accountant of the information available, he names himself as one who "aspires to the title of historian"; he refers to the "united aid of medals, manuscripts, and inscriptions, I am enabled to say, positively, that the borough of Vondervotteimittiss has existed, from its origin, in precisely the same condition which it at present preserves."[70] The narrator-historian cannot give any other details with certainty, neither the date of the borough's foundation nor the origin of its name, but he gives sources to consult and suggestions of the possible etymology of Vondervotteimittiss, to comply with his promise that, as historian, he will do the best he can with the materials available. Given that the town's name is a homophonic joke—it sounds like "wonder-what-time-it-is" in a faux German accent—the careful reader would immediately distrust this narrator's capacity to detect irony.

Clarice opens with a narrator who rejects the title of historian and actively claims the lack of knowledge that Poe's narrator dissembles about. Instead of the institutionalized historiography that governs the frame of the source text, her narrator rejects the utility of those claims to authority and instead cultivates a casual, forgetful, exclamatory, and overall oral register of storytelling.

> A cidade chamava-se Vondervotteimittiss. Não sei quase nada sobre o seu significado. Se algum leitor estiver interessado em saber, poderei indicar as fontes de informação. Não creio, porém, que a consulta vá adiantar muito. É tudo muito complicado. E desnecessário. O que interessa mesmo, ah, esqueci de dizer logo no início: é o melhor lugar do mundo. Ou *era*. E é sobre isso que lhes quero falar. . . . Não sou historiador. Portanto, não lhes falarei da data de sua origem, de

> sua importância no meio das outras cidades. Esse é mesmo um caso à parte.[71]
>
> (The city was called Vondervotteimittiss. I know almost nothing about its meaning. If any reader should be interested to know, I could indicate some sources. But I don't believe any consultation will do much good. It's all very complicated. And unnecessary. What really matters, ah, I forgot to say back at the start: it's the best place in the world. Or it *was*. And that's what I want to tell you about. . . . I'm not a historian, so I won't talk about any founding dates or its importance compared to other cities. This really is a special case.)

Unlike Poe's "aspiring historian," Lispector constructs a voice of indifference, generality, and limited attention. While both narrators draw from the classic rhetorical device of humility and self-deprecation, and their pose of not fully claiming authority should thus be held at critical distance, I read Lispector's narrator as constructing a second-level rejection of authority: where Poe's narrator aspires to historian status, Lispector's finds it all "unnecessary." Her narrator does not want to get into the complications of historical materials and sources, although Poe's narrator delights in doing so. Instead, this narrator barely remembers to emphasize that the important fact about this town is that they have preserved their traditions, that nothing has changed there, ever. The haphazard storyteller Lispector cultivates evokes the same critiques leveled against her translation work.

Lispector also alters significantly the linguistic markers that characterize the people inhabiting this place and makes no attempt to re-create the qualities of the language Poe uses, which include the production of a faux Dutch or German accent during the direct speech of his characters. Poe constructs their voices as combining accented English and German, counting along with the clock: "'Dree! Vour! Fibe! Sax! Seben! Aight! Noin! Den!'"[72] In a few moments, the narrator slips into the same accented discourse as the townsfolk, revealing he likely has close ties to the town and its traditions, despite his scholarly distance displayed in the opening pages. After the invading stranger has danced his way up to the clock tower, the terrible event occurs: "'*Thirteen*! said he. . . . 'Der Teufel!' groaned they, 'Dirteen! Dirteen!!—Mein Gott, it is Dirteen o'clock!!'"[73] Exclaiming in German "The Devil!" and "My

God!" the residents and the narrator alike register this event as a catastrophe of epic proportion, where the habitual striking of the bell becomes a nightmarish supplement and disturbance to the order of the town, which, as its name "Vondervotteimittiss" indicates, lives to "wonder-what-time-it-is."

While she does not domesticate this joke and leaves the name of the town in Poe's faux Dutch or German, Lispector's version otherwise eliminates the accented speech register: "'—O Diabo!—gemeram. Treze! Treze! Santo Deus, são treze horas!'"[74] She does not construct any accented dialect for the townsfolk, and instead of using German words, *Der Teufel* or *Mein Gott*, she directly translates them as "O Diabo" and "Santo Deus," domesticating what was foreign in the source text. In her translation, all of the characters in the story including the narrator speak the same Brazilian Portuguese as readers of Lispector's version.

Lispector's version also domesticates and even reverses the description of the foreigner come to town, this supplemental stranger who causes the beloved clock to strike thirteen. Poe depicts him as an immediate object of fascination with sartorial markers of wealth, an air of foreignness in his movements, and racialized traits associated with antisemitic descriptions of Jewish people. Lispector also racializes the foreigner but using Afro-Brazilian features, and she transforms him into a poor, insignificant, and uninteresting invader.

Poe describes him as "a very odd-looking" and "droll object," and although small, he attracts a great deal of attention: "Everybody had soon a good look at him."[75] Dressed richly in fabrics that draw the eye—"a tight-fitting swallow-tailed black coat, (from one of whose pockets dangled a vast length of white handkerchief), black kerseymere knee-breeches, black stockings, and stumpy-looking pumps, with huge bunches of black satin ribbon"—he carries luxury objects, including "a huge *chapeau-de-bras*" and "a fiddle nearly five times as big as himself" and "a gold snuff-box."[76] Poe's description of his skin color, facial features, and hair evokes the figure of the Jew: "His countenance was of a dark snuff-color, and he had a long hooked nose, pea eyes, a wide mouth, . . . and his hair neatly done up in *papillotes*" or paper-curls. His movements are quick, unusual, and wildly out-of-step with the orderly townsfolk. When he first appears, "he capered down the hill, cutting all manner of fantastical steps," and his physicality is depicted using increasingly foreign terms to describe the hyperactive presence: "What mainly occasioned a righteous indignation was, that the scoundrelly popinjay, while he cut a fandango here, and a whirligig there, did not seem to have the remotest idea in the world of such a thing as *keeping time* in his steps."[77] Poe uses an abundance of loan-words in this passage to enrich his description of the physicality of the invading stranger with an air of an exoticized dancer, doing the fandango or ballet steps: he "gave a *chassez* here, and a *balancez* there; and then, after a *pirouette* and a *pas-de-zephyr*, pigeon-winged himself right up into the belfry."[78] Subject to multilingual descriptors, his language of movement betrays his foreignness without him uttering a word. He arouses curiosity, indignation, suspicion: "Many a burgher who beheld him that day, would have given a trifle for a peep beneath the white cambric handkerchief which hung so obtrusively from the pocket."[79] The citizens feel a collective urge to police him, to subject him to further scrutiny.

In her version, Clarice's narrator also racializes the strange interloper, yet he represents an internal threat to an ordered society: he embodies the displaced poor. His features as described in her Portuguese are those associated with Afro-Brazilians rather than the antisemitic tropes in Poe's story. Again, she describes the stranger with less detail than Poe, a choice that aligns with the general mode of abridgment or adaptation. Yet these changes also support a major alteration to this central character: her stranger is insignificant, whereas Poe's was fascinating. While he comes down the hill at the same speed, "he truly was the most insignificant person, the least, that anyone had ever seen" (era realmente a pessoa mais insignificante, menor, que se vira por ali); "his skin was dark, curved nose, round eyes, wide mouth. He lived laughing from ear to ear" (sua pele era escura, o nariz recurvo, olhos redondos, boca larga. Vivia rindo, de orelha a orelha); and he had "curly hair" (cabelos encaracolados).[80] Lispector's description of the invader is less rich in detail, and his racialized characteristics are more associated with a Black body. What makes this character most remarkable is his poverty and utter insignificance: he carries nothing, certainly no gold snuff-box, and his shoes have no "satin ribbons" but are *sapatilhas achatadas* (broken-down, worn-out shoes). He also appears with none of the "self-satisfaction" of Poe's visitor he is not a "sight for the honest burghers," he does not "excite suspicion" or "righteous indignation" or any reaction at all; instead, he is the "most insignificant person." His poverty, his racialized characteristics, and his insignificance cast him as a completely different figure within Brazilian society: the subaltern individual from the interior who arrives in the big city unseen and unwanted. He resembles Manuelinho, the subject of her *crônica* about the extrajudicial killing of a Black murder suspect, shot thirteen times; he recalls Lispector's character Macabea from *The Hour of the Star*. The stranger is an invader from within, a threat to order not for his whimsical, foreign dance steps but for his sinister, familiar-but-insignificant poverty. Lispector translated this story in 1974 or 1975, when Brazil was in the midst of a military dictatorship, while working on her novel about Macabea, the humble migrant from the Northeast whose desires and habits are unimaginable to her educated narrator. Lispector's intersectional translation gives Poe's story a treatment that connects it to Brazilian realities and tensions between desire for stability amid vast social and economic inequality—and a fascist demand for order and conformity in response.

In Poe's source text, expelling the foreign element will restore order, and the narrator appeals to the reader to aid in maintaining the formality of register and precision he prizes. In Lispector's translation, the expulsion of the unstable element will restore tranquility, and the appeal to the reader is articulated in an informal, oral register, a voice of neighborhood gossip, the most powerful form of social policing. When Poe concludes his story, the narrator confirms his alliance with the residents of Vondervotteimittiss: "Affairs being thus miserably situated, I left the place in disgust, and now appeal for aid to all lovers of correct time and fine kraut. Let us proceed in a body to the borough, and restore the ancient order of things in Vondervotteimittiss by ejecting that little fellow from the steeple."[81] Lispector's narrator concludes with similar sentiments, again emphasizing the oral register by the use of the diminutive and sentence fragments, and adding in the value of peace and tranquility once this new element is expelled: "Com as coisas neste lamentável estado, parti daquele lugar, com grande desgosto. Agora peço a ajuda de todos os que amam a hora certa e uma boa conserva de repolho. E a tranqüilidade. Vamos seguir juntos para lá e restaurar a antiga ordem de coisas em Vondervotteimittiss, expulsando aquele sujeitinho da torre do grande relógio."[82] Lispector's version adds the short phrase "E a tranqüilidade" (And tranquility), an informal, incomplete sentence that stands out, breaks up the rhythm of the text, an additional supplement contrasting with her elimination of words and phrases elsewhere. Drawing attention to this emphatic love of tranquility, her translation questions the perversity of a society that seeks to create peace and order by expelling some of its subjects, specifically *aquele sujeitinho*, the "littlest nobody," the smallest, poorest, and weakest element of a social body.

Lispector's publisher critiqued her translation manual for being haphazard or inaccurate, and her published translations have been dismissed by subsequent scholarship. But by paying close attention to the material she adds to Poe's stories, what gifts she brings to the field of translational exchange, we can better see that her process was not careless; rather, it was designed to fit her political moment and her own writerly interests. In other words, scrutiny demonstrates that her Poe adaptations were not meant merely to fit a new public, a children's market, by simplifying the material. Nor does her translation demonstrate an inattentive or *mocosuena* approach—although elements of sound and orality do signify. Instead, her changes show that she was thinking about her own literary sensibilities: she makes changes that complicate rather than simplify, she draws from her own interests to enhance certain aspects of Poe's works, and she transforms Poe's hypermasculine historian-narrators into narrative frames oriented around her own ambivalent and instinctual literary self-fashioning.

GENDERED EXCLUSION FROM LITERARY RECIPROCITY

Despite their positions as respected authors, when they turned to the task of translation, Clarice Lispector and Rosario Castellanos were not afforded the privilege of assumed mastery by the literary circles of their time. When they made creative choices, including the same choices celebrated in other translators of the day—to prioritize aesthetic information, to cut, to personalize, alter, or to reframe—these choices were ascribed to lack of attention, ignorance, immaturity, and poor taste. Paying attention to these feminized translations that are denied the privilege of being read as creativity points out the use of the strategies of cannibal translation as a part of a larger project of self-authorization for female authors during this period.

Castellanos and Lispector were not the only Latin American authors who achieved prominence but were still rejected along gendered lines for their translation work: Silvina Ocampo received a similar treatment at the hand of Jorge Luis Borges. Her privileged position as member of the literary founding family of *Sur* and her long-standing collaboration with Adolfo Bioy Casares and Borges did not prevent the dismissal of her translations. The first edition of her translations of Emily Dickinson included a preface by Borges in which he damns her work with faint praise by dismissively associating Ocampo's translations with "the concept of a literal version," which he rejects in his own writings on translation. He writes:

> I have always suspected that the concept of a literal version, unknown to the ancients, derives from those faithful disciples who dared not change a word dictated by the Spirit. Emily Dickinson seems to have inspired an analogous respect in Silvina Ocampo. In this volume, we nearly always have the original words in the same order. It doesn't happen every day that a poet translates another poet, and Silvina Ocampo is, beyond a doubt, the greatest Argentine poet. The cadence, intonation, and modest complexity of Emily Dickinson await the reader of these pages by a stroke of luck: a successful transmigration.[83]

Although his prologue ends on a note of high praise for Ocampo, Borges does not endorse her translation method. Describing her practice paradoxically as putting "the original words in the same order," he implies that her translations lack creativity, daring, or craft. The publisher must have seen this assessment as less than positive as well: Tusquets chose not to include Borges's prologue in any of the subsequent reprintings of Ocampo's 1985 publication.

The reception of Deborah Smith's translation of *The Vegetarian* by Han Kang (published in Korea 2007, translated 2015) serves as a more contemporary example of the way creative translation techniques might be rejected using the rhetoric of feminized immaturity. Due to the different racialized positions of a Korean author and her white US translator, the charges of mistranslation from a critical race perspective do invoke an important critique of Smith for colonial appropriation through the privilege of her competence with English. Yet the intersectional analytical lens I advocate for in this chapter also accounts for the way the gender position of the translator opened her up to charges of ignorance and careless mistake rather than reading the distance between source and target texts as creative choices, productive failures, or considered transculturation to fit the target culture.[84]

We continue to write, read, and work in an environment in which power, identity, race, and gender intersect to impact the reception of literary production. Who has the privilege of being unfinished, in process, or experimental? When do we interpret errors or strangeness in translated writing as aesthetic choices and when do we code these qualities as amateurism? Castellanos and Lispector both embraced and rejected the easy association between their biographical femininity, their otherness as authors, and their works themselves. Yet within this ambivalence, their self-reflexive intersectional translation practices remind us to incorporate an understanding of translator positionality into our analysis, to trouble any unexamined assumption of an objective translator, and to question who is accorded the privilege of translating with the creative techniques of cannibal translation.

CHAPTER 4

Translingual Editing for a Latin American Canon at Biblioteca Ayacucho

Mexican translator Héctor Olea (b. 1945) captures the tensions and utopian aspirations built into translating Brazilian literature into Spanish in the "Posfacio" for his 1977 Spanish transcreation of *Macunaíma* by Mário de Andrade (1928). He writes, "Assimilating ourselves to the idea of the *Homo brasilicus* is an attempt to ritualize the American myth. To reflect on our own reflection. To reveal and redeem priceless traditions for all to see. To identify a utopia we have in common in a pluralistic language that rediscovers its own transplant."[1] Tangling up the directionality and agency of assimilation, in Olea's translation commentary, the "*Homo brasilicus*" is not absorbed by the target Hispanophone culture but, rather, vice versa: Who is eating whom? Olea discusses the particularities of translating *Macunaíma*—a Brazilian *modernista* cannibalization of Indigenous oral tradition in a celebrated if contested avant-garde package—into a pan–Spanish American lexical variety he invents for this project. An avid reader and student of both Haroldo de Campos and Octavio Paz, Olea frames his translation task as reinventing a shared tradition common among Latin Americans of different languages, seeing the self in the mirror of the other. For him, a translation between Brazil and Spanish America must operate on the level of the linguistic and the sociocultural: the ritual of translation performs reciprocal repair.

Uruguayan literary critic Ángel Rama (1926–83) had his own utopian vision for the cultural integration of Latin America. While he commissioned translations from Olea and shared his interest in translation between Brazil and Spanish America as key to undoing colonial and neocolonial divisions, Rama's broader epistemological aims did not always mesh smoothly with Olea's translation approach. Where my prior chapters focused on cannibal translations circulating in specialized literary journals or in limited editions, this chapter examines cannibal translation practices in the service of institutionalized cultural production at the Venezuelan press Biblioteca Ayacucho. Founded in 1974 under Rama's leadership, this state-sponsored publishing house commissioned translations of key Brazilian texts into Spanish for the Colección Clásica, envisioned as a new Latin American canon. I analyze the translingual editing process—per Karen Emmerich's term—for three Brazilian volumes through letters Rama exchanged with volume editors Aracy Amaral, Haroldo de Campos, Antonio Candido, and Gilda de Mello e Souza; and translators Santiago Kovadloff, Héctor Olea, and Márgara Russotto. These translators and editors have divergent and sometimes competing translation manuals; I demonstrate how cannibal translation as an editorial style allows multiple translations to coexist and continues the contested nature of Brazilian cannibalistic art-making into Latin American Spanish.

Rama strove to represent the foundational polemics informing Latin American lettered culture in his new autochthonous, interdisciplinary, and socioculturally inclusive canon. This chapter illuminates the way the translation process itself manifested its own polemic. Haroldo's interest in a purely intratextual transcreation sometimes clashed with Rama's editorial interest in creating a pedagogical framing to promote cultural integration. I associate Rama's guiding principles with the concept of "thick translation" defined by Kwame Anthony Appiah for translation in a decolonial setting.[2] Appiah locates the need for thick translation in pedagogical contexts where a translation "should preserve for us the features that make it worth teaching"; in his specific context of English translations from the Twi language in Ghana, this requires "a thick and situated understanding of oral literatures" because the literary tradition there relies on an oral tradition of proverbs.[3] He argues that thickly descriptive glosses and contextual information best support decolonial pedagogy by making up for both the information deficit and received notions of epistemological superiority created by power imbalances between source and target cultures. Given Rama's expressed interest in using translation to redress the divisiveness of colonialism and to elevate the contributions of Indigenous and African oral traditions within Latin American literature, his frequent editorial instruction to add more notes, more glosses, more contextual information comports with Appiah's notion of thick translation.

The practices I unite under the broader concept of cannibal translation—which the Ayacucho translators variously describe as transcreating, transsaying or transspeaking, and version-making—shine through the publisher's archive as productive debates that remained unresolved. I highlight the information contained in the internal inconsistencies and multiple options present in the published works. For example, where Olea draws on Haroldo's method of transcreation to repeat the aesthetic games in his Brazilian source texts and actively rejects the need for explanatory footnotes, Rama conversely encourages editors to add copious notes so the Biblioteca Ayacucho volumes thoroughly contextualize Brazilian letters for the Spanish American reader. His editorial style may not reach the extreme of Vladimir Nabokov and his excessively annotated approach to translating Pushkin, with "footnotes reaching up like skyscrapers to the top of this or that page."[4] Yet Rama does emphasize with all of his Brazilian interlocutors the need to accommodate significant information gaps the Spanish American reader will have when encountering the Brazilian tradition. Operating at impressive speed, the editor also seeks to make up for lost time by moving Brazilian letters into the Spanish American public sphere as quickly as possible. Conversely, Olea associates the Amerindian structures of his source texts with a need to work patiently, to carefully "rethink to re-create" wordplay, and to avoid footnotes by finding simple word shifts. He names his process with the neologism *tradecir* ("transsaying" or "transspeaking"), by which he means "deducing the tradition, reinventing patience, slow things."[5] These conflicting translation modes coexist in the Ayacucho project.

A reader operating within translation norms oriented around smoothness or consistency could look at the Ayacucho edition of Mário de Andrade and find it lacking for the internal inconsistencies on display, where multiple translations of key phrases put the paratexts and the literary works in conflict. A cannibal translation reading practice instead asks what these inconsistencies reveal about the relationship between Brazilian literature and a Latin American literary canon in Spanish, and how decolonial translation, an ethical position shared by Rama and Olea, might produce multiple approaches to the same goal.

To translate Brazilian *modernismo* into Spanish, the editors and translators must mediate between experimentalism and canonicity, between aesthetic elements and an ethnographic gaze. Drawing from the archives at this state-sponsored publishing house, I reconstruct negotiations between the translator's aesthetic values and the editor's pedagogical aims of bringing Brazilian *modernismo* to Spanish American readers with rich cultural context. In the course of this translingual editorial process, the letters reveal a significant polemic about the right way to produce a translation of the literary avant-garde. Reading the resulting volumes through these letters, I understand editorial inconsistencies not as flaws but as signals that cognitively highlight cannibal translation at work. At Ayacucho, competing readings and translation methods coexist, and reciprocal exchanges match mobile untranslatables across Latin American language cultures and literary spheres.

My analysis of the translator's archive illuminates the work of constructing a pan–Latin American canon as a multilingual practice aimed toward reciprocity. In his aspiration to retrospectively integrate movements, aesthetics, and intellectual camps previously unknown to one another, Rama echoes the translationship between Paz and Haroldo in chapter 2, which first took the form of a reciprocal literary exchange and was eventually drawn into their political moment. In this chapter the translingual intellectual friendships on display perhaps represent the opposite movement. Rama and his major Brazilian interlocutors, Antonio Candido and Darcy Ribeiro, shared a political agenda for their scholarship, and the need for translation between Spanish and Portuguese resulted from that shared goal of cultural integration to support political and economic solidarity.

These translations also contrast with the framework of the so-called Boom in Latin American literature, which Rama facilitated through his journal *Marcha* but ultimately rejected due to the capitalist logic driving that literary marketing phenomenon. He regretfully writes about the unintended effects of the Boom: "By promoting some few writers, it marginalizes the rest and displaces poetry and the Latin American essay, disseminating almost solely novels."[6] Unlike the norms of Latin American literature translated into English under the aegis of the Boom—or what now fits the broader framework of the "global novel"—the Ayacucho project made no assumption of translatability; instead, multiple versions of mobile untranslatables proliferate in these volumes.

The chapter ends with the case of *Macunaíma* (1928) by Mário Raul de Morais Andrade (1893–1945) as translated by Mexican poet-translator Héctor Olea. When Rama buys the rights to Olea's artful transcreation published in 1977 by the Spanish publishing house Seix Barral to republish it with Biblioteca Ayacucho, he also commissions an extensive critical apparatus: prologue, footnotes, bibliography, and a chronology. In short, the norms of thick translation are layered on top of a transcreation as the work travels from Barcelona to Caracas—an imposition the translator Olea strenuously objects to in vehement letters to Rama. By including two translation approaches—transcreation and thick translation—the Ayacucho edition remains consistent with the unresolved paradoxical treatment of cultural hybridity at the heart of the text. The translation into Spanish fulfills the author Mário de Andrade's aim to depict the localized culture of the Orinoco delta as more valuable than the arbitrary borders between Venezuela, British Guiana, and Brazil—or between Spanish, English, and Portuguese. The editorial process for this work does result in moments of unsmoothness in the final publication, which ultimately allow the Ayacucho "translingual edition" to emphasize the proliferation of voices, translation techniques, and cultural forms possible within cannibal translation.

ÁNGEL RAMA'S CULTURAL INTEGRATION AS A RECIPROCAL TRANSLATION PROJECT

Rama planned Biblioteca Ayacucho's Colección Clásica as a pedagogical tool, a thick translation that would provide the needed framework "to integrate, retrospectively, the intellectual efforts Latin America lived through separately, divided into regional or national camps."[7] Facing globalization in the context of Cold War polarization, Rama views the cultural integration of Latin America as a vital internal support for any extension into global economic systems.[8] Venezuela took on a unique position within the Latin American economic and political landscape at this time, 1973–83. The "Revolución de la OPEP" of 1973, in reaction to oil embargos on Middle East nations, resulted in a financial bonanza for Venezuela, while Argentina, Brazil, Chile, and Uruguay suffered through military dictatorships.[9] President Carlos Andrés Pérez framed the Venezuelan oil boom as a broader continental restitution within the global economy, one that should benefit all of Latin America.[10] After the joint blows to pan–Latin American leftist solidarity represented by the 1971 fall from grace of the Cuban Revolution as capitulated by the Caso Padilla and the 1973 fall of Salvador Allende's government to Pinochet, Venezuela became the most politically stable and economically fertile ground for pan–Latin Americanist economic and cultural solidarity. When President Pérez established the "Ley Nacional de la Cultura," the benefits of Venezuelan petroleum nationalization extended to artists and intellectuals.[11] Under these political and economic conditions, Rama could promulgate his vision for Latin American cultural integration at the Biblioteca Ayacucho, the most prominent remaining counterpoint to the publishing of Latin American letters from Spain or Paris.

Understanding the danger of accepting a Latin American canon formed under a "world literature" rubric framed by academics outside Latin America, at Biblioteca Ayacucho Rama worked from the "revolutionary intent" of constructing a usable past for the projected ideal future and the regional unity necessary for maintaining self-determination. My fascination is with the underexamined translation practices and the reciprocal imaginary that underwrite Rama's vision. Mariano Siskind questions the stability of Rama's binary opposition between the cosmopolitanism of authors who seek to join the world by performing mastery of European-facing literary practices and the integrationist utopianism of transculturators, authors who look inward to appropriate local cultural elements. As Siskind points out, while Rama invests himself in Fernando Ortiz's transculturation as a mode of elevating Latin American cultural difference, he also "recognizes a common modernizing anxiety in both transculturalizing and cosmopolitan narratives."[12] I see the translation politics operating within Biblioteca Ayacucho as playing both sides of this coin—seeking external visibility in the form of potential reciprocity with Brazilian letters while also shoring up internal self-knowledge.[13] Rama's stewardship of the Colección Clásica indeed includes three volumes translated from the Indigenous languages Nahuatl, Maya, and Quechua, one from English, and three from French.[14] However, Brazil figures as the only source of Latin Americanist textual production that also represents a destination of translatable literary reciprocity: while he hoped to inspire a Brazilian Portuguese version of his project, Rama never envisioned a translation of the entire Colección Clásica into Quechua, English, or French.

Translation figures as an underlying support for each of the five guiding principles Rama outlines for this canon-building series. First, he aims for a "culturalist Latin American criteria" that would include a transhistorical mix of genres and disciplines across the humanities and social sciences that define Latin American letters as a unique cultural production of interdisciplinary and indeterminate genres; the multilingual colonial era requires significant translation from Indigenous languages.[15] Second, he incorporates all social strata of Latin American society, which necessitates the inclusion of oral traditions, soldier-chronicles, texts by mestizos with informal education, texts that incorporate multiple languages or registers. Again, to frame these multiple registers of Spanish requires the "thick translation" approach—even within one language—to adequately convey the richness of these oral traditions.[16] Third, he includes works written by visitors to the region, texts by Alexander von Humboldt and William Hudson translated from French and English that left their mark—either as relevant outside perspectives or as distorted images of Latin America that call for correction. In order to achieve integration into "universal culture," this foreign gaze shows that Latin America was never isolated at all, but in fact always constitutive of a global world picture.[17] Fourth—and the most overtly reliant on translation practice—Rama depicts the cultural integration of Latin American letters as a decolonial struggle:

> Since the origins of Latin America, everything has conspired to hinder internal communication and the development of a shared cultural sphere: starting from the evolving colonial administrative system and the monopolizing regimes of the Spanish and Portuguese monarchies and conflicts between them; to the subsequent fragmentation from wars of independence; to imperialistic interventions aimed at consolidating internal divisions and strengthening separation; and most recently the intervention of monopolistic economic policies. . . . Perhaps Brazil represents the best example of this elusive integration.[18]

Finally, he wants the Ayacucho canon to unify multiple sociocultural and political positions, past and present, to "give a calibrated vision of opposed ideological, artistic, and educational paradigms, since none have exhausted their relevance, and they continue to orient the contradictory weave of our current societies."[19] Naming as his primary example the diversity of nineteenth-century political thought, he references the five collected volumes on political independence, socialist utopianism, conservative thought, independence poetry, and Latin Americanist positivism—all of which include representative thinkers from Brazil in Spanish translation. Each of these five guiding principles relies on translation, yet scholarly analysis of Rama's Ayacucho project has not contended with the material, intellectual, and collaborative work involved in this translation effort.[20] I am interested in elevating the role of the Ayacucho publishing project in developing and deploying Latin Americanist translation theories in the service of Rama's integration of Brazilian cultural forms into Latin American culture.

Other contemporary pan–Latin American canon-building editorial houses also sought to support and distribute Spanish American literature more widely, but none aimed for the same multidisciplinary and politically pluralistic representation of the ethnic, social, educational, and national mosaic of Latin America.[21] Rama himself distinguishes the broader cultural panorama at Ayacucho from the more exclusively literary series Biblioteca Americana published in Mexico by the Fondo de Cultura Económica.[22] While he praises the Colección Latinoamericana organized by the postrevolutionary Cuban publishing house Casa de las Américas, a press that published many of his works during the 1960s, his goal of political pluralism for Ayacucho opposes the singular ideological framework of the Cuban collection.[23] Furthermore, as Jessica Gordon-Burroughs points out, after the military coups of the mid-1970s, Biblioteca Ayacucho took on both the left-wing political mantle and the exiled intellectuals of three Southern Cone editorial houses: Centro Editorial America Latina (CEAL) and Ediciones de la Flor in Buenos Aires and Quimantu in Chile.[24]

Yet none of these projects ever elevated Brazilian letters to the same extent as Ayacucho, and Rama's communications with those involved in planning and executing the Colección Clásica reflect the urgency with which he understood the translation demands of his project. Writing in 1974 to his major Brazilian collaborator Antonio Candido de Mello e Souza (1918–2017), Rama proposed Brazil's contribution to the Ayacucho project could eventually benefit the Brazilian cultural sphere as well, hoping that a Brazilian publisher or other institution might translate and publish the same collection in Portuguese for the mutual benefit of Brazilian readers.

> One of our dreams is the possibility that a Library similar to Ayacucho could be taken on in Brazil by some editors or a reputable institution—which would need to be independent, none of this rejecting Mariátegui because he was a communist. I would appreciate your opinion on this: what could be

> done to urge Brazil to also publish the same Biblioteca Ayacucho, major works of the Latin American past, and many of them perhaps for the first time.[25]

Rama would repeat this same reciprocal intention again in his 1981 essay about the publishing project.[26] While Rama's vision of a Brazilian counterpart to the Biblioteca Ayacucho did not come to fruition during his lifetime, the volume *América Latina: Palavra, literatura e cultura* (1995) edited by Ana Pizarro and published in Portuguese and Spanish took shape in conversation with Rama during this period.[27] This form of reciprocal readership grounded in a translatability based on expert attention from both source and target cultures distinguished the Ayacucho project not only from other internally facing Latin Americanist canon-building editorial projects in Spanish but also from the Paris-based literary journal *Mundo Nuevo* edited by Emir Rodríguez Monegal, another internationalist publication circulating Latin American literature for export but critiqued by Rama as underwritten by US political interests.[28]

While Rama's presence in Caracas afforded him this unique publishing opportunity, he landed there by necessity. The military coup in Montevideo on June 27, 1973, forced Rama to remain in exile in Caracas, where he held a visiting teaching appointment since 1972.[29] Although he took many visiting appointments in the United States, the State Department's anticommunist agenda thwarted his desire to build a career there. Rama always identified as a socialist and not as a communist, but when the University of Maryland invited him to join their faculty, first as a visiting member and then with a tenured post, the State Department denied him visas and permanent residency.[30] Although his time at US universities earlier in the 1970s proved useful for his research, Rama expressed dismay at the provincialism and ignorance he encountered even in the government center of DC and the treatment of Latin America as an invisible territory.[31] During my visit to this archive in 2013, the sting of this expulsion was still manifest. Editor Elizabeth Coronado described Rama's relationship with the US academy as the painstaking recuperation of the cultural heritage of Latin America held in the archives and libraries of Europe and the United States, where Rama often transcribed by hand materials only available there. While consulting the Ayacucho editorial archive, I was asked to use only a pencil and paper to take notes, no computer was permitted, nor could I take photographs of documents. When explaining this policy, the staff referenced Rama's experience; I could only access material in the manner that Rama could, in a reciprocal restriction on materials.

As an Uruguayan exile, still recovering from the blows of losing his country to dictatorship and his expulsion from the possible stability of a faculty position in the US, Rama built an editorial team of scholars dispersed and displaced across the Americas, and his editorial leadership always mediated between a Venezuelan nationalist position and a pan–Latin American pluralist and integrationist platform. Ayacucho has always sought a more international than national profile; their continued participation in book fairs all over the continent and the participation of academics from all over Latin America in their editorial projects exemplify this commitment.[32] The editorial project at Rama's Ayacucho fashions a Latin American literary canon around the revolutionary act of integration, while also giving Venezuela pride of place as the cradle of Latin America's revolutionary history and nineteenth-century independence movements with Simón Bolívar figured as savior. Rama inaugurated the publishing house in 1974 to recognize the 150th anniversary of the Battle of Ayacucho in 1824, celebrated as a decisive victory against the Spanish by Bolívar and South American independence fighters.[33] The first volume of the Colección Clásica is indeed the *Doctrina del Libertador* by Simón Bolívar (1979); the first one hundred volumes include eleven by Venezuelan authors, a near match to the ten Brazilian works.

Translation into Spanish grounds Rama's cultural integration framework, where he aims to present as one coherent whole the multilingual contributions to Latin American culture written in English, French, Maya, Nahuatl, Portuguese, Quechua, Spanish, and more—and written in multiple varieties, registers, and grammatical paradigms of these languages.[34] Not only will translation be a central part of this new canon—displacing the hegemony of Hispanidad, Spain, and the Spanish language as the sole repository of cultural heritage—Rama seeks a translation paradigm that does not shy away from the complexities of the Latin American varieties of these languages. Whereas the publishing model and the translation paradigm into English of the so-called Boom tended to reward smoothness, literary autonomy, and an easy legibility within the target culture, Rama's choice to include significant paratextual apparatus in his publications operates even within texts written in Spanish to defamiliarize language and elevate the materiality of production. For example, Argentine novelist Roberto Arlt (1900–1942) crafted complex Buenos Aires–specific voices, including *lunfardo*, the unique working-class dialect spoken by Italian and other immigrants to the city. The author's widow Mirta Arlt praised Rama's editorial choice to leave his writing "uncombed," unabridged, just as difficult in its new frame—which included a glossary of *lunfardo* vocabulary.[35] The materiality of the translator's archive represents a rich corpus to understand the professional, material, and political nuances that went into the production of this canon: translating but not "combing" or abridging; expanding from Portuguese into Spanish without eliminating, covering over, or domesticating the creative relationship with the source culture; maintaining it, instead, as an ongoing, reciprocal link.

READING AYACUCHO'S ARCHIVES: BRAZILIAN *MODERNISMO* IN SPANISH AMERICA

Under Rama's editorial vision, translating Brazilian works into Spanish represented a decolonial act: to correct internal divisions separating Latin American spaces with shared cultural history, and to repair fractures imposed by Iberian colonial competition and reinforced through periods of independence and modernization by neoliberal economic interests.[36] His aspirations extended beyond the Venezuelan publishing firm, and as he envisioned the canon he was creating there, he thought it could itself prove translatable into Portuguese through a possible reciprocal publishing project in Brazil. While this ultimate vision was not achieved before his untimely death in 1983, the cornerstone series Colección Clásica had in less than ten years published 101 volumes, including five of Latin American political theory that include Brazilian writings and ten of Brazilian literature and cultural studies.[37] Three of the ten Brazilian volumes were devoted to Brazilian *modernismo*, a challenging literary movement to translate. Given the transhistorical scope of the Colección Clásica, it may seem surprising that three volumes were devoted to this brief period. Yet Rama saw its pedagogical value for his cultural integration goals, since Brazilian *modernismo* ties together strains from Indigenous, Afro-Brazilian, precolonial, and European influence. In fact, literature students in Brazilian universities *begin* with this avant-garde movement before studying earlier periods, so the Ayacucho canon also translates that Brazilian centrality into Spanish. The approaches to translation on display in these volumes—both theoretically and practically, as I emphasize by reading the publications through the archive—highlights the translingual nature of the source texts as well as the target culture. The three volumes of Brazilian *modernismo* draw from Amerindian narratives, diverse Brazilian regionalisms, and storytelling inflected with orality, and they reflect unresolved debates over this historical avant-garde literary movement. Seen in this light, Brazilian *modernismo* was never only Brazilian, nor does it become fully Spanish American in translation; instead, it remains a literary practice of shape-shifting and mutual exchange—much like cannibal translation itself.

In their analysis of the epistolary archive at the Biblioteca Ayacucho, genetic criticism scholars Carlos Pacheco and Marisela Guevara Sánchez emphasize the value of these documents for understanding the intellectual network underpinning this enormous undertaking and Rama's personal involvement in nearly every aspect of bringing the catalog to fruition. Including approximately 1.5 million pieces organized by volume, these materials offer a rich and largely untapped archival source for understanding the production of Latin American thought during the period.[38] My resources for understanding the Ayacucho "translation manual" include unpublished letters held in their archive as supplemented by published volumes of correspondence between Ángel Rama and his major Brazilian interlocutors, Antonio Candido and Darcy Ribeiro.[39] During a visit to the Biblioteca Ayacucho offices in July 2013, I read through folders of correspondence exchanged during the editorial process for the critical editions of three volumes representing Brazilian *modernismo*.[40] The values and priorities expressed by the participants in this bilingual conversation—along with the allocation of financial resources, legal considerations about copyright, concerns about the legibility of Brazilian literature—all contribute to a picture of the publishing house's formal and informal translation manual at that time. The archival record shows the way translators shared their work in progress, threatened to quit, reframed the terms of their participation, and changed the final outcome of the Brazilian editions through these negotiated collaborations.

Rama's initial exchanges with his Brazilian interlocutors introduce them to the larger stakes of the project. When inviting Antonio Candido, Gilda de Mello e Souza, Haroldo de Campos, Darcy Ribeiro, and Aracy Amaral to participate as volume editors, he takes pains to enlist them in an opportunity for Latin America to tell its own story, rather than have its story routed through German anthropologists, French literary magazines, US intellectuals, or Spanish publishing houses. Rama generally writes in Spanish and Candido, Ribeiro, and Mello e Souza in Portuguese, and their friendly translingual correspondence reaffirms a shared intention to "strengthen ties between our two peoples of América."[41]

In his process of selection, Rama's initial ambition was that the Colección Clásica catalog would include twenty volumes in the first one hundred from Portuguese America to fully match the contribution from Spanish America.[42] In his first letter to Candido about the Ayacucho project, Rama emphasizes the urgent need to start working on translations as soon as possible. After inviting him to Caracas for an editorial meeting to plan the Biblioteca Ayacucho on November 17–21, 1975, he asks Candido for a quick list of representative Brazilian works:

> I need you to draw up a preliminary selection for me, the one you already know by heart, off the top of your head: the twenty Brazilian titles that are indispensable to a Library of this kind. I want to get ahead on this point because we have before us a complicated translation task, and it will be to our advantage to forge ahead: obtaining the books, finding the right translators who we will need to search for throughout Latin America, etc. etc.[43]

While Rama prioritized finding the "right" translators, he does not define what skills these ideal translators would bring.

Although he first nominates Candido to serve as his primary Brazilian collaborator—"as you well know, you are our man in Brazil, guide and advisor to our library"—Rama also invites at least four Brazilian interlocutors to create their own lists of the Brazilian texts necessary for the new Latin American canon.[44] In communication with Candido, Rama requests strong representation from the colonial and imperial eras, as well as texts with historic, sociological, and folkloric importance; he does not specifically ask for any literary genres. Asking Brazilian anthropologist Darcy Ribeiro for help in that field, he also invites Ribeiro himself as featured contributor.[45] Writing to Gilda de Mello e Souza at first through her husband, Antonio Candido, he secures her participation as editor for the Mário de Andrade volume by the end of 1975.[46] Rama began reaching out to Haroldo de Campos in 1976, asking for the same list of Brazilian authors, also asking him to serve as editor for the Oswald de Andrade volume, which predetermines his response to include Brazilian *modernismo*. When Haroldo agrees to participate, he suggests Héctor Olea as translator for Oswald, and emphasizes that their most challenging task will be translation.

While in each case Rama asks his Brazilian collaborators to produce a list of the most important Brazilian materials needed for inclusion, he does not always take their advice. For example, when he asks Aracy Amaral, at first she tries to convince Rama to include more recent poetic movements, including concretism and neo-concretism. Responding to her claim that Brazilian *modernismo* has received enough scholarly attention, Rama insists: "I'll explain myself: for you, this period is practically spent. I have carefully followed the bibliography for the fifty-year anniversary [of the 1922 Semana de Arte Moderna], and I agree with your perception. But you must understand: for Spanish America, 'Brazilian Modernism' is an unknown animal."[47] Apparently, Rama needed to make this argument repeatedly and broadly even with his Spanish American collaborators.[48] Both translation from Brazilian Portuguese and recirculation of locally consecrated but still internationally unknown figures required negotiation between national contexts and an integrated pan–Latin American canon.

The letters speak to the urgency and speed with which Rama was producing these critical editions. This urgency only increases after the "Brazilian delegation" could not appear at the initial meeting in Caracas November 1975 to plan the contribution from Portuguese America to the Biblioteca Ayacucho, when the Brazilian government denied Caio Prado Junior, Carlos Drummond de Andrade, and Antonio Candido visas to travel.[49] Rama tries to motivate his Brazilian interlocutors to help him accelerate the process, hoping the Colección Clásica could make a strong showing and demonstrate the incorporation of Brazil at an upcoming national event celebrating the 150th anniversary of the 1826 Congreso de Panamá meeting of newly independent Latin American nations convened by Bolívar.[50]

Even in his increasing haste, Rama continues to emphasize the need for careful "thick description" surrounding the Brazilian cultural context; if producing a translingual edition involves multiple stages of selection, translation, and editorial review, then translation figures as a primarily practical concern while the paratextual scholarship poses a greater intellectual problem. In his letters with Brazilian specialists and translators, first about the selection of Brazilian texts and second about the paratextual apparatus surrounding those texts, Rama repeatedly reminds all participants that they need to keep in mind a Spanish American audience that knows nothing of Brazil. Writing to Mello e Souza, he emphasizes: "Don't forget that Mário de Andrade is unknown in Hispanophone America; things you find obvious are precisely what nobody knows and what readers will need to be informed about."[51] Producing a thick translation necessitates including contextual information beyond the norms of a critical edition.

Rama certainly shaped the resulting translingual editions by choosing the participants, guiding their contributions, motivating them with attentions and exchanges of cultural and social capital, and contracting future work to keep editors and translators going. Yet each individual participant also exerted a high level of choice and creative, intellectual control; each editor and translator operated independently with myriad ways of subverting the directives or the authority of Rama—the translation archive shows that centralized planning, at least where translation projects are concerned, proves challenging. Translation appears at first to represent a merely practical challenge rather than an intellectual problem on the same order of magnitude as the selection, curation, and paratextual presentation of these texts. The process will soon show otherwise.

NEGOTIATING METHODS: TRANSCREATION OR THICK TRANSLATION

Comparing the divergent aesthetic values displayed by different translators at work on Brazilian *modernismo* for the Biblioteca Ayacucho demonstrates their capacity to intervene even when editorial oversight seeks to normalize or standardize. The prologues for the Brazilian Colección Clásica texts, often based on recent scholarship written for the Brazilian public, placed even more importance on the annotated translations to achieve Rama's goal of reframing this material for a broader Latin American readership.[52] Some translators took this task on; others saw their role differently.

Rama encourages his volume editor Mello e Souza to give as much context as possible and she responds in kind, writing, "I am finishing the notes for *Macunaíma*, which ended up being a lot, perhaps too many," and she offers to eliminate some before sending her manuscript.[53] In response, Rama emphasizes that he wants to retain the responsibility and control to decide which notes are necessary for the Spanish American reader. He refers to a prior experience with Walnice Nogueira Galvão, who did not provide enough information for the translated edition of *Os sertões*, an issue he wants Souza to avoid.[54]

However, her footnotes do not coincide with Olea's transcreation. Rama writes to Mello e Souza, raising her honorarium, and explaining the problem: "When coordinating the notes with the text, we have found that in some cases, as we anticipated, they are not necessary because the solution found in Spanish is explicit enough; in other cases, we have contradictions between the translator's solution and the interpretation you offer."[55] Then Rama writes to Olea asking him to review the notes with the same concerns in mind, offering Olea the chance to correct any errors in the Seix Barral edition, and he raises the rate for his translations.[56] Olea's work on the Oswald project edited by Haroldo had already caused some disagreements between Rama and the translator over deadlines and payment.[57] When Rama wrote to Olea asking him to review the notes by Mello e Souza, Olea responded with a detailed and emphatically critical letter, explaining his views on translation as diametrically opposed to those in place at Ayacucho. Voicing surprise that he was not consulted sooner, Olea explains that his transcreation made notes unnecessary and strenuously objects to the editor's attempt to define untranslatable phrases: "Annotating PORÉM JACARÉ ABRIU? NEM ELES! (literally untranslatable into Spanish) demonstrates a naïve position of skeptical arrogance, not only with respect to translation itself but also an aprioristic ignorant blindness to colloquial Spanish and the diffusion of popular linguistic forms across borders."[58] In this complaint, he asserts that Spanish-speaking readers could find meaning in these phrases by applying their own understanding of popular speech. The untranslatable phrase "But did the caiman open [the door]? Not for them!" repeats in the text, where this "caiman," an Amazonian alligator, repeatedly shows up, followed by different verbs, to express playful disdain and refusal to obey. An English transcreation could be some combination of "Later, alligator" and "No way, José." Olea's transspoken version in Spanish reads: "¿Ustedes creen que abrieron? Lagarto!" (Do you think they opened [the door]? Lizard!), a choice that conveys the mood of jocular rejection contextually. While he does not use his neologism in this letter, I associate the translator's defense of the reader's ability to comprehend orality with his depiction of his method as "transspeaking" or "transsaying," in which his process of deduction remade the source text's oral qualities within Spanish. For Olea, a thick translation of the text risks obscuring its poetic lightness and irony: "To explain a good poem shows a lack of faith in poetry."[59]

In the specific case of the repeated "Lagarto!" joke, a transspoken version of orality, Rama accepted Olea's point: the published edition contains no footnote explaining the lizard. Yet the notes about Indigenous words, flora, and fauna were largely maintained. Olea also argues that these footnotes mislead the reader by explaining specific words in Portuguese that come from Tupi-Guarani words with Spanish "equivalents" where no equivalence was desirable or necessary, especially in the case of Amazonian flora or fauna. "It's not the same to say: IANDU CARANGUEJEIRA is a poisonous spider, because the text itself left that implicit."[60] Olea points out the ethical dimension to this concern; he claims that "Andrade was only interested in these terms for their specific use-value in the contemporary metaphoric symbiosis of Luso-Tupi terms in the profuse Brazilian lexicon. If the author only included these words for their character as Luso-Tupi hybrid terms, then to translate them is to create foreignness in the translation where none existed in the original."[61] Remarkably, Mello e Souza also draws on the author's voice to support her critical apparatus; in her footnotes, she references a set of materials Mário de Andrade prepared in 1930 for a never-completed English translation by Margaret Hollingsworth.[62] Treating this unpublished, incomplete translation as an idealized ghost, Mello e Souza gives her footnotes an aura of authorized legitimacy, even though these explanations were for an Anglophone readership, not the Hispanophone Ayacucho public.

Using Andrade's self-analysis as evidence also presumes that, if possible, authors would make the best translators of their work—an assumption that cannibal translation destabilizes. An author's perspective on their own work in translation could be useful, but need not be privileged. As in this case, the author might justify multiple modes of translation. In cannibal translation, where the act of translating takes a creative and destructive pose and makes it possible to add the cultural history of translation to the translation itself, the author would not have access to that necessary critical layer of their own work. Olea and Mello e Souza both reference authorial intention only to buttress the translation approaches they prefer. For Olea, Andrade already engaged in an act of transspeaking when incorporating Luso-Tupi lexicon into his literary text; for Mello e Souza, Andrade's explanations for the English-language translator provide readers in any language with helpful background information. From their perspectives, they are diametrically opposed. From the perspective of cannibal translation, Olea's rejection of marking anything as "foreign" and Mello e Souza's insistence on providing the text's trajectory through many hands and languages ultimately work together to show the translingual nature of the text and the long journey it took on the way to becoming a work of Latin American—and world—literature.

Although the archival record shows that Rama sought Olea's help to find common ground between the critical apparatus and the translation, the volume itself has many inconsistencies. While the Ayacucho archive contained no response from Rama where he defended his editorial approach, Olea's general complaint remained unaddressed: there are over four hundred notes in the Ayacucho edition, and despite the after-the-fact effort to align the transcreation with the paratextual material, it remains evident that the volume editor created the footnotes largely with the Portuguese source text in mind rather than the Spanish version.

Given this process of producing translations separately from their paratexts, Mello e Souza's notes predictably caused the same inconsistencies with the translations by Santiago Kovadloff of the other texts for the Mário de Andrade *Obras escogidas* volume. Yet where Olea reacted with shock and insult on an ethical and almost personal level, Kovadloff responded with more disinterest, ceding responsibility. An Argentine psychiatrist, Kovadloff practiced literary translation without the same connection to universities or other institutions that the editors enjoyed. During the late 1970s and early '80s, as the economic situation in Argentina declined, he continued to ask for more compensation. While he does not respond favorably, Rama does acknowledge Kovadloff's requests, albeit in a handwritten note appended to the letter, a postscript or afterthought.[63] Reading through his correspondence with Kovadloff and other translators, Rama often organizes communication strategically: most of his letters discuss their shared intellectual project, positioning translation as a task undertaken for its own reward. He then relegates practical questions of timeline and pay rate to postscripts, downplaying the conditions of their labor.

When Rama writes to Kovadloff to ask him to do the same editing process as Olea, he emphasizes concern about regionalisms and register:

> In some cases, it's simply a matter of opting for a more universal term that includes all of Spanish America (less regional). . . . I ask you to examine it with close attention. There are also cases imposed by the annotations by Gilda de Mello: if she is noting that the language of a character is popular, responding to phonetics associated with lower class, we find this has generated incoherence between the note and the translation rendered in fluid, correct Spanish.[64]

This letter demonstrates that Rama wanted Kovadloff to alter his translation rather significantly: to make it more like Olea's, more responsive to varied registers of formality and voice in the source, more inventive of a pan-Hispanoamerican Spanish rather than his own Argentine regionalisms—and to make it more like the Brazilian text described in Mello's notes.

Kovadloff replies with less frustration than Olea, but he largely rejects Rama's assignment and simply accepts the changes and suggestions from Rama, Souza, and the Ayacucho style editor. In the few cases he asks for clarification, he does not personalize the differences in interpretation, simply asking, "Does that really say the same thing?" Yet Kovadloff avoids taking responsibility for reviewing his translation, never commenting on the issue of register Rama raised, and suggesting that other readers might be equally equipped to review his work and ensure a sufficiently "universal" Spanish: "I repeat, in global terms, the work done on my translation seems right to me. I don't think it's essential that I read all the material unless you consider it indispensable. Perhaps it would be enough for your style editor to check with some Rioplatense you must have there in Caracas to eliminate the gravest doubts."[65] Kovadloff has already asked for higher wages for his work, several times, and so he is justifiably unwilling to take on the painstaking process Rama requested to check his translation for alignment in register and lexicon with Mello e Souza's notes. Several months later, he writes sadly that, due to his personal circumstances caused by the Argentine financial crisis, he can no longer translate for Ayacucho.[66]

Olea and Kovadloff's different responses to the layer of "thick translation" added to their work also contrasts with the work of two in-house translators at Ayacucho: Márgara Russotto and Marta Traba. A renowned critic in her own right, Rama's wife Traba was almost completely absent from the archival record.[67] Though she was credited as translator of the *Arte y arquitectura* volume, the archival materials did not show any payment for her translation work, unlike the other three translators involved. Much like the "traducción lunar" dynamic personified by Ulalume González de León and described in the prior chapter, the feminine translators play a more shadowy role in the translations of Brazilian *modernismo*. Ayacucho could not issue a reprint of the *Arte y arquitectura* volume because none of the permissions for publication or translation were secured, and it contained hundreds of photos and other images.[68] I read Rama's choice to simply publish this translation as quickly as possible with the translator closest at hand without securing rights as his reaction to the challenges he faced in editing the other two volumes of Brazilian *modernismo*.

Although Olea was initially invited to translate both Oswald novels, *Memórias sentimentais de João Miramar* and *Serafim Ponte Grande*, the latter was ultimately translated by the Ayacucho employee Márgara Russotto and labeled "Versión al castellano."[69] In contrast to the resentful letter Olea writes to Rama, attempting to reject the editor's footnotes, Russotto includes over one hundred footnotes of her own, many of which simply state "Así en el original (N. de la T.)" to indicate that a phrase was already in a language other than Portuguese. While these "Notes by the Translator" emphasize the novel's multilingual aesthetic, the overall effect is mechanistic, a repetitive reminder to the reader that the source text was just as polyglot as the translation in a line of identical footnotes stretching up from the bottom of a particularly playful page. While she does remind the reader that the translator in this case is "la traductora," the fact remains that unlike Olea or Kovadloff she was never asked to review the paratextual materials added to her translation. This general absence from the translator's archive of both Traba and Russotto speaks to their presence in the editorial project as feminized, invisible, and "lunar," as transparent conveyors of the creative work of others rather than creators in their own right.

Olea's approach to footnotes in his translation of Oswald's "Manifiesto Antropófago" differs from both his transcreation of *Macunaíma* and the work of Russotto. He only includes three, and he trusts the reader to deduce that any text not in Spanish appeared that way in the source text.[70] Instead, his notes focus on providing the comparative angle for the Spanish-speaking reader familiar with literary *indigenismo* or *vanguardismo* in Spanish American contexts. For example, to the phrase "En el país de la 'víbora-víbora'" he adds the footnote "the Great Cobra (víbora-víbora) is a mythological figure in Brazilian *indigenismo*, feared for its evil-doing, such as when it flips over ships at sea when it takes the form of a viper. Similar to the Jagüey from the riverside legends in Cuba (Translator's Note)."[71] Elsewhere Olea positions himself heatedly against the explanatory footnote, yet in this case the source text itself encloses the phrase *víbora-víbora* in quotation marks, flagging it as something that might need a gloss. Olea's notes are fewer than Russotto's, and they tend to focus on moments in the text that reference Indigenous Brazilian culture.

Olea also uses translator footnotes to support Haroldo's interpretation of Oswald's works, in which he reads the cannibalist incorporation of Tupi poetry into this manifesto as illuminating Brazilian concrete poetry before the fact. Unlike the words in English and French that he does not translate or mark as different, when Oswald's manifesto incorporates a poem in Tupi-Guarani, Olea does choose to give this citation a full translation and gloss. Unlike Oswald, who never translated this text he cannibalized, Olea wants readers to understand not just the words but also his own understanding of the reasons behind including them. The aphorism begins with the claim "We already had Communism. We already had Surrealist language. The Golden Age."[72] A poem in Tupi-Guarani follows, standing as proof of the axiom:

> Ya teníamos comunismo. Ya teníamos lengua surrealista. La edad de oro.
>
> Catiti Catiti
> Imara Notiá
> Notiá Imara
> Ipeyú[73]
>
> [Nota] Este poema *tupí-guaraní*/pre-concreto (como lo definiera Haroldo de Campos) fue extraído por O. de Andrade del libro *O Selvagem*, de Couto de Magalhães, dentro del mismo espíritu con el que el autor se valió de textos de cronistas del Brasil colonial. Se trata de una invocación a la Luna nueva:
>
> Lunanueva Lunanueva
> *Arresopla* en fulano
> En Fulano arresopla
> Recuerdos de mí[74]
>
> ([Note] O. de Andrade extracted this *tupí-guaraní*/pre-concrete poem (as Haroldo de Campos would define it) from the book *O selvagem* by Couto de Magalhães, in the same spirit with which the author availed himself of the texts by the chroniclers of colonial Brazil. It is an invocation of the New Moon:
>
> New Moon New Moon
> Snatch-gust-blow on mister so-and-so
> On Mister So-and-So snatch-gust blow
> Memories of me)

Going beyond an informative translation of the poem, Olea's note adds an interpretation, and even an expansion on the concept. Oswald used the Tupi poem to posit an Indigenous "Golden Age" before the European invasion, a flourishing culture that had already achieved "communism" and "surrealist language." Olea adds the idea that this "Golden Age" also included concrete poetry: Indigenous cultures had already invented every literary and political innovation that contemporary Brazilians (or their European colonizers) could claim. Unlike Russotto, Olea assumes the reader will understand enough of the English, French, or Italian, peppering the text—but not the Tupi-Guarani poem. Furthermore, this footnote actually expands on the concrete elements of the source poem, emphasizing the shape on the page not present in other printings of the poem. Olea makes this ode to the New Moon more of a concrete poem than ever.[75] Given his frustration when Rama imposes thick translation paratexts on his transcreation of *Macunaíma*, I view these additions to the Oswald manifesto as the cannibal translator's reassertion of creative authority and control.

DETERRITORIALIZED TRADITIONS: WORLD LITERATURE AS MOBILE UNTRANSLATABLES

Transcreating, transspeaking, or transsaying *Macunaíma* without explanatory footnotes, Olea emphasizes underlying connections between the Brazilian and Spanish American cultures in their shared incorporation of Indigenous cultures, an accessible shared past that can be mined in the present day through the colonial languages of Spanish and Portuguese, "conscious of separation, but at the same time attempting to reunite what was dismembered."[76] Olea describes his practice as unifying what colonial history split apart, while remaining conscious of that legacy of division. Olea works from what I have been calling "mobile untranslatables" by drawing out different Indigenous vocabularies and oral idioms in Spanish and mixing them with similar untranslatables in Brazilian Portuguese—he achieves transplantation without translating, mirroring untranslatable kernels of cultural knowledge between an expanded pan–Latin American space.

Scholarly debate around *Macunaíma*—extended by the Ayacucho project into a debate around how to translate the work—included questions of the nature of the author's incorporation of Indigenous myth, practices, and lexicon. Mário de Andrade's novel follows Macunaíma on an ambivalent journey from his home in the Amazon through São Paulo, Rio de Janeiro, and back again, only to leave the terrestrial plane entirely to become a constellation. The character succeeds in his quest to recover a powerful amulet stolen by his antagonist, the cannibal giant and Peruvian Italian merchant collector Piaimã Venceslau Pietro Pietra—but he loses it again. Trickster hero Macunaíma acquires regional idioms and habits through contact with new communities, yet he ultimately fails to realize any stable character or retain any material gains. I follow Alfredo Cesar Melo in centering this paradox in the text, to focus on exchanges between subaltern spaces within South America rather than the hybridism of European and Indigenous cultures.[77] The journey of *Macunaíma*—both the character and the book—shines through the Ayacucho edition as a series of exuberant, proliferating translations, a celebration of cultural contact that also critiques assimilation.

Macunaíma traveled from São Paulo through the Seix Barral publication in Barcelona to land in Caracas as a newly consecrated Latin American classic in Spanish at the Biblioteca Ayacucho.[78] The work has a longer history in becoming world literature, however, in the two-step process defined by David Damrosch.[79] Andrade completed the first step of reading a source text as literature when he rewrote Indigenous legends collected by German ethnographer Theodor Koch-Grünberg as literary rather than ethnographic material. In *Vom Roraima zum Orinoco: Ergebnisse einer Reise in der Nordbrasilien und Venezuela in den Jahren 1911–1913* (published 1916–24), Koch-Grünberg collected stories from Indigenous cultures including the Taulipangue and Arecuná along the Orinoco River, which runs through Venezuela and the state of Roraima in northern Brazil. Mário invented a style of literary orality to weave together stories that included many untranslatable flora, fauna, place-names, and character names in what Haroldo calls a "mosaic," an "archifábula, una *fábula ómnibus*."[80]

The Brazilian literary field continues to debate *Macunaíma* and its representation of Brazilian modes of cultural hybridity; the divergent views of Haroldo de Campos and Gilda de Mello e Souza capture the debate.[81] Haroldo centers his interpretation on *Morphology of the Folktale* by Russian formalist Vladimir Propp, in which the "proto-fable" elements of fairytales obey a "law of transferability," serving the same function in multiple stories; he sees Andrade's artistic achievement in his elaboration of an "arch-fable" where elements of Indigenous legends maintain their function when combined in a larger mosaic. Mello e Souza counters Campos's description of the work as a "mosaic," instead labeling it "bricolage" as defined by Claude Lévi-Strauss. For her, the piece borrows structurally from Portuguese music, novels of chivalry (*caballerías*), and the picaresque: she asserts that the text's "central nucleus continues to be *firmly European*" (emphasis in the source).[82] She adopts a psychoanalytic approach, and her analysis relies on interpreting the ending as melancholic. When the character Macunaíma abandons Brazil, she views this conclusion as a satirical comment on an inability to construct the right national "mask" rather than a celebratory conflagration of past influences. Even when she questions nationalistic readings of the novel—citing the author's pride at borrowing from multiple geographies—she does not explore the Venezuelan connection that author Mário de Andrade himself emphasized, when he wrote:

> Nobody could say the protagonist of this book is Brazil. I extracted him from the work of the German Koch Grünberg. He is as much Venezuelan as he is ours, if not more so. He is so unaware of the stupidity of borders that he wanders into the "land of the English," as Macunaíma calls British Guiana. The fact that the protagonist may not be absolutely Brazilian pleases me greatly.[83]

Mello e Souza ultimately upholds the conflation of the character with the Brazilian nation; yet she reverses Haroldo's vision, arguing that the work is indeed Brazilian because of its bricolage of European cultural sources rather than its structural deployment of Indigenous myth.[84]

Olea's transcreation, however, responds to the text as already both fundamentally pan–Latin American, responsive to Iberian colonization, but also highly localized to the protagonist's origins on the Orinoco River. Lúcia Sá understands the central narrative as a "language quest" rather than a "magical object" quest. As Macunaíma changes shape and location, his language also transforms, and this linguistic journey becomes visible only when the non-European formal elements are studied.[85] Sá claims that all debates over *indigenismo* in literary or sociopolitical spheres stem from concern over land rights. If Brazilian and Spanish American literatures share Indigenous mythic structure—more than shared European heritage—this integrated cultural grounding has implications for Indigenous cultural demands that go beyond visibility to also support claims to rights and land sovereignty.[86]

TRANSSAYING/TRANSSPEAKING: HÉCTOR OLEA DEDUCING THE TRADITION IN *MACUNAÍMA*

Olea had a truly utopian aim in his transcreation practice. He describes his deterritorialized Spanish as an artistic act promoting a shared cultural imaginary in the Americas, asserting that translating this Brazilian work into Spanish American idioms represents new myth-making. "America is a mirror that invents itself," he claims; translating Brazilian literature allows Spanish America to "reflect on its own reflection."[87] Referring to Haroldo's theories, Olea's transcreation strategies include linguistic re-creation of orality by transferring phonemes or deforming words through apheresis or other forms of stretching Spanish syntax to imitate oral speech much like Andrade stretched Portuguese; inventing new portmanteaus and rewriting wordplay; and "desgeografización" or geographic displacement through the interpolation of Spanish American expressions, idioms, dialects, or folkloric details. For example, Olea points out his use of Spanish diction marked by the gaucho culture that straddles both sides of the Brazilian and Argentine border.[88] He also includes various names for flora and fauna to expand regional associations through multiple Indigenous language cultures.[89] For example, after researching manioc and popcorn, two widely adopted staples of Amerindian food culture, he places alternative names for the same root or grain in different parts of the work.[90] Olea avoids notes with these techniques, while he also freely invents, combines words, or alters orthography. Because many of these stylistic details have "scant functional meaning," Olea re-creates effects rather than translating for semantic information.[91]

Adhering to the poetic, experimental, and cannibalistic sides of *Macunaíma*, Olea transspeaks Andrade's work as a practice, as an elaboration of ideas rather than a completed whole. He draws on connections between literary traditions: "*Reconstruction and restoration* of oral or popular literature are constants in the work of the modernist writer [Mário de Andrade]. His ethnographic and musicological studies are faithful demonstrations of his interest in *mobile or movable traditions*."[92] Olea treats the source text as a series of experimental representations of oral speech in written text, representations he re-creates in Spanish.[93] He emphasizes the Indigenous, Afro-diasporic, oral, and profane elements of the novel, molding a poetic trajectory. Privileging these aesthetic elements, he uses "untranslatables" as points of contact between Brazil and Spanish America. In a linguistic analysis of Olea's treatment of Indigenous terms, Márcia Moura da Silva finds that his translation displays the greatest fidelity with the Tupi linguistic interpolations and posits that Olea gave himself greater freedom to intervene into the work because he prioritized creating a convincing transcreation of Indigenous characteristics.[94]

Once I read the letters exchanged by the agents of translation at Ayacucho, I could see the *Obra escogida* volume in a different light, alert to the different translation manuals at play. When one treats Olea's transcreation as a direct mirror of the source text, the references Mello e Souza adds do successfully provide contextual framing that would aid pedagogy. In some instances, however, the "thick translation" ignores or negates the creative rendering Olea chose—resulting in a proliferation of competing translations within the same text.

For example, Mello e Souza describes the two catchphrases Macunaíma repeats as "inversely symmetrical" key concepts expressing the "profound ambivalence" of the work; Kovadloff translates them in her prologue as "¡Ay qué pereza!" (What laziness / I'm so tired / I'm such a slacker) and "Mucha hormiga y poca salud son los males de Brasil" (Many ants and meager health are the banes of Brazil).[95] Mello e Souza positions Macunaíma's slogans as opposites; the first is an "apologia for idleness," whereas the second references chronicles by colonial administrators bemoaning the poor health of the region, their fears that their investment might infect and kill them. In his notes for the uncompleted English translation, Andrade asserts that the phrase is relevant to "the satirical sense of the book and has been created rhythmically in the form of a proverb."[96] Kovadloff includes the Portuguese phrase and explains his translation in the context of Mello e Souza's prologue even further: "The phrase in Portuguese says: 'Muita saúva e pouca saúde os males do Brasil são.' The *saúva* is a type of giant, voracious ant common to Brazil (N. del T.)"[97]

While her analysis glosses these invented proverbs, Mello e Souza does not account for Olea's transcreation into colloquial Spanish. For the prologue, Kovadloff chooses the most direct translation of "Ai! que preguiça . . . !" which is "¡Ay qué pereza!" But Olea opts for another Spanish word: "—Ay! qué flojera!"[98] Particularly common in Mexico, *flojera* expresses the same laziness or enervation as *pereza* but also connotes physical or intellectual slackness or weakness. Given that Macunaíma and his family frequently complain of hunger and food insecurity, the term *flojera* fits their everyday lives even better than *preguiça* does. Olea also invents a rhyming idiom—just as Andrade did—to convey the whimsical nihilism of Macunaíma's worldview: "'Mucha tambocha y poco bizcocho, / Luchas son que al Brasil dejan mocho'" (Lots of ants and few biscuits / Are the struggles that make Brazil fall short).[99] Olea's transcreation, unlike Kovadloff's version, maintains the playful rhyme, or "aesthetic information," while altering "semantic information." Olea removes the reference to health, adding instead the idea of food scarcity, an apt choice given the prevalence of hunger in *Macunaíma*.

In one example of interpolation, Olea adds references to Afro-Cuban Santería where the source text represented Afro-Brazilian religion. When Macunaíma journeys to Rio de Janeiro, he attends a *candomblé* ritual for Exú to gain strength to get his amulet back. Olea interpolates "la Virgen Caridad de Cobre," the patron saint of Cuba, where Mário de Andrade includes the Saint of the Azores, "Nossa Senhora da Conceição."[100] As Heloisa da Costa Milton points out, the chapter title "Macumba" in Portuguese appears as "Bembé-Macumba" in Spanish; these references to Cuban Santería and other local beliefs "effectively fulfill the function of a glossary or a collection of footnotes with respect to the reception of the text."[101] Olea also adds Afro-Cuban author Nicolás Guillén to a list of "macumberos" where the source text included only Brazilian and French artists practicing *négritude*.[102]

> E pra acabar todos fizeram a festa juntos. . . . Então tudo acabou se fazendo a vida real. E os macumbeiros, Macunaíma, Jaime Ovalle, Dodô, Manu Bandeira, Blaise Cendrars, Ascenso Ferreira, Raul Bopp, Antônio Bento, todos esses macumbeiros saíram na madrugada.[103]
>
> Y para acabar todos hicieron el bochinche juntos. . . . Entonces todo acabó volviéndose a la vida real. Y los macumberos, Macunaíma, Jaime Ovalle, Dodó, Manú Bandeira, Blaise Cendrars, Ascenso Ferreira, Raúl Bopp, Antonio Bento, Pierre Verger, Peque Lanusa, Nicolás Guillén, todos esos bemberos salieron hacia la madrugada.[104]
>
> (And everyone ended up partying together. . . . Then everything went back to real life. And the macumba-players Macunaíma, Jaime Ovalle, Dodó, Manú Bandeira, Blaise Cendrars, Ascenso Ferreira, Raúl Bopp, Antonio Bento, Pierre Verger, Peque Lanusa, Nicolás Guillén, all those bemberos went out until dawn.)

Mello e Souza adds a note that flags this passage as one where the author mixes "real and fictitious elements," providing biographical information about the poets listed by Andrade—yet she does not point out Olea's expansion of Andrade's metaliterary game or gloss his three additional bemberos.[105] He adds Pierre Verger (1902–96), a French photographer and student of African religious diasporas who initiated himself into *candomblé* in his adopted home of Salvador. Including Verger reminds readers that to look at an Afro-Brazilian ritual means looking at a forcefully transplanted cultural form that many have since adopted and adapted. Peque Lanusa likely refers to Argentine poet José Luis Lanuza (1903–76); he wrote *cancioneros* and studied the gaucho tradition in Argentina. By adding Lanuza, Olea connects the Argentine gaucho, another racialized subaltern subject, with *bembero* culture in Brazil. Given Mário's study of music, *gauchesco* poetry and *negrismo* have a logical connection because both poetic traditions incorporate popular musical forms into a literary culture that gets elevated to the level of celebrated national heritage. Nicolás Guillén (1902–89) is the best-known parallel Olea adds. In *Motivos de son* (1930) and *Sóngoro cosongo* (1931) Guillén incorporates Afro-Cuban music into his poetry, thematically and aesthetically, against prevailing cultural and legal interdictions seeking to suppress African cultural forms within dictatorship-era Cuba.[106] Olea's Spanish transcreation interpolates recognizable but geographically displaced representations of Afro-Latinidad to draw in the Spanish American reader.

In his "Posfacio," Olea writes about this parallelism available between the Afro-Cuban poetic voice created in the same period by poet Nicolás Guillén. Olea's persistent search for a connection already available in the literature of the Spanish-speaking Americas bespeaks his conviction that translation—especially in the Brazilian mode—can reveal connections.

> Another technique of creative translation—oft used by pre-Romantic Brazilian poet Odorico Mendes—is interpolation, which introduces citations from other poets when their images match the source's phrase. This was how he could accommodate Homeric hexameters in heroic hendecasyllables by grafting lines from Camões. Mário de Andrade undeniably took great care to place mixed-raced culture within his ample essays and investigations on the subject of blackness, of *négritude*. So Nicolás Guillén, among others, was no stranger to him.[107]

When Olea adds the name of Nicolás Guillén along with other artists of his period interested in circulating Black diaspora cultural forms, it represents the translator interpolating his corpus of references, just as Andrade was citing his own sources. Although he introduces a problematic equivalence superficially traced between various and contested representatives of distinct literary and artistic movements uplifting the African influence in Latin American cultural forms, the transcreation does interpolate new information to draw the Spanish American reader closer to the Afro-Brazilian experience presented in this chapter of *Macunaíma*.

Olea uses the strategy of interpolation in another scene featuring musical performance, where he transcreates a Northeast Brazilian dance custom, the "Bumba-meu-boi," by adding different lyrics from a parallel Guatemalan version, the "Danza de toritos." For Mello e Souza, this song performs Brazil's Portuguese heritage, placing Brazilian folk rounds as descended from songs by Portuguese *jograis* (troubadours), proof of the European heritage of the work. Although Olea acknowledges the shared cultural history from the Iberian Peninsula, rather than tracing those origins he offers a comparative vision of the many iterations these cultural forms have taken in Latin America. Olea claims greater authenticity for his interpolation of a "cantiga hispanoamericana" rather than translating the Brazilian folkloric verses: "I found it more authentic to intercalate into the Mariandradian text the ready-made of some fragments of the refrains sung in the Dance of the Bull instead of trying to reproduce in Spanish the stanzas that appear in the rhapsody."[108] Using the term "rhapsody," he recalls the author's description of work as *uma rapsódia* rather than a novel, justifying his own variations on the theme. Just as with the addition of Guillén, Olea applies a Brazilian translation technique of interpolation, borrowed from Odorico Mendes and learned from Haroldo de Campos, to translate a Brazilian text and to emphasize the shared legacy of cultural mixture with Spanish American folk songs.

Recalling Appiah's initial framing of "thick translation" as a way to provide context for the use of Twi proverbs in literature, Olea harvests parallel idioms from popular speech in Spanish America into the text where there are Brazilian idioms, using interpolation rather than adding notes. For example, he remixes a Brazilian nursery rhyme with a similar game from Central America, reproducing the aesthetic function of wordplay and repetition—recognizable elements of a childhood game even if the reader does not know the song. Where the source text reads "chegou o domingo pé-de-cachimbo," Olea adds the nonsense word *chingolingo* borrowed from a dice game from Central America.[109] His transcreated rhyme reads: "llegó el domingo-chingolingo pie-de-cachimbolimbo."[110] Mello e Souza adds a note that glosses only Mário's version while also adding her own:

> La expresión "Domingo pé de cachimbo" pertenece a una cuarteta infantil que dice: "Hoje é domingo / pé de cachimbo / cachimbo é de barro / que bate no jarro." Trasladado al castellano en forma más o menos textual e intentando preservar el ritmo, tendríamos "Hoy es domingo / pata de pipa / pipa de barro / que rompe el jarro."[111]
>
> (The expression "Domingo pé de cachimbo" pertains to a nursery rhyme. . . . Translated to Spanish in a more or less textual way that also tries to preserve the rhythm, we would have: "Today is Sunday / leg of pipe / pipe made of clay / that breaks the jug.")

In this case, her note offers her own values of translation, alternative to the translation in the body of the text, where Olea preserves the mood without explanation; Mello e Souza explains the context but also translates creatively to "preserve the rhythm." The Ayacucho edition includes all three versions rather than resolving them into one solution, enriching the reader's experience.

At times Olea chooses phrases associated with Mexican Spanish, such as the verb *ningunear*. Macunaíma causes a commotion at the São Paulo Stock Exchange, tricking his brothers into attempting to hunt tapir in this inhospitable forest of financial institutions of steel and cement. When a mob tries to lynch him for the disturbance, he deflects their rejection with typical aplomb and insists on his belonging, even there in the city center. The source text registers his strong reaction with repetitive, emphatic orality: "'O que! quem que é desconhecido!' berrou Macunaíma desesperado com a ofensa" ("What?! which who is the stranger!" bellowed Macunaíma, exasperated at the insult).[112] In his translation, Olea maintains the orality, but transspeaks it into a specifically Mexican register "'Qué qué! a mí ninguno me ningunea!' berreó Macunaíma desesperado por la patochada" ("What what?! nobody nobodies me!" bellowed Macunaíma, exasperated at the slap in the face).[113] The expression Olea chooses fits the context perfectly.

Analyzed by Octavio Paz in his treatise on Mexican identity *Labyrinth of Solitude*, *ningunear* means "to ignore, to give the cold shoulder"—literally, to turn another person into a nobody. Olea took the opportunity to interpolate this idiomatic Mexican expression where none appears in the source. Paz defines the *ninguneo* as the powerful, internalized silence inherent to Mexico as a former colony, where the absent but influential father, the Spaniard don Nadie (Sir Nobody), has abandoned his son, Ninguno (Nobody Either). "Don Nadie, Spanish father of Ninguno, possesses grace, guts, honor, a bank account, and he speaks with a strong, sure voice. Don Nadie fills the world with his empty, vainglorious presence. . . . Banker, ambassador, businessman, . . . functionary, influencer—he has an aggressive, conceited way of not being."[114] Not only does the decolonial figure Macunaíma speak with a specifically Mexican Spanish, but Olea also gives him the vocabulary to voice a rejection of this colonial father, come to life in the São Paulo financial district. Returning to Paz's description of the experience of being "nobodied" or *ninguneado*, as Macunaíma forcefully rejects, he places this silence at the core of Mexican national identity, above all other recognizable symbols of both Indigenous and colonial historical monuments: "Ninguno is always present. He is our secret, our crime, our remorse. . . . The shadow of Ninguno extends over Mexico . . . more resilient than the pyramids and sacrifices, the churches, the rebellions and the popular songs, silence returns to reign."[115] Introducing this culturally specific term in his translation, without any indicators or labels, Héctor Olea breaks from the national identification of the *ninguneo* to produce it here, in Macunaíma's experience in São Paulo, and at the stock exchange, a fitting place to reencounter Don Nadie, or perhaps Dom Ninguém, the absent Portuguese colonial father. Olea matches these two literary moments of decolonial reflection on being exploited and then left behind like a nobody, building a bridge from Paz to Andrade. He also takes the character of Macunaíma as a space through which to invite the Mexican trope of the *ninguneado* or "nobodied" people to speak out through an ostensibly, ambivalently Brazilian figure. This is a fitting expansion of the work's subtitle; *Macunaíma: O herói sem nenhum caráter*, or *The Hero with No Character*, was always aligned with other Ningunos scattered around Latin America.

Biblioteca Ayacucho's *Obra escogida* by Mário de Andrade may not present a seamless whole. Instead of regarding its inconsistencies as failures, I understand them as a productive negotiation between distinct cannibal translation practices—from transcreation and transspeaking or transsaying to thick translation—with the shared interest in crafting a decolonial Latin American canon that would highlight historical colonial and present-day neoliberal divisions while rejecting and resisting both. Whereas translation of Latin American literatures into English, especially during the heyday of the Boom in the 1960s and 1970s, rewarded the smooth presentation of an art object as in the Seix Barral *Macunaíma*, the Ayacucho re-edition elevates opacity, colloquial or nonstandard language, Indigenous lexicon, and local referents by doubling their interpretative layer with footnotes that introduce multiple versions. Olea transspeaks the novel: he reproduces the orality of the text and puts it into motion rather than making the narrative transparent for a wider audience. The very unsmoothness of the Caracas publication speaks to the polyvocal Brazilian *modernismo* movement. The creative devouring of the source text remains visible as Olea uses the Brazilian mode of cannibal translation to make this Brazilian work legible in Spanish as a canonical work of Latin American literature.

CHAPTER 5

Approximation, Untranslation, and World Literature as Heteronym

In his poem "La flecha" ("The Arrow"), José Emilio Pacheco (1939–2014) traces the arc through space created by an arrow's release. Imagining that it would be better if the arrow never landed, never killed the hunted animal, never caused harm, this poem could be read through a politics of nonviolence or through Zeno's paradox, where a destination can never be reached because only half the distance can be covered at a time. Instead, I understand this poem as a visualization of the Mexican writer's theory of translation.

> No importa que la flecha no alcance el blanco.
> Mejor así.
> No capturar ninguna presa,
> no hacerle daño a nadie,
> pues lo importante
> es el vuelo, la trayectoria, el impulso,
> el tramo de aire recorrido en su ascenso,
> la oscuridad que desaloja al clavarse,
> vibrante,
> en la extensión de la nada.[1]

(It doesn't matter if the arrow never hits the target.
Better that way.
Not capturing any prey,
not hurting anyone,
so what matters
is the flight, the trajectory, the impulse,
the stretch of air traveled on its ascent,
the darkness displaced as it pierces,
quivering,
through the extension of nothing.)

Perhaps proper translations of world literature should resolve, cohere, land on a "target language," but in Pacheco's anthology *Aproximaciones* (1984) "what matters / is the flight."

In his own translation anthology, *O anticrítico* (1986), Augusto de Campos also draws on the image of an arrow in flight to define "porous prose," a genre of "literary criticism through creative translation" where he pairs translations with poem-like commentary. While he may direct the "arrow of his 'anti'" against critics who "illuminate nothing," his true "aim is something other, my aim is poetry: color, sound, failure of success."[2] For Pacheco and Augusto, source and target matter less in translation than the long flight between moments of poetic expression, and the capacity of their languages to carry that flight. Adam Shellhorse reads Augusto's arrow image as a nod to the Nietzschean concept that "a great thinker shoot an arrow into the heavens as an untimely yet necessary gesture. In his or her wake, a new thinker picks up this arrow and reconfigures it, shooting it once more into the distance. Untimely yet urgent, the writer's present inscription marks this debt, this lesson, to an interruptive genealogy of radical thought."[3] The same can be said of Pacheco; in translation practice, both poets are more interested in the thought itself—anonymous, collective, reciprocal, and extraterritorial rather than directional, intentional, originated or owned anywhere. Freeing the poet-translator from the critic's desire to land an argument, or the translator's task to carry everything across, their cannibal translation anthologies instead show a creative blend of their own voices speaking through various authorial masks to make world literature on their terms.[4]

Pacheco and Augusto displace more than the "target" of translation: both authors also performatively destabilize their source texts by creating a relationship between translation and heteronym. Heteronyms are invented personalities who write; Portuguese poet Fernando Pessoa (1888–1935) championed this practice, crafting many heteronyms with unique biographies, voices, and relationships to poetic traditions. Augusto never used the literary device himself, explaining that "for a Portuguese-speaking author, after Fernando Pessoa, it is difficult to use the expression 'heteronym' without sounding pretentious."[5] However, he does imagine translation as akin to inventing another persona to inhabit and write from: "Translation for me is persona. Almost a heteronym. Climb inside the pretender's skin to refine all over again, pain for pain, sound for sound, color for color. That's why I never set out to translate everything. Just what I feel."[6] While Augusto considers translation only "almost" a heteronym, in *O anticrítico* he translates mere fragments of much longer texts, reformatting them to add visual concrete poetic qualities, illuminating Augusto's vision of what is important, undervalued, or forgotten about these source texts by other critics. In this sense, he turns canonical authors of world literature—Dante, Omar Khayyám, Lewis Carroll, Emily Dickinson—into his own heteronyms. For his part, Pacheco makes a well-studied use of heteronyms within his own volumes of poetry, flagging for readers their invented status.[7] Yet in his translation collection *Aproximaciones*, Pacheco takes the next step and adds several heteronyms to great names of world literature; in this case, the heteronyms are the invented authors of what are essentially pseudotranslations.[8] A pseudotranslation proports to be a translation but has no source text in any language; for example, Cervantes presents much of *Don Quixote* as a pseudotranslation from Arabic written by Cide Hamete Benengeli.[9] In his translation anthology, Pacheco mixes heteronyms together with renowned authors and lesser-known poets—including some of Pacheco's own translators—without differentiating between them.[10] Much like the "skin" Augusto wears of the source author's persona, Pacheco claims that "poems are only remote, ancient, or foreign when we don't make them our own by any lawful or unlawful means, if we don't take them by assault in the most savage and civilizing of all tasks."[11] Pacheco and Augusto describe the loving destruction of ventriloquizing another author's voice, making it their own—both anthologies present readers with the radical condition of accepting that the authors included have become heteronyms for their translator, recognizable literary costumes to wear and perform in.

Reading Pacheco and Augusto together illuminates the potential of cannibal translation techniques to contest hierarchies and assumptions built into the structures of world literature anthologies. Going even further than the self-reflexive intersectional translations of Castellanos and Lispector, or the multivocal translingual editing at Biblioteca Ayacucho, their anthologies never let readers forget the mediated perspective presented in any translation. Their critical approach to world literature raises an important question: What does it mean to acknowledge that, in translation, the source author becomes an invented heteronym, a projection into the target language? Pacheco and Augusto deploy cannibal translation techniques of approximation, porous prose, and untranslation to reimagine colonial relationships between languages, to emphasize the complex role translation plays in the incorporation of subaltern figures into the literary frame, and to play with abandoning and usurping authorship and authority.

APROXIMACIONES AND *O ANTICRÍTICO* AS CRITICAL WORLD LITERATURE ANTHOLOGIES

I read these idiosyncratic anthologies of Pacheco and Augusto together to underscore the potential for cannibal translation techniques to offer world literature anthologies alternative strategies that critique their own colonial or assimilationist history. Pacheco's approximations index the violently one-sided history of contact between Indigenous and colonizing cultures in the Americas. He critiques Spanish as an instrument of assimilation and draws on translation to reconfigure relationships between Indigenous and colonial epistemological systems. In Augusto's untranslations and porous prose, he selects fragments from poems and prose works to transform them into concrete pieces. I focus on his cannibalization of the Brazilian literary canon where he reinvents verbose classics by Gregório de Matos and Euclides da Cunha, emphasizing elements of their work he sees as undervalued or suppressed by the critical tradition. Reading these translation projects together, I highlight their conceptual use of fragmentation and translational heteronyms to critique the framing of other world literature anthologies. Pacheco's term "approximation" foregrounds the tensions inherent in translation: the verb "to approximate" signifies drawing near but always holding apart, never "to duplicate" or "to bring over." An approximation never quite gets there; the arrow of Pacheco's translation never quite arrives at its target. Once more, their tactics of what I call cannibal translation emphasize the "becoming" of these translated works, which is never resolved into "being" or into a stable or uncontested placement in a world literary canon.

To be clear, neither poet-translator claims the label of "anthology" or of "world literature." I find it productive to understand them as cannibal translation anthologies of world literature because they frame their collections in ways that both mimic and critique conventions of canonical structuring in a world literature anthology. To recall Haroldo's definition of the cannibal as critic, they take on the pose of the polemicist and the anthologist, lovingly cutting up and reassembling world literature to the measure of their own poetic concerns.

Both *Aproximaciones* and *O anticrítico* participate in the organizational norms of many world literature anthologies. These traits include a chronological organization that spans centuries; uniting literatures from many languages into one; retranslating canonical figures; and framing works with biographical, critical, and literary commentaries. Yet their cannibal translation approach to world literature differs because it centers on translation history, highlights the problematic trajectory of literary consecration built on a logic of colonialism, and thwarts expectations of translation as a transparent act in the service of the anthology. Instead, sources may be combined, invented, or so mediated as to be contested and undermined; or the genre of the translation may differ from the genre of the target text. Furthermore, they include their respective target cultures—Mexico and Brazil—not simply as passive receivers of literary genius originating elsewhere but also as a filter, mediator, and producer of world literature. In this gesture, they counter what Theo D'haen warns against: the "radical dissociation of an 'internal' and an 'external' canon" in which a national canon for export gets shaped "under 'world literature' pressure" and diverges from a national canon for internal consumption.[12] Instead of patterning themselves on world literature produced in the Anglophone sphere, they respond to Mexican and Brazilian canons, incorporating a critique of translation history (Pacheco) and local classics in creative translation (Augusto).

Anthologies tend to be "reflective of the laws of their domain."[13] The *Longman Anthology of World Literature* (first edition 2004; most recent edition 2019) exemplifies enduring Eurocentric values by providing "comprehensive coverage of key works of the Western literary tradition" and merely "the best, core enduring works" from the rest of world.[14] Although the aim of such volumes is pedagogical coverage for an English-speaking readership, the anthology does little to problematize English as the receiving language: contextual materials place works historically and within literary movements, but language remains a transparent conveyor and the translator a neutral or invisible figure.

Translation studies and anthology studies have common cause but are only recently being brought to bear together, particularly as the publication of anthologies in Western languages showed prominent increase in the 1990s and 2000s.[15] I analyze two anthologies through the lens of cannibal translation to show how they exemplify a unique approach to world literature from the geo-linguistic standpoint of Latin America. Pacheco and Augusto elaborate alternative practices—approximations, untranslations, porous prose—that counter the model of translation as a transparent procedure, a one-to-one reflection of a text, author, or language. Instead, translation becomes a constantly repositioning action that calls into question where authors and readers should place themselves. David Damrosch suggests an elliptical approach to world literature could avoid the extremes of either a "self-centered construction of the world or a highly decentered one," imagining instead an anthology in which the dual centers of the reader and the world provide a self-reflexive experience in which "we read in the field of force generated between these two foci."[16] Already in the mid-1980s, Pacheco and Augusto draw on cannibal translation practices to generate this elliptical force.

Anthologies gather previously published selections, whereas collections assemble new works; an anthology creates new relationships between texts through selection, ordering, and framing.[17] The collections published by Biblioteca Ayacucho or as a result of the translationship between Octavio Paz and Haroldo de Campos framed new translation work with the trace materials of the process; this chapter discusses cannibal translation as an anthologizing gesture, reframing previously published works with new paratexts and through juxtaposition. The term "anthology" comes from the Greek for "bouquet" and referred initially to collections of poetry.[18] Paradoxically, unlike anthologies of other genres, anthologies of world poetry tend to evade that classification, opting for more metaphoric or creative labels, as Ana Maria Bernardo demonstrates in her analysis of nineteenth- and twentieth-century poetry anthologies.[19] Both *Aproximaciones* and *O anticrítico* amply fit these genre descriptors of a world poetry anthology. Choosing iconoclastic titles, the authors also claim that these volumes emerged not as the result of a planned organizing principle but after the fact out of translation activity previously published elsewhere. Pacheco translated for a monthly literary supplement, "Poesía para todos" ("Poetry for All"), in *Comunidad Conacyt*, and he emphasizes the same democratic spirit when he describes his translation anthology as "a book of collective poetry."[20] Augusto tells a similar origin story, collecting previously published works united by the genre-mixing style of his porous prose, and covering poetry "from Dante to Cage."[21] Reading these two projects together, I illuminate cannibal translation as a technique to build counter-hegemonic world literature anthologies and reading strategies.

APPROXIMATING OTHER AMERICAS: TRANSLATING THE COLONIALITY OF RACISM

Much like his Brazilian contemporaries Augusto and Haroldo de Campos, José Emilio Pacheco calls his translations "inseparable from my own poetry"; while he claims Octavio Paz as a model, he directly opposes Paz's translation dictum when he states: "from poems in other languages, I tried to make poems in my own."[22] His poetry collections all include approximations, and he continued to edit and change this translation work as assiduously as his own poems. Translation practice held so central a place in his career that he chose to read only approximations rather than any so-called original poems at one of his last public readings, the 2009 Feria International del Libro (FIL) in Guadalajara.[23] Yet this work has been largely sidelined by critical reception.[24] Unfortunately, his translations were not included in the most recent editions of his collected poetry; I hope continued interest in Pacheco will also turn attention to his approximations as objects of study and as an art form, as the author saw them.[25]

On the surface, his anthology *Aproximaciones* appears organized under world literature principles—yet a careful reading of his paratexts shows that Pacheco constantly introduces themes of Indigenous reclaiming of land, rights, and recognition in the face of an enduring colonial logic of translation as embedded in a conflict between the "civilized" and the "barbarous" and as wavering between the violence of nonconsensual occupation and a vital, generative act of generosity that keeps the "body of poetry" alive. The fraught question of how to translate Indigenous texts for a postrevolutionary Mexico goes through cycles of hope and cynicism; I read Pacheco's approximations as performing both sides of that cycle. Gordon Brotherston describes the widespread and lasting influence of the translations by Ángel Garibay of *Cantares mexicanos* and *Poesía nahuatl* (1965–68) or of Miguel León-Portilla's *La visión de los vencidos* (1959) on Mexican letters. He understands their work as a corrective to the culturally biased translations of an earlier generation, especially the nineteenth-century US historian W. H. Prescott, who "had given an ideological twist to the 'laments' of the poet-king Nezahualcóyotl (1402–72), seeing in them covert yearning for Cortés and his religion."[26] Whereas Brotherson reads the translation work of Garibay and León-Portilla as correcting the hegemonic ideological position of previous translations and replacing them with a new and more authentic vision of life for the Nahuatl-speakers of pre-Columbian and colonial times, Ignacio M. Sánchez Prado evaluates this moment of retranslation as still problematic and equally imbricated as other historical moments in a hegemonic process of constructing the Indigenous past to serve the purposes of present-day political realities.[27] For him, these translations are utilized by a state project of identity politics, in which the Mexican state-sponsored imaginary can celebrate an Indigenous past while politically empowering a mestizo present based on a political hegemony that excludes and disenfranchises present-day Indigenous communities.

As a translator, Pacheco negotiates between the less critical position of Brotherston and the more skeptical perspective of Sánchez Prado. He both celebrates the importance of translating from Indigenous languages and also uses those translations to highlight all the cultural baggage projected onto the figure of the Indigenous person: connection with the past, the open wound of colonialism, and the ongoing structural inequalities that disadvantage Indigenous Mexicans—and Indigenous Americans in a range of different national contexts. Pacheco ends his introductory note placing himself in a long line of Indigenous and bicultural translators into Spanish: "Through your humble Mexican interpreter—one more, another in a long chain that began when Fernando de Alva Ixtlixóchitl translated his great-grandfather Nezahualcóyotl's poems into the lyric verse of Fray Luis [de León] and has not been interrupted nor will it cease—the true author of these approximations is the Spanish language."[28] This statement both celebrates the transcultural translation efforts inherent in transforming poetry not just from Nahuatl to Spanish but from an Indigenous literary tradition to the peninsular lyric verse forms of the time—but it also reminds readers of the status of Spanish as a colonial instrument of assimilation. Pacheco places himself in that tradition, self-consciously: he does the same act of shaping Indigenous texts to the measure of poetry in Spanish, but he also invents poems of his own and attributes them to the Apache, introducing heteronym and suspicion into all his translations.

Pacheco ends *Aproximaciones* with "Catorce poemas indígenas de Norteamérica," selected from an English translation anthology by John Bierhorst, *In the Trail of the Wind* (1971). He gives these approximations pride of place and frames them as a "humble homage" to "Indigenous Americans"—yet he also emphasizes self-critique, placing himself as translator inside the "us" who has usurped the power to represent "them," Indigenous people subjected to this repeated historical treatment: "It was not enough to defeat them, dispossess them of their land, exterminate them. They were also converted into a spectacle for our entertainment."[29] These approximations share some of what Brotherston describes as the "corrective" ideology of the Garibay and León-Portilla project—Pacheco's selection and editing of Bierhorst's works reflect this ideology. However, when he adds a pseudotranslation, he critiques the translation project as inevitably an invention, in a way that is closer to Sánchez Prado's position, while also making the reader complicit in his ambivalence. His series of "Catorce poemas" measures the distance between the moment of his translations (1984) and the earlier moment that celebrated the Garibay translations (1965–68) or the translation collection by Bierhorst (1971). The 1960s and 1970s represent a high point in the incorporation of Indigenous poetries into the writing of both US and Mexican poetry.[30] But by 1984, Pacheco cannot have the same celebratory attitude about the translation of Indigenous texts; he can no longer uncritically applaud or participate in cultural recognition of Indigenous people when they were being increasingly exploited through new economic relations with the United States. While his translations present works from North American Indigenous cultures located in territories outside the national boundaries of Mexico, his critique extends to Mexican instrumentalization of Indigenous cultural forms.

Just as his frame places translation on the shaky ground of discourses of power, inside his approximations Pacheco makes no pretense of objectivity or representative choices: his cannibal translations alter his sources significantly, with strategies of repunctuation and fragmentation, to recast prose into poetic lines and to shift meaning. In one example of relineation that demonstrates Pacheco's focus on poetic qualities in the target language, his "Canción de amor de los Kwakiuti" only loosely approximates Bierhorst's "Love Song of a Young Man." Where the English source is stiff and unremarkable, Pacheco uses line breaks to trace a meandering shape on the page, evoking the listlessness of the lovelorn:

Si como,
como el dolor de tu amor, amada.
Si duermo,
sueño el dolor de tu amor, amada.
Si yazgo,
yazgo en el dolor de tu amor, amada.
Dondequiera que voy
piso el dolor de tu amor, amada.[31]

Compared to the prosaic lines of Bierhorst's translation, Pacheco's approximation conveys more emotion through presentation on the page and word choice, making the restless meandering of the lovesick visible and audible, whereas in Bierhorst's version merely repeats:

Whenever I eat, I eat the pain of your love, mistress.
Whenever I get sleepy, I dream of my love, my mistress.
Whenever I lie on my back in the house, I lie on the pain of your love, mistress.
For whenever I walk about, I step on the pain of your love, mistress.[32]

Pacheco's poem sounds more like a song and speaks more to the extremity of love experiences than Bierhorst's version. In Pacheco's version the lines begin with *si* (if), leaving open the possibility that the speaker will not eat or sleep for the pain of this love, whereas Bierhorst's speaker claims to experience the pain of love "whenever I eat." The intensity of lovesickness intensifies for Pacheco's speaker, who will either eat the pain of love or eat nothing and experience the redoubled pain of hunger and love at once. The speaker might even avoid these human needs in effort to escape the pain of love, but that attempt will also be fruitless. Pacheco also ends the poem with a more global expression: *dondequiera que voy* means "wherever I go," not "whenever I walk about," as in Bierhorst's line. The speaker experiences the same pain everywhere and anywhere, rather than only in those moments as detailed in the source text. In addition, his choice of *amada* (beloved) instead of "mistress" crafts a more consistent poetic register in Spanish, rather than the informality of Bierhorst's "get sleepy," which clashes with the euphemistic formality of "mistress."

Even when Pacheco translates without making new line breaks or stabilizing diction, his translations demonstrate the same ideology Brotherston identifies in the translations by Garibay and León-Portilla, to correct the record of previous translations by removing a tone of lament and desire for the oppressor. In his approximation of "Profecía (*Iroqueses*)" Pacheco silently eliminates the end of the poem before it places the collective poetic voice of the Indigenous people in the irretrievable past. Bierhorst ends with the lament confirming their cultural demise, "Here we will gather, here live, and here die."[33] But Pacheco cuts off before the prophesy is fulfilled: "Hace muchos inviernos nuestros sabios ancestros lo predijeron: el monstruo de ojos blancos llegará del oriente. Al avanzar consumirá la tierra. Este monstruo es la raza blanca. La profecía está a punto de cumplirse."[34] He places Indigenous culture in the present rather than in a doomed past.

In Pacheco's most invasive translation choice, he adds a poem of his own creation and attributes it to the Apache. By introducing a pseudotranslation and using the Apache as a heteronym, Pacheco opens his entire anthology to suspicion, implicating even translations with sources in this irreverent act of ventriloquism, and critiquing the vision of a world literature anthology that would make this possible. When Pacheco ascribes this pseudotranslation to the Apache, he also signals the questionable status of that cultural label, which has itself always been a harmful invention, a cultural mistranslation. A term that came into English through Spanish, "the Apache" refers to the Indigenous peoples making their lives on the Great Plains of the US Midwest and Southwest, regions between the United States and Mexico both before and after the Louisiana Purchase. Much like the Carib people, who were branded as cannibals, the "Apache" were defined as the most "bellicose" Indigenous people in the region.[35] Labels given to Indigenous cultures by settler colonizers tend to be fraught mistranslations—or, as in the case of the Apache, pseudotranslations—of what a people called themselves.

The title "Cantos a las corrientes de la tierra" ("Songs for the Currents of the Earth") would signal to suspicious readers an ambiguous authorship: "Apache" evokes arid landscapes, and those familiar with Pacheco's poetry might recognize rivers and flows among his favored lyrical themes. The very word *corriente* also encapsulates the problem of fluctuation and stability germane to literary translation: like a current flowing from its source, a translation changes everything while remaining within the container of a riverbed. Incorporating multiple opposites, *corriente* in Spanish can mean both "stylish, up-to-date" or "common, cheap," both constant movement and a stable pathway or trajectory.[36] European powers also exploited the currents of the earth for global navigation. *Corriente* encapsulates the fable of Herodotus: one cannot step into the same river twice; the current signifies both constant movement and consistent direction. The title contains the elegant concept that even things that do not appear to have any motion or "currents" actually are in constant flux. The poem reads:

Cantos a las corrientes de la tierra (*Apaches*) 1 El manso arroyo esbelto, convertido en torrente, alaba con su bramar tumultuoso la generosidad de la Madre Lluvia.	(Songs to the Earth's Currents (*Apaches*) 1 The tame and slender stream, transformed into a torrent, praises with its tumultuous howl the generosity of Mother Rain.
2 No he de volver a verte, río. Seguirás fluyendo sin mí, sin mí. Tan sólo otra mirada que se añadió a tus aguas.[37]	2 I need not return to see you, river. You will continue flowing without me, without me. Only another look added to your waters.)

Pacheco's pseudotranslation uses repetition and negation to create an unstable poetic speaker primarily known through absence, movement, loss, and haunting. The repetition of "sin mí, sin mí" evokes the repeated stepping into the river, a different river each time, where every repetition implies a difference. It also speaks through a doubled or tripled poetic voice. The anthology by Bierhorst encouraged a nonliterary reading of these works even as he presented them as poems—he claimed the "us" or the "we" spoke as a collective voice of the "culture" passing knowledge through generations.[38] When Pacheco writes that the Apaches wrote this line "without me, without me," however, he creates a multiplicity of positions for the poetic speaker of this work, and implicitly for all of his other approximations. The line imagines a river left behind by an Indigenous speaker absented through forced displacement or extermination, or a poem abandoned by its author, who has left behind his creation, signed it with an anonymous name, and disguised it as a translation. Reading the line as a lyric construction relates the poem to the long history of other elegiac poetic works expressing the nostalgia for a lost home, the *saudade* of the navigator always looking out to sea. The collectivity of this poetic speaker, therefore, would include opposing figures that mutually exclude one another—the native and the traveler, the individual poetic speaker and the expression of collective sentiment. Through pseudotranslation, Pacheco succeeds in constructing works where texts matter more than authors—yet not in the ahistorical manner of New Criticism. For Pacheco, the historical context matters more than the biographical authors, and he frames his approximations in the historical embeddedness of the Spanish language as processed through the experience of linguistic and cultural colonialism in Mexico.

CANNIBAL TRANSLATIONS REORIENTING THE SO-CALLED WILD WEST

Using the mouthpiece of an invented Brazilian heteronym, Pacheco makes a similar critique of Mexican ideologies of racial hierarchies and the conventional images circulated by the Hollywood western. Aurelio Azevedo Oliveira (1938–81), Uruguayan born of Brazilian parents and paradoxically "perfectly bilingual, he never wrote a single line that was not in Brazilian Portuguese," serves Pacheco as the mask of a Brazilian poet exactly of his generation who shares his political concerns.[39] In the "posthumous" chapbook *Bugraria* (1983), which Pacheco "translates" in full, he takes his title from the derogatory Portuguese word *bugre*. Referring to an urbanized or semiassimilated Indigenous person, depicted as attempting but failing to gain the social capital of the occupying colonizing culture, this word recalls a history of dehumanizing language used to describe Indigenous peoples after forced displacement. Pacheco glosses the offensive word *bugre* as a Brazilian equivalent of *naco*, the term used in Mexico to express similar racialized judgment, revealing that he is not translating from the "Brazilian Portuguese" but inventing a voice through which to talk about Mexico.[40] He also borrows from a longer tradition of Brazilian literature focused on urban poverty: the full name of this heteronym, Aurelio Azevedo Oliveira, recalls the naturalist Aluísio Azevedo (1857–1913), author of Brazilian classics *O mulato* (1881) and *O cortiço* (1890). The latter novel depicts social realities of a Rio de Janeiro neighborhood where Portuguese immigrants, Indigenous people, the formerly enslaved, and mixed-race people live in close quarters. Pacheco's heteronymous Azevedo does not take the naturalist, localized approach of his namesake; instead, he writes caustic poetry taking a global vision of struggles against social disenfranchisement. For example, "Rue Vaugirard" is about the hope of a change in social and economic relations, which continues to be unfulfilled, from May 1968 in Paris to October 1968 in Mexico.[41]

In the poem "Western," the mass-produced Hollywood trope of "cowboys and Indians" figures to critique creative conventions, in which various forms of art-making—from a crowd-pleasing movie to poetry and its translation—all participate in upholding a limited and stereotyped image that supports the shared Western Hemispheric experience of cultural genocide of Indigenous peoples. Pacheco already referred to this poem to introduce his translations from the Bierhorst collection. By connecting the Bierhorst translations with a poem about Hollywood movies, Pacheco implicates the former in the same project as the latter: setting up and perpetuating a series of genre conventions that clearly divide the good from the bad, the civilized from the savage. The poem "Western" sets a scenario that asks why and how the moviegoing audience—and by extension the reader—became so prone, so accustomed to this image.

> Y a tal punto estamos compenetrados
> con la presentación de un mundo ajeno
> que somos los defensores de aquel fuerte
> erguido en tierra apache: somos los cruzados
> de la última frontera: los depredadores
> de esta parte de América: la nuestra[42]
>
> (And we are complicit to such an extent
> with the representation of this alien world
> that we are the defenders of that fort
> erected in Apache land: we are the crusaders
> on the last frontier: the predators
> of this part of América: ours)

The audience of children, *compenetrados* (complicit, in rapport with, identifying with) this stereotyped presentation of a *mundo ajeno* (alien world), cannot see outside the racist frame of the film to the reality of Indigenous experience covered over by the conventions of the Hollywood Western, projected onto Indigenous Americans and circulated globally.

Sin convención no hay arte: todos sabemos
que en ese instante va a escucharse el clarín
los jinetes azules llegarán a salvarnos[43]

(Without convention, there is no art: we all know
that at any moment we will hear the bugle call
the blue-uniformed horsemen will ride in to save us)

Pacheco invokes convention in two key ways. First, he reproduces the widespread, damaging discourse of barbarism versus civilization. Second, he generalizes the concept that conventions are always necessary to produce art. These two perspectives on convention implicate Pacheco's own poetic practice and that of any translator. By convention, we must believe that a source text exists when we are reading something labeled a translation. Yet this pseudotranslation attacks that convention both structurally and within the text of the poem that performs the use of conventions to encode racialized scripts, hierarchies, and stereotypes.

In the final stanza, the speaker erases all the previous markers of place and time, transposing the conventions into wider and wider geographies until the frame itself breaks down:

Inesperadamente no hay clarín ni película
no hay fuerte en tierra apache: sólo favelas
en torno a Río como un arco de fuego:
O quizá es lo contrario y aún seguimos
en aquel viejo cine:
la multitud de apaches son los pobres del mundo:
De repente se clava
una flecha incendiaria en nuestro asiento.[44]

(Unexpectedly there is no bugle or movie
no fort in Apache territory: only favelas
around Rio like a ring of fire:
Or perhaps it is the opposite and we are still there
in that old theater:
the Apache multitude is the world's poor:
Suddenly our seat
is pierced by a flaming arrow.)

Pacheco's heteronym Azevedo Oliveira expands the image from the burning fort on screen to the favelas around Rio de Janeiro to all the poor of the world, collapsing the security of artistic convention. At the end of the pseudotranslation, the use of *nuestro asiento* (our seat) implicates readers along with the audience members in the poem in their position occupying a shared seat of power, identified with those who consume the conventional spectacle of the western as entertainment—or the comforting conventions of poetry, translation, or world literature. "Flecha" can be read as a weapon of revolt or as an instrument for writing, implicating both poetry and translation into the critique of convention.[45] As a genre with its own conventions, poetry has not always been as democratic as Pacheco wants to make it, as he shows through his approximations. "Western" tends to conform to line lengths of seven, eleven, and fourteen syllables—and the poem most notably turns to these classic structures of Iberian Baroque lyric poetry precisely when the speaker claims that "we are the defenders of that fort / erected in Apache territory," implying that poets and translators participate in the conventions upholding this invading, colonizing force. While Pacheco does not resolve these concerns, he does use heteronyms, pseudotranslations, and approximations that never claim to reach the target but instead maintain a posture of active interrogation in the face of the construction of cultural authority. The genre of the approximation can be flexible enough to include works that Pacheco wrote himself but does not claim—works that allow him to ventriloquize other poetic discourses and critique the language politics of translations for a world literature anthology.

THE MEXICAN PAST OF T. S. ELIOT'S AMERICAN MIDWEST IN PACHECO'S NOTES

Pacheco does not just use the device of heteronym in the cannibal translation anthology *Aproximaciones*. A lifelong reader and translator of T. S. Eliot, Pacheco annotates his versions of Eliot in such a way as to use the author as a heteronym, adding extensive notes to *Four Quartets* reminiscent of Eliot's own notes to *The Waste Land*—in short, Pacheco translates Eliot as though wearing his persona. These notes question the nature of the Mississippi River as a "border" or a "frontier" and the ideologies of racial superiority and US Manifest Destiny encoded in that space.

After publishing a celebrated translation of Eliot's *Four Quartets* in 1989, Pacheco significantly revised this work, adding extensive annotations over two decades later, publishing his new versions in the prominent cultural magazine *Letras Libres* in 2011 and 2014, the last year of his life.[46] These annotated approximations represent what Helen Vendler calls a "last look" back through his poetic itinerary.[47] The belated yet extensive revision work on his Eliot translations affirms Pacheco's placement of his approximations on par with his own "original" poetry; the paratextual additions confirm his playful and pointed willingness to use an author's voice for his own purposes.

The provenance and value of the explanatory notes in the first published edition of *The Waste Land* represent an intractable discussion in Eliot scholarship: where some see revelatory paratextual information, others see a distracting addition.[48] Pacheco's notes share with Eliot's the fertile mixture of useful citation that help readers discover the poem by explicating sources and other notes that are obscurantist red herrings, tangents and trivia providing little interpretive guidance. Pacheco makes the boundary between translation and source text more porous; the relevance of Eliot to Mexican literature is more direct, and the importation of Mexicanisms or other references to the Spanish language appears more a matter of excavating connections that were buried and forgotten within the poem rather than importing localisms or "domesticating" Eliot for Mexico.

Pacheco's annotations dwell on the sources of the source text (such as the Spanish San Juan de la Cruz) but also problematize the US geography depicted by the Anglo-American modernist. In his annotated approximation of "The Dry Salvages," Pacheco transforms some of Eliot's geographical references. Conflating spaces and times even more vertiginously than his source poem does, he expands on the landscape evoked by Eliot's title "The Dry Salvages." The explanatory note that Eliot resisted adding to the source text asserts the origin of that place-name as a homophonic, or sound-based translation from French.[49] Eliot's note reads: "The Dry Salvages—presumably *les trois sauvages*—is a small group of rocks, with a beacon, off the N.E. coast of Cape Ann, Massachusetts. *Salvages* is pronounced to rhyme with *assuages*."[50] His gloss on pronunciation emphasizes the place-name as a unit of poetry, and Eliot takes pains to distance his title from the English word "savages." In the first appearance of this note in the fourth manuscript, Eliot wrote that it rhymes with "rampages," but then changed that to "assuages" in the proofs. While both words provide the homophonic information, the word "rampages" relates to the semantic field of "savages," while "assuages" relates to "salvages."[51] With this edit, Eliot attempts to protect the image of a craggy New England coastline from that of the "savage" inhabitants. Conversely, Pacheco's annotation directly refers to what he calls *los pieles rojas* or "redskins," naming the "savages" that Eliot avoided mentioning: "In the seafaring dialect of New England, they call the rocks that stand out even at high tide 'dry.' Because of the danger they represent, navigators called this formation 'savage' because the stones evoked the danger of the 'redskins.' George Williams points out that, thanks to his lighthouse, the 'three savages become salvages: means of salvation against shipwreck.'"[52] Pacheco provides precisely the explanation that Eliot's note eschews: where Eliot downplays the "savage" in the *trois salvages*, even insisting on a specific pronunciation to assure that distance, Pacheco's approximation puts several savages back into the poem through his annotations.

Pacheco further transforms the spaces depicted in "The Dry Salvages" when he repositions the Mississippi River as depicted within the US literary canon. The Mississippi River in Eliot's poem is a transporter of commerce and a frontier marking the East–West expansion of the nation into an empty wasteland. In Pacheco's cannibal translation, the same Mississippi represents a perpetrator of human trafficking of enslaved people and a contested border between the United States and its unacknowledged or exterminated neighbors. Pacheco's annotations place another coordinate on the map: the South. In Pacheco's Eliot, the Mississippi River traces the North–South routes of the slave trade and marks the memory of the territorial expansion of the United States into what was Mexico prior to the 1803 Louisiana Purchase.

Eliot describes the Mississippi River as a "strong brown god," already evoking a global and multiracial spiritual figure. But Pacheco transforms the significance of that river when he draws attention to its diverse meanings for different observers. The Mississippi River represents a frontier from the Anglocentric US perspective that sees the "wild West" as an uninhabited expanse—but for Mexicans and Indigenous people living in that Western region, the river might represent a border instead. While *frontera* can carry both meanings in Spanish, Pacheco's annotation makes it clear that in his approximation the river is a "border" marking two regions with settled communities before the Louisiana Purchase, whereas in Eliot's source text it is a "frontier" between a place, the United States, and an empty wasteland.

> I do not know much about gods; but I think that the river
> Is a strong brown god—sullen, untamed and intractable,

Patient to some degree, at first recognised as a frontier;
Useful, untrustworthy, as a conveyor of commerce;
Then only a problem confronting the builder of bridges.
The problem once solved, the brown god is almost forgotten
By the dwellers in cities—ever, however, implacable,
Keeping his seasons and rages, destroyer, reminder
Of what men choose to forget.[53]

No sé mucho de dioses, pero creo que el río
Es un dios pardo y fuerte,
Hosco, intratable, indómito,
Paciente hasta cierto punto,
Al principio reconocido como frontera;
Útil, poco de fiar como transportador del   comercio.
Después solo un problema para los constructores de puentes.
Ya resuelto el problema
Queda casi olvidado el gran dios pardo
Por quienes viven en ciudades
—Sin embargo, es implacable siempre,
Fiel a sus estaciones y sus cóleras,
Destructor que recuerda
Cuanto prefieren olvidar los humanos.[54]

One effective and poignant choice Pacheco makes in this approximation of Eliot places more weight on the word *comercio* (commerce) through spacing, bringing home the disturbing history of the river. By leaving a gap or pause in the line, he delays the revelation of what is transported on this river, inviting the reader to pause to remember that one of the major motors of commerce for the river was the system of chattel slavery.

Then, in his annotations, Pacheco takes the reader back through the history of the landscape as it exchanged hands between imperial powers of Europe. His note redefines the Mississippi River of the landscape in the first section of Eliot's poem as the border between what would be Mexico and the United States, between two places rather than merely the frontier of the United States in a westward expansion into a wasteland:

> *Only a problem confronting the builder of bridges.* The Eads Bridge (1867–1874), made entirely of iron, was considered

> one of the new wonders of the world. . . . St. Louis, Missouri was named in honor of Louis XV, occupied by the French and then the Spanish. In 1803, Napoleon sold it to the United States as a part of the Louisiana Purchase that doubled the initial territory of the new country. When Eliot was born, St. Louis—border between the Anglo-Saxon world and the "savage west" of the Indians and Mexicans—already had 450,000 inhabitants.[55]

Pacheco's reference to Eads Bridge likely comes from Gardner, who traces Eliot's representation of the Mississippi as a "brown god" to his introduction to *Huckleberry Finn* published in 1950. In that introduction, Eliot connects the Mississippi River to the historical trauma of that landscape, to its complicity moving enslaved people downriver as a part of the brutal plantation slavery system. But Pacheco also frames the river as the boundary between "the Anglo-Saxon world and the 'savage west' of the Indians and Mexicans," conflating the space of the poem's title—the savage Atlantic coast—with the new frontier of the savage West. Where Eliot's poem connects the New England coast with the Mississippi River at St. Louis through biographical connection and memory, Pacheco conflates these two spaces and historical traumas even further through the repetition of the word *salvaje* in relation to the Mississippi.[56] When he repeats the word *salvaje* in his gloss about the river, he ties together these two geographies in a new way, replacing what for Eliot was a simple East-West vector, a frontier marking westward expansion into empty territory. In Pacheco's cannibal translation, this frontier becomes a border that also marks a North-South relationship, considering the United States from the Mexican side and from the perspective of Indigenous cultures whose land sovereignty was foreclosed on by multiple nations that refuse to see them.[57] Reading world literature through his lens, we must contend with the settler-colonial framework written into the languages of these geographies.

POROUS PROSE, ANTICRITICISM, AND UNTRANSLATIONS BY AUGUSTO DE CAMPOS

Where cannibal translation techniques allow Pacheco to anthologize world literature centered on a complex ambivalence around the role of translation in any placement of Indigenous cultures within Mexican,

Spanish American, and Western Hemispheric literary spheres, Augusto de Campos also incorporates the Brazilian canon into his parallel anthology, as an innovative translation zone and a source of world literature. My first chapter studied Augusto's project focused on E. E. Cummings, which began in the mid-1950s and produced his concept of *intradução*, a lifelong engagement with a single author. I end by analyzing his anthology *O anticrítico* (1986) and another genre of translation he explores: *prosa porosa* (porous prose). In this eclectic and sparsely studied volume, Augusto applies a unique mode of translation as criticism to a range of figures in world literature, where each section opens with a porous-prose introduction to the author and poses an argument about their work, followed by a hyperfragmented translation that illustrates concepts explored in the essay-poem.[58]

Read as a whole, this volume counters world literature in three main ways: centering translation traditions rather than transparently presenting works in translation; emphasizing concrete possibilities within works that did not have visual elements; and including Brazilian literatures as source texts also in need of the porous-prose style of translation. In the mood of the musical remix, other versions, translations, or reactions are layered together. His anthology includes the world literature classics Dante, John Donne, and *The Ruba'iyát of Omar Khayyám* by Edward Fitzgerald; fellow minimalists Emily Dickinson, Marcel Duchamp, and John Cage; language innovators Lewis Carroll, Stéphane Mallarmé, Paul Verlaine, Gertrude Stein; the avant-garde poets Vicente Huidobro and Oliveiro Girondo; and Brazilian literary figures João Cabral de Melo Neto and Gregório de Matos. With the Brazilian authors, he magnifies the presence of subaltern figures and aesthetic traits that have not always lent themselves to translation. In their fragmented style, Augusto's translations tend to be minimalist and condensed, unlike Haroldo's expansive and completist translation projects.[59] Gonzalo Aguilar draws this same distinction between the poetic projects of the two brothers: where Haroldo tends toward "serial expansion," Augusto pursues "minimalist synthesis."[60]

While I read this minimalist, fragmented anthology as a critique of translation practices of world literature, Augusto presents it primarily as a challenge to literary criticism, where he asserts that his translations themselves are a form of critical engagement. In his introduction, "Antes do anti," Augusto defines *prosa porosa* as an alternative route to literary criticism, drawing from Buckminster Fuller's term "ventilated prose."[61] He insists that although "many thought they were poetry," these works were actually "porous prose," which he started writing and publishing in journals in 1971.[62] Defending the indeterminacy of this genre, he writes: "If, despite my best intentions, poetry leaked in and contaminated this so-called prose, it is just the deformation of the avid amateur, still preferable to the professional deformation produced by the impenetrable language of the critic thanks to the imposition and imposterism of seriousness."[63] The Portuguese *amador*, which I have translated here as "amateur," also connotes "fan," capturing the pose of the supportive, creative reader as opposed to the seriousness of the professional critic. Where Pacheco claimed a "savage" position for his irreverent translation games—or claimed the collective and responsibility-eschewing position of anonymity—Augusto uplifts the pose of the amateur, emphasizing lightness, flight, informality, and playfulness as opposed to the heaviness or self-restraint of the sober literary critic. Through the porous-prose introductions to each author, he explores the suggestion he attributes to John Cage: "'The best critique of a poem is a poem.'"[64] Throughout the volume, translation intertwines with criticism to produce "criticism via creative translation": playful, cannibal translations that respond to familiar literary works.

All of his fourteen entries have their own "aim" or argument, but they share an approach, a vector that points in the opposite direction from an unmediated presentation typical of the invisible translation work in world literature anthologies. For example, as I have argued elsewhere, his versions of Huidobro and Girondo and their porous-prose introduction titled "a contra-boom da poesia" perform an alternative trajectory for a translingual Latin American literary history rooted in a shared avant-garde tradition in order to circumnavigate the surrealist moment and better incorporate Brazilian poetics.[65] In other cases he locates unusual precursors for his concrete aesthetics, as when he reads John Donne as a concrete poet, emphasizing the visual and sonic redoubling of letters in "The Expiration."[66] For his more obvious progenitor Lewis Carroll, he untranslates *Doublets* (1880) not by translating the semantic content of his source text but by transforming the word game into a page filled with fourteen new "doublets" in Portuguese (see fig. 11).

The rules of the game are clear and inviting: one word transforms into its opposite, one letter at a time, where the intervening words must also signify something, but only have an oblique and arbitrary connection to those before and after. Once again, as with Cummings, Augusto shows interest in breaking language down to the level of individual letters, a poetic procedure only a cannibal translation technique can approximate. I highlight here two examples based on key words for

DOUBLETS

LONGE	FOGO	CÉU	MANHÃ
monge	foro	cem	manha
monte	fora	com	manda
ponte	fura	cor	mando
ponto	aura	dor	bando
porto	agra	dar	bardo
PERTO	ÁGUA	MAR	tardo
			TARDE
			ta*rdo
CERTO	DEUS	SIM	tordo
curto	meus	vim	mordo
furto	maus	vem	morto
farto	mais	nem	morte
falto	cais	neo	norte
FALSO	CAOS	NÃO	NOITE
TERRA	LIXO	BEM	
torra	luxo	sem	PRESO
torta	luto	som	prego
morta	puto	sol	prega
morte	puro	sal	praga
MARTE	OURO	MAL	traga
			trava
			toava
		SOL	toara
		sul	tiara
PROSA	TUDO	sua	fiara
presa	lodo	LUA	fibra
preta	lado	loa	libra
poeta	nado	soa	livra
POEMA	NADA	SOL	LIVRE

Fig. 11. Augusto de Campos, "DOUBLETS," inspired by Lewis Carroll's *Doublets: A Word Puzzle* (1879), in *O anticrítico* (1986). © Augusto de Campos.

Augusto's own poetry, accompanied by my own semantic (i.e., noncannibal) translations:

LIXO	(TRASH
luxo	luxury
luto	mourning
puto	boyslut
puro	pure
OURO	GOLD

PROSA	PROSE
presa	prey
preta	black
poeta	poet
POEMA[67]	POEM)

Beginning with a reference to his famous concrete poem "lixoluxo" (1965), this new "Doublet" moves from *lixo* (trash) to *ouro* (gold); the second recalls his initial introduction for the volume by revisiting the porous nature of any boundary between "prose" and "poem." Where other translators may have ignored the "nonsense" poems of Carroll in favor of other works, Augusto draws on them as generative practices, crafting a full new page of "doublets" in the style of Carroll, and inviting readers to play along.

Augusto not only translates from other translations, just as Pacheco did; he also emphasizes his retranslations as a response to prior translations rather than claiming a direct relationship with an "original." For example, in the chronological organization of his world literature anthology, he places his translation of *The Ruba'iyát of Omar Khayyám* not in the order of the eleventh-century lifetime of the "original" author but in that of Edward Fitzgerald, the nineteenth-century English translator, the author of Augusto's source text, credited with recirculating the "astronomer-poet of Persia" in his verse translation. Even here, he zooms in on an anagram and creates a concrete poem out of a lyric verse in his piece titled "homage to edward fitzgerald" (see fig. 12).[68]

The essay poem and the translation focus on the English text and the challenge it poses to re-create anagrams, alliteration, and repetitive rhyme. He claims that the Fitzgerald text "solidifies signifiers and signifieds / through an anagramatic chain."[69] Along with Carroll's *Doublets*, *The Ruba'iyát* becomes a precursor to Brazilian concrete poetry in Augusto's anthology. Far from the domestication process typical of a world literature anthology, he performs the hypervisible and creative remixing of the cannibal translator.

In the case of Dante, Augusto does not simply update other Portuguese translations—he places himself within a tradition of Brazilian translators to argue for specific translation values that determined his approach. In his porous-prose essay poem "dante: um corpo que cai," he compares his translation of the final line of canto 5 to the solutions other translators have found to render this key line in Portuguese.[70] First, he turns that final line into a concrete poem that traces an arc of homage to edward fitzgerald

S

E

I

L I F E

F

Fig. 12. Augusto de Campos, "homage to edward fitzgerald," from *The Rubá'iyát of Omar Khayyám*, in *O anticrítico* (1986). © Augusto de Campos.

descent down the page, the words "and I fell like a dead body falls," first in his Portuguese and then the Italian source:

e
caí
como
corpo
morto
cai

e
caddi
come
corpo
morto
cade[71]

Ignoring the Portuguese translators of Dante to cite three other Brazilian versions—Xavier Pinheiro's from 1888, Dante Milano's from the 1950s, and Cristiano Martins's from 1976—Augusto emphasizes the particular translation vector of Dante in Brazil.[72] He points out the difference between his translation and theirs, and the consequences of a single translation choice. Where they chose to reverse the order of the line, and end the canto on the adjective *morto* (dead), he instead hews closer to the source text by ending with the verb "fall":

"e tombei, como tomba corpo morto"	("and I tumbled down, as tumble bodies dead"
(xavier pinheiro)	(xavier pinheiro)
"e tombei como tomba um corpo morto"	"and I tumbled like tumbles a body dead"
(dante milano)	(dante milano)
"e caí, como cai um corpo morto"	"and I fell, like falls a body dead"
(cristiano martins)	(cristiano martins)
o desejo	the desire
de chegar mais perto	to approximate more closely
da precisão especular do original	the reflective precision of the original
. . . .	. . . .
me levou a traduzir o canto V do *inferno*	had me translate canto V of the *inferno*
de trás para diante	from back to front
a partir do último verso[73]	starting from the last line)

To achieve the falling syntax he admires in the source text, he must determine the rhyme scheme of the *terza rima* from the final word, *cai* (fall). By ending with *morto* rather than *cai*, unlike his own version, these three prior translations could not be read as concrete poems, with a descending arc landing on the verb "fall." Recalling Augusto's fascination with the poem "l(a" by E. E. Cummings, which dramatizes a falling leaf with the vertical layout of letters, Augusto introduces into Dante not only his own concrete aesthetics but also those of Cummings. Furthermore, the "sustain" of the arrow shot by Dante and traveling through older translations remains a part of his own iteration—the new insight to translate from the last word backward rises out of seeing the example of other Brazilian translators and choosing a different vector.

One way to read world literature includes an examination of the paths it has traveled; Augusto retranslates this fragment of a classic and builds a place for the translation tradition within his new version, from the present back to the first Brazilian translator.

In all these cases of untranslation-as-retranslation, Augusto emphasizes the visual and insists on the role of repetition and active readership in the making of a critical world literature. The opening work in his challenging anthology in fact untranslates from another Brazilian poet and salutes the idea of a "contrary reader"—a reader positioned both against and in favor of the text or the writer. Dedicated to João Cabral de Melo Neto (1920–99), Augusto's poem "a joão cabral: agrestes" honors a member of the Brazilian "Generation of '45," a poetic moment marked by a return to form and bridging the explosive experimentalism of *modernismo* with the visual condensation of *concretismo*.[74] Melo Neto was prized for his tight-knit formal verse, a return to traditional structure after the rupture of the avant-garde. Augusto's poem represents a counter-gift for the poem Melo Neto dedicated to Augusto to introduce his contemporaneous volume of poetry *Agrestes* (1985). In a strict octosyllabic meter, Melo Neto's metapoetic dedicatory poem explicates its own structure, the steel-like formal precision it performs, and places itself opposed to Augusto's poetry. But it ends by imagining that Augusto—this contrary reader—will nevertheless be his best reader, even though Augusto's own concrete poetry actively writes against the formal structures of Melo Neto's poetics. The poem asks and then answers a crucial question: Who does the poet write for? Why does Melo Neto dedicate his book to Augusto, someone who crafts such a different kind of poetry, "a quem faz uma poesia / de distinta liga de aço?" (to the one who makes a poetry / of a different steel alloy?).[75] In the concluding lines of his poem, Melo Neto imagines that only "o leitor contra, maugrado" (the contrary, frustrated reader) will "know how to read / revolutionary poets with acuity."[76] Augusto's reply also elevates the role of readership from a position of contrariness—and performs the same action, drawing most of its vocabulary from Melo Neto's piece but cutting away many elements of its source poem while also leaving behind the key concept: that a poet's preferred reader might be those who are most resistant, contrary, but active.

In Augusto's reciprocal gift, an homage poem both concrete and in a lyric fixed form, he celebrates what he has learned from Melo Neto with a skewed sonnet, a fourteen-line rhymed poem with lines of only four words (see fig. 13).

uma	fala	tão	faca
fratura	tão	ex	posta
tão	ácida	tão	aço
osso	tão	osso	só
que eu	procuro	e não	acho
o ad	verso	do que	faço
o	concreto	é o	outro
e	não	encontro	nem
palavras	para	o	abraço
senão	as	do	aprendiz
o	menos	ante o	sem
que	só aqui	contra	diz
nunca	houve	um	leitor
contra	mais	a	favor

Fig. 13. Augusto de Campos, "a joão cabral: agrestes," in *O anticrítico* (1986). © Augusto de Campos.

Although Augusto will later incorporate this poem his collection *Despoesía* (1994) grouped with a set of *profilogramas*, or brief poetic profiles of other poets, it was composed for this cannibal translation anthology and can be read within that practice.[77] Augusto's concrete poem functions as an untranslation because it draws almost entirely from the favored semantic field of his predecessor: the words *fala*, *faca*, *fratura*, *ácida*, and *aço* (speak, knife, fracture, acid, and steel) echo Melo Neto's poem; the final line in the figure of "um leitor contra" (a contrary reader) does the same. From left to right, a literal translation would read:

> such knife-like speech
> fracture so ex posed
> so acidic so steel
> bone so only bone
> that I seek and don't find
> ad verse to what I do

concrete is the other
and I can't discover any
words for the embrace
except those of the apprentice
the less before without
that only here contradicts
never was there a reader
against more in favor.

As a noun, *agrestes* refers to fallow fields, rustic woodlands; as an adjective, it evokes uncultivated roughness or even wildness—the titles of Melo Neto's volume and Augusto's homage poem both imply *poemas agrestes*, poems that are unplowed, simple, unrefined. However, the visual impact of Augusto's four cultivated lines running down the page evokes four rows of tilled soil. In this untranslation of his contemporary, Augusto plays with writing his version of a fixed-verse form that he himself would never use. Much like Rosario Castellanos describes, translators may take pleasure inhabiting a style they would have been ashamed to actually adopt. Augusto ends with the line that most directly cites Melo Neto: "nunca houve um leitor / contra mais a favor" (never was there a reader / against more in favor). While they may have opposing approaches, they share a similar goal: forging revolutionized language with steel-like precision. The cannibal translation Augusto gifts back to Melo Neto shows how he can match the aesthetic but also destroy it and incorporate it into his own. Augusto's contrary readership finds and emphasizes through fragmentation the kernel of "revolutionized" experimental language inside Melo Neto—and inside the other texts included in *O Anticrítico*. From the first poem in this anthology, Augusto presents a world literature aimed toward a critical readership, the "contrary reader."

INTRALINGUAL UNTRANSLATIONS AND SUBALTERN FIGURES IN THE BRAZILIAN CANON

Augusto's translation approach draws in both translation history and a critical consideration of the Brazilian literary canon. His "arte final para gregório" crafts a visual poem out of a verse by Gregório de Matos, and his essay-poem introduction emphasizes alternative, forgotten fragments of the Baroque poet's work. Matos figures for Augusto and Haroldo as the suppressed origin of the Brazilian canon, the "first experimental cannibal" who dared to cut up pieces of sonnets by the early modern Spanish poet Luis de Góngora to reassemble them after his own fashion and explode the Iberian poetic tradition from within.[78] Augusto dissects and operates on Matos in a similar fashion (see fig. 14).

Augusto calls this poem a "blow-up" that emphasizes the "rich linguistic texture of the poet."[79] Putting Augusto in dialogue with Pacheco emphasizes the way his untranslation zooms in on an indefensible racist image in Matos and blows up this cruel satire to draw attention to the problematic racial and gender hierarchies at the core of this founding figure in Brazilian literature.[80] The first two repeated stanzas roughly translate as "prickly feet covered up with silk / goat hair powdered with marble," an image of an animalized racial other dressed up in the fine trappings of luxury and authority.[81] In his essay-poem, Augusto provides the context that Matos's poem satirizes the figure "Marinícolas," a leader of Bahian society, homophobically caricatured here as a *ninfo gentil* (genteel nymph) and as a racialized other, a mixed-race Indigenous and Portuguese person.[82] Augusto insists that, while scholars and editors never fail to put Matos in dialogue with the categories of Baroque poetry of *culteranismo* or sacred verse, his satirical verse is given short shrift: it is included in just a few examples, only "mild satires" that are "soft or

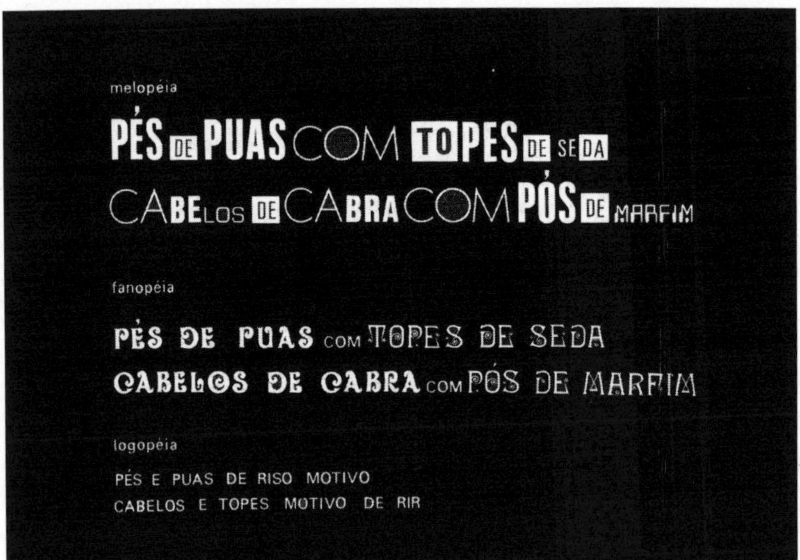

Fig. 14. Augusto de Campos, "arte final para gregório," in *O anticrítico* (1986). © Augusto de Campos.

softened by suppression and reticence."[83] Augusto also points out that this is only one version of this text, the one that has "prickly feet" (*pés de puas*), whereas other versions have "flea's feet" (*pés de pulgas*). By including both animalized versions of this poem in his analytical porous-prose analysis, he emphasizes that there is a proliferation in Matos's poetry of racist language that has not been contended with in the scholarly work surrounding this Baroque poet—where the most complex but also unsavory and violent portions of his work are erased from his body of work. Augusto's visually striking untranslation magnifies aspects of Matos's poetry that are often underexamined or even actively erased from the scholarly tradition—the anti-Black, racist, homophobic, and sexist comedy in his satirical poems and the circulation of his work as anonymous broadsides posted in public spaces around the city. By "blowing up" this racist strain within Matos, he emphasizes the need for Brazilian literature to recognize and work through this part of the canon.

The title, "arte final para gregório," refers to the process of finalizing visual qualities before sending a text to the printer. This process has intrigued Augusto since the earliest days of the Noigandres group, in which the poets used an experimental technique for producing multicolored prints using a movable-type printing system. Furthermore, his use of different fonts and sizes recalls the cutups taken from newsprint of a ransom note or other anonymous and perhaps threatening missive. In much the same way that some of Matos's poems were pasted around the city of Bahia, anonymously denigrating various public figures, Augusto's untranslation fills the page with a dramatic black background, accusing the reader and the poet alike with its anti-Black language. This visual translation draws out a moment in which the popular-culture satirical voice and material of Matos is elevated over and outside his Baroque form. In his porous-prose introduction, Augusto meditates on the different layers of Matos's reception, pointing out that the established critical apparatus brought to bear on his work emphasizes his sacred and lyrical poetry and analyzes it within the established categories of *conceptista* and *culturanista* Iberian poetics. The satirical poetry, however, tends to be segregated from the rest:

> generally
> relegated to the kitchen
> far from the anterooms
> where they hang
> the pious sonnets.[84]

Although he does not reject any one approach, Augusto does point out the limitations of the erudite literary critical tools of evaluating this Brazilian Baroque writer within the Iberian poetic tradition, or the scholarly historical tools of debating through comparison of manuscripts and codices which of the poems attributed to Matos "belong" in his corpus. These methods miss the musical, comical, and popular elements embodied in Matos's work—elements that Augusto's untranslation draws out by "blowing up" these two couplets characteristic of what he calls the *musa crioula* (creole muse) or *musa praguejadora* (swearing, cursing muse) to do justice to Matos's satirical poems.[85]

Nevertheless, Augusto does obliquely anticipate the racialized qualities of the works excised from Matos's corpus when he describes them as "relegated to the kitchen." This phrase evokes the ongoing Brazilian cultural legacy of the social division between enslavers and those they enslaved. Sociologist Gilberto Freyre defines various spatial divisions that produce and reinforce segregation through strict boundaries between the *casa grande* (big house) and the *senzala* (fields). With his cannibal translation, Augusto not only draws a critical eye to the anti-Black racist language at the center of his own literary tradition; he also accuses the canon-makers of reproducing a problematic racialized division, elevating only the more "pious" elements of Matos's poetry and censoring or rejecting from anthologies those parts of his works that show the homophobic, anti-Black racist language embedded in Brazilian poetry. This "blow-up" of one stanza emphasizes a form of readership that would be unafraid to look again at the underemphasized parts of a canonical figure. In the Michelangelo Antonioni film *Blow-Up* (1966), based on the Julio Cortázar short story "Las babas del diablo" (1959), a photographer accidentally witnesses a crime by photographing it in the remote background. The focus and zooming-in action Augusto applies to Matos here, which follows the movie's title and plot, magnifies the crime of despicable and animalizing language for racial and sexual minorities.[86] Just as Pacheco creates a Brazilian heteronym to zoom in on racist language in Mexico from an oblique angle, Augusto blows up this section of Matos to ask how the literary tradition—and Brazilian culture writ large—has failed to contend with its own anti-Black history.

Augusto deploys the same techniques of selection, reduction, and reconfiguration in a series of untranslations he creates from a classic of the Brazilian canon, *Os sertões* (1902) by Euclides da Cunha. In this geographical-historical essay on the War of Canudos (1896–97) in the Brazilian *sertão*, or northeastern backlands, da Cunha reports on the dramatic rise of charismatic leader Antonio Conselheiro and the violent suppression of his community by the Brazilian army. His dense naturalist description, peppered with concepts from eugenics and liberalism, both connects the aridity of the land with racialized "mental defects" of the rebel leader and his followers and decries the violence with which the state massacres its most vulnerable citizens.[87]

In *Os sertões dos Campos: Duas vezes Euclides* (1997) by Augusto and Haroldo de Campos, Augusto uses what Jakobson calls "intralingual translation," or translation within one language, to craft brief, poetic untranslations out of this hefty sociohistorical treatise.[88] He describes these poems as "obtained without alteration to the text or punctuation."[89] Along with Augusto's untranslations, Haroldo contributes an essay about translating *Os sertões* into German; together, the paired sections posit that translation within one language can be critically revealing and that a translation into another target language can still relate to the source culture.[90]

Published as a joint work by Augusto and Haroldo, the volume puts the twin concepts of "translation as criticism" and "criticism as translation" into dialogue. In his introduction, Haroldo calls Augusto's work a "rereading" and his own a "transposition"; together their pieces form "a reciprocally complementary double reading."[91] Haroldo describes Augusto's operation as intending to "retraçar as veredas de poesia" (retrace the paths of poetry) in the source; the word *veredas* (paths) in this context of the writing and rewriting of Brazilian canonical literature echoes the title of a later work set in the same region, *Grande sertão, veredas* (1956) by João Guimarães Rosa.[92]

Augusto's untranslations ask what kinds of "form" can be found in the "inform" text of the source text as well as in the wild beauty of the *sertão* itself: these poems challenge notions of where beauty comes from in Brazil and how it may circulate. As Krista Brune contends, the space of the northeastern *sertão* tends to be underrepresented in English translation, even though the Brazilian canon uplifts the region as the central source of national authenticity.[93] By exploring an irreverent, cannibal translation treatment of this canonized work, these untranslations question the nation's utilization of the space of the *sertão* as quintessentially Brazilian while also ignoring the material precarity of this region and those who live there.

In these intralingual untranslations, Augusto draws on two models of reception. First, he follows the operation of Oswald de Andrade's avant-garde *Pau Brasil*, which cannibalizes colonial documents.[94] Second, he rejects a scholarly trend that evaluates the poetic content and style of *Os sertões* as a deficit, instead elevating the creative language contained within *Os sertões*, the unusual style Euclides da Cunha applied to material typically addressed in the more scientific language of reportage, geographical analysis, and sociological theories. Brazilian critics Augusto Meyer and Eugenio Gomes dismissed the Parnassian or excessively poetic qualities of this historiographic essay as though they were weak points of the work.[95] According to Augusto, however, these scholars fail to appreciate the genius of da Cunha when they reject his poetic language; to prove his point, Augusto writes poems that encapsulate da Cunha's work within the very same lines of verse that these other critics have disparaged as superfluous. In his method of harvesting lines of poetic verse from da Cunha's prose, Augusto is following in the footsteps of another avant-garde poet, Guilherme de Almeida, who did a similar experiment in 1946.[96] Again, Augusto takes a cue from a Brazilian tradition of translation, as with his pursuit of similar translation techniques as Gregório de Matos or Paulo Miranda. Augusto also uses his intralingual translation to remove the overemotionality of the style of da Cunha's writing without removing the poetic density of embodiment, rhythm, and description. Although the qualities Augusto and Haroldo reject from Spanish American poetry were present in this classic Brazilian narrative, in Augusto's untranslated versions, the political impact remains without the emotional manipulation of lyricism or surrealistic detail. Augusto also cites another frequent touchstone: the minimalist experimental modernism of John Cage and his concept of "'writing through' foreign texts, as a critical-pragmatic operation."[97] "Writing through" evokes Pacheco's heteronyms, the literary mask of a Brazilian poet he invents to critique Mexican racialized language denigrating the urbanized Indigenous population, parallel to the *sertanejos* depicted in *Os sertões*. Yet unlike Pacheco, Augusto assertively dispels the notion that his poems might be inventions by providing page numbers from his source text for each poem. His selections dwell on the *sertanejos*, the subaltern figures fighting a doomed war, especially horsemen and prisoners. By "writing through" another author's words, Augusto emphasizes the need to pay closer attention to the poetry of this work, which also allows a closer examination of the embodied experiences of the participants and the victims of this violent state oppression.

Although many world literature anthologies will abridge canonical texts, often providing only the best-known or most representative fragments of longer works, Augusto's method of fragmentation counters the canonical reading that critiques these poetic passages as less objective, sociological, or historically accurate. Not simply converting prose into poetry, in fact, he argues that he is not transforming anything but, rather, laying bare what is already present: his procedures "denude the poetic extracts."[98] More than a transformation based on rules outside the source text, his untranslations demonstrate that these poetic structures in fact organize and structure the text: "In many of the most soaring passages of his book, precisely those where he proves himself most original and persuasive, Euclides resorted to poetic methods."[99] Augusto argues that, contrary to previous readings, these poetic stretches shift the work from didactic reportage to the realm of literature.[100] Much as Pacheco does with the Indigenous poetry of North America, Augusto includes but also critiques former readings of his source material through his cannibal translation.

In many of the poems, Augusto uses the technique of relineation to emphasize meter and other poetic qualities already present in the prose source text, one of the same strategies Pacheco draws on in his approximations. For example, the first poem, "Soldado," includes a repeated line, "braços longamente abertos" (arms wide open), prompting readers to think about how repetition is used even in prose to slow down the pace, emphasize an image, or create a sense of the monotony of war that the author experienced.[101] The metric choices in the poem "Rodeio" create the jerk-stop motion of a rodeo—or the threatening sound of being encircled and surprised by horsemen, the other meaning of the title. This effect comes through using numerous *esdrújulas* (dactylic words with the accent on the third from last syllable) and *pie quebrado* (one-word lines marking sharp line breaks), two sonic effects that punctuate the phrase:

> De repente
> estruge ao lado um
> estrídulo tropel de cascos sobre pedras
> um
> estrépito de galhos estralando[102]

> (Suddenly
> roared in from one side a
> shrill clatter of hooves on stone
> a
> din of branches crashing)

In my translation, "shrill" and "din" fail to capture the rhythmic charm of the two matching dactyls in Augusto's version of da Cunha's Portuguese. While the prose text did not include the line breaks to emphasize the two galloping words, *estrídulo* and *estrépito*, da Cunha did choose matching rhythmic words to describe the dramatic arrival of the horsemen, announcing their entrance with these noisy words before they even appear on the page.

"O prisioneiro" stands out as a visual poem with notable *mise-en-page* qualities that contribute centrally to the work. Augusto writes that he "took the most liberties" with this poem, but still only modified placement of words on the page.[103] He builds this concrete poem by drawing on the many commas to create line breaks, fragmenting da Cunha's description of a prisoner in the Canudos War, placing lines in the shape of a Christ figure on the cross. Without changing any semantic information, he elevates the aesthetic parallel between the subaltern disciples of Christ and the Canudos *cangaceiros*—"indigents" or "outlaws"—the derogatory term journalists attached to the rebellious followers of Antonio Conselheiro.

um
suspenso
pelas axilas entre duas praças
meio
desmaiado
tinha
diagonalmente
sobre o peito nu
a desenhar-se num recalque forte
a lâmina do sabre que o abatera[104]

Many of Augusto's line breaks were already implied by the commas; the poem was already present in da Cunha's text. The source version reads: "Um, suspenso pelas axilas entre duas praças, meio desmaiado, tinha, diagonalmente, sobre o peito nu, a desenhar-se num recalque forte, a lâmina do sabre que o abatera" (One, suspended by his armpits between two posts, half-fainted, had, diagonally, across his bare chest, the drawing of a strong impression, the blade of the saber that felled him).[105]

The poem's title, "O prisioneiro," clarifies the dangling modifier "um, suspenso" (one [prisoner], suspended). When the same poem graces the back cover, Augusto also labels it an untranslation, giving it amplified graphic elements and a different title: "Intradução: Prisioneiro de Euclides." Displaying two versions of the text, one layered atop the other, this concrete untranslation in red lettering stands out against the prose sentence in larger gray font. Augusto's technique of untranslation draws out a latent element in the source text: a teleological retelling of the Christ narrative that the rebels were drawn to in the charismatic figure of the Conselheiro (see fig. 15).

However, while all the words remain the same, Augusto's interpolation of his concrete aesthetics also obscures or crafts aesthetic distractions around the violent scene depicted. The word *diagonalmente* refers to the mark or wound left by a saber's blow to the prisoner's body. Placing this word at a diagonal and transforming the phrase into the figure of Christ on the cross, Augusto's untranslation transforms the adjective "diagonal" into his legs set at an angle, or into a drape of cloth modestly covering him, or a combination of the two. The diagonal in Augusto's

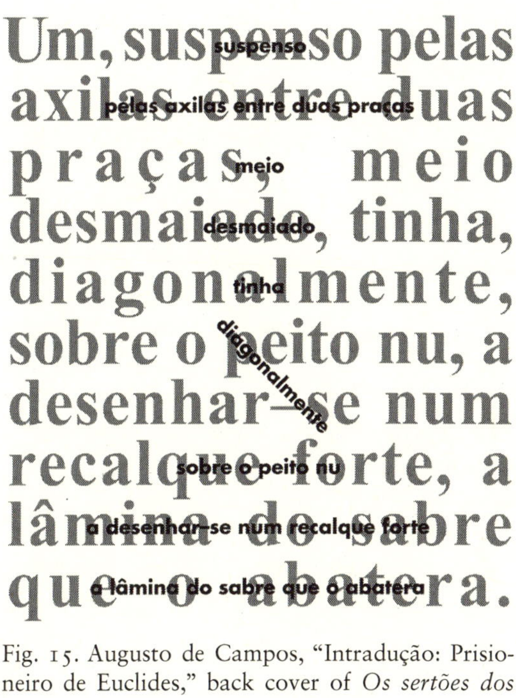

Fig. 15. Augusto de Campos, "Intradução: Prisioneiro de Euclides," back cover of *Os sertões dos Campos* (1997). © Augusto de Campos.

poem forms the body of the prisoner, whereas in the source text, it refers to the vicious wound left by the armed forces on their prisoner. This choice makes the violence of the text both more visible and less visible. It connects the drama of the leader of the Canudos War, the prophet-like Conselheiro, with the very Christian teleology his movement exploited. But it also camouflages the wound of the secular prisoner, turning his saber wound not into the stigmata of Christ but into his clothing or his body. Telling the story of the Canudos War in Brazil allegorically risks erasing the more widespread and banal violence of the historically specific event. This cannibal translation both performs this rewriting and erasure while making the cut visible. As with Augusto's "blow-up" of Matos, these repositioned fragments magnify the embodied experiences of the subaltern subjects of the Brazilian canon.

Augusto de Campos and José Emilio Pacheco work with literary traditions that encode various epistemological and physical forms of violence. Their cannibal translation anthologies never present themselves as neutral, transparent, complete, or representative images of world literature. Instead, they inscribe the violence of prior translation cultures, in which imperialist erasure denied many Indigenous or enslaved peoples their linguistic and epistemological self-determination. Using heteronyms, or turning major authors into heteronyms, they devour their source texts while loving them, translating against the logics of their sources.

Cannibal translations celebrate translingual writing with all its strange features, elisions, and failures as a part of the fabric and texture of text-making that critically considers contemporary language politics. To critique a translation for clumsiness or inaccuracy—or to refrain from translation in fear of appropriation—is to reject the impulse to pick up the arrow again, to offer another solution, a different vector. Although Pacheco was not in direct dialogue with the brothers de Campos, his translation practice takes some of their ideas further. Where Augusto translates *as though* he is writing from another persona or a heteronym, Pacheco takes the next step of inventing other poets to translate. Creating world literature anthologies from a stance of casual, fragmentary playfulness, they both hold space open for the history and limitations of translation—and they challenge their readers to search for the inventions, selections, and erasures implicated in any approximation of the voice of another.

Their use of fragmentation and heteronym as creative strategies elevates, underscores, and zooms in on the racial and class subaltern subjects within their own societies often left out of the Latin American texts most widely circulated in Anglophone world literature. By placing these devices within the familiar frame of the anthology, they also draw attention to the hypermediation and contested multiplicity of authorship in any other world literature anthology. Pacheco and Augusto invite readers to become participatory fans and amateur critics, never willing to fully accept any representation of a source text. Ultimately, reading their cannibal translations requires greater involvement and responsibility, becoming "um leitor contra mais a favor," the contrary reader who favors the text the most.

CONCLUSION

Cannibal Translation Futures

This book has traced cannibal translation from its origins in the Brazilian avant-garde and its revival by Haroldo and Augusto de Campos through to Spanish American translators adopting these practices and applying them to Brazilian and world literatures. Cannibal translation now comprises a set of translation strategies rooted in reciprocity, loving destruction, and nonassimilation. As an editorial practice, cannibal translation shows the process, leaves inconsistencies present as valuable elements of meaning-making, and imagines a return to source cultures rather than extraction. Finally, cannibal translation serves as a heuristic device for reading translations as such, looking for the positionality of translators, including translation tradition alongside literary tradition, and demanding productive suspicion and a self-questioning awareness of convention from readers. It is not that cannibal translation simply reactivates the historical avant-garde's gesture of treating readers as co-creators; rather, I see this Latin American praxis as an invitation to use that gesture in literary translation and in our readership of world literature in translation.

As a creative practice, cannibal translation implicates translators and authors in an ethical translationship, an encounter without assimilation that alters both the source culture by remaining implicated within it and the target language by stretching it to include another. The different approaches available to translators Augusto and Paz, whose loving destruction of E. E. Cummings allowed them to theorize their process, showing translation to be generative of new ideas and aesthetic gains, and staging the Latin American languages of Brazilian Portuguese and Spanish as affording the potential to create through translation in a different way than the European translators were imagining for French or German. The horizon of possibility of cannibal translation also included a historical correction, placing Latin American languages in direct contact through Paz and Haroldo de Campos, rather than separate poetic traditions only triangulated through English or French.

As a reading practice, cannibal translation provides a framework that facilitates reading translations for their particular qualities, which may include self-reflexive, intersectional traces of the translator's own position, tastes, or needs. Women translators Rosario Castellanos and Clarice Lispector show us that without reading their translations as creative acts we would not see the elements of themselves they added to source texts, or their critique of literary languages that reinforce gendered and racialized hierarchies or fail to include marginalized voices.

As an editorial framework, cannibal translation provided Biblioteca Ayacucho with a way to present multiple perspectives, techniques, and approaches at once, resulting in translingual editions of Latin American cultural history that honor its polyglot complexity and stage the challenges of the translation process. In their world literature anthologies, Pacheco and Augusto imagine authors as practically heteronyms of their translators, provoking productive suspicion and critiquing the same selective tools of world literature they themselves are using by centering their work on what traditionally has been left out of Mexican and Brazilian canons.

Where else could cannibal translation go? What can cannibal translation lovingly devour next? How can we imagine future applications of this creative, decolonial approach to translating texts in a way that emphasizes becoming over being, that seeks to produce an ethical encounter in which space is made for another inside the self? I conclude with two examples from growing spheres of nontraditional publication, and I end with an invitation.

The generative possibilities of cannibal translation anticipated the twenty-first century's expanded access to the publication and distribution of literary works; my concluding examples draw from two distinct self-publication frameworks: the DIY community-engaged practice of *cartonera* book-making with recycled cardboard; and the glossy, digital platforms of social media where writers find new audiences through immediate international availability. In a *cartonera* book published as an homage after Haroldo's death, editor Gonzalo Aguilar puts into practice the cannibal translation blend of transcreation, a laboratory of texts involving multiple actors, and an editorial framework that includes the sociopolitical context. For his part, Augusto continues to expand his poetic reach through the visual, digital medium of Instagram, where he again untranslates works by E. E. Cummings, this time framed as commentary on the political crisis facing Brazil under the government of Jair Bolsonaro. These cases extend cannibal translation practices into twenty-first-century modes of circulation, two of many potential models for contemporary translators.

In loving homage after Haroldo's death in 2003, the Spanish and Portuguese bilingual *cartonera* book *El ángel izquierdo de la poesía* (2005) recognizes his impact in Brazil, Latin America, and worldwide as a writer, founder of concrete poetry, and ambitious translator.[1] Editor Gonzalo Aguilar draws the title from Haroldo's poem "o anjo esquerdo da história," and the logic of the entire collection commemorates Haroldo's translation theories. The translingual edition included eight translators and writers; mixing together essays, translations, and poetry, it fulfills Haroldo's vision for a "laboratory of texts" in which participants from distinct disciplines generate multiple responses to source texts. For example, Aguilar translates into Spanish Haroldo's Portuguese transcreation of Vladimir Mayakovski's long poem "A Serguei Esenin," confirming the status of the transcreation as a work of literature in its own right, authored by the translator.[2]

Held at UCLA Special Collections, the edition I consulted features an eye-catching cover with metallic gold foil paper decorating the cardboard covers of the hand-bound book. Published in Lima by Sarita Cartonera, this initiative was inspired by the Eloísa Cartonera publishing collective founded by Washington Cucurto, Javier Barilaro, and Fernanda Laguna in 2003 in Buenos Aires in response to the 2001–2 financial crisis in Argentina. This particular book was designed as a part of an initiative to include Peruvian plastic artists in the local *cartonera* project, and Juan Osorio created this cover for the series "Libros fascinantes" (see fig. 16).

The method of *cartonera* publishing quickly spread across Latin America and the United States as practice for collective, community-driven intellectual production. Taking their name from the *cartoneros*, people who gather cardboard to sell this recyclable material, groups like Sarita Cartonera buy cardboard at higher rates than usual to construct creatively decorated cardboard book covers. Publishing both new works

Fig. 16. Cover of *cartonera* book *El ángel izquierdo de la poesía: Poética y política. Antología bilingüe* (2005), translations of political poetry by Haroldo de Campos, edited by Gonzalo Aguilar. Designed by Juan Osorio for the series Libros fascinantes produced by Sarita Cartonera in Lima, Peru. Held at Charles E. Young Research Library Special Collections, UCLA.

and classics, the signature style of *cartonera* publications includes packaging each volume with a one-of-a-kind cardboard cover decorated to promote unique, personalized relationships with books as objects. Furthermore, instead of merely representing marginalized subjects as characters in literary works, *cartonera* publishing projects "incorporate their labor—more generously compensated than on the open market, as the cardboard books' copyright pages insist—into the sphere of literary production itself."[3] *Cartonera* book-making collectives reject a hierarchical relationship to literary culture and instead involve people in making books from materials at hand, a fitting package for the cannibal translation inside.

The *cartonera* frame of *El ángel izquierdo de la poesía* and the political gesture of community-based literature evoke the urgency of the poem referenced in the title, composed as a protest poem and first published in the Worker's Party Journal, *PT Notícias*, in 1996.[4] In "o anjo esquerdo da história," Haroldo treats the theme of historical progress through the relationship between land sovereignty and human self-determination, drawing specific language for the piece from the context of the Brazilian Movimento dos Trabalhadores Rurais Sem Terra (MST; Movement of Rural Landless Workers). This labor movement officially consolidated in 1984 along with Brazil's return to democracy, but it has roots in 1970s activism during the military dictatorship. Haroldo composed this political poem of denunciation and outrage in the aftermath of a massacre by the police of nineteen landless workers in the northern Brazilian state of Pará.[5] The poem's key word, *terra*, evokes the social movement of the MST within Brazil, but as the poem unravels the word, as it disintegrates and adheres to a range of images and concepts that determine our legal, affective, and material relationship to land, Haroldo's poem becomes a globally recognizable and relevant statement against settler colonialism and in favor of decolonization.

While each version of the *cartonera* book might bear a unique cover crafted with available recycled materials, this particular cover (see figure 12) provides a reflective surface, signaling the self-reflection provoked by the collected poems and their consideration of the political positions of readers and subjects. The title poem ends with a reference to Paul Klee's "Angelus Novus," described by Walter Benjamin as the angel of history, and invokes readers to keep our eyes fixed on the graveyard of history and past forms of writing this history down, even as we are blown backward toward a future. For Haroldo, careful examination of the translations of the past challenge the translations of the future to find new practices of just collaboration rather than exploitative appropriation, whether in the realm of the aesthetic or the material. While masquerading as an expensive art book with a shiny gold-plated embossed cover, the *cartonera* volume actually performs the wide circulation and democratic accessibility of cannibal translation.[6]

To trace the routes of cannibal translation into the digital sphere, I end with Augusto's redeployment of his translation practice online.[7] Augusto's work transfers easily to Instagram—many of his poems already used the square format—and his account @poetamenos shares new works, reframes older work, and posts video clips allowing viewers to skim glimpses of larger book projects.[8] On this digital, multilingual, transnational platform, Augusto continues to push the boundary between creation, plagiarism, ready-made, translation, and cultural critique of Brazilian political realities.[9] In a poem posted on Instagram with the title "CLÁUSULA PÉTREA ready made" (see fig. 17), Augusto gives the Brazilian Constitution the same "untranslation" treatment he used with *Os sertões*.

Fragmenting the text of this controversial clause of the Brazilian Constitution, the shape of Augusto's untranslation evokes an hourglass

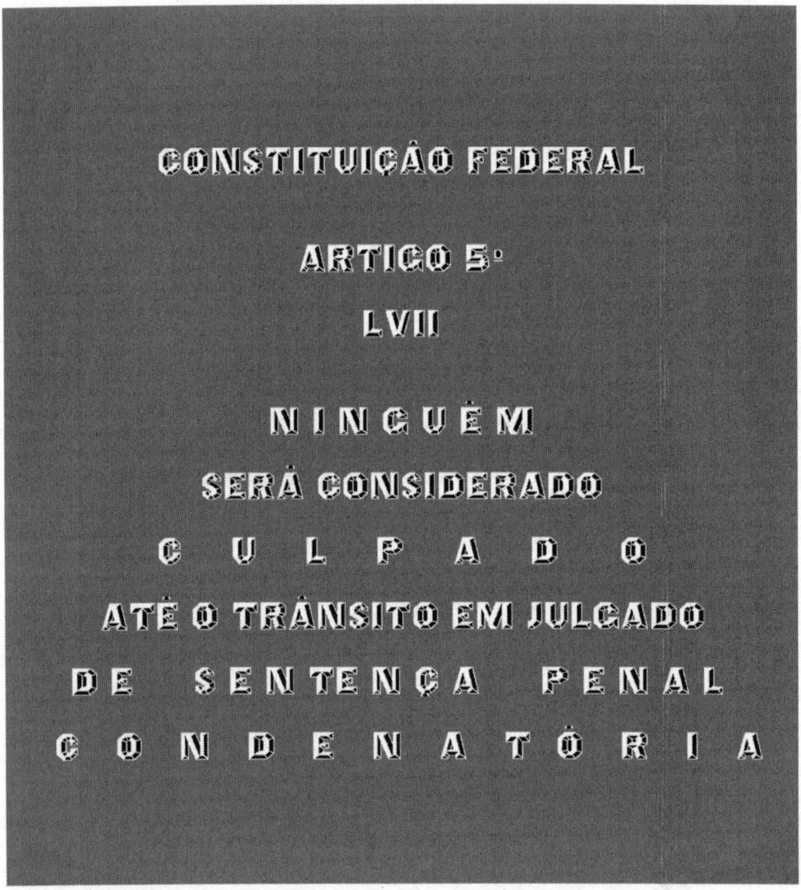

Fig. 17. "CLÁUSULA PÉTREA ready-made (poema de 2 abril de 2018)," posted to Augusto de Campos's Instagram account, @poetamenos. © Augusto de Campos.

where time is almost running out, evoking urgency, demanding action. Throughout 2018 and 2019, Augusto shared multiple versions and colors of this "ready-made" he titles "Cláusula Pétrea" (Set-in-Stone Clause), referring to one of several articles of the 1988 Brazilian Constitution that cannot be changed.[10] Reacting to the dictatorship's practices of imprisoning dissidents indefinitely, this clause "says 'no one shall be considered guilty until their case is fully adjudicated' and gives defendants the right to remain free as long as appeals are pending."[11] Augusto first shared this work in response to the Brazilian Supreme Court ruling of March 29, 2018, which had allowed the then former president Lula (Luiz Inácio Lula da Silva) to be jailed after only one appeal had upheld his sentence for corruption.[12] Augusto also exhibited a series of colorful, large-scale versions of this poem in a São Paulo gallery, Luciana Britto, yet the pieces reached far more people online.

Beyond these untranslations of Brazilian source texts as "ready-mades," Augusto also registered his concern over the changing political climate in Brazil by composing this new untranslation of E. E. Cummings titled "intradução: humanimais" and posted to Instagram in October 2019. He selected a charming font called Velcro that recalls the playful aesthetic of flower-power psychedelia associated with the Tropicália movement of the 1960s and 1970s; the text itself draws out the first stanza of a longer lyric published in the 1950s (see fig. 18).

Tied together with other poems branded as *contrapoemas* on Instagram, in which the poet issues scathing critiques of contemporary Brazilian political life, this untranslation is also a transhistorical mash-up, writing through and untranslating Cummings to express a more contemporary concern, that blindly seeking progress puts humanity at risk. Augusto's Portuguese reads:

> de todas as bênçãos que à human
> idade o progresso espalma
> uma é a suprema: um ban
> do de humanimais sem alma[13]

These lines translate the Cummings poem:

> of all the blessings which to man
> kind progress doth impart
> one stands supreme i mean the an
> imal without a heart.[14]

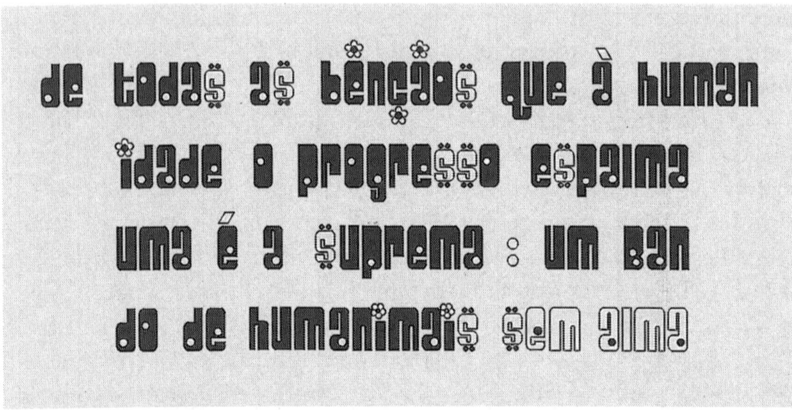

Fig. 18. "intradução: humanimais (e. e. cummings) inédito. outubro 2019," posted to Augusto de Campos's Instagram account, @poetamenos. © Augusto de Campos.

Maintaining the line breaks that fragment words, where Cummings creates a rhyme between "man" and "an," Augusto keeps that aesthetic detail. Yet he adds a key neologism with his title "humanimals," a concept that dramatically transforms the central figure of the poem, from "man as a heartless animal" to "humankind as a humanimal without a soul." The green floral print evokes an ecological reading of the poem, tied to Brazilian movements protesting the Bolsonaro administration for accelerating environmental crises and climate change. The source text is masculinist, speaking only of "mankind"; Augusto shifts to the more inclusive "humanity" and expands the responsibility from a singular human to a collective *bando*. Implicating humanity as a collective in relationship with a natural environment, this untranslation imagines that any solution to the false promise of progress must also confront individualism and the presumed uniqueness of the human species.

With these Instagram remixes, Augusto performs cannibal translation as an ongoing relationship between multilingual spaces. Although the platform is certainly flawed—just as flawed as the framing apparatus of the world literature anthology—I see Augusto's work, along with that of other cannibal translators, as crafting an audience for an alternative language politics centered in a critical Latin American translation praxis. In the context of rapidly expanding access to the digital production and consumption of texts, we are hyperaware of the collectivity, reciprocity, and instability of the written word. Readers begin to see translation as one of many performances of a work, for different readerships, on different platforms, where elements of generosity, destruction, and reciprocity all shape literary translation as a generative practice that holds a work open.

Yet even more than the possibilities explored and explorable by any given translator, cannibal translations operate on readers to require their participation, calling for an attentive, active, suspicious, or contrary reader. Whether through the inclusion of the process in a publication, refusal to settle into one final version, emphasis on the positionality of translators, the interpolation of invented heteronyms or pseudotranslations, the hyperfragmentation of a counterpunch to world literature, all these cannibal translation techniques challenge our reading practices. As translators explore different modes of circulation as another way of holding literary works in process and in common—from local communities crafting *cartonera* to globalized digital platforms—how can new translations that are properly improper imagine and create new publics?

I end with an invitation that I hope will whet your appetite: What could you translate that would remain in reciprocal relationship with the source culture? How would your readers know to read it as a translation? How could you read with eyes attuned to the details that reveal the work of a translator, the traces of the techniques used to lovingly devour the source text, to show the history of power relations that brought that translation to your hands, to leave behind internal inconsistencies, to refuse assimilation, to show their own presence implicated in the work?

Notes

ABOUT THE ARTIST FEATURED ON THE COVER

A sculpture by Adriana Varejão titled *Azulejaria em Carne Viva* or *Tilework in Live Flesh* (1999; oil on canvas and polyurethane on wood and aluminum) graces the cover. Inspired by the Brazilian Baroque, this piece stages the Portuguese colonial material world of fine porcelain tiles layered over but failing to cover up a raw meat interior, the collective memory of violence in the Brazilian historical experience. An internationally renowned artist working in multiple hybrid forms including ceramic, painting, sculpture, and video, based in her hometown studio in Rio de Janeiro, Varejão received the Order of Cultural Merit from the Brazilian Ministry of Culture in 2011.

INTRODUCTION

All translations or back-translations provided without attribution are my own. In accordance with Brazilian scholarly norms, when two authors have the same last name (Augusto and Haroldo de Campos, who are brothers; Mário de Andrade and Oswald de Andrade, who are not related), I will respectfully refer to them by their first names.

1. Walter Benjamin, "The Critic's Technique in Thirteen Theses," in *One-Way Street and Other Writings*, trans. Edmund Jephcott and Kingsley Shorter (London: NLB, 1979), 67.

2. Haroldo de Campos, "Anthropophagous Reason: Dialogue and Difference in Brazilian Culture," trans. Odile Cisneros, in *Novas: Selected Writings*, ed. Antonio Sergio Bessa and Odile Cisneros, foreword by Roland Greene (Evanston, IL: Northwestern University Press, 2007), 160.

3. Augusto de Campos, "Verso, reverso, controverso," in *Verso, reverso, controverso* (São Paulo: Editora Perspectiva, 1978), 7–8.

4. See Carlos A. Jáuregui, *Canibalia: Canibalismo, calibanismo, antropofagia cultural y consumo en América Latina* (Madrid: Iberoamericana, 2008), 49–50. For more on colonial accounts, which often represented only the aftermath and detritus of cannibalism, see Peter Hulme, "Introduction: The Cannibal Scene," in *Cannibalism and the Colonial World*, ed. Francis Barker, Peter Hulme, and Margaret Iversen (Cambridge: Cambridge University Press, 1998), 1–38.

5. See Roberto Fernández Retamar, "Caliban: Notes towards a Discussion of Culture in Our America," in *Caliban and Other Essays*, trans. Edward Baker (Minneapolis: University of Minnesota Press, 1989), 3–45.

6. See Charles A. Perrone, *Seven Faces: Brazilian Poetry since Modernism* (Durham, NC: Duke University Press, 1996), in particular "Chapter 4. The Orphic Imperative: Lyric, Lyrics, and the Poetry of Song," in *Seven Faces*, 87–116, and Charles A. Perrone and Christopher Dunn, eds., *Brazilian Popular Music and Globalization* (London: Routledge, 2001). For a comparative analysis of Cuban and Brazilian deployment of cannibal art practice, see Luís Madureira, *Cannibal Modernities: Postcoloniality and the Avant-Garde in Caribbean and Brazilian Literature* (Charlottesville: University of Virginia Press, 2005).

7. See Zita Nunes, *Cannibal Democracy: Race and Representation in the Literature of the Americas* (Minneapolis: University of Minnesota Press, 2008).

8. Robert J. C. Young points out the proliferation of words in English, Greek, German, and Latin to describe the process commonly known as translation, a foundational problem where "discussions of translation proceed as if the concept were as universally transparent as earlier philosophical discussions of truth," and he asks whether "translation itself [is] a translatable term, or does meaning only attach to it loosely, lightly, in a volatile way." Maria Tymoczko identifies an "erosion of translation communities" taking place on intranational and global scales and sees this form of epistemicide as "leading to new conceptual shifts that recolonize minds around the world through hegemonic remapping of the domains of cross-cultural concepts." See Robert J. C. Young, "Philosophy in Translation," and Maria Tymoczko "Cultural Hegemony and the Erosion of Translation Communities," in *Companion to Translation Studies*, ed. Sandra Bermann and Catherine Porter (Chichester, UK: Wiley-Blackwell), 52 and 174–75.

9. One of Roman Jakobson's three translation types, "interlingual translation or *translation proper* is an interpretation of verbal signs by means of some other language." Roman Jakobson, "On Linguistic Aspects of Translation," in *The Translation Studies Reader*, 2nd ed., ed. Lawrence Venuti (New York: Routledge, 2004), 139.

10. Cannibal translators anticipate in practice Naoki Sakai's insight that Jakobson's concept undergirds the image of languages as distinct or naturally present, which "validates the ethno-linguistic unity of 'natural' language." Naoki Sakai, "Dislocation in Translation," *TTR: Traduction, terminologie, rédaction* 22, no. 1 (2009): 172–73.

11. Oswald de Andrade, "Cannibalist Manifesto," trans. Leslie Bary, *Latin American Literary Review* 19, no. 38 (July–December 1991): 38–44.

12. Translation modified; I shifted Leslie Bary's choice of "Galli Mathias" for "gallimatias" or "nonsense" instead to "Balder Dash," to keep the joke. Oswald, "Cannibalist Manifesto," 41.

13. Before the Cannibalist phase (1924–28) came the International or Heroic phase (1922–24), inaugurated by the 1922 Semana de Arte Moderna in São Paulo; after it came the Nationalist phase (1928–45). For a complete discussion, see Haroldo de Campos, "Uma poética da radicalidade," in *Obras completas: Poesias reunidas*, by Oswald de Andrade (Rio de Janeiro: Civilização Brasileira, 1971), 9–59; Benedito Nunes, "Antropofagia ao alcance de todos," in *Obras completas de Oswald de Andrade: A utopía antropofágica* (São Paulo: Secretaria de Estado da Cultura, 1990), 5–39; and for the canonization of the phase after cannibalism, see Randal Johnson, "The Dynamics of the Brazilian Literary Field, 1930–1945," *Luso-Brazilian Review* 31, no. 2 (1994): 5–22.

14. Augusto de Campos, Haroldo de Campos, and Décio Pignatari, "Pilot Plan for Concrete Poetry," trans. Jon Tolman, in Haroldo, *Novas*, 218. For discussion of the lifelong trajectory of Augusto's "verbivocovisual" poetics, see Adam Shellhorse, "The Verbivocovisual Revolution: Anti-Literature, Affect, Politics, and World Literature in Augusto de Campos," *CR: The New Centennial Review* 20, no. 1 (Spring 2020): 147–84.

15. The phrase in the "Plano Piloto" refers to Paulo Prado's preface to Oswald's *Poesía Pau Brasil*: "It's a great day for Brazilian letters: to take, in pill form, minutes of poetry. Interrupt the balance." Paulo Prado, "Poesía Pau Brasil," in Oswald de Andrade, *Poesias reunidas*, vol. 4 of *Obras completas*, ed. Haroldo de Campos (São Paulo: Civilização Brasileira, 1974), 70.

16. Augusto de Campos, "Revistas Re-vistas: Os Antropófagos," in *Poesia Antipoesia Antropofagia & Cia* (São Paulo: Companhia das Letras, 2015), 145–46. He claims that the writers of the previous stage merely imitated European futurism, and the more nationalist "verde-amarela" *modernistas* took a step backward from the peak of cannibalism.

17. Augusto, "Revistas Re-vistas," 154.

18. Augusto actually paraphrases his fellow concrete poet Décio Pignatari: "A antropofagia 'virou carne de vaca,' e a diluição e o consumo se encarregaram de banalizar o tema, que no entanto é mais sério do que parece." Augusto de Campos, "Pos-Walds," in *Poesia Antipoesia Antropofagia & Cia*, 261. The banalization of Oswald's cannibalistic literary tradition went hand in hand with a studied forgetting of other experimental movements, including Augusto's own literary production. In the opening note to their major collection on his work, Flora Süssekind and Júlio Castañon Guimarães write that the prior lack of critical focus on Augusto de Campos "responds to a pseudoconsensual, deaf movement of cultural rejection of the vanguard tradition and experimental artistic practices perceptible in Brazilian literary life today." Flora Süssekind and Júlio Castañon Guimarães, eds., *Sobre Augusto de Campos* (Rio de Janeiro: Edições Casa de Rui Barbosa / 7 Letras, 2004), 7.

19. Benedito Nunes describes cannibalism as a productive psychoanalytic metaphor for the Brazilian subject, both diagnosis and therapy. B. Nunes, "Antropofagia ao alcance de todos," 15–16. Outside Brazil, readers including Edwin Gentzler and Randal Johnson center on the national reading of the manifesto, through which "Brazil marked the first step in the creation of an original Brazilian national culture and a separate Brazilian identity." Edwin Gentzler, *Translation and Identity in the Americas* (London: Routledge, 2008), 78; Randal Johnson, "Tupy or Not Tupy: Cannibalism and Nationalism in Contempo-

rary Brazilian Literature and Culture," in *Modern Latin American Fiction*, ed. John King (London: Faber and Faber, 1987), 41–60.

20. "Tupi cannibalism stands as an obstacle to all possibilities of synthesis. . . . Tupi cannibalism breaks with the imaginary (mirror) function of Jacques Lacan." Sara Castro-Klarén, "A Genealogy for the 'Manifesto antropófago,' or The Struggle between Socrates and the Caraïbe," *Nepantla: Views from the South* 1, no. 2 (2000): 312.

21. Castro-Klarén cites Eduardo Viveiros de Castro on the place of cannibalism within Araweté metaphysics, where he describes "a universe where Becoming is prior to Being and unsubmissive to it." Eduardo Viveiros de Castro, *From the Enemy's Point of View: Humanity and Divinity in an Amazonian Society*, trans. Catherine V. Howard (Chicago: University of Chicago Press, 1992), 4. Quoted in Castro-Klarén, "A Genealogy," 311. Viveiros de Castro would later expand his investigation to put the sacred cannibalism of the Araweté in dialogue with the cannibalistic social ritual of the Tupinambá to rethink anthropology from Indigenous perspectives. He posits an Amerindian alter-anthropology centered on perspectivism and multinaturalism, which "affirms not so much a variety of natures as the naturalness of variation—variation *as* nature," and in which the reciprocity of the cannibal act is central: "What was eaten was the enemy's relation to those who consumed him; in other words his *condition as enemy*. In other words, what was assimilated from the victim was the signs of his alterity, the aim being to reach his alterity as point of view on the Self. Cannibalism and the peculiar form of war with which it is bound up involve a paradoxical movement of reciprocal self-determination through the point of view of the enemy." Eduardo Viveiros de Castro, *Cannibal Metaphysics: For a Post-Structural Anthropology*, trans. and ed. Peter Skafish (Minneapolis: Univocal, 2016), 74 and 142–43.

22. Haroldo, "Anthropophagous Reason," 165.

23. Haroldo de Campos, "Translation as Creation and Criticism," trans. Diana Gibson and Haroldo de Campos, in Haroldo, *Novas*, 318.

24. Haroldo de Campos, "Tradução, Ideologia e História," in *Transcriação*, ed. Marcelo Tápia and Thelma Médici Nóbrega (São Paulo: Editora Perspectiva, 2013), 39.

25. Thelma Médici Nóbrega and John Milton, "The Role of Haroldo and Augusto de Campos in Bringing Translation to the Fore of Literary Activity in Brazil," in *Agents of Translation*, ed. John Milton and Paul Bandia (Amsterdam: John Benjamins, 2009), 260.

26. Odile Cisneros, "From Isomorphism to Cannibalism: The Evolution of Haroldo de Campos's Translation Concepts," *TTR: Traduction, terminologie, rédaction* 25, no. 2 (2012): 30–33.

27. Z. Nunes, *Cannibal Democracy*, 6–14.

28. While scholarly consensus places translation as intimately imbricated in the poetic and critical production of both Augusto and Haroldo de Campos, the theoretical and practical implications of their engagement with the discourses of Oswaldian cannibalism provoke ambivalence. For example, the most recent volume on Haroldo de Campos specifically "confirms the linkage, the integration, and the coexistence of [poetry, criticism, and translation,] three

conceptual areas of literary work in the oeuvre of Haroldo . . . which has drawn the attention of a new generation interested in concepts of *Gesamtkunstwerk* and *World Literature*." Eduardo Jorge de Oliveira and Kenneth David Jackson, "Haroldopédia ou a educação do poeta," in *Poesia-Crítica-Tradução: Haroldo de Campos e a educação dos sentidos*, ed. Eduardo Jorge de Oliveira and Kenneth David Jackson (Berlin: Peter Lang, 2022), 16. Yet in her chapter, Melanie Strasser studies the anthropophagic trope in Haroldo's writing on translation to demonstrate the fundamental ambivalence and caution with which he related to that tradition, concluding that "the translation poetics of Haroldo de Campos can be read as a suspension of cannibalism, where suspension takes the triple-meaning of German (*Aufhebung*): raise up, conserve, and abolish." Melanie Strasser, "Tradução canibal? Sobre a poética da tradução de Haroldo de Campos," in *Poesia-Crítica-Tradução: Haroldo de Campos e a educação dos sentidos*, ed. Eduardo Jorge de Oliveira and Kenneth David Jackson (Berlin: Peter Lang, 2022), 326–27.

29. Susan Bassnett and Harish Trivedi define postcolonial translation as grounded in a refusal to be merely failed copies of Europe, so that the cannibal metaphor frames translations as "both a violation of European codes and an act of homage." Susan Bassnett and Harish Trivedi, "Of Colonies, Cannibals, and Vernaculars," in *Post-colonial Translation Theory*, ed. Bassnett and Trivedi (London: Routledge, 1998), 5. Else Ribeiro Pires Vieira names "cannibalistic translation" a "philosophy of nourishing from two reservoirs, the source text and the target literatures." Else Ribeiro Pires Vieira, "A Postmodern Translational Aesthetics in Brazil," in *Translation Studies: An Interdiscipline*, ed. Mary Snell-Hornby, Franz Pöchhacker, and Klaus Kaindl (Amsterdam: John Benjamins, 1994), 72. Rainer Guldin asserts that instead of merely inverting power relations, cannibalism establishes cultural identity based on a two-way flow between source and target cultures, to "devour the very border between the foreign and the familiar, devour the devourer and the act of devoration itself." Rainer Guldin, "Devouring the Other: Cannibalism, Translation and the Construction of Cultural Identity," in *Translating Selves: Experience and Identity between Languages and Literatures*, ed. Nikolau Paschalis and Maria-Venetia Kyritsi (London: Continuum, 2008), 120–22. In perhaps the first deployment in English of the cannibal trope in reference to translation, Serge Gavronsky does not even make a stop in Brazil to describe the replacement of the pious Judeo-Christian translator with a new Nietzschean cannibal translator, the "aggressive translator who seizes possession of the original, who savors the text, that is, who truly feeds upon the words, who ingurgitates them, and who, thereafter, enunciates them in his own tongue, thereby having explicitly rid himself of the original creator." Serge Gavronsky, "The Translator: From Piety to Cannibalism," *SubStance* 6–7, no. 16 (Summer 1977): 60. Note that while his metaphors and bellicose vocabulary may resemble those of the cannibal translators in my corpus, Gavronsky is still operating from the standpoint of the total otherness of the cannibal by leaving no space for reciprocity. In his reading, the act of cannibal translation culminates in the erasure of the creator, rendering it final rather than one of continual becoming as in the Tupi metaphysical source of the trope of cannibal translation as I route it through Brazil.

30. For Tápia, outside Brazil Haroldo's procedure of "transcreation" has been mislabeled as "cannibalism." He instead proposes "plagiotropia" to describe translation as both copy and creation in Haroldo's work, also aiming to free Haroldo's thought from his precursor Oswald. Marcelo Tápia, "O eco antropofágico," in Haroldo, *Transcriação*, 149. Thayse Leal Lima elevates Haroldo's concept of the "ex-centric" that emphasizes his positionality as not "of the center" but a position that "allows us to rethink world literature as an open matrix of texts traveling in multiple directions constantly 'feeding and re-feeding' one another." Thayse Leal Lima, "Translation and World Literature: The Perspective of the 'Ex-Centric,'" *Journal of Latin American Cultural Studies* 26, no. 3 (2017): 475.

31. John Milton, "Literary Translation Theory in Brazil," *Meta: Journal des traducteurs / Meta: Translators' Journal* 41, no. 2 (1996): 198.

32. Gabriel Borowski demonstrates how Haroldo distanced himself from any cannibalistic theory of translation, preferring to cite others, because "the 'theory' in question does not actually come from his own writings or from Brazil, but is instead ascribed to them as a Western theoretical construct." Gabriel Borowski, "Beyond Cannibalism: Reviewing the Metaphor of Anthropophagy in Contemporary Translation Studies," paper presented at "Poetry, Criticism, Translation: Haroldo de Campos" conference, Yale University, New Haven, CT, December 13–14, 2019, 5–6.

33. In *Canibalia* (2008) Carlos A. Jáuregui traces the term *caníbal* through its colonial origins as the first New World neologism and the subsequent history of reclaiming this Eurocentric epithet as a badge of Latin American–specific cultural creativity. Drawing from over five centuries of material, Jauregui traces the different mobilizations of the Latin American trope of the cannibal, from a justification for colonial domination, evangelization, and extermination, to the resignification of this key concept as autochthonous identity formation and cultural production.

34. Augusto, "Revistas Re-vistas," 154. For Augusto, the challenge Oswald's philosophy of cannibalism faces is the continued resurgence of the taboo; his work seeks to revive what he calls the "totemic banquet" of Oswald's *Revista da Antropofagia*.

35. See Mimi Sheller on the vilification of Caribbean bodies—depicted as cannibals, zombies, sources of disease, or a general threat—as a form of consuming radical alterity or otherness. Mimi Sheller, *Consuming the Caribbean: From Arawaks to Zombies* (London: Routledge, 2003), 143–49. See also Alan Rice and Vincent Woodard on the Black Atlantic. Rice reads the cannibal trope in literature as a retelling of the violence of the Middle Passage and the forced enslavement of African people. White enslavers would use force-feeding to prevent suicide, which the enslaved people understood as a precursor to being eaten. Alan Rice, "Who's Eating Whom? The Discourse of Cannibalism in the Literature of the Black Atlantic from Equiano's *Travels* to Toni Morrison's *Beloved*," *Research in African Literatures* 29, no. 4 (1998): 109. In other cases, the desire of white men for Black bodies was figured as a gustatory metaphor. Vincent Woodard, *The Delectable Negro: Human Consumption and Homo-*

eroticism within U.S. Slave Culture, ed. Justin A. Joyce and Dwight A. McBride (New York: New York University Press, 2014), 35.

36. Viveiros de Castro details the social nature of Tupinambá cannibalism as a "very elaborate system for the capture, execution, and ceremonial consumption of their enemies. Captives of war, who frequently shared both the language and the customs of their captors, lived for long periods among the latter before being subjected to solemn, formal execution . . . followed by the ingestion of his body by those in attendance—guests from neighboring villages as much as their hosts." Viveiros de Castro, *Cannibal Metaphysics*, 140–41.

37. Even Gentzler's chapter on Brazilian translation theories lands the argument in a parallel between Derrida and Haroldo as seekers of a third way out of binaries of capitalism vs. communism or nationalism vs. internationalism during the 1980s and their shared interrogation of translation as a language of philosophy. Gentzler, *Translation and Identity in the Americas*, 92–97.

38. Augusto, "Revistas Re-vistas," 153.

39. David Damrosch, *What Is World Literature?* (Princeton, NJ: Princeton University Press, 2003), 1.

40. Franco Moretti, "Conjectures on World Literature," *New Left Review*, no. 1 (January 2000): 54.

41. Moretti, "Conjectures on World Literature," 55–56.

42. Moretti, "Conjectures on World Literature," 58.

43. Pascale Casanova, *The World Republic of Letters*, trans. M. B. DeBevoise (Cambridge, MA: Harvard University Press, 2007), 24.

44. Casanova writes, "Translation, like criticism, is a process of establishing value. . . . Translators thus contribute to the growth of the literary heritage of nations that enjoy the power of consecration: critical recognition and translations are weapons in the struggle by and for literary capital." Casanova, *The World Republic of Letters*, 23.

45. Even through what Edwin Gentzler calls the macro-turn to "global and transnational translation research" in translation studies to incorporate a more diverse body of literatures and languages, the field still focuses on translations involving English or European languages or in relation to the coloniality of European powers. Edwin Gentzler, "Macro- and Micro-turns in Translation Studies," *Translation and Interpreting Studies* 6, no. 1 (2011): 122. Walter Mignolo and Freya Schiwy also insist that despite the scholarly inattention to the contrary, "certainly there have been translations from Chinese to Taiwanese or from Argentinean Spanish to Brazilian Portuguese." Walter Mignolo and Freya Schiwy, "Transculturation and the Colonial Difference: Double Translation," in *Translation and Ethnography*, ed. Tullio Maranhão and Bernhard Streck (Tucson: University of Arizona Press, 2003), 4. Aamir R. Mufti claims that by uncritically embracing the "global anglophone," world literature studies risks unlearning the critical intervention Said's *Orientalism* made to knowledge production. Aamir R. Mufti, *Forget English!* (Cambridge, MA: Harvard University Press, 2016). Rebecca Walkowitz places translation and translatability at the center of the frame of contemporary world literature, but her analysis still centers the ways literary works make themselves legible in English. Rebecca

Walkowitz, *Born Translated: The Contemporary Novel in an Age of World Literature* (New York: Columbia University Press, 2015).

46. Damrosch, *What Is World Literature?*, 4–6.

47. Bermann draws on the work of Gloria Anzaldúa, Édouard Glissant, and Maria Tymoczko to show how many foundational texts first demonstrate "errantry" before being subsumed by nationalist readings. Sandra Bermann, "World Literature and Comparative Literature," in *The Routledge Companion to World Literature*, ed. Theo D'haen, David Damrosch, and Djelal Kadir (London: Routledge, 2011), 176–78.

48. Cheah writes, "Following Goethe, I suggest that we should conceive of the world not only as a spatio-geographical entity but also as an ongoing dynamic process of becoming, something that possesses a historical-temporal dimension and hence is continually being made and remade." Pheng Cheah, *What Is a World? On Postcolonial Literature as World Literature* (Durham, NC: Duke University Press, 2016), 42.

49. Emily Apter, *Against World Literature: On the Politics of Untranslatability* (New York: Verso, 2013), 7.

50. "As a model of deowned literature, [translation] stands against the swell of corporate privatization in the arts, with its awards given to individual genius and bias against collective authorship. A translational author—shorn of a singular signature—is the natural complement, in my view, to World Literature understood as an experiment in national sublation that signs itself as collective, terrestrial property." Apter, *Against World Literature*, 15.

51. Haroldo anticipates Casanova's disentanglement of literary and economic spheres and draws from Engels, Marx, and Goethe's *Weltliteratur* to define world literature as "a meeting point of discourses, a necessary dialogue and not a monologic xenophobia. . . . Anthropophagous reason [is] a theory proposing the critical devouring of universal cultural heritage, formulated not from the submissive and reconciled perspective of the 'noble savage' (idealized following the model of European virtues in the 'nativist' vein of Brazilian Romanticism . . .), but from the disabused point of view of the 'bad savage,' devourer of whites, the cannibal." Haroldo, "Anthropophagous Reason," 158–60. The Brazilian Romanticism Haroldo cites is all Moretti's distant reading method finds in Brazil. It bears brief mention the numerous fields beyond the literary which benefit from theoretical innovations born out of Brazilian cultural contexts; Robert Stam and Ella Shohat list the following internationally influential Brazilian theories and practices: "dependency theory in economics (where future president of Brazil Fernando Henrique Cardoso played a major role), social geography (Josué de Castro's 'geography of hunger'); education theory (Paulo Freire's 'pedagogy of the oppressed'), radical theater (Augusto Boal's 'theater of the oppressed'), cinema (Glauber Rocha's 'aesthetics of hunger'), anthropology (Viveiros de Castro's Indigenous 'perspectivism'), and music (bossa nova, Tropicália)." Robert Stam and Ella Shohat, *Race in Translation: Culture Wars Around the Postcolonial Atlantic* (New York: New York University Press), 272.

52. "Só me interessa o que não é meu. Lei do homem. Lei do antropófago." Oswald de Andrade, "Manifesto antropófago," *Revista de Antropofagia* 1, no. 1 (May 1928): 3.

53. Octavio Paz to Haroldo de Campos, March 14, 1968, in Octavio Paz and Haroldo de Campos, *Transblanco (em torno a "Blanco" de Octavio Paz)* (Rio de Janeiro: Editora Guanabara, 1986), 96.

54. "Rival systems of analytical hypotheses can conform to all speech dispositions within each of the languages concerned and yet dictate, in countless cases, utterly disparate translations; not mere mutual paraphrases, but translations each of which would be excluded by the other system." Willard Van Orman Quine, *Word and Object* (Cambridge, MA: MIT Press, 1960), 73–74. Working from Quine's insight, Efraín Kristal understands these "translation manuals" as the set of written or unwritten guidelines a publisher, grant institution, or translator may impose on the process. Efraín Kristal, "Philosophical/Theoretical Approaches to Translation," in *A Companion to Translation Studies*, ed. Sandra Bermann and Catherine Porter (Chichester, UK: Wiley-Blackwell, 2014), 37–39.

55. Apter's "translation zone" "provokes serious reflection on what constitutes the limits of a discrete language, not just in terms of original and target, or native and 'foreign,' but more precisely in terms of language as a border war conditioned by the clash between plurilingualism and corporate standardization." Emily Apter, *The Translation Zone: A New Comparative Literature* (Princeton, NJ: Princeton University Press, 2006), 9.

56. Here, Olea anticipates the use of untranslatables as a reading strategy that for Apter is an antidote to the "bulimic drive to anthologize and curricularize the world's cultural resources." Apter, *Against World Literature*, 3. Olea's transcreation of *Macunaíma*—and the interest in translating Brazilian modernism at Ayacucho—flies against Casanova's analysis of the novel centered on its "national ambition" for which "translation proposals aroused little interest abroad." Casanova, *The World Republic of Letters*, 289. Ellen Jones focuses on multilingual works like *Macunaíma* and their draw to translation because of rather than in spite of the untranslatable content, producing "translation as multiple, moving, and layered; readers will recall Barbara Cassin's definition of 'untranslatability' not as that which cannot be translated but as that which one continues endlessly to translate, as that which is 'unable to finish being translated' . . . 'the untranslatable is rather what one keeps on (not) translating.'" Ellen Jones, *Literature in Motion: Translating Multilingualism Across the Americas* (New York: Columbia University Press, 2022), 155. She cites here from Rebecca L. Walkowitz, "Translating the Untranslatable: An Interview with Barbara Cassin," *Public Books*, June 15, 2014; and Barbara Cassin, ed. *Dictionary of Untranslatables: A Philosophical Lexicon*, trans. Emily Apter, Jacques Lezra, and Michael Wood (Princeton, NJ: Princeton University Press, 2014), xvii.

57. For example, if "code-switching" represents an oral practice of moving between languages and/or registers of formality, and literary code-switching does the same in text, cannibal translation might offer manners of translating these literary devices; Olea seeks to use Spanish American details alongside Brazilian Portuguese moments in his Spanish translation to craft a polyvocal Latin American version of Mário de Andrade's *Macunaíma*.

58. Paulo Moreira analyzes "deep undercurrents" that are not necessarily reciprocal; he sees Reyes placing Brazil and Mexico in comparative dialogue with the "particular gaze of a foreigner who is also a fellow Latin American."

Paulo Moreira, *Literary and Cultural Relations between Brazil and Mexico: Deep Undercurrents* (New York: Palgrave, 2013), 38.

59. Moreira's *Literary and Cultural Relations between Brazil and Mexico* positions both countries as outside many formulations of Latin America and studies early twentieth-century exchanges by cultural brokers and ambassadors, including Ronald de Carvalho and Alfonso Reyes. Robert Patrick Newcomb's *Nossa and Nuestra América: Inter-American Dialogues* (West Lafayette, IN: Purdue University Press, 2012) focuses on the genre of the essay and its development in Spanish and Portuguese as Cuban and Brazilian thinkers develop the concept of Latin America and their troubled place in it. Sergio Delgado Moya's *Delirious Consumption: Aesthetics and Consumer Capitalism in Mexico and Brazil* (Austin: University of Texas Press, 2017) and Adam Shellhorse's *Anti-Literature: The Politics and Limits of Representation in Modern Brazil and Argentina* (Pittsburgh: University of Pittsburgh Press, 2017) place Brazilian concrete aesthetics in dialogue with other Spanish American anticapitalist aesthetic movements.

60. Mariano Siskind, *Cosmopolitan Desires: Global Modernity and World Literature in Latin America* (Evanston, IL: Northwestern University Press, 2014), 21.

61. "Imperialism is supposed to have brought the novel everywhere. Is the novel form identical with 'literature'? I think the real problem with this identification, between writing good reference tools for the novel form on the one hand and for the entire discipline on the other, is a denial of collectivity. The others provide information while we know the whole world. . . . This *is* nationalism, US nationalism masquerading as globalism." Gayatri Spivak, *Death of a Discipline* (New York: Columbia University Press, 2003), 108.

62. Kristal emphasizes Rubén Darío's role in circulating *modernismo* in Spanish, French, and English on both sides of the Atlantic to show that in poetic spheres of influence, Latin America takes on the quality of center rather than periphery. Efraín Kristal, "'Considerando en frío . . .': Una respuesta a Franco Moretti," in *América Latina en la "literatura mundial,"* ed. Ignacio M. Sánchez Prado (Pittsburgh: Instituto Internacional de Literatura Iberoamericana, 2006), 104.

63. Ignacio M. Sánchez Prado, "The Persistence of the Transcultural: A Latin American Theory of the Novel from the National-Popular to the Global," *New Literary History* 51 (2020): 351. See also Ignacio M. Sánchez Prado, "'Hijos de Metapa': un recorrido conceptual de la literatura mundial (a manera de introducción)," in *América Latina en la "literatura mundial,"* ed. Sánchez Prado (Pittsburgh: Instituto Internacional de Literatura Iberoamericana, University of Pittsburgh, 2006), 20–21.

64. Nóbrega and Milton, "The Role of Haroldo and Augusto de Campos in Bringing Translation to the Fore," 272. From its earliest framing in the "Pilot Plan," concrete poetry "aims at the lowest common denominator of language" or a "coincidence and simultaneity of verbal and nonverbal communication." Augusto, Haroldo, and Pignatari, "Pilot Plan," 218. For an international account of the intertwined nature of concrete poetry and translation, see John Corbett and Ting Huang, eds., *The Translation and Transmission of Concrete Poetry* (London: Routledge, 2019). "The practice and appreciation of concrete

poetry 'unites and connects' across cultures and languages, enriching both, in part by presenting translation challenges that have demanded creative, ingenious solutions." Corbett and Huang, *The Translation and Transmission of Concrete Poetry*, 1.

65. Mariano Siskind, "The Genres of World Literature: The Case of Magical Realism," in D'Haen, Damrosch, and Kadir, *The Routledge Companion to World Literature*, 346; Siskind, *Cosmopolitan Desires*, 83.

66. Gerard Aching points out in the Caribbean literary field a legacy favoring opacity, orality, and other nonstandard linguistic styles, modes that have not been well served by broader circulation in the languages of literary consecration, English and French. Gerard Aching, "The 'Right to Opacity' and World Literature," *1616: Anuario de Literatura Comparada* 2 (2012): 33–47. Aching draws primarily from Édouard Glissant and Derek Walcott's conversations about opacity in translation from and between Creoles. Krista Brune has argued the same for Brazilian literature, while also celebrating the new twenty-first-century translation projects that are changing this trend. Krista Brune, "The Necessities and Dangers of Translation: Brazilian Literature on a Global Stage," *Comparative Critical Studies* 15, no. 1 (2018): 5–24.

67. Eric Hayot treats "non-Western literature" as so much scholarly broccoli: vegetables might be "interesting, even 'important'" or "good for you" but nobody could build a meal or a new literary paradigm around them—"that importance has not mattered much to the making of literary history." Eric Hayot, *On Literary Worlds* (New York: Oxford University Press, 2012), 1–6. When Moretti tests his distant reading approach on Brazil, he reads in Antonio Candido's "Literature and Underdevelopment" the confirmation of his own preconceived notion. He cites Candido's claim that "'we [Latin American literatures] never create original expressive forms or basic expressive techniques, in the sense that we mean by Romanticism, on the level of literary movements; the psychological novel, on the level of genres; free indirect style, on that of writing.'" Antonio Candido, "Literature and Underdevelopment," in *Latin America in Its Literature*, ed. César Fernández Moreno, Juilo Ortega, and Ivan A. Shulman, trans. Mary G. Berg (New York: Holmes & Meier, 1980), 272–73. Cited in Moretti, "Conjectures on World Literature," 65. While Moretti draws also from Roberto Schwarz to bolster his reading of Brazilian Romanticism as derivative, he relies only on Candido's model of a Brazilian literature that began with the Romanticism of the so-called good savage, ignoring Haroldo's reading of the longer tradition of cannibal aesthetics, starting from Gregório de Matos in the Baroque era.

68. Sandra Bermann cites Judith Butler in "Performing Translation," in *A Companion to Translation Studies*, ed. Bermann and Catherine Porter (Chichester, UK: Wiley-Blackwell, 2014), 293–95. Emphasis in the original.

69. Paul Ricoeur, *On Translation*, trans. Eileen Brennan (London: Routledge, 2006), 23–24.

70. Damrosch writes that "my claim is that world literature is not an infinite, ungraspable canon of works but rather a mode of circulation and of reading, a mode that is as applicable to individual works as to bodies of material, available for reading established classics and new discoveries alike." Damrosch, *What Is World Literature?*, 5.

71. Emphasis mine. Lawrence Venuti, "World Literature and Translation Studies," in D'Haen, Damrosch, and Kadir, *The Routledge Companion to World Literature*, 191.

72. Her term "translingual edition" elevates the translator's editorial role, expanding the insight that stable originals never exist from fields like classical studies, or from nonliterary texts, to apply to any work transformed by the process of publication, including modern and contemporary literatures. Karen Emmerich, *Literary Translation and the Making of Originals* (New York: Bloomsbury Academic, 2017), 9.

73. Moretti writes that "the study of world literature is—inevitably—a study of the struggle for symbolic hegemony across the world." Moretti, "Conjectures on World Literature," 64. Cannibal translation instead struggles against symbolic hegemony through practices of translation that focus on process and not publication or sales, on becoming and not being.

74. María Constanza Guzmán calls for investigation into "translator sociographies" to include "the interplay between the intimate and personal and socio-historical [and to] underscore situatedness [and] the translator's self-understanding." María Constanza Guzmán, "Translation North and South: Composing the Translator's Archive," *TTR: Traduction, terminologie, rédaction* 26, no. 2 (2013): 188. In her notions of the importance of the translator's sociography within an analysis of the translator's archive, she draws from Daniel Simeoni's articulation of the translator as an agent of cultural production, "moving from a predominantly linguistic/semiotic outlook towards a broader, 'contextualizing' comprehension not only of translation but of all textual production." Daniel Simeoni, "Translation and Society: The Emergence of a Conceptual Relationship," in *In Translation: Reflections, Refractions, Transformations*, ed. Paul St-Pierre and P. C. Kar (Amsterdam: John Benjamins, 2007), 14–15. Quoted in Guzmán, "Translation North and South," 173. My approach sees a reciprocal relationship between the linguistic/semiotic and the sociological in translation studies.

75. John Milton and Paul Bandia propose that "agents of translation are much more than gate-keepers" and that inclusion of these diverse agents into translation analysis will also incorporate their unintentional consequences and the "casual and personal way in which ideas gain currency." John Milton and Paul Bandia, "Introduction: Agents of Translation and Translation Studies," in *Agents of Translation*, ed. Milton and Bandia (Amsterdam: John Benjamins, 2009), 10–12.

76. Several single-translator volumes establish the prolific and influential translation praxis of Jorge Luis Borges: see Efraín Kristal's *Invisible Work: Borges and Translation* (Nashville: Vanderbilt University Press, 2002) on Borges's translation projects as testing grounds for his own writing process. For insight on Borges's translations and the impact of that work on reception of authors of world literature such as Walt Whitman and Edgar Allan Poe in Latin America, see Emron Esplin, *Borges's Poe: The Influence and Reinvention of Edgar Allan Poe in Spanish America* (Athens: University of Georgia Press, 2016); David E. Johnson, *Kant's Dog: On Borges, Philosophy, and the Time of Translation* (Albany: State University of New York Press, 2012); and Sergio

Waisman, *Borges and Translation: The Irreverence of the Periphery* (Lewisburg, PA: Bucknell University Press, 2005). Translator Gregory Rabassa inspired a monograph and also wrote his own memoir: see María Constanza Guzmán, *Gregory Rabassa's Latin American Literature: A Translator's Visible Legacy* (Lewisburg, PA: Bucknell University Press, 2010) and Gregory Rabassa, *If This Be Treason: Translation and Its Dyscontents: A Memoir* (New York: New Directions, 2006). Translator Suzanne Jill Levine illuminates her own translator's archive and the impact of her work in *The Subversive Scribe: Translating Latin American Fiction* (Champaign, IL: Dalkey Archive, 2009). Heather Cleary and Martín Gaspar each explore fictional translators within Latin American narratives: see Heather Cleary, *The Translator's Visibility: Scenes from Contemporary Latin American Fiction* (New York: Bloomsbury Academic, 2021) and Martín Gaspar, *La condición traductora* (Rosario, Argentina: Beatriz Viterbo, 2014). In an informative meditation on the understudied intersection of translation and mass culture, Gaspar analyzes young adult fiction as translated in Latin America to interrogate the nature of the writerly education that translations of world literature impart on "minor" readers. See Martín Gaspar, "Minor Translations and the World Literature of the Masses in Latin America," in *Translation and World Literature*, ed. Susan Bassnett (London: Routledge, 2019), 109. Lastly, the comparative approach is implied and made possible but not engaged with in the excellent collection *Voice-Overs*, which unites essays about translation by the authors and translators already mentioned and many more, including the contributions of Latinx writers and translators to the field. See Daniel Balderston and Marcy E. Schwartz, eds., *Voice-Overs: Translation and Latin American Literature* (Albany: State University of New York Press, 2002).

77. Walter Benjamin, "The Task of the Translator: An Introduction to the Translation of Baudelaire's *Tableaux Parisiens*," trans. Harry Zohn, in Venuti, *The Translation Studies Reader*, 80.

78. Frances R. Aparicio identifies the "versión" in Latin America with the *modernista* movement of the late nineteenth century, when Manuel Gutiérrez Nájera admonished Spanish American poets to imitate less from Spanish poets and adapt styles from other languages, so their poetry "would be invigorated by intermixing"; for her, the Spanish American *versión modernista* predates the US modernist version. Frances R. Aparicio, *Versiones, interpretaciones y creaciones: Instancias de la traducción literaria en Hispanoamérica en el siglo veinte* (Gaithersburg, MD: Ediciones Hispamérica, 1991), 34–36. Lawrence Venuti names Ezra Pound the originator of the "poet's version," where "departures from the source text that were motivated by the imposition of a different poetics or by mere ignorance of the source language." Lawrence Venuti, "The Poet's Version; or, An Ethics of Translation," *Translation Studies* 4, no. 2 (2011): 231.

79. See Tom Boll on how Hispanophone translators of Eliot crafted an aesthetically smoother but more politically radical Eliot; for her part, Marjorie Perloff places the Brazilian concrete poets as some of the best readers of Ezra Pound, placing their project in a trajectory she builds from Pound through Brazilian concretism and Tropicália to John Cage. Tom Boll, *Octavio Paz and T. S. Eliot: Modern Poetry and the Translation of Influence* (London: Legenda Modern Humanities Research Association and Maney Publishing, 2012); and

Marjorie Perloff, *Unoriginal Genius: Poetry by Other Means in the New Century* (Chicago: University of Chicago Press, 2012).

80. Haroldo, "Translation as Creation and Criticism," 315. The term "transcreation" was added to this English translation; it is not present in the Portuguese source text from 1962. In Haroldo's work, *transcriação* does not appear until "Píndaro, hoje" (1969). See Nóbrega and Milton, "The Role of Haroldo and Augusto de Campos in Bringing Translation to the Fore," 259. "Transcreation" was a definitive key term for Haroldo, but even in the 1985 essay "Da transcriação: Poética e semiótica da operação tradutora," he still associates transcreation with a broader practice of neologisms for artistic translation procedures from the initial framing of "re-creation." See Haroldo, *Transcriação*, 79. Although "transcreation" may be as unstable a term in his thought as "cannibal translation," the specificity of transcreation as technical practice remains clear.

81. Paulo Rónai, *Escola de tradutores* (Rio de Janeiro: Livraria São José, 1956), 17. Cited in Haroldo, "Translation as Creation and Criticism," 315.

82. Haroldo, "Translation as Creation and Criticism," 325.

83. Kwame Anthony Appiah, "Thick Translation," in Venuti, *The Translation Studies Reader*, 389–400.

84. José Emilio Pacheco, *Aproximaciones*, ed. Miguel Ángel Flores (Mexico City: Editorial Penélope, 1984), 7–8.

85. Augusto de Campos, "Antes do anti," in *O anticrítico* (São Paulo: Companhia das Letras, 1986), 10.

CHAPTER 1

1. Augusto de Campos to E. E. Cummings, October 31, 1956, box 4, folder 127, E. E. Cummings Papers (hereafter cited as EECP), series 1, Letters to E. E. Cummings, Houghton Library Special Collections, Harvard University, Cambridge, MA.

2. Octavio Paz, "e. e. cummings: Seis poemas y un recuerdo," in *Puertas al campo* (Mexico City: Universidad Nacional Autónoma de México, 1966), 90.

3. Octavio Paz to E. E. Cummings, May 23, 1958, box 21, folder 1001, EECP, series 1, Letters to E. E. Cummings.

4. Augusto de Campos generously allowed me to consult his personal papers related to his Cummings project when I visited him in São Paulo on June 13, 2019. These materials included letters from Cummings and Marion Morehouse, copies of his own letters, letters and instructions exchanged with the printer at the Ministry of Education in Rio de Janeiro, eight rounds of corrected proofs for *10 poemas* (1960), letters he received from readers including the French translator D. Jon Grossman, press clippings from Brazilian newspapers on the death of Cummings, and more.

5. William Carlos Williams translated numerous poems from Spanish in his lifetime; he translated Paz for *Evergreen Review* in 1955 and included the Mexican poet in his anthology *The Penguin Book of Spanish Verse* in 1956. For further detail, see William Carlos Williams, *By Word of Mouth: Poems from the Spanish, 1916–1959*, ed. Jonathan Cohen (New York: New Directions, 2011), 150–52.

6. Portugal left Cummings unimpressed during a visit in 1921. As John Dos Passos describes him in his memoir, "'New Englander to the core, he was re-

pelled by the rankness of the Manueline style . . . some ancestral phobia against popery came to the surface.'" Christopher Sawyer-Lauçanno, *E. E. Cummings: A Biography* (Naperville, IL: Sourcebooks, 2004), 186. Cummings recalls that trip: "many years ago I made a 23day [*sic*] voyage by freighter from New Bedford to Lisboa with John Dos Passos, who proved so linguistically gifted that my subsequent Portuguese rarely transcended the equivalent of 'typewriter'—which in fact . . . may explain why I've never adventured Brazil." E. E. Cummings to Isolda Hermes da Fonseca, 1954, box 3, folder 172, E. E. Cummings Additional Papers (hereafter cited as EECAP), series 1, Letters by EEC to Various Correspondents.

7. Augusto to Cummings, November 20, 1956, box 4, folder 127, EECP, series 1, Letters to E. E. Cummings.

8. Augusto's papers record his sending to Cummings *Noigandres* nos. 2, 3, and 4 when they came out, in February 1955 and in 1956, and the note of thanks he received May 14, 1955. Unfortunately, these rare issues are not in the E. E. Cummings Papers at Houghton Library, nor is it clear exactly when Augusto sent the typescript translations, as they are archived along with the 1958 letters but are associated with the earlier correspondence.

9. Eva Hesse writes from Munich, US Zone, that despite her efforts as a translator "I have, however, so far not been able to break down the prevailing literary prejudice against yourself, Wallace Stevens, and Ezra Pound, who are to my mind the three leading poets in the English language at present—(I would also include T.S. Eliot as a fourth, but as he is 'accepted' by our professorinos I have not had any trouble on his account)." Eva Hesse to E. E. Cummings, April 25, 1949, box 13, folder 575 (1), EECP, series 1, Letters to E. E. Cummings.

10. Augusto's letters more consistently avoid capital letters; where Cummings opts for normative capitalization when writing the address and date, Augusto addresses himself to "dear mr. e.e. cummings." This typographic choice to never capitalize is consistent with Augusto's own use of only the lowercase, as in *O anticrítico* (1986).

11. The extra spaces added between "and   now   new" are too thoughtfully placed for dramatic effect to be the unintended error of an unpublished typescript.

12. Cummings to Augusto, November 6, 1956, box 1, folder 62, EECAP, series 1, Letters by E. E. Cummings to Various Correspondents.

13. Augusto to Cummings, November 20, 1956, box 4, folder 127, EECP, series 1, Letters to E. E. Cummings.

14. Greg Barnhisel, "*Perspectives USA* and the Cultural Cold War: Modernism in Service of the State," *Modernism/Modernity* 14, no. 4 (2007): 739.

15. The Cummings poems featured in the French *Profils* are not the same as in the United States–based *Perspectives*; only three poems appear in both; perhaps certain poems were already translated or fit the French audience better.

16. D. Jon Grossman to Edouard Roditi, August 9, 1952, box 50, folder 80, EECP, series 4, Other Letters.

17. The second issue exemplified the clash between the board's financiers and Laughlin's aims. Critic Alice Widener called the journal "'a vehicle for the writings of many well-known pro-Communists, . . . the literary avant-garde who pride themselves on a lack of appreciation for American life, . . . and the 'unintel-

ligible . . . unsuitable' modernist verse by poets such as cummings." Greg Barnhisel, *Cold War Modernists: Art, Literature, and American Cultural Diplomacy* (New York: Columbia University Press, 2015), 210; third ellipsis in the original.

18. Typescript of translations by D. Jon Grossman, box 109, folder 31, EECP, series 10, Other Manuscripts. The poem begins with the line "the communists have fine Eyes," but actually is titled in French with a time and place: "16 heures / l'Etoile." E. E. Cummings, in *Complete Poems 1904–1962*, ed. George J. Firmage (New York: Liveright, 1991), 273. As in other cases, the French language featured prominently in the source text might have drawn Grossman's interest in translating, but the content prompted him to reconsider inclusion.

19. Cummings, "he does not have to feel because he thinks," in *Complete Poems*, 406.

20. Barnhisel, *Cold War Modernists*, 194–95.

21. Typescript of translations by D. Jon Grossman, box 109, folder 30, EECP, series 10, Other Manuscripts.

22. E. E. Cummings to D. Jon Grossman, March 23, 1951, box 3, folder 159 (3), EECAP, series 1, Letters by E. E. Cummings to Various Correspondents.

23. D. Jon Grossman to Edouard Roditi, August 9, 1952, box 50, folder 80, EECP, series 4, Other Letters.

24. Augusto to Cummings, September 4, 1958, box 4, folder 182, EECP, series 1, Letters to E. E. Cummings.

25. Eva Hesse to Brandt & Brandt, June 5, 1953, box 50, folder 103, EECP, series 4, Other Letters.

26. E. E. Cummings to Eva Hesse, January 29, 1958, box 39, folder 301, EECP, series 2, Letters from E. E. Cummings.

27. Eva Hesse to E. E. Cummings, January 11, 1960, box 13, folder 575, EECP, series 1, Letters to E. E. Cummings.

28. "Concerning the Langewiesche (bilingual) volume, provided its publisher can & will guarantee me as many proofs of my own poems—versus the translations—as I may demand." E. E. Cummings to Eva Hesse, April 26, 1957, box 39, folder 301, EECP, series 2, Letters from E. E. Cummings.

29. James Laughlin to Alain Bosquet, November 3, 1955, box 50, folder 123, EECP, series 4, Other Letters.

30. Hesse to Cummings, February 12, 1962, box 13, folder 575, EECP, series 1, Letters to E. E. Cummings.

31. Attributed to E. E. Cummings, this quote features on the title page of Grossman's *En traduction* draft. This page also describes the poems as "traduits de l'américaine par D Jon Grossman et l'auteur." Typescript of translations by D. Jon Grossman, box 109, folder 31, EECP, series 10, Other Manuscripts.

32. "The lower the quality and distinction of its language, the larger the extent to which it [the source text] is information, the less fertile a field is it for translation, until the utter pre-ponderance of content, far from being the lever for a translation of distinctive mode, renders it impossible. The higher the level of a work the more does it remain translatable." Benjamin, "The Task of the Translator," 82.

33. Cummings to Augusto, December 1, 1956, box 1, folder 62, EECAP, series 1, Letters by E. E. Cummings to Various Correspondents.

34. In fact, all three translate "love is more thicker than forget" and "Since feeling is first," but Paz's Spanish translations alter, adapt, and re-create these works, while the German and French stick closer to the source.

35. Augusto de Campos, "30 anos, 40 poemas," in *40 poem(a)s* by E. E. Cummings, expanded ed. (São Paulo: Editora Brasiliense, 1986), 11.

36. Augusto foregrounds violence in the epigraph he selects from Cummings's *Is 5* (1926): "my theory of technique, if I have one, is very far from original; nor is it complicated. I can express it in fifteen words. . . . 'Would you hit a woman with a child?—No, I'd hit her with a brick.' Like the burlesk [*sic*] comedian, I am abnormally fond of that precision which creates movement." Augusto de Campos, trans., epigraph to *10 poemas*, by E. E. Cummings (Rio de Janeiro: Ministério de Educação e Cultura, 1960), 8.

37. "Organic structure, expressionism of vocabulary (typographical gesticulation), disfiguring (not always surpassing) the discursive." Augusto, "Olho e fôlego," in *10 poemas*, 7.

38. Augusto, "Olho e fôlego," 5.

39. Cummings, "twi-," in *Complete Poems*, 351; Augusto, trans., "crep-," by Cummings, in *10 poemas*, 17.

40. Cummings, "birds(," in *Complete Poems*, 448; Augusto, trans., "aves(," by Cummings, in *10 poemas*, 25.

41. Cummings, "un," in *Complete Poems*, 463; Augusto, trans., "a," by Cummings, in *10 poemas*, 29. Both source and target poems split up the phrase into brief lines of only three to five letters each, with the word "slowliest" or "lentamente" interpolated in between; I gloss the phrase to emphasize Augusto's grammatical shifts, which allowed him to maintain the number of letters in most lines.

42. Cummings, "(fea," in *Complete Poems*, 653; Augusto, trans., "(plu," by Cummings, in *10 poemas*, 31.

43. Cummings, "i will be," in *Complete Poems*, 195; Augusto, trans., "eu estarei," by Cummings, in *10 poemas*, 11.

44. Corrected page proofs for *10 poemas*, private collection of Augusto de Campos.

45. Cummings, "i will be," in *Complete Poems*, 195.

46. Augusto, trans., "eu estarei," by Cummings, in *10 poemas*, 11.

47. Cummings, "i will be," in *Complete Poems*, 195.

48. Augusto, trans., "eu estarei," by Cummings, in *10 poemas*, 11. Augusto does refrain from using line breaks to introduce the even more explicit translingual possibility, which could have been "crep ús culo," but that would perhaps have been a step too far.

49. Cummings, "o pr," in *Complete Poems*, 392.

50. Augusto, trans., "ó pr", by Cummings, in *10 poemas*, 19. Of course, with the accent mark, in the first line Augusto reads the source text title "o pr" as "oh pr" as in the exclamation "oh progress" not yet the definite article it would become in "O Presidente" or "The President."

51. Augusto to Cummings, November 20, 1956, box 4, folder 127, EECP, series 1, Letters to E. E. Cummings.

52. Cummings corrected the English of the citation Augusto planned to use as an epigraph and the formatting of his draft of "birds(" in the second and

third pages of his letter dated November 20, 1956. The two pages were returned to Augusto with Cummings's letter dated December 1, 1956, private collection of Augusto de Campos.

53. In the translations by Grossman, he does appear drawn to selections that include French in the source texts. In cases when he wants to correct errors that Cummings made in French—errors that seem to be errors more than choices—he then asks permission to correct the French in his translations.

54. Augusto de Campos to E. E. Cummings, November 20, 1956, box 4, folder 127, EECP, series 1, Letters to E. E. Cummings.

55. The undated pages are catalogued from 1958, but Augusto believes they were sent sometime in 1955 along with the rare *Noigandres* 2. The poems include "Semi de Zucca" by Haroldo de Campos translated into English and "com/som" by Augusto de Campos in French. Cummings replied with a thank-you postcard dated May 14, 1955, private collection of Augusto de Campos.

56. The authorship of these typescript translations is ambiguous, and Augusto does not remember. Perhaps he composed them personally for Cummings; equally probable they were a collective effort of three *Noigandres* poets, perhaps roughly compiled in conversation and typed up by Augusto. To my knowledge these poems were not published in English or French until the 1960s, making these typescripts among the earliest translations of the concrete poets. Unsigned typescript, box 109, folder 10, EECP, series 10, Other Manuscripts.

57. The proof is captioned "e.e. cummings personally reviewed the proofs for this edition. this in fact was the only requirement he made to the translator. the present *fac-simile* illustrates the rigorous care the american poet took with the preservation of his extremely personal spatial architecture." Augusto, trans., *10 poemas*, 37.

58. Augusto writes that he "never asked license to use the proofs Cummings sent." Email message to author, November 7, 2019.

59. This page was from the first set of proofs worthy of the author's attention—in fact, the third produced for the project, which ultimately took eight tries to meet with mutual satisfaction of author and translator. After Cummings mailed the corrected proofs back to São Paulo, Augusto would recopy and translate the corrections onto both the English and the Portuguese versions so he could send them to the printer in Rio and keep the originals.

60. D. Jon Grossman to Augusto de Campos, January 15, 1967, private collection of Augusto de Campos.

61. Grossman to Augusto, January 15, 1967, private collection of Augusto de Campos.

62. Augusto, trans., *10 poemas*, 37.

63. For a more extensive discussion of this term, see Isabel C. Gómez, "Anti-surrealism? Augusto de Campos 'Untranslates' Spanish American Poetry," *Mutatis Mutandis* 11, no. 2 (2018): 376–99.

64. Cummings to Augusto, postcards, December 7 and 26, 1959, private collection of Augusto de Campos.

65. Cummings to Augusto, typescript draft of a letter, July 15, 1960, box 39, folder 299, EECP, series 2, Letters from E. E. Cummings. I use italics here to indicate the words emphasized in red type in the source.

66. After this meeting, Paz developed an interest in plays written by Cummings. He wanted to translate and produce *Santa Claus* in Mexico City; this project did not come to fruition due to lack of funding.

67. It may be unlikely Paz ever wrote anything without considering its eventual publication; he did publish the six Cummings translations first in 1966, after the poet's death, still writing that they were composed "for myself and a few friends." Paz, "e. e. cummings: Seis poemas y un recuerdo," 90.

68. Octavio Paz to E. E. Cummings, May 23, 1958, box 21, folder 1001, EECP, series 1, Letters to E. E. Cummings.

69. Cummings to Paz, June 2, 1958, box 41, folder 477, EECP, series 2, Letters from E. E. Cummings.

70. Paz, "e. e. cummings: Seis poemas y un recuerdo," 93.

71. "Me he acercado a sus originales con respeto y amor. Más lo último que lo primero. No sé si mis traducciones sean literalmente fieles; por lo menos he procurado ser fiel al espíritu si no a la letra." Octavio Paz to E. E. Cummings, May 23, 1958, box 21, folder 1001, EECP, series 1, Letters to E. E. Cummings.

72. Paz, "e. e. cummings: Seis poemas y un recuerdo," 93.

73. Paz, "e. e. cummings: Seis poemas y un recuerdo," 95; ellipsis in the original.

74. Paz, "e. e. cummings: Seis poemas y un recuerdo," 90.

75. Paz, "e. e. cummings: Seis poemas y un recuerdo," 91.

76. Typescript of translations by Octavio Paz, box 114, folder 66, EECP, series 10, Other Manuscripts.

77. Paz, "e. e. cummings: Seis poemas y un recuerdo," 96.

78. Cummings, "in spite of everything," in *Complete Poems*, 289.

79. Octavio Paz, "A pesar de todo," in *Obras completas*, vol. 12, *Obra poética II (1969–1998)* (Mexico City: Fondo de Cultura Económica, 2004), 400.

80. Cummings, "in spite of everything," 289.

81. Paz, "A pesar de todo," 400.

82. Paz, "Amor es más espeso que olvidar," in *Obra poética II*, 400.

83. Cummings, "love is more thicker than forget," in *Complete Poems*, 530.

84. Paz, "Amor es más espeso que olvidar," 400.

85. Cummings, "love is more thicker than forget," 530.

86. Cummings, "love is more thicker than forget," 530; Paz, "Amor es más espeso que olvidar," in *Obra poética II*, 401.

87. Octavio Paz, "Translation: Literature and Letters," trans. Irene del Corral, in *Theories of Translation: An Anthology of Essays from Dryden to Derrida*, ed. Rainer Schulte and John Biguenet (Chicago: University of Chicago Press, 1992), 158.

88. Octavio Paz, *Versiones y diversiones* (Mexico City: Joaquín Mortiz, 1974), 9.

89. Paz, *Traducción: Literatura y literalidad* (Barcelona: Tusquets, 1971), 16. I translate from the Spanish source text by Paz in this case because the English translation by Irene del Corral does not reproduce this phrase "before his eyes."

90. Octavio Paz, *Versiones y diversiones*, 2nd ed. (Mexico City: Joaquín Mortiz, 1978), 8. In her analysis of Paz's translations of Nerval, Fabienne Bradu writes that Paz allows readers to choose between form sacrificed to preserve

content or content sacrificed to preserve form, an "unsolvable dilemma that surely motivated Paz to publish the two versions together, as if to leave that impossible decision up to the reader." Fabienne Bradu, *Los puentes de la traducción: Octavio Paz y la poesía francesa* (Mexico City: Universidad Nacional Autónoma de México, 2004), 30. I would contend that, in a reading practice oriented through cannibal translation and where both options are present, that choice is rendered unnecessary and irrelevant.

91. "Cummings more and more came to dread the return to Manhattan in the fall—after the leaves had fallen in New Hampshire. . . . The one(li)ness he could feel at Joy Farm was also a harbinger of the loneliness he associated with the lack of natural beauty in New York." Sawyer-Lauçanno, *E. E. Cummings*, 519.

92. Paz, "s (u," in *Obra poética II*, 399. It bears mention that Paz does still normalize Cummings's punctuation, even in this more experimental selection, adding a space between the letter and parenthesis of his title line "s (u" where no space is present in the original "l(a."

93. Cummings, "l(a," in *Complete Poems*, 673.

94. The six poems Paz sent to Cummings were first published as "e. e. cummings: Seis poemas y un recuerdo" in *Puertas al campo* (1966) and reprinted in the first edition of *Traducción: Literatura y literalidad* (1971). By the 1973 edition, he adds the seventh poem and retitles the piece "siete poemas y un recuerdo" to include "s (u," his translation of "l(a," now the first of the seven Cummings translations.

95. Augusto added the two-tone green color scheme to a later version for a poster by Omar Guedes for the exhibition *Transcriar* organized by Julio Plaza and shown in the São Paulo Museo de Arte Contemporáneo in 1985. Augusto de Campos, trans., *40 poem(a)s*, by E. E. Cummings (São Paulo: Editora Brasiliense, 1984), 29. The title "so l(a (cummings) (1984)" accompanies the poem in *Despoesia*, where the poet places the work in a section of "intraduções." Augusto de Campos, *Despoesia*, Coleção Signos, ed. Haroldo de Campos (São Paulo: Editora Perspetiva, 1996).

96. In his essay introducing *40 poem(a)s*, Augusto distinguishes "minha intradução" (my untranslation) from the others by excluding it from the "count" of total poems. "In the first edition from 1960, there were only 10. (I began translating them in 1954.) The second edition (1979) grew to 20. Now there are 40 Cummings poems that I have turned into Portuguese—not to mention my untranslation." Augusto, "30 anos, 40 poemas," in *40 poem(a)s*, 11.

CHAPTER 2

1. My own translation from Haroldo's selective vision of Paz. "Uma linguagem que corte o fôlego. Rasante, talhante, cortante. Um exército de espadas. Uma linguagem de aços exatos, de relâmpagos afiados, de esdrúxulas e agudos, incansáveis, reluzentes, metódicas navalhas. Uma linguagem guilhotina. Uma dentadura trituradora que faça uma pasta dos eutuêlenósvósêles." Octavio Paz, "Trabalhos do Poeta" (1949), in *Constelação*, by Paz and Haroldo de Campos, trans. Haroldo (Rio de Janeiro: AGGS Industrias Gráficas, 1972), 71. "Un len-

guaje que corte el resuello. Rasante, tajante, cortante. Un ejército de sables. Un lenguaje de aceros exactos, de relámpagos afilados, de esdrújulos y agudos, incansables, relucientes, metódicas navajas. Un lenguaje guillotina. Una dentadura trituradora que haga una masa del yotúélnosotrosvosotrosellos." Octavio Paz, from section 10 of *Libertad bajo palabra* in *Obras completas*, vol. 11, *Obra poética I (1935–1970)* (Mexico City: Fondo de Cultura Económica, 1997), 152.

2. Octavio Paz, "Recapitulaciones," in Paz and Haroldo, *Constelação*, n.p. This epigraph Haroldo selects splits apart a section from *Corriente alterna* in which Paz draws on Buddhist thought to consider poetic practice; Haroldo takes out the Buddhism just as he will seek to take out the surrealism in his selections of Paz.

3. Magdalena Edwards, "The Translator's Colors: Elizabeth Bishop in Brazil and Elsewhere" (PhD diss., University of California Los Angeles, 2007), 256. In the case of Paz's poem "Objects & Apparitions," Bishop transposes two stanzas, a choice Paz applauded and reproduced in Spanish in subsequent editions of the poem; "her intervention is indicative of the kind of translationship she and Paz enjoyed, where both poets got their hands dirty with the other's work as poet-translators, not simply as translators." Edwards, "The Translator's Colors, 229.

4. Odile Cisneros traces the two poet-translators' theoretical similarities: their shared affirmation of the autonomy of translations as works of literature; affinities between their translation concepts, Paz's "analogous" and Haroldo's "isomorphic" relationship with the original; and their vision of translation as a deep form of critical reading. However, her analysis of *Transblanco* along with translations of Mallarmé and E.E. Cummings concludes that where Haroldo and Augusto follow these theories in practice and take translation as "an opportunity for creative possibilities and mutually enriching intercultural exchange," Paz instead does not take full advantage and in practice exhibits greater "timidity and solemnity" than both the de Campos brothers and his own theories. Maria Esther Maciel contrasts their cosmographic metaphors to understand the "plurality and hybridity" of Latin American cultural production by distinguishing between Paz's analogic approach from Haroldo's anthropophagic approach—a distinction which also characterizes their translation concepts. Klaus Meyer-Minnemann studies *Transblanco* as a perfect expression of Haroldo's transcreation concept, in which there is a dual operation to not only express the work in a target language but also to reveal and recreate the "poetic function" of the source. Marjorie Perloff reads Paz's *Blanco* (1966), their collaborative *Transblanco* (1986), and Haroldo's epic poem *Galáxias* (1984) as divergent responses to their shared interest in Ezra Pound and his ideogram, finding that Paz rejected Pound's ideogram as a translation concept that betrays the "arrogance of the conquistador" whereas Haroldo embraced the ideogram as a productive exercise of juxtaposition. Analyzing Haroldo's translations and correspondence with Paz, Severo Sarduy, and Julio Cortázar, Jasmin Wrobel distinguishes this intra–Latin Americanist dialogue as combatting a shared peripheral experience and supporting the Brazilian author in developing his concept of "world literature without center or periphery and the Baroque as a point of departure for Latin American literatures." See Odile Cisneros, "Traducción y poéticas radicales: El caso de Octavio Paz y el grupo *Noigandres*," in *Estudios hispánicos en*

el siglo XXI, ed. Jelena Filipović et al. (Belgrade: University of Belgrade, 2014), 222–23; Maria Ester Maciel, "América Latina Reinventada: Octavio Paz e Haroldo de Campos," *Revista Iberoamericana*, 64, nos. 182–83 (1998): 222; Klaus Meyer-Minnemann, "Octavio Paz-Haroldo de Campos *Transblanco*: Punto de intersección de dos escrituras poéticas de la Modernidad," *Poligrafías: Revista de Literatura Comparada* 3 (1998–2000): 105; Marjorie Perloff, "Refiguring the Poundian Ideogram: From Octavio Paz's *Blanco/Branco* to Haroldo de Campos's *Galáxias*," *Modernist Cultures* 37, no. 1 (2012): 41–52; and Jasmin Wrobel, "Desde *Transblanco* até *Un tal Lucas*; Três exemplos dos frutíferos diálogos inter-americanos de Haroldo de Campos," *Cadernos de Literatura Comparada* 32 (2015): 207. For further discussion of the translationship between the two poets beyond the *Transblanco* volume, including essays, remembrances, and poetic responses, see Jamille Pinheiro Dias, Marília Librandi, and Tom Winterbottom, eds. *Transpoetic Exchange: Haroldo de Campos, Octavio Paz, and Other Multiversal Dialogues* (Lewisburg, PA: Bucknell University Press, 2020).

5. Octavio Paz to Haroldo de Campos, inscription in a book held at the Casa das Rosas in São Paulo, Acervo Haroldo de Campos, vol. 6538, William Carlos Williams, *Veinte poemas*, trans. Octavio Paz (Mexico City: Ediciones Era, 1973), title page.

6. Some of their letters were written with an eye toward eventual publication. While the first set of letters from 1968 to 1970 remain merely personal, the second set from 1978 to 1981 begins with Paz accepting Haroldo's plan to translate *Blanco* and publish it alongside their correspondence and extends through Paz's approval of a final version.

7. "In 1920, the avant-garde lived in Spanish America; in 1960, in Brazil." Octavio Paz, "¿Poesía latinoamericana?," in *Obras completas*, vol. 3, *Fundación y disidencia: Dominio hispánico* (Mexico City: Fondo de Cultura Económica, 1994), 71. "In Brazil there truly exists an authentic and rigorous avant-garde: the concrete poets." Paz, "Los nuevos acólitos," in *Fundación y disidencia*, 361.

8. Octavio Paz to Haroldo de Campos, Delhi, March 14, 1968, in Paz and Haroldo, *Transblanco*, 96–97.

9. Paz to Haroldo, Delhi, March 14, 1968, in Paz and Haroldo, *Transblanco*, 101.

10. The translations into Portuguese of all letters by Paz and other Hispanophone interlocutors are unattributed.

11. Haroldo adds references to Augusto's "Mallarmé: O poeta em greve" (1967), which predates Paz's "Soneto en ix" (1968). Paz and Haroldo, *Transblanco*, 107, 133. They each translate this same complex sonnet by Mallarmé, "Ses purs ongles très haut dédiant leur onyx." Odile Cisneros discusses Augusto's choice to maintain the "ix" rhyme but lighten the diction as opposed to Paz's elimination of the main rhyme but elevation of the poem's indeterminacy. See Odile Cisneros, "Traducción y poéticas radicales," 218–20. In another example of Brazilian primacy, Haroldo claims the filmic qualities of Paz's *Blanco* are predated by Augusto's "Poetamenos," which he described as "filmletras" as early as 1957. Paz and Haroldo, *Transblanco*, 130.

12. Paz to Haroldo, Delhi, March 14, 1968, in Paz and Haroldo, *Transblanco* 100.

13. Peter Sloterdijk connects rage with the denial of thymos, the sociocultural exclusion from the human desire, privilege, and right to give and receive worthily. Peter Sloterdijk, *Rage and Time: A Psychopolitical Investigation*, trans. Mario Wenning (New York: Columbia University Press, 2010), 10–17.

14. Haroldo to Paz, São Paulo, February 24, 1968, in Paz and Haroldo, *Transblanco*, 94.

15. Paz writes that "the peculiar relationship between poetry and criticism that defines concrete poetry does not separate it from the tradition of Western poetry: it converts it into its complementary contradiction." Paz to Haroldo, Delhi, March 14, 1968, in Paz and Haroldo, *Transblanco*, 97.

16. Paz to Haroldo, Delhi, March 14, 1968, in Paz and Haroldo, *Transblanco*, 98.

17. With the exception of Edgard Braga and Pedro Xisto, who produce work less in need of explication, Haroldo provides commentary for all the Brazilian and Portuguese-language poets listed.

18. Haroldo defines "poesia para" as a "committed poetry, without giving up the devices and technical achievements of concrete poetry." Haroldo de Campos, "Servidão de passagem (1961)," trans. Edwin Morgan, in *An Anthology of Concrete Poetry*, ed. Emmet Williams (New York: Something Else Press, 1967), n.p.

19. Haroldo de Campos, note to "preto" by José Lino Grunewald (1957), in E. Williams, *An Anthology of Concrete Poetry*, n.p.

20. Paz to Haroldo, Delhi, March 14, 1968, in Paz and Haroldo, *Transblanco*, 98.

21. Haroldo to Paz, São Paulo, February 24, 1968, in Paz and Haroldo, *Transblanco*, 94–95. Haroldo's first letter ends with questions about the words *rejegas* in the poem "Las palabras" and *librero* in the poem "Animación" from *Lección de cosas*. In this second case, he also doubts the English translation by Muriel Rukeyser: where she has used "bookseller," Haroldo thinks it should be "bookshelf." Haroldo implies superiority as a translator and performs his methodology, consulting translations into other languages in a "laboratory of texts." In his response, Paz answers these specific questions—but he does not take up the critique of the other translator implied in Haroldo's question. "*Rejego* é um mexicanismo: quer dizer: obstinado, teimoso, indócil; se aplica em geral aos animais, às mulas em particular. *Librero* é um armário no qual se colocam livros." Paz to Haroldo, Delhi, March 14, 1968, in Paz and Haroldo, *Transblanco*, 101.

22. Haroldo to Paz, undated letter, likely sent between November and December 1968, in Paz and Haroldo, *Transblanco*, 109.

23. Paz, "Las palabras," in *Obra poética I*, 66–67.

24. Haroldo, "As palavras" by Paz, in Paz and Haroldo, *Constelação*, 67.

25. Paz, "Las palabras," 66–67.

26. Haroldo, "As palavras," 67.

27. Paz, "Las palabras," 66–67.

28. Haroldo, "As palavras," 67.

29. Paz to Haroldo, Delhi, March 14, 1968, in Paz and Haroldo, *Transblanco*, 100.

30. Paz writes: "I believe that with these poems concrete poetry makes its appearance in Spanish America. (That of Goeritz is more plastic arts)." Paz to Haroldo, Delhi, undated letter on letterhead of the Mexican Embassy, likely sent between March and October 1968, in Paz and Haroldo, *Transblanco*, 102–3. Mexican architect and artist Mathias Goeritz appeared in the Emmet Williams anthology represented by the poem and a photograph of a sculpture, from *Mensajes de Oro* (1960) and "el eco del oro" (1961). Haroldo concurs with Paz that Goeritz is not concrete poetry but, rather, plastic arts. Haroldo, "Notas," in Paz and Haroldo, *Transblanco 130*.

31. Sergio Delgado Moya reads the concrete poetry of Paz during this period, including *Blanco* (1966), *Topoemas* (1968), and *Discos visuales* (1968), as a culmination of Paz's concern with mass media and technology—advertising with *Discos visuales* and film with *Blanco*. Delgado Moya, *Delirious Consumption*, 132–52.

32. Paz to Haroldo, in Paz and Haroldo, *Transblanco*, 102–3.

33. Octavio Paz to Celso Lafer, Kasauli, India, June 11, 1968, in Paz and Haroldo, *Transblanco*, 142.

34. Paz writes that "the lone participation of the unconscious in making a poem converts it into a psychological document; the sole presence of thought, frequently empty and speculative, evacuates it. Neither academic discourse nor sentimental vomit: monotonous arguments in verse, sad leftovers of the word, produce the same disgust in us as the turbulent dark waters of the unconscious." Octavio Paz, "Poesía de soledad y poesía de comunión," in *Obras completas*, vol. 13, *Miscelánea I: Primeros escritos* (Mexico City: Fondo de Cultura Económica, 1999), 243.

35. The copy of the limited first-run edition of *Topoemas* held in MIT's collection comes from Roman Jakobson's library and includes this inscription in Spanish: "To Roman Jakobson, these texts at the limit of the 'poetic function.' Octavio Paz, Delhi, October 8, 1968." Octavio Paz, *Topoemas* (Mexico City: Imprenta Madero, 1968). From the library of Roman Jakobson Papers, 125 of an edition limited to 150 copies. MIT Institute Archives, Cambridge, MA.

36. The Topoemas were first published as a supplement in the *Revista de la Universidad de México* (1968); Paz includes a set of final "Comentarios" to the set of visual poems, stating that "in their entirety, these topoemas are an implicit homage (now explicit) to ancient and modern masters of poetry . . . to Apollinaire, Arp, and cummings, and to Haroldo de Campos and the group of young Brazilian poets from *Noigandres* and *Invenção*." Paz, *Obra poética I*, 553.

37. Haroldo de Campos, "Topogramas," in *Antologia do verso à poesia concreta 1949–1962: Noigandres 5*, ed. Décio Pignatari, Haroldo de Campos, and Augusto de Campos (São Paulo: Massão Ohno, 1962), 79.

38. Paz discusses toponyms in translation through an Unamuno poem and its empty assertion of untranslatability. The poem, almost entirely made up of Spanish cities ("Ávila, Málaga, Cáceres / Játiva, Mérida, Córdoba"), ends by celebrating "the untranslatable marrow / of our Spanish tongue." Paz insists that this poem is "perfectly translatable since its image is universal" and points out that it "is remarkable that the untranslatable essence of Spain should consist of

a succession of Roman, Arabic, Celtiberian and Basque names." Paz, "Translation: Literature and Letters," 155–56.

39. Paz, "Comentarios" to the *Topoemas*, in *Obra poética I*, 553. Citation from the Guide to the Royal Botanical Gardens in English in the source text.

40. Haroldo to Paz, undated letter, in Paz and Haroldo, *Transblanco*, 108–9.

41. The English explanation was simply "An essay of poetic crystallography. The metaphorical hunger of form and form as a kind of hunger. Crystal as the ideogram of the process." Haroldo, "Cristal" in E. Williams, *An Anthology of Concrete Poetry*, n.p. The expanded Spanish explanation, again encapsulating the translation process of mirroring within the concrete poem, reads, "In this poem, we have the ideogram of a process. Made from the symmetrical repetition of the word 'crystal,' it offers a prismatic structure. Poetic crystallography triggers semiotic transformation through the permutation of the words that design the central virtual rectangle: 'hunger' and 'form.' From the metaphorical 'hunger for form' the poem is born which, in turn, is a 'form of hunger,' and so on, in a perpetual game of semantic mirrors." Haroldo de Campos, in "Poesía concreta: Configuración / textos," special issue, *Plural* 8 (May 1972): 26.

42. Augusto de Campos, "Cidade (1963)," in Augusto and Haroldo, eds., "Poesía concreta: Configuración / textos," trans. Antonio Alatorre, special issue, *Plural* 8 (May 1972): 23.

43. Paz to Haroldo, Paris, March 10, 1969, in Paz and Haroldo, *Transblanco*, 110.

44. For more on this cultural turning point and its lasting place in the Mexican imaginary see Samuel Steinberg, *Photopoetics at Tlatelolco: Afterimages of Mexico, 1968* (Austin: University of Texas Press, 2016), and Susana Draper, *1968 Mexico: Constellations of Freedom and Democracy* (Durham, NC: Duke University Press, 2018).

45. Paz to Haroldo, Delhi, October 9, 1968, in Paz and Haroldo, *Transblanco*, 104.

46. Paz to Haroldo, in Paz and Haroldo, *Transblanco*, 103. As Haroldo's annotation clarifies, "The letter is undated, but it was sent with a copy of the *Topoemas*, where one can read 'Delhi, March 20, 1968.'" Paz and Haroldo, *Transblanco*, 131n8.

47. While I focus on the Brazilian translations and publications of Paz's protest letters, with the *New York Review of Books* as a counterpoint in the United States, Paz also placed this open letter and poem in the *Times Literary Supplement* (London) and in *La Cultura* (Mexico). See Claire Brewster, *Responding to Crisis in Contemporary Mexico: The Political Writings of Paz, Fuentes, Monsiváis, and Poniatowska* (Tucson: University of Arizona Press, 2005), 57. Paz also implored Carlos Fuentes to have it published in a French newspaper in a good translation; he suggested that Fuentes have it translated by Claude Esteban or Jean-Clarence Lambert. See Ángel Gilberto Adame, ed., *Octavio Paz en 1968: El año axial. Cartas y escritos sobre los movimientos estudiantiles* (Mexico City: Taurus, 2018), 88.

48. For a complete discussion of the many communications involved in this process, see Guillermo Sheridan, *Poeta con paisaje: Ensayos sobre la vida de Octavio Paz*, vol. 1 (Mexico City: Ediciones Era, 2004), 485–95.

49. See Guadalupe Nettel, *Octavio Paz: Las palabras en libertad* (Barcelona: Taurus, 2014), 259. For more information about representations of this event in the Mexican press, see Claire Brewster, "The Student Movement of 1968 and the Mexican Press: The Cases of *Excélsior* and *Siempre!*," *Bulletin of Latin American Research* 22, no. 2 (2002): 183–84.

50. Sheridan, *Poeta con paisaje*, 493.

51. Brewster, *Responding to Crisis*, 56–61.

52. "Paz maintained 'I'm not a political militant.' He was not, nor had he ever pretended to be, an icon of the left. In 1968, he had simply followed his conscience." Brewster, *Responding to Crisis*, 61.

53. In addition to Haroldo de Campos, these included Argentine author and translator José Bianco; Spanish poet and translator Pere Gimferrer; his old friend Manuel Moreno Sánchez, a Mexican writer and politician who did not break as clearly with the state; French poet, critic, and translator Jean-Clarence Lambert; the British poet Charles Tomlinson, with whom he collaborated on *Renga*, the quadrilingual poetic experiment; and James Laughlin, the editor and founder of New Directions, Paz's longtime US publisher. See Adame, *Octavio Paz en 1968: El año axial*, 84–117; and Guillermo Sheridan, "Corresponder," in *Habitación con retratos: Ensayos sobre la vida de Octavio Paz*, vol. 2 (Mexico City: Ediciones Era, 2015), 75–171.

54. Paz to Haroldo, Delhi, October 9, 1968, in Paz and Haroldo, *Transblanco*, 104–5.

55. Paz to James Laughlin, Delhi, October 7, 1968, in Sheridan, *Habitación con retratos*, 170.

56. Paz to Charles Tomlinson, Delhi, October 8, 1968, in Adame, *Octavio Paz en 1968: El año axial*, 90.

57. Paz to Haroldo, Delhi, October 9, 1968, in Paz and Haroldo, *Transblanco*, 104–5.

58. Paz and Haroldo, *Transblanco*, 132.

59. First published through international newspapers, "México: Olimpiada de 1968" would soon be collected in Octavio Paz's *Ladera este* (Mexico City: Joaquín Mortiz, 1969), 68–69. The dedication to Dore and Adja Yunkers, friends of the author and politically committed visual artists, places the poem in the company of formally experimental art with a political agenda. Adja Yunkers would participate in the art-book production of "Blanco" translated by Eliot Weinberger, one of the two English translations Haroldo would consult for *Transblanco*.

60. Paz, "Intermitencias del oeste (3) (México: Olimpiada de 1968)," in *Obra poética I*, 374.

61. Paz and Haroldo, "México: Olimpíada de 1968," in *Transblanco*, 133.

62. Mark Strand, trans., "The Shame of the Olympics" by Octavio Paz, *New York Review of Books*, November 7, 1968.

63. Paz, "Intermitencias (3) (México: Olimpiada de 1968)," 374.

64. Paz and Haroldo, "México: Olimpíada de 1968," in *Transblanco*, 133.

65. Strand, "The Shame of the Olympics."

66. Paz, "Intermitencias (3) (México: Olimpiada de 1968)," 374.

67. Paz and Haroldo, "México: Olimpíada de 1968," in *Transblanco*, 133.

68. Strand, "The Shame of the Olympics."

69. See Victoria Carpenter's analysis of Paz's Buddhist period in India; she connects the colors mentioned in or connected to the poem with white (the blank page), yellow, and black bile and thus with human states of being in Buddhist thought. The poem travels from an enlightened blank page to a black, violent morass. Read backward, it depicts the reverse journey—from black to yellow to white—indicating the value of anger and shame for a process of enlightenment. Victoria Carpenter, "The Echo of Tlatelolco in Contemporary Mexican Protest Poetry," *Bulletin of Latin American Research* 24, no. 4 (2005): 503.

70. Paz, "Intermitencias (3) (México: Olimpiada de 1968)," 374.

71. Paz and Haroldo, "México: Olimpíada de 1968," in *Transblanco*, 133.

72. Strand, "The Shame of the Olympics."

73. Paz, "Intermitencias (3) (México: Olimpiada de 1968)," 374.

74. Paz and Haroldo, "México: Olimpíada de 1968," in *Transblanco*, 133.

75. Strand, "The Shame of the Olympics."

76. Paz to Haroldo, Delhi, October 9, 1968, in Paz and Haroldo, *Transblanco*, 104.

77. "Otávio Paz faz poesia sobre México," *Jornal do Brasil*, November 16, 1968.

78. "Poeta da Olympiada faz versos de protesta," *Folha de São Paulo*, October 25, 1968.

79. "Poeta da Olympiada faz versos de protesta."

80. Vladir Dupont would later translate a collection of essays by Paz which he would gift to Haroldo: Vladir Dupont, *A outra voz* (São Paulo: Siciliano, 1993), tombo 75, Haroldo de Campos Collection, Casa das Rosas.

81. Vladir Dupont, "México, mistérios e encantos," *Folha de São Paulo*, October 25, 1968.

82. Eliot Weinberger, trans., "Interruptions from the West (3) (Mexico City: The 1968 Olympiad)," in "Paz in Fury, 1968," *Los Angeles Times*, October 14, 1990. I have chosen to focus on the Mark Strand translation because it is more contemporaneous with the initial circulation of Paz's protest poem—and because I prefer Strand's translation of the key term as "clarity" to the choice Weinberger makes, to render *limpidez* as "lucidity." The Weinberger translation was previously published in *The Collected Poems of Octavio Paz: 1957-1987*, ed. Eliot Weinberger, trans. Eliot Weinberger, Elizabeth Bishop, Paul Blackburn, Lysander Kemp, Denise Levertov, John Frederick Nims, and Charles Tomlinson (New York: New Directions, 1987), 261.

83. Pablo Neruda, "Explico algunas cosas," in *Obras completas: Tercera edición aumentada* (Buenos Aires: Editorial Losada, 1967), 277.

84. From "Otávio Paz faz poesia sobre México," *Jornal do Brasil*, November 16, 1968.

85. Paz and Haroldo, "México: Olimpíada de 1968," in *Transblanco*, 133.

86. Paz and Haroldo, "México: Olimpíada de 1968," in *Transblanco*, 133.

87. Paz added a note to "Himachal Pradesh (3)," the poem between his dark homage to the Olympics and the French-language "Intermitencia del oeste (4) (Paris: les aveugles lucides)," dating it to "May of 1968 during the student movement in Paris." Octavio Paz, *Obra poética I*, 549. This poetic series aligns with Paz's controversial "Posdata" (1970) epilogue to *El laberinto de la soledad*

in taking stock of the tumultuous moment. Both political camps critiqued the essay for its excoriation of Mexican politics within a frame of sociohistorical self-examination as opposed to activist or reformist leadership.

88. Nettel, *Octavio Paz*, 260.

89. Haroldo to Paz, undated letter, likely sent between November and December 1968, in Paz and Haroldo, *Transblanco*, 107.

90. Haroldo to Paz, Austin, TX, April 20, 1981, in Paz and Haroldo, *Transblanco*, 127.

91. For example, Paz reads a translation from *Galaxias* into French in the journal *Change*, and he highlights a line he likes enough to choose as a motto: "The word is my fable." Paz to Haroldo, Cambridge, UK, September 30, 1970, in Paz and Haroldo, *Transblanco*, 111. Haroldo adds a footnote stating that he cannot take full credit for the line, as the Portuguese version is totally distinct from this part of the French translation Paz admired. Haroldo, "Notas," in Paz and Haroldo, *Transblanco*, 134.

92. "On reading you, I affirm once more that poetry is the word spoken and heard: a profoundly spiritual and physical activity in which lips and sound intervene. A sensual, muscular, spiritual activity. So I am doubly grateful to you: for your splendid translation and your luminous explanations." Paz to Haroldo, May 7, 1981, in Paz and Haroldo, *Transblanco*, 128.

93. Paz to Haroldo, December 8, 1983, in Paz and Haroldo, *Transblanco*, 9. Campos often gives his translations original titles that add his perspective, foregrounding his idea of translation as criticism and blurring the lines between writing and translation. For discussion of his unconventional titles for translations, see Else Ribeiro Pires Viera, "Liberating Calibans: Readings of *Antropofagia* and Haroldo de Campos' Poetics of Transcreation," in *Post-colonial Translation Theory*, ed. Susan Bassnett and Harish Trivedi (London: Routledge, 1998), 106.

94. Haroldo, "Nota de Haroldo de Campos à Tradução," in Paz and Haroldo, *Transblanco*, 90.

95. For further theorization of the concepts of *traducción pura* and *traducción para* in response to the translation theories of Haroldo as explored by other Latin American translators commemorating his legacy, see Isabel C. Gómez, "A Laboratory of Texts: The Multilingual Translation Legacies of Haroldo de Campos," in *The Routledge Handbook of Latin American Literary Translation Studies* (London: Routledge, 2023), 364–66.

96. Paz to Haroldo, Mexico City, March 26, 1981, in Paz and Haroldo, *Transblanco*, 119.

97. Paz to Haroldo, Mexico City, March 26, 1981, 119.

98. Paz to Haroldo, Mexico City, March 26, 1981, 120.

99. Paz to Haroldo, Mexico City, March 26, 1981, 120.

100. Paz to Haroldo, Mexico City, March 26, 1981, 119.

101. Paz to Haroldo, Mexico City, March 26, 1981, 120.

102. "All suprahistorical kinship of languages rests in the intention underlying each language as a whole—an intention, however, which no single language can attain by itself but which is realized only by the totality of their intentions supplementing each other: pure language." Benjamin, "The Task of the Translator," 78.

103. Benjamin, "The Task of the Translator," 80.

104. Paz disagrees with Haroldo's choice of the words *áscua*, *mulher*, *sisuda*, *brecha*, and *centelha*; the first is the only correction Haroldo accepts. Paz to Haroldo, Mexico City, March 26, 1981, in Paz and Haroldo, *Transblanco*, 120.

105. Haroldo to Paz, Austin, TX, April 20, 1981, in Paz and Haroldo, *Transblanco*, 124.

106. Haroldo to Paz, Austin, TX, April 20, 1981, in Paz and Haroldo, *Transblanco*, 124.

107. "*Som* e *são*, unfolded in my language, respond to the two shades of *son* in your text and remind Brazilian readers of *Cante a palo seco* by João Cabral de Melo Neto and the 'one-note samba' in the voice of our master bossa nova singer, the cool virtuoso João Gilberto." Haroldo to Paz, Austin, TX, April 20, 1981, in Paz and Haroldo, *Transblanco*, 127.

108. Haroldo, "Nota prévia," in Paz and Haroldo, *Transblanco*, 7.

109. Enrico Mario Santí, ed., *Archivo Blanco*, by Octavio Paz et al. (Madrid: Ediciones Turner, 1995).

110. Tombo 4123, vol. 2, Haroldo de Campos Collection, Casa das Rosas, São Paulo, Brazil. In the book itself, Santí also acknowledges in his biography of Haroldo that *Transblanco* was "the model and inspiration for this edition and archive." Santi, *Archivo Blanco*, 328.

111. The brothers shared many interests and writing projects; the resemblance was multifaceted: "Professor K. David Jackson, a close friend for many years, reported that in his last hours, [Haroldo] de Campos called his brother Augusto, his '*Siamême* twin,' and proposed that they translate the *Commedia* by telephone." Antonio Sergio Bessa and Odile Cisneros, introduction to Haroldo, *Novas: Selected Writings of Haroldo de Campos*, xxxv.

CHAPTER 3

1. The anonymous author further pronounces: "It would have been better had Castellanos stuck to reading Perse and enjoying him in her own way." "Mocosuena," *Plural*, no. 13 (October 1972): 40.

2. "Mocosuena," 40.

3. Benjamin Moser, *Why This World: A Biography of Clarice Lispector* (New York: Oxford University Press, 2009), 340.

4. Lori Chamberlain examines gendered metaphors used to describe translation and reveals the extent to which they maintain a hierarchy in which production is valued over reproduction, reinforcing both the gender binary and images of originality and power as forms of masculinity. See Lori Chamberlain, "Gender and the Metaphorics of Translation," in Venuti, *The Translation Studies Reader*, 306–21. For the relationship between feminism and translation theory, see Sherry Simon, *Gender in Translation: Cultural Identity and the Politics of Transmission* (London: Routledge, 1996); and Luise von Flotow and Hala Kamal, eds., *The Routledge Handbook of Translation, Feminism, and Gender* (New York: Routledge, 2020).

5. In this work, I follow Luise von Flotow's proposition that the intersectionality framework of "multiple inequalities" can respond to the question of "how

can the individual case with all its intersections be made meaningful and applicable at a macro-cosmopolitan level." Luise von Flotow, "Contested Gender in Translation: Intersectionality and Metramorphics," *Palimpsestes* 22 (2009): 248.

6. In a roundtable discussion opening a new collection on translation and gender, the discussants admit that "the existing Eurocentric feminist translation scholarship has largely adhered to a gender-only focus in its theories and practices and only recently, both with the emergent geopolitical expansion of the field and with the deep interrogation and transformation of Western feminist praxes by the intersectional critiques of feminists of color, queer feminists, and third world feminists, feminist translation scholars have explicitly begun to claim intersectionality as a crucial sign post for their translation practices." Emek Ergun et al., "Women (Re)Writing Authority: A Roundtable Discussion on Feminist Translation," in von Flotow and Kamal, *The Routledge Handbook of Translation, Feminism, and Gender*, 10.

7. Kimberlé Crenshaw, "Demarginalizing the Intersection of Race and Sex: A Black Feminist Critique of Antidiscrimination Doctrine, Feminist Theory, and Antiracist Policies," *University of Chicago Legal Forum* 1, no. 8 (1989): 139–67.

8. Sumi Cho, Kimberlé Crenshaw, and Leslie McCall, "Intersectionality: Theorizing Power, Empowering Theory," *Signs* 38, no. 4 (Summer 2013): 797.

9. Haroldo, "Anthropophagous Reason," 165; Haroldo, "Translation as Creation and Criticism," 318; and Augusto, "Revistas Re-vistas," 154.

10. Castellanos died in Tel Aviv in 1974, alone in her apartment electrocuted by a lamp, and her death was officially determined an accident, although no formal investigation was conducted despite several requests. Cynthia Steele reconsiders the mysteries and suspicions (that her death was a suicide, that she was being followed in the days leading up to her death, that many of her papers and works-in-progress were destroyed with the exception of one letter that appeared to confirm the suicide explanation, etc.) surrounding this tragic early end to her life by evaluating newly available materials, including personal memoirs, interviews, and letters. See Cynthia Steele, "Power, Gender, and Canon Formation in Mexico," *Studies in 20th Century Literature* 20, no. 1 (1996): 65–100. Lispector died of untreatable ovarian cancer in 1977 in ways that eerily echo the death of Macabéa, the heroine of *The Hour of the Star*, published just before her passing. See Moser, *Why This World*, 381.

11. In her comparative work on Castellanos, Cecília Meireles, and Gabriela Mistral, Karen Peña identifies Castellanos as one who connects language itself with "patriarchal institutions [that] forbid women to convey their realities." Karen Peña, *Poetry and the Realm of the Public Intellectual: The Alternative Destinies of Gabriela Mistral, Cecília Meireles, and Rosario Castellanos* (Leeds, UK: LEGENDA / Modern Humanities Research Association / Maney Publishing, 2007), 1. Mary Louise Pratt includes Castellanos in a generation of female essay writers in Latin America who used the genre to wrest self-determination away from male writers "obsessively" interested in writing about women. "'No me interrumpas': Las mujeres y el ensayo latinoamericano," trans. Gabriela Cano, *Debate Feminista* 21 (2000): 70–88. Joanna O'Connell summarizes Castellanos's work within three forms of feminist discourse: writing about women's

lives, critiquing cliched tropes that masculine writers perpetuate about women, and performing her status as a female public intellectual by debating with other producers of Mexican culture as their equal. Joanna O'Connell, *Prospero's Daughter: The Prose of Rosario Castellanos* (Austin: University of Texas Press, 1995), 209.

12. The hundreds of columns, essays, and articles Castellanos wrote for the *Excélsior* and other journals represent a rich and still understudied corpus of her work; they were only recently collected in *Mujer de palabras: Artículos rescatados de Rosario Castellanos*, 3 vols., ed. Andrea Reyes (Mexico City: Conaculta, 2004, 2006, 2007).

13. Emily Hind, Femme*nism and the Mexican Woman Intellectual from Sor Juana to Poniatowska: Boob Lit* (New York: Palgrave, 2010), 35–50, 52.

14. *Plural* never bothered to review *Poesía no eres tú* (1972) in full before or after this infantilizing critique of her translations; when *Plural* conducted a poll to identify the best Mexican literature published that year, eight writers (all male) ranked their favorite books: none of the eleven winning books are written by women, and Octavio Paz's translation project *Renga* won. "Encuestas de *Plural*," *Plural* 16 (January 1973): 45–46.

15. The appraisal of her merits despite her identity does acknowledge her role opening space in the public sphere for others in marginalized positions: "Como las minorías que se esfuerzan por ganar reconocimiento a fuerza de méritos indiscutibles, muy pronto [Castellanos] se hizo respetar como gente seria a pesar de ser joven, abierta a pesar de ser católica, de un talento innegable a pesar de ser mujer. Nunca subió dando la espalda a lo que era o había sido. Por el contrario, parecía actuar como quien abre brecha para otros que no han ganado el debido reconocimiento." Yet this faint praise, always "in spite" of her identities, singles out Castellanos in a triple obituary that commemorates with more respect Salvador Novo and Jaime Torres Bodet, two other Mexican writers who died that year. Gabriel Zaid, "Poetas ejemplares," *Plural* 36 (September 1974): 92. To be fair, Castellanos was widely mourned, and another obituary honoring the same three figures describes her with greater respect, although still gendered praise; neither Novo nor Torres Bodet receive comment on their looks. "Rosario had it all: sensitivity, intelligence, sense of humor, physical beauty, an unusual degree of culture free from all pedantry. Everything except good luck, as her absurd death has shown." Manuel Durán, "In Memoriam: Jaime Torres Bodet, Salvador Novo, Rosario Castellanos," *Revista Iberoamericana* 41, no. 90 (January–March 1975): 82.

16. A premier journal in Mexican and Latin American literary fields, *Plural* was defined by Paz as "a Latin American journal in Mexico that would be open to the world," which was "as much a community of translators as it is a community of poets or critics." John King, *The Role of Mexico's* Plural *in Latin American Literary and Political Culture: From Tlatelolco to the "Philanthropic Ogre"* (New York: Palgrave, 2007), 1, 147–49.

17. "They denied Rosario Castellanos her merits as a writer for many years. Including when she began to translate . . . instead of valuing her efforts, they dedicated themselves to pointing out how her translations were bad." Juan Armando Epple, "Las voces de Elena Poniatowska: Una entrevista," *Confluen-*

cia 5, no. 2 (1990): 128. See also Cynthia Steele, "Entrevista" (interview) with Elena Poniatowska, *Hispamérica* 18, nos. 53–54 (1989): 89–105.

18. Poniatowska quoted in Steele, "Entrevista," 90–91.

19. For example, in a dossier on fellow poet-translator Charles Tomlinson, Paz translates the poetry and González de León translates the literary criticism. See Charles Tomlinson, "Textos y poemas," trans. Ulalume González de León and Octavio Paz, *Plural* 22 (July 1973): 3–5. Paz's *Plural* published his translations of Ezra Pound, William Carlos Williams, and Elizabeth Bishop; José Emilio Pacheco's approximations of Italo Calvino and Greek and Latin fragments; Antonio Alatorre's translations of Brazilian poetry; Gerardo Deniz's translations of French erotica and Hölderlin; and much more.

20. Ulalume González de León, trans., "Los Totum Revolutum" by Edward Lear, *Plural* 15 (December 1972): 9.

21. Rosario Castellanos, "Traduciendo a Claudel," in *Mujer que sabe latín . . .* (1973; repr., Mexico City: Fondo de Cultura Económica, 1995), 191.

22. Castellanos, "Traduciendo a Claudel," 191.

23. Castellanos, "Traduciendo a Claudel," 191.

24. Castellanos, "Traduciendo a Claudel," 192.

25. Rosario Castellanos, "Divagación sobre el idioma," in *El uso de la palabra*, ed. José Emilio Pacheco (Mexico City: Ediciones de Excélsior, 1975), 152.

26. Rosario Castellanos, "Notas al margen: El lenguaje como instrumento de dominio," in *Mujer que sabe latín . . .* , 172.

27. Castellanos, "Notas al margen," 175. This second citation comes from the same essay but from the second section, which is subtitled "El lenguaje, posibilidad de liberación."

28. Martha LaFollette Miller observes that Castellanos consistently pairs any discussion of her achievements as a writer with expressions of her vulnerabilities or doubt about her skills expressed in gendered terms. Martha LaFollette Miller, "The Ambivalence of Power: Self-Disparagement in the Newspaper Editorials of Rosario Castellanos," in *Reinterpreting the Spanish American Essay: Women Writers of the 19th and 20th Centuries*, ed. Doris Meyer (Austin: University of Texas Press, 1995), 168–71.

29. The essay includes four translations; five more were first published in *Materia memorable* (Mexico City: Universidad Nacional Autónoma de México, 1969); all nine Dickinson translations are included without edits in her book of collected poems: *Poesía no eres tú: Obra poética, 1948–1971* (Mexico City: Fondo de Cultura Económica, 1972), 223–27. The essay was not reprinted until Andrea Reyes's *Mujer de palabras: Artículos rescatados de Rosario Castellanos*, vols. 1–3 (2004–7).

30. Rosario Castellanos, "Emily Dickinson: Una mujer singular," in Reyes, *Mujer de palabras*, 1:258.

31. In this essay, Castellanos cites Sor Juana's Romance 48: "si es que soy mujer, / ninguno lo verifique" (27), that is, "if it's true I'm a woman / let nobody verify it." Rosario Castellanos, "Otra vez Sor Juana," in *Juicios sumarios: Ensayos* (Xalapa, Mexico: Universidad Veracruzana, 1966), 27.

32. Castellanos, "Emily Dickinson," 260.

33. Castellanos, "Dos veces antes se cerró mi vida," in *Poesía no eres tú*, 225. In her translation, Castellanos eliminates the space between the two stanzas of Dickinson's poem, another choice contributing to the emotional amplification of her version, speeding the reader towards the infernal end of the lyric poem.

34. Emily Dickinson, "My life closed twice before it's close" (#1732), in *The Poems of Emily Dickinson: Reading Edition*, ed. Ralph W. Franklin (Cambridge, MA: Belknap Press of Harvard University Press, 1999), 630–31. Dickinson's idiosyncratic spelling is on display in the first line of this poem; I cite from the definitive reading edition based on her manuscripts, where all choices of spelling, capitalization, and punctuation are the poet's. As the editor's introduction highlights, Dickinson knew what she was about: "'I spelt a word wrong in this letter,' she teased her brother, Austin, in 1854, 'but I know better, so you need'nt think you have caught me' . . . A spaced hyphen, rather than an en or em dash, has been used as appropriate to the relative weight of her dashes in most of the poems. The apostrophes in many contractions are misplaced, as in *hav'nt* and *did'nt* (perhaps indicative of how her ear divided the sounds), or not used at all, as in *dont*, *wont*, and *cant* (no division). In certain possessive forms, apostrophes appear by analogy: *her's*, *your's*, *it's*. The single form *it's* served her as both a possessive pronoun and a contraction of 'it is.'" Ralph W. Franklin. "Introduction," in *The Poems of Emily Dickinson*, 9–10.

35. The latter was in fact the choice Silvina Ocampo makes in another Spanish version of the same poem, where she translates the lines as "si la inmortalidad revela / un tercer evento para mi," (#1732), in *Poemas* by Emily Dickinson, trans. Silvina Ocampo (Barcelona: Tusquets Editores, 1985), 361.

36. Rosario Castellanos, "El zipper: Hora de la verdad," in Reyes, *Mujer de palabras*, 3:311–12.

37. The vocabulary of Dickinson anticipates her arrival in the Castellanos poem. The "páramos de Ávila" could be described in many ways—when Castellanos uses the word *páramo*, she connects this poem of her own with her translation "Jamás he visto un páramo," which is her version of the Dickinson poem "I never saw a Moor" (#800); and with the Mexican literary touchstone *Pedro Páramo* (1959) by Juan Rulfo. The first two lines read "I never saw a Moor. / I never saw the Sea -," which Castellanos translates as "Jamás he visto un páramo / y no conozco el mar." *The Poems of Emily Dickinson*, 355; Castellanos, *Poesía no eres tú*, 226. Ocampo opts for *brezal* rather than *páramo*, and her version reads "Nunca vi un brezal — / nunca vi el mar —." Ocampo, *Poemas*, 274. Ocampo perhaps crafts a closer fit with *brezal* for the mist-laden grassland image of Dickinson's "moor"; her choice would have been a better match also for the green rolling hills of medieval Ávila than the dry wasteland evoked by *páramo* in Castellanos's translation, in particular if we are reading her through Rulfo. Yet Ocampo's version lacks the rhythm and swing of Dickinson as rendered by Castellanos.

38. Castellanos, "Meditación en el umbral," in *Poesía no eres tú*, 316.

39. Maureen Ahern, trans., "Meditation on the Brink," in *A Rosario Castellanos Reader: An Anthology of Her Poetry, Short Fiction, Essays, and Drama*, ed. Ahern (Austin: University of Texas Press, 1988), 111.

40. Ahern, "Meditation on the Brink," 111.

41. Castellanos, "Canción," in *Poesía no eres tú*, 204.

42. Dickinson, "'Tis not that Dying hurts us so" (#528), in *The Poems of Emily Dickinson*, 240.

43. Castellanos, "Morir no hiere tanto," in *Poesía no eres tú*, 224.

44. Ahern connects this use of state-sponsored formal language to the professional roles Castellanos took on and her strategies of ironizing these formal qualities as a part of her critique of power. "The years that Castellanos worked within the Mexican government sharpened her talent for re-creating bureaucratic formats and the officialese of its administrative documents and press releases." Ahern, "Reading Rosario Castellanos: Contexts, Voices, and Signs," in *A Rosario Castellanos Reader*, 25.

45. Castellanos, "Nota roja," in *Poesía no eres tú*, 199.

46. The translations of her works into English and Spanish have received increased scholarly attention. Tace Hedrick advocates for new translations that would depart from concepts of "écriture féminine" and preserve the details of her stylistics in English translations; Edgar Cézar Nolasco interrogates her writing as a process of translating her reading habits, interpreting her last novel, *A hora da estrela* (1977), as a translation or a rewriting of the French novel *La Dentellière* (1974) by Pascal Lainé. See Tace Hedrick, "'Mãe é para isso': Gender, Writing, and English Language Translation in Clarice Lispector," *Luso-Brazilian Review* 41, no. 2 (2004): 56–83; and Edgar Cézar Nolasco, "Clarice Lispector Tradutora," *Revista Cerrados* 16, no. 24 (2007): 263–72.

47. These new translations feature introductions by prominent cultural figures such as writer Colm Tóibín, director Pedro Almodóvar, and musician Caetano Veloso; the project began with five of Lispector's best-known novels: *The Hour of the Star* (trans. Benjamin Moser, 2011), *The Passion according to G. H.* (trans. Idra Novey, 2012), *Água Viva* (trans. Stefan Tobler, 2012), *A Breath of Life* (trans. Johnny Lorenz, 2012), and *Near to the Wild Heart* (trans. Alison Entrekin, 2012). *The Complete Stories of Clarice Lispector* (trans. Katrina Dodson, 2015) received the 2016 PEN Translation Prize for Prose.

48. Magdalena Edwards, "Benjamin Moser and the Smallest Woman in the World," *Los Angeles Review of Books*, August 16, 2019.

49. Lispector first published seven stories in 1974 as *7 de Allan Poe* (Technoprint); she added eleven more in 1975, under the title *O gato preto e outras histórias de Allan Poe* (Ediouro). In 1985 the publisher changed the title of the subsequent editions and reprintings to *Histórias extraordinárias de Allan Poe* (Bottman). Lispector's translations of Poe remain in print and in wide circulation; I cite from the fifteenth edition (Ediouro, 1996). See Denise Bottmann, "Alguns aspectos da presença de Edgar Allan Poe no Brasil," *Tradução em Revista* 8, no.1 (2010): 1–19.

50. Severino J. Albuquerque, "Reading Translation Queerly: Lispector's Translation of *The Picture of Dorian Gray*," *Bulletin of Hispanic Studies* 76, no. 5 (1999): 694–95.

51. Fernando Arenas, "Being Here with Vergílio Ferreira and Clarice Lispector: At the Limits of Language and Subjectivity," *Portuguese Studies* 14 (1998): 187.

52. "She began to translate English and French works, often for Álvaro Pacheco's Artenova. For another publisher, she adapted classics for children." Moser, *Why This World*, 339.

53. "The story of Mrs. Chagall's childhood in Vitebsk, today in Belarus, would have kindled the memories of the stories her family told her about their own past." Moser, *Why This World*, 339.

54. Moser, *Why This World*, 339.

55. Moser supports the reading that Clarice did not complete these "bad" translations herself, but only as rumors that cannot be substantiated. "Rumor has it that in order to help her friend, Olga Botelli's sister Helena did many of her translations for her." Moser, *Why This World*, 433n17.

56. Moser, *Why This World*, 340. The citations at the end of the passage come from a letter by Anna Maria da Silva Telles Watson at Editora Artenova dated April 26, 1976.

57. Lispector quoted in Edwards, "Benjamin Moser and the Smallest Woman in the World," n.p.

58. Studies of Poe's reception in Brazil include Lispector's translations, but they tend to set her work aside as adaptation without illuminating any insights achieved through her translation choices. Carlos Daghlian affords Lispector only a brief comment that classifies her translation work as rewriting for commercial success, not art. "Lispector rewrote, successfully, eleven stories by Poe for the juvenile public." Carlos Daghlian, "A recepção de Poe na literatura brasileira," *Fragmentos* 25 (2003): 46. Fabiano Bruno Gonçalves systematically compares eight translations of Poe's story "The Tell-Tale Heart" into Portuguese; frequently, he analyzes a citation in the other seven versions only to say that the passage was omitted in Lispector's adaptation. Where she did translate the passage in question, he finds her translation "the most spontaneous, perhaps because it's for an adaptation." This may be the case, but it is equally possible that Lispector's translation is the most "spontaneous" as a chosen effect. Fabiano Bruno Gonçalves, "Tradução, interpretação e recepção literária: Manifestações de Edgar Allan Poe no Brasil" (PhD diss., Universidade Federal do Rio Grande do Sul, 2006), 101.

59. Élida Paulina Ferreira and Karin Hallana Santos Silva, "Edgar Allan Poe em português: Os limites entre tradução e adaptação," *Domínios de lingu@gem: Revista Eletrônica de Linguística* 5, no. 3 (2011): 20–37.

60. Ferreira and Silva, "Edgar Allan Poe em português," 34.

61. Clarice Lispector, trans., *Historias extraordinárias de Allan Poe: Textos selecionados e reescritos por Clarice Lispector*, 15th ed., by Edgar Allan Poe (Rio de Janeiro: Ediouro Publicações, 1998); Charles Baudelaire, trans., *Histoires extraordinaires*, by Edgar Allan Poe (Paris: A Quantin, 1884).

62. Her epigraph to "O gato preto" ("The Black Cat") draws from "Matter, Spirit, and Divine Will"; the epigraph "Parece porque é" ("It seems because it is") from Poe's "Eureka" introduces "A máscara da morte rubra" ("Masque of the Red Death"); translated lines from Poe's epic poem "Al-Aaraaf" reframe "The Oval Portrait"; to "O caso do Valdemar" she adds a quote from "The Pit and the Pendulum," a Poe story she does not translate.

63. Nearly all of the eighteen stories she translates were translated by Baudelaire; the epigraphs she adds are frequently drawn from the additional essays he

translated, and she tends to add new material without remark where he adds footnotes.

64. "The soul does not reside only once in a sensing body: as for the rest—a horse, a dog, even a man, it is nothing more than the barely tangible resemblance of these animals." Edgar Allan Poe, *The Complete Stories*, ed. John Seelye (New York: Knopf, 1992), 37.

65. The epigraph in Poe's story comes from Martin Luther; Lispector translates it into Portuguese rather than leaving it in Latin. Consistent with her general "translation manual" to move everything into Portuguese, she even translates his name: "'Vivo, era uma peste. Morrendo, serei tua morte.' *Martinho Lutero*." Lispector, "Metzengerstein," in *Historias extraordinárias de Allan Poe*, 147.

66. It continues to say: "In India, the human soul, a piece of the universal soul, must suffer the trials of a great number of lifetimes, much like a purification of its virtue and heart, before reuniting once again with the universal soul. Many agree that the soul is immortal and has as a field of activity an incommensurable series of worlds." Lispector, "Metzengerstein," 147.

67. Baudelaire, *Histoires extraordinaires*, 305–6n2.

68. Edgar Allan Poe, "The Devil in the Belfry," in *The Complete Stories*, 422.

69. Poe, "The Devil in the Belfry," 426.

70. Poe, "The Devil in the Belfry," 419.

71. Lispector, "O Diabo no campanário," in *Historias extraordinárias de Allan Poe*, 134. Emphasis in the original.

72. Poe, "The Devil in the Belfry," 425.

73. Poe, "The Devil in the Belfry," 425.

74. Lispector, "O Diabo no campanário," 138–39.

75. Poe, "The Devil in the Belfry," 423.

76. Poe, "The Devil in the Belfry," 423.

77. Poe, "The Devil in the Belfry," 423–24.

78. Poe, "The Devil in the Belfry," 423–24.

79. Poe, "The Devil in the Belfry," 423–24.

80. Lispector, "O Diabo no campanário," 138.

81. Poe, "The Devil in the Belfry," 426.

82. Lispector, "O Diabo no campanário," 140.

83. Jorge Luis Borges, "Prologue," in Silvina Ocampo, trans., *Poemas*, by Emily Dickinson (Barcelona: Editorial Tusquets, 1985), 12.

84. Charse Yun draws from both Korean and Anglophone press reviews to summarize the criticism of her errors of diction, but he raises greater concerns over her stylistic changes, elevating sentiment and description; he equates Smith's translation with Pound's *Cathay*—unfairly, to my mind, given that Pound had no knowledge of the source language. Charse Yun, "How the Bestseller 'The Vegetarian,' Translated from Han Kang's Original, Caused an Uproar in South Korea," *Los Angeles Times*, September 22, 2017. Jiayang Fan strikes a balance, presenting the widespread charges of mistranslation, Yun's critiques of cultural colonialism, and the commentary Smith and Han have made about the emotional projection within translation. Jiayang Fan, "Han

Kang and the Complexity of Translation," *New Yorker*, January 15, 2018. Sneja Gunew draws on *The Vegetarian* to ask how translation might accommodate the cultural specificity of affect, and in fact proposes we consider "affect as a modality of translation," 18. Sneja Gunew, "Excess of Affect: In Translation," *Hecate* 42, no. 2 (2016): 7–22.

CHAPTER 4

This chapter relies on archival materials consulted at the Biblioteca Ayacucho during a visit in 2013. Citations from letters are included with the permission of Director Luis Edgar Páez on behalf of the Biblioteca Ayacucho Foundation; all translations from Spanish and Portuguese into English are my own. The closing sections of this chapter focused on *Macunaíma* were previously published in an earlier version in my article "Brazilian Transcreation and World Literature: *Macunaíma* Journeys from São Paulo to Caracas," *Journal of World Literature* 1, no. 3 (2016): 316–41, included here with permission.

1. Héctor Olea, "Posfacio," in *Macunaíma* by Mário de Andrade (Barcelona: Seix Barral, 1977), 241.

2. Appiah's term is adapted from anthropologist Clifford Geertz's concept "thick description." Kwame Anthony Appiah, "Thick Translation," in Venuti, *The Translation Studies Reader*, 394.

3. Appiah, "Thick Translation," 398, 400.

4. Vladimir Nabokov, "Problems of Translation: 'Onegin' in English," in Venuti, *The Translation Studies Reader*, 127.

5. Olea, "Posfacio," 245.

6. Carina Blixen and Alvaro Barros-Lémez, *Cronología y bibliografía de Ángel Rama* (Montevideo: Fundación Ángel Rama, 1986), 46.

7. Ángel Rama, "La Biblioteca Ayacucho como instrumento de integración cultural latinoamericana," in *30 años de Biblioteca Ayacucho (1974–2004)*, ed. Oscar Rodríguez Ortiz (Caracas: Biblioteca Ayacucho, 2004), 85.

8. "Within the process of building what Wallerstein has called a 'world-economy,' founded on the European conquest of the American continent, any solution to Latin American solidarity must apprehend the fundamental need for not only economic but also broad cultural integration into an international sphere. But the role played by Latin America will be merely ancillary, lacking in autonomy or creativity, if that external pole is not compensated by another internal one that balances and regulates it." Rama, "La Biblioteca Ayacucho," 69.

9. Carlos Pacheco and Marisela Guevara Sánchez, "Ángel Rama, la cultura venezolana y el epistolario de la Biblioteca Ayacucho," *Estudios: Revista de Investigaciones Literarias y Culturales* 22–23 (2003–4): 101–7.

10. "[Pérez] was aware that economic development could not happen in an isolated country, that it needed to be a continental Latin American project. He pointed out that 'Venezuela acts in complete solidarity with international struggles for justice. . . . We are an example of a new concept of international solidarity that repudiates all forms of exploitation.'" Pacheco and Sánchez,

"Ángel Rama, la cultura venezolana y el epistolario de la Biblioteca Ayacucho," 106.

11. "'This morning I enacted the National Law for Culture, a campaign promise equal in scope to the monumental initiative of the nationalization of oil. . . . Today I want to bring artists and intellectuals into the national celebration of the nationalization of oil.'" Carlos Andrés Pérez, "Discurso de la nacionalización petrolera," (1975), in Pacheco and Sánchez, "Ángel Rama, la cultura venezolana y el epistolario de la Biblioteca Ayacucho," 107.

12. Siskind, *Cosmopolitan Desires*, 13.

13. Rama included texts written in English or French because "the integration of Latin America to universal culture must be recognized, and these works testify to the fact that our culture is not segregated from the universal ensemble nor can it be apprehended outside of the parameters of thought developed in its different metropolises." Rama, "La Biblioteca Ayacucho," 79–80.

14. Translated from Nahuatl, Maya, and Quechua are #28 *Literatura del México antiguo* (1978), #57 *Literatura maya* (1980), and #78 *Literatura quechua* (1980); from English, #63 William Hudson's *La tierra purpúrea; Alla lejos; y Hace tiempo* (1980); and from French, #44 Francisco García Calderón's *Las democracias latinas de América* (1979), #74 Alexander von Humboldt's *Cartas americanas* (1980), and #99 Amadeo Frezier's *Relación del viaje por el mar del sur* (1982).

15. Rama, "La Biblioteca Ayacucho," 71–73.

16. Rama, "La Biblioteca Ayacucho," 73–78.

17. "In the cases where they caused gross distortions, they allow us to confront them and proceed to self-definition in opposition to those external discourses." Rama, "La Biblioteca Ayacucho," 79.

18. Rama, "La Biblioteca Ayacucho," 80–81.

19. Rama, "La Biblioteca Ayacucho," 89.

20. Scholars of Ángel Rama's contribution to Latin American studies through his editorial role at Biblioteca Ayacucho celebrate his inclusion of Brazil and other regions often left out of the picture, yet none investigates the translations themselves. Marcela Croce elevates the multilingual approach of Ayacucho, naming its three greatest achievements as incorporating Filipino, Brazilian, and Haitian literatures; Nora Fernández and Facundo Gómez describe Biblioteca Ayacucho as "mestizo *arielismo* supporting a notion of Latin American identity that is open, diverse, politically committed, inclusive of all classes and of cultural production traditionally excluded from Latin American studies like that of Brazil and the Philippines," referring to the utopian gesture of incorporating Brazil; Jessica Gordon-Burroughs focuses on the materiality of covers, printing, and circulation; and Haydée Ribeiro Coelho highlights the comparative literary potential explored through the Brazilian volumes. See Marcela Croce, "Ángel Rama: La utopía americana destellando en un momento de peligro," in *Latinoamericanismo: Canon, crítica y géneros discursivos*, ed. Marcela Croce (Buenos Aires: Corregidor, 2013), 127–62; Nora Fernández and Facundo Gómez, "Biblioteca Ayacucho: La utopía de América," in *Latinoamericanismo*, 41–78; Jessica Gordon-Burroughs, "Monuments and Ephemera: The Biblioteca Ayacucho," *A Contracorriente* 11, no. 3 (2014): 90–118; and Haydée Ribeiro

Coelho, "O Brasil na 'Biblioteca Ayacucho': Vertente literária e cultural," *O eixo e a roda* 18, no. 2 (2009): 85–103.

21. Rama, "La Biblioteca Ayacucho," 71–72.

22. The Fondo de Cultura Economica (FCE) in Mexico City, established in 1934, did not wholly oppose a Hispanist model of cultural canonization and in fact worked with the Casa de España. Rather than the FCE press as a whole, Rama associates the Biblioteca Ayacucho project with the FCE series "Biblioteca Americana," designed by Dominican intellectual Pedro Henríquez Ureña (1884–1946) in his last year of life. The inaugural book in the series, a translation of the Popol Vuh by Adrian Recinos, was published in 1947, and as a volume of Indigenous religious faith it represents the distinct direction of this series departing from Hispanism.

23. Rama resists both the framework of literature as an independent sphere (from *Mundo Nuevo*) and as a singular ideological representation of one political agenda overriding literary considerations (as in *Casa de las Américas*; "in 1974 [*Casa de las Américas*] had a poetry section that Rama described in his diary as 'desoladora [heartbreaking],' published alongside 'editoriales seudo revolucionarios [pseudo-revolutionary editorials],' replete with 'pacotilla retórica [shabby rhetoric]'"). Gordon-Burroughs, "Monuments and Ephemera," 97.

24. CEAL, founded in 1966 by Boris Spivacow, counted on the participation of all the major Southern Cone intellectuals; Ediciones de la Flor was founded in 1966 by Ana Maria Kuki Miler and Daniel Divinsky; Divinsky also served at Ayacucho after he left Argentina; it remains in operation as an independent publisher. Salvador Allende's government founded the Editorial Nacional Quimantu in 1971 with a mission to democratize print culture.

25. Rama to Candido, September 17, 1974, in Pablo Rocca, ed., *Un proyecto latinoamericano: Antonio Candido y Ángel Rama, Correspondencia* (Montevideo: Editora Estuario, 2016), 70.

26. "This effort enriches Spanish American culture where the Biblioteca Ayacucho will circulate, bringing high quality works from the (as yet unknown) Portuguese-speaking neighboring zone—and at the same time it represents a challenge to Brazilian culture to attempt a similar task of systematically disseminating Spanish American letters, philosophy, and history—a body of works they currently lack." Rama, "La Biblioteca Ayacucho," 83.

27. See Pacheco and Sánchez, "Ángel Rama, la cultura venezolana y el epistolario de la Biblioteca Ayacucho," 131–32. Based on meetings in Caracas and Campinas in 1980 and 1983 and initiated with Rama's sponsorship and through circles around him at Ayacucho, Pizarro's project took shape later and now stretches to an extensive online volume.

28. Studying Latin American and US intellectual relations during the Cold War, Deborah Cohn demonstrates that institutional and ideological alliances did not always match or maintain clear boundaries, as when accusations arose that the journal *Mundo Nuevo* received CIA funding. Deborah Cohn, *The Latin American Literary Boom and U.S. Nationalism during the Cold War* (Nashville: Vanderbilt University Press, 2012), 17–24.

29. Blixen and Barros-Lémez, *Cronología y bibliografía de Ángel Rama*, 47–49.

30. For further detail on legislation and immigration regulations that resulted in severely curtailing the circulation of many Latin American intellectuals in the United States, see Cohn, *The Latin American Literary Boom*, 37–63.

31. On letterhead from the University of Maryland Department of Spanish & Portuguese, Rama wrote to Candido: "It's the peace of the ghetto, like all universities in the USA, with great libraries and nice service, but marginalized from the world. But the whole country behaves this way: since I've been here I haven't seen a single news article on Latin America in the *Washington Post* I receive every day, except when President Carter visited Mexico." Rama to Candido, February 26, 1979, in Rocca, *Un proyecto latinoamericano*, 118.

32. Argentine Daniel Divinsky, who cofounded Ediciones de la Flor in 1966, was its first director of distribution and later was exiled in Venezuela; Uruguayan Hugo García Robles also worked in distribution, to name a few examples beyond the Brazilian scholars and Mexican and Argentine translators already named in this chapter.

33. The concept also revived the 1924 project by Venezuelan *modernista* Rufino Blanco Fombona, another editor who included Brazilian literatures within his canon. The name creates a teleological heritage, from the Battle of Ayacucho, to the commemoration by Fombona, to Rama's renewal of a Venezuelan publishing firm compiling a Latin American canon of continental and hemispheric scope. Oscar Rodríguez Ortiz, "Presentación," in Ortiz, *30 años*, 12–14.

34. The first description of Ayacucho that Rama writes to Candido defines the project as a three-hundred-volume library of the "literature, history and thought of Nuestra América (Spanish, Portuguese, and French) from its origins through today." Rama to Candido, September 17, 1974, in Rocca, *Un proyecto latinoamericano*, 69–70.

35. Thanking Rama, Mirta Arlt writes with a telling combination of reaching to European world literature for a suitable comparison for the heft of the edition ("it seems like *War and Peace* for the size!") and celebrating the unique, untutored style of Arlt's writing: "I think you did right to not 'comb' him. Few writers can write that way and be great writers." Arlt to Rama, July 9, 1978, in Gordon-Burroughs, "Monuments and Ephemera," 90.

36. Rama describes the collection as a "struggle against fragmentation and lack of communication that has lasted for centuries." Brazil is only the most obvious of example of internal cultural divisions; Puerto Rico and the Caribbean also represent deliberate fragmentation from a Latin American cultural whole. Rama, "La Biblioteca Ayacucho," 80.

37. To integrate parallel experiences, these five volumes present "vast intellectual or political movements that were lived simultaneously by all the nations on the continent, but also separately, without perceiving the connections between their actions." Ortiz, *30 años*, 84–85; #23–24 *Pensamiento político de la emancipación (1790–1825)* (1977); #26 *Utopismo socialista (1830–1893)* (1977); #31 *Pensamiento conservador (1815–1898)* (1978); #59 *Poesía de la independencia* (1979); and #71–72 *Pensamiento positivista latinoamericana* (1980). The works of Brazilian literature are #11 Gilberto Freyre, *Casa-grande y senzala*, ed. Darcy Ribeiro, trans. Benjamin de Garay and Lucrecia Manduca

(1977); #25 Manuel Antonio de Almeida, *Memorias de un sargento de milicias*, ed. Antonio Candido, trans. Elvio Romero (1977); #33 Machado de Assis, *Cuentos*, ed. Alfredo Bosi, trans. Santiago Kovadloff (1978); #47 *Arte y arquitectura del modernismo brasileño (1917–1930)*, ed. Aracy Amaral, trans. Marta Traba (1978); #49 Lima Barreto, *Dos novelas*, ed. Francisco de Assis Barbosa, trans. Haydeé M. Jofre Barroso (1978); Machado de Assis, *Quincas Borba*, ed. Roberto Schwarz, trans. Juan Garcia Gayo (1979); #56 Mário de Andrade, *Obra escogida: Novela, cuento, ensayo, epistolario*, ed. Gilda de Mello e Souza, trans. Santiago Kovadloff, Héctor Olea, and Márgara Russotto (1979); #79 Euclides da Cunha, *Los sertones*, ed. Walnice Nogueira Galvão, trans. Estela dos Santos (1980); #84 Oswald de Andrade, *Obra escogida*, ed. Haroldo de Campos and K. David Jackson, trans. Santiago Kovadloff, Héctor Olea, and Márgara Russotto (1981); and #93 Silvio Romero, *Ensayos literarios*, ed. Antonio Candido, trans. Jorge Aguilar Mora (1982).

38. According to Pacheco and Sánchez, the archive was first organized from Rama's perspective, all correspondence grouped together and ordered chronologically up to 1988. In 2001 Marisela Guevara began to organize the collection based on the volumes in the catalogue. Pacheco and Sánchez, "Ángel Rama, la cultura venezolana y el epistolario de la Biblioteca Ayacucho," 122. Each volume folder I examined includes documents and correspondence from the conception of a project to sending approved proofs to the printer, though not the proofs themselves.

39. Pablo Rocca's collection of correspondence between Rama and Candido flags missing material from 1974 to 1977, when Rama wrote from Ayacucho in his official capacity; the letters from those days are in the Biblioteca Ayacucho Archive. Both published volumes are largely drawn from letters at the Ángel Rama Foundation in Montevideo.

40. In some cases, different projects from different folders converged, as the translators and editors communicated about multiple elements of different projects at once. The three volumes focused on Brazilian *modernismo* are #47 *Arte y arquitectura del modernismo brasileño (1917–1930)* (1978); #56 Mário de Andrade, *Obra escogida* (1979); and #84 Oswald de Andrade, *Obra escogida* (1981).

41. Candido to Rama, August 6, 1975, folder 56, *Obra escogida* by Mário de Andrade, Biblioteca Ayacucho Archive (hereafter cited as BAA).

42. He maintained this proportional ambition throughout, expressing disappointment at falling below the mark: "20 Brazilian volumes were hoped for in the first 100 (and only 10 appeared!) so I'm asking you now to suggest new volumes and editors given our delinquency in the plan. In the 500 volumes no fewer than 100 should be Brazilian." Rama to Candido, January 23, 1983, in Rocca, *Un proyecto latinoamericano*, 19.

43. Rama to Candido, September 17, 1974, in Rocca, *Un proyecto latinoamericano*, 70.

44. Rama to Candido, January 20, 1976, folder 56, *Obra escogida* by Mário de Andrade, BAA.

45. Rama invites Riberio as volume editor of *Casa-Grande e Senzala* by Gilberto Freyre, knowing that his friend wrote critically of this founding Brazilian

sociologist; true to his interest in polemic, he promises to also publish Ribeiro's *Las Américas y la civilización*, ed. María Elena Rodríguez Ozán, trans. Renzo Pi Hugarte (1992), #180.

46. Rama to Candido, November 20, 1975, in Rocca, *Un proyecto latinoamericano*, 84–85.

47. Rama to Aracy Amaral, June 29, 1976, folder 47, *Arte y arquitectura del modernismo brasileño, 1917–1930*, BAA.

48. Citing from his diary, Gordon-Burroughs registers Rama's uneasiness about the Ayacucho project stemming from some intellectuals' resistance to the idea of a "continental cultural heritage"; for example, "Escovar Salom questions the first title, Bolívar's writings, with this: they're already so well-known! I'm astonished, but it's useless to tell him that the Biblioteca should precisely be made up of the most well-known works. I merely argue that unfortunately in other parts of the continent Bolívar isn't equally well-known (!)." Ángel Rama, *Diario: 1974–1983*, ed. Rosario Peyrou (Montevideo: Trilce, 2001), 42. Cited in Gordon-Burroughs, "Monuments and Ephemera," 99.

49. Rama's letter to Candido during the meeting speaks to his misgivings that the pan–Latin American scope of the project will be foreclosed: "The unfortunate absence of the Brazilian delegation has provoked grave concern." Rama to Candido, November 20, 1975, in Rocca, *Un proyecto latinoamericano*, 84. Writing to Darcy Ribeiro, he expresses the same frustration that the Brazilian government denied their visas, positing a potential meeting in São Paulo. Rama to Ribeiro, November 25, 1975, in Haydée Ribeiro Coelho and Pablo Rocca, eds., *Diálogos latino-americanos: Correspondência entre Ángel Rama, Berta e Darcy Ribeiro* (São Paulo: Editora Global, 2014), 63.

50. "It would be a real shame if the date of the sesquicentennial of the Congreso Anfitiónico arrived and among the volumes published there were no Brazilian authors. That's why I would appreciate your help with the preparation of a volume dedicated to Mário de Andrade. I need Gilda de Mello to select his works, including *Macunaíma*, and for you to obtain the needed authorization from the family to publish it in Spanish." Rama to Candido, November 20, 1975, in Rocca, *Un proyecto latinoamericano*, 85.

51. Rama to Mello e Souza, September 10, 1976, in Rocca, *Un proyecto latinoamericano*, 150.

52. The prologues represent a complex case of simultaneous audience. For Haroldo and Mello e Souza, their prologues on Oswald and Mário respectively were published in Brazil nearly simultaneously with the Ayacucho Spanish translation. See Ribeiro Coelho, "O Brasil na 'Biblioteca Ayacucho,'" 87–88. In the case of Darcy Ribeiro's introduction to *Casa-grande e senzala*, the plan to translate it into Spanish formed a part of the text's initial production: in fact, "Rama was Ribeiro's first reader" for this work on the Brazilian sociologist Gilberto Freyre. See Haydée Ribeiro Coelho, "A vida em movimento: A correspondência entre Ángel Rama, Berta, e Darcy Ribeiro," in Ribeiro Coelho and Rocca, *Diálogos latino-americanos*, 28.

53. Mello e Souza to Rama, October 7, 1976, folder 56, *Obra escogida* by Mário de Andrade, BAA.

54. "With respect to the annotations, I suggest you do not cut too much of what you have done, as it may be better to leave it to us: this task relies on understanding the Spanish American reader. We've had a bad experience with Walnice Nogueira Galvão, who turned in a set of notes too slim for a book so in need of historical, geographic, and linguistic information as *Os sertões*, such that we had to ask her to redo the work." Rama to Mello e Souza, October 18, 1976, folder 56, *Obra escogida* by Mário de Andrade, BAA.

55. Rama to Mello e Souza, October 2, 1978, folder 56, *Obra escogida* by Mário de Andrade, BAA.

56. Rama to Olea, October 3, 1978, folder 56, *Obra escogida* by Mário de Andrade, BAA. Called an honorarium, the translation rate was six Venezuelan dollars per five hundred words; Rama raised it here to ten dollars, but the total was still far from the $3,500 Olea had previously requested for the two Oswald novels. Olea to Rama, September 27, 1977, folder 84, *Obra escogida* by Oswald de Andrade, BAA.

57. Although his letters to Rama often appear go unanswered according to the archival record, Olea remains committed to the project. Haroldo seemingly mediates between the two parties, ultimately proposing the resolution that Olea receive Ayacucho Colección Clásica volumes in addition to his honorarium for his translations for the Oswald volume.

58. Olea to Rama, November 11, 1978, folder 84, *Obra escogida* by Oswald de Andrade, BAA.

59. Olea to Rama, November 11, 1978, folder 84, *Obra escogida* by Oswald de Andrade, BAA.

60. Olea to Rama, November 11, 1978, folder 84, *Obra escogida* by Oswald de Andrade, BAA.

61. Olea to Rama, November 11, 1978, folder 84, *Obra escogida* by Oswald de Andrade, BAA.

62. Gilda de Mello e Souza, "Notas a *Macunaíma*," in Mário de Andrade, *Obra escogida*, ed. Mello e Souza (Caracas: Biblioteca Ayacucho, 1979), 113.

63. "We have not changed our rates, nor do I anticipate we will do so for the rest of the year. At least it is better with poetry than prose." Rama to Santiago Kovadloff, April 6, 1978, folder 56, *Obra escogida* by Mário de Andrade, BAA.

64. Rama to Kovadloff, November 15, 1978, folder 56, *Obra escogida* by Mário de Andrade, BAA.

65. Kovadloff to Rama, November 25, 1978, folder 56, *Obra escogida* by Mário de Andrade, BAA.

66. Kovadloff wrote to Eloy Romero rather than Rama: "The economic situation my country is going through is so catastrophic that the remuneration the Biblioteca offers for my work has become ridiculous. . . . Perhaps in the future I might be able to return to take on other such exciting literary projects. As I've said, that is no longer possible for me at the moment. Reality demands that I carefully redefine my means of earning a living." Kovadloff to Eloy Romero, May 15, 1979, folder 56, *Obra escogida* by Mário de Andrade, BAA.

67. Her work was not represented in the archival materials for these translations from Brazilian *modernismo*, nor did they appear in the folder for the other translation she completed of Humboldt's *Cartas americanas* (1980).

68. Aracy Amaral made Rama aware of this difficulty in April 1977, but he did not take any action at that time to secure the necessary rights. Amaral to Rama, October 21, 1977, folder 47, BAA. In 2001, the Ayacucho President Alfredo Chacón exchanged memos with chief editor Oscar Rodríguez Ortiz about rereleasing this out-of-print volume. Ortiz responds that it will be impossible: "We are faced with a serious problem of copyright: proper authorizations were not sought or obtained at the time (1978) for either the texts or photographic reproductions, nor are they in our files for this volume. Although another Copyright Law was in place in Venezuela at the time, Ayacucho was aware of the problem, and it is mentioned in a letter by volume editor Aracy Amaral dated April 24, 1977." Ortiz to Chacón, October 23, 2001, folder 47, BAA.

69. Oswald de Andrade, *Obra escogida*, ed. Haroldo de Campos and K. David Jackson (Caracas: Biblioteca Ayacucho, 1981), 161.

70. The best-known example, of course, would be the line "Tupí or not tupí, that is the question": the reader will understand even without any footnote that this phrase was always in English. Oswald de Andrade, "Manifiesto antropófago," trans. Héctor Olea, in *Obra escogida*, 67.

71. Oswald, "Manifiesto antropófago," 68.

72. Oswald, "Cannibalist Manifesto," 40.

73. Oswald, "Manifiesto antropófago," 69.

74. Oswald, "Manifiesto antropófago," 69n2. While Haroldo indeed defines this work as preconcrete, he does not present the poem in the shape of the new moon, as Olea does in his translation.

75. Olea dissembles that his source did not know the meaning of the Tupi words; he translates from elsewhere in the poem and adds *arresopla*, or *arrebatar* plus *resoplar*. The Portuguese translation offered is "Lua Nova, o Lua Nova! assoprai em fulano lembrança de mim; eis-me aqui estou em tua presença; fazei com que eu tão somente occupe [*sic*] o seu coração" (New Moon, New Moon! blow on so-and-so's memory of me; here I am in your presence; make me the only one occupying his heart). Couto de Magalhães, *O selvagem* (Rio de Janeiro: Typographia da Reforma, 1876), 142. The nineteenth-century ethnographer read this text as evidence of prolonged contact between Portuguese and the Indigenous language Guaraní: "The mixture is already almost imperceptible. All of it is in good modern Guaraní, however the rhyme and the meter are Spanish." Magalhães, *O selvagem*, 144. The assimilationist perspective on display here privileges the less perceptible "mixture" as opposed to the *groseiro* (coarse) linguistic hybridity evidenced in other texts—precisely the opposite use that Oswald makes of the poem, where his importation of Tupi is overt.

76. Olea, "Posfacio," 259.

77. "The novel contains elements that elevate Brazilian hybridity and at the same time critically examines the aims of anthropophagic appropriations and suggests another type of hybridism for Brazilian culture, which I call subaltern, which valorizes cultural exchanges between countries of the Southern Hemi-

sphere." Alfredo Cesar Melo, "*Macunaíma*: Entre a crítica e o elogio à transculturação," *Hispanic Review* 78, no. 2 (2010): 205.

78. Although he was not the first to translate *Macunaíma*, Olea succeeded most in incorporating his transcreation into another literary system through the dense dialogue with Rama and the incorporation into the Ayacucho collection. Prior translations include the Italian by Giuliana Segre Giorgi (1970) and the French by Jacques Thiérot (1975). Margaret Richardson Hollingsworth translated several chapters into English during Andrade's lifetime, but she did not complete or publish her translation. The Argentine artist Carybé produced a Spanish translation along with illustrations; his images appeared in an illustrated Portuguese edition in 1957, but to my knowledge his translation remains unpublished. See Têle Porto Anacona Lopez, "Traduções de *Macunaíma*," in Mário de Andrade, *Macunaíma: O herói sem nenhum caráter*, ed. Têle Porto Anacona Lopez (Rio de Janeiro: Livros Técnicos e Científicos, 1978), 407–9. Unfortunately, colonialist ideology mars the first English translation by E. A. Goodland (New York: Random House, 1984), where words like "devilish" characterize Afro-Brazilian cultural forms, which are celebrated in the source text, not demonized. See Albert Braz, "Traducing the Author: Textual (In)fidelity in E. A. Goodland's Translation of *Macunaíma*," *Graphos* 9, no. 1 (2007): 190. Katrina Dodson has carefully crafted an artful and thoroughly researched new translation, which is certain to provide the English-reading public with better access to this classic of Brazilian *modernismo*. Katrina Dodson, trans., *Macunaíma. The Hero with No Character*, by Mário de Andrade, intro. by John Keene (New York: New Directions, 2023).

79. Damrosch, *What Is World Literature?*, 6.

80. Haroldo de Campos, "Prefacio. *Macunaíma*: La fantasía estructural," in *Macunaíma* by Mário de Andrade (Barcelona: Seix Barral, 1977), 15.

81. Mello e Souza bases her analyses in Marxist thought; Haroldo's approach was more formalist.

82. She furthermore frames the transculturation present in these traditions as conflict rather than cross-pollination or creative expansion. "I am convinced that, when composing *Macunaíma*, Mário de Andrade transposed to literature, in an intentional and critical manner, the conflict he observed in music between the European tradition inherited from Portugal and the local, popular, Indigenous, or African manifestations." Gilda de Mello e Souza, "Prólogo: El tupí y el laúd," in Mário de Andrade, *Obra escogida*, ed. Mello e Souza (Caracas: Biblioteca Ayacucho, 1979), xxxv.

83. Mário qtd. in Mello e Souza, "Prólogo," xxii.

84. Debates over this novel continue. Kimberle López concludes that the cosmopolitan authors of *modernismo*, while Brazilian, viewed Indigenous cultures with the same "imperial eyes" as European authors, and questions "whether, in his cannibalistic appropriation of material from Koch-Grünberg, Andrade can avoid adopting the same sort of ethnographic authority." Kimberle López, "*Modernismo* and the Ambivalence of the Postcolonial Experience: Cannibalism, Primitivism, and Exoticism in Mário de Andrade's *Macunaíma*," *Luso-Brazilian Review* 35, no. 1 (1998): 32. Conversely, José Luiz Passos connects the novel to a Brazilian narrative tradition, using *Macunaíma* to identify a series of

central tenets in its precursors: the *malandro* or trouble-maker protagonist, the centrality of racial mixture, and morbid irony. "After Mário de Andrade, Manuel Antônio de Almeida, José de Alencar, and Machado de Assis can be read in a Macunaimac way." José Luiz Passos, *Ruínas de linhas puras: Quatro ensaios em torno a "Macunaíma"* (São Paulo: Annablume, 1998), 19.

85. Lúcia Sá draws out the "language quest," which "can only be understood if we carefully read those stories that others have considered unimportant in the narrative structure or have disregarded in favor of supposed European prototypes . . . a hero whose behavior changes from situation to situation." Lúcia Sá, *Rain Forest Literatures: Amazonian Texts and Latin American Culture* (Minneapolis: University of Minnesota Press, 2004), 67–68.

86. "Claiming the historical importance of Indians in the formation of Brazilian society, one is dangerously close to accepting their ancestral rights to land." Sá, *Rain Forest Literatures*, xxv. The same goals appear in the Ayacucho collection of colonial documents Darcy Ribeiro edited, *La fundación de Brasil: Testimonios, 1500–1700*, ed. Darcy Ribeiro (Caracas: Biblioteca Ayacucho, 1992).

87. Olea, "Posfacio," 241.

88. Olea, "Posfacio," 250.

89. By turning different synonyms from different Indigenous languages into mobile untranslatables, Olea also reflects what Harris Feinsod identifies as a shift in the deployment of Indigenous cultural forms, from a usable past ready to be mined for national identity formation to an interest in broader pan–Latin American and present-day Indigenous living traditions, such as, in Olea's case, food and plants as localized cultural knowledge. Feinsod focuses on the cultural and literary use of Indigenous ruins, which switches from a nationalist to a pan-American frame in the 1950s, what he calls "a midcentury culture of pre-Columbian ruins." Harris Feinsod, *The Poetry of the Americas: From Good Neighbors to Countercultures* (New York: Oxford University Press, 2017), 139.

90. Olea, "Posfacio," 255.

91. Olea, "Posfacio," 244.

92. Olea, "Posfacio," 245; emphasis in the source text.

93. Heloisa Costa Milton compares Olea's Spanish and Andrade's Portuguese and demonstrates his many departures from semantic meaning in order to preserve elements of rhyme and rhythm. She characterizes his translation as an "homage to the Brazilian writer [that] activates a circuit which reaches at least two poles in two directions: Brazilian and Spanish American narrative in their possibilities of dialogue." Heloisa Costa Milton, "*Macunaíma* no reino hispânico (A propósito de tradução)," *Revista de Letras* 33 (1993): 69.

94. Márcia Moura da Silva, "Análise da tradução de termos indígenas em Macunaíma de Mário de Andrade na tradução de Héctor Olea para o espanhol" (PhD diss., Universidade Federal de Santa Catarina, 2009), 122.

95. Mello e Souza, "Prólogo," xxx–xxxi.

96. Mário de Andrade qtd. in Mello e Souza, "Prólogo," xxxi.

97. Mello e Souza, "Prólogo," xxxi.

98. Mário, *Obra escogida*, 3. The English translation by Goodland "Aw! What a fucking life!" is more profane and angry than the Portuguese catch-

phrase; this choice exemplifies that first English translation's imposition on the text to create a threatening other in the Brazilian trickster-hero. Goodland, *Macunaíma*, 3. In her new translation, Katrina Dodson renders his saying as "Ah! just so lazy!"; she includes an endnote (unmarked in the body of the text but available for curious readers) that reactivates the multilingual nature of the source text: "The hero's catchphrase, Ah! just so lazy! (*Ai! que preguiça!*), contains a bilingual pun linking Portuguese and Tupi. A sloth is called a *preguiça* in Portuguese, and in Tupi it is called *aig* (also transliterated as *ai* and *aígue*)." Dodson, trans., *Macunaíma*, 250.

99. Mário, *Obra escogida*, 52.

100. Mário, *Obra escogida*, 37; Mário de Andrade, *Macunaíma: O herói sem nenhum caráter*, ed. Têle Porto Anacona Lopez (Rio de Janeiro: Livros Técnicos e Científicos, 1978), 55.

101. H. C. Milton, "*Macunaíma* no reino hispânico," 64.

102. Along with adding three *bemberos*, Olea interpolates the Central American colloquialism *bochinche* to express their party-making, where Andrade used a more commonplace phrase *fazer a festa* in the source text.

103. Mário, *Macunaíma*, ed. Têle Porto Anacona Lopez, 63.

104. Mário, *Obra escogida*, 41.

105. Mello e Souza, "Notas a *Macunaíma*," 126n170.

106. Unfortunately, Olea ignores the contributions of Lydia Cabrera, the Cuban ethnographer whose work provided foundational research for Guillén and other artists and writers interested in Afro-Cuban cultures.

107. Olea, "Posfacio," 245.

108. Olea, "Posfacio," 247.

109. Mário, *Macunaíma*, ed. Têle Porto Anacona Lopez, 82.

110. Mário, *Obra escogida*, 55.

111. Mello e Souza, "Notas," in *Obra escogida*, 130.

112. Mário, *Macunaíma*, ed. Têle Porto Anacona Lopez, 92.

113. Mário, *Obra escogida*, 62.

114. Octavio Paz, *El laberinto de la soledad*, ed. Enrico Mario Santí (Madrid: Cátedra, 1993), 180–81.

115. Paz, *Laberinto*, 181.

CHAPTER 5

1. José Emilio Pacheco, *Tarde o temprano: Poemas 1958–2009*, 4th ed. (Mexico City: Fondo de Cultura Económica, 2009), 187.

2. Augusto, "Antes do anti," 10.

3. Shellhorse, *Anti-Literature*, 74.

4. Ana Cristina Cesar compares Augusto's translation anthology to Manuel Bandeira's in order to emphasize the difference between them, particularly Augusto's contrarian, antitradition approach to translation. See Ana Cristina Cesar, "Bastidores de la traducción," in *El método documental*, ed. and trans. Teresa Arijón and Bárbara Belloc (Buenos Aires: Manantial, 2013), 179–91.

5. Augusto de Campos, email message to author, November 7, 2019.

6. Augusto, *Verso, reverso, controverso*, 7.

7. Pacheco features poetry by two heteronyms Julián Hernández and Fernando Tejada within the "Apéndice: Cancioneiro Apócrifo" section of his chapbook *No me preguntes cómo paso el tiempo (Poemas 1964–1968)* (Mexico City: Joaquín Mortiz, 1969), 111–122. As Hugo Verani points out, Pacheco signals the literary game afoot when he introduces these poems with epigraphs drawn from Antonio Machado and Fernando Pessoa, the Spanish and Portuguese poets most associated with this literary practice. See Hugo Verani "José Emilio Pacheco: La voz complementaria," *Revista de Crítica Literaria Latinoamericana* 24, no. 47 (1998): 284–85. For further exploration of Pacheco's dispersion of poetic authority even in his own "original" poetry through strategies of appropriation, heteronym, and reciprocity, see also: Mary Docter, "José Emilio Pacheco: A Poetics of Reciprocity," *Hispanic Review* 70, no.3 (2002): 373–92; and José Miguel Oviedo, "José Emilio Pacheco: La poesía como 'Ready-Made,'" *Hispamérica* 5, no. 15 (1976): 39–55.

8. Appearing only in his 1984 translation collection *Aproximaciones*, while Gordon Woolf, Piero Quercia, and Azevedo Oliveira may receive less critical attention than the two heteronyms featured first in his 1969 chapbook, these figures still represent what Verani calls "new textual masks." See Verani, "José Emilio Pacheco: La voz complementaria," 286.

9. Susan Bassnett cites Gideon Toury, who defines "pseudotranslations" as texts presented as translations with no corresponding source texts in any language. See Susan Bassnett and André Lefevere, *Constructing Cultures: Essays on Literary Translation* (Clevedon, PA: Multilingual Matters, 1998), 28.

10. Pacheco translated works by authors who translate from Spanish: Edward Dorn, Alastair Reid, George McWhirter (who had translated Pacheco himself), Archibald MacLeish, Michael Schmidt, Tom Raworth, Charles Tomlinson, Kenneth Rexroth, and Elizabeth Bishop (who had translated other Latin American poets). Recognized world literary greats Petrarch, Goethe, Rilke, and Apollinaire appear in *Aproximaciones*; Robert Lowell, W. H. Auden, William Carlos Williams, Matthew Arnold, Mallarmé, Rimbaud, Baudelaire, Nerval, and John Donne appear in *Tarde o temprano* (1980). See Isabel C. Gómez, "José Emilio Pacheco and Reciprocity between Literary Cultures: Gift Theory as Translation Studies Methodology," *Transfer* 14, nos. 1–2 (2019): 73–99.

11. Pacheco, *Aproximaciones*, 6.

12. Theo D'haen, "Anthologizing World Literature in Translation: Global/Local/Glocal," *Forum for World Literature Studies* 9, no. 4 (2017): 539, 553.

13. Jeffrey R. Di Leo, "Analyzing Anthologies," in *On Anthologies: Politics and Pedagogy*, ed. Di Leo (Lincoln: University of Nebraska Press, 2004), 1.

14. From the back cover: "This concise anthology combines comprehensive coverage of key works of the Western literary tradition and the best core, enduring works of the literatures of China, Japan, India, the Middle East, Africa, and native Americas." David Damrosch and David L. Pike, eds., *The Longman Anthology of World Literature* (New York: Pearson/Longman, 2008). https://www.worldcat.org/title/180314582.

15. For data on literature anthologies published in Europe from 1900 to 2011, see Teresa Seruya et al., "Introduction: Translation Anthologies and Collections. An Overview and Some Prospects," in *Translation in Anthologies and*

Collections (19th and 20th Centuries), ed. Teresa Seruya, Lieven D'hulst, Alexandra Assis Rosa, and Maria Lin Moniz (Amsterdam: John Benjamins, 2013), 1–2.

16. "World Literature has oscillated between extremes of assimilation and discontinuity: either the earlier and distant works we read are really *just like us*, or they are unutterably foreign, curiosities whose foreignness finally tells us nothing and can only reinforce our sense of separate identity." Damrosch, *What Is World Literature?*, 44.

17. Di Leo, "Analyzing Anthologies," 3–4.

18. Seruya et al., "Introduction: Translation Anthologies and Collections," 3; Di Leo, "Analyzing Anthologies," 2–3.

19. Ana Maria Bernardo, "Poetry Anthologies as *Weltliteratur* Projects," in Seruya, D'hulst, Assis Rosa, and Lin Moniz, *Translation in Anthologies and Collections*, 109.

20. Pacheco, *Aproximaciones*, 8.

21. Augusto, "Antes do anti," 10.

22. Pacheco begins *Aproximaciones* (1984) with the above-cited reversal of the last phrase of Paz's introduction to *Versiones y diversiones* (1974), and he continues: "In my youth I learned this art from Octavio Paz and Jaime García Terrés. . . . Since then it has been inseparable from my own work in poetry." Pacheco, *Aproximaciones*, 5.

23. Pacheco read from his unpublished approximations at the 2009 Feria Internacional del Libro (FIL), a month after receiving the Premio Cervantes. Norma Gutiérrez reports that he read all translations: one by Wisława Szymborska, five from Charles Baudelaire, one approximation of Catullus, and a final poem from his large corpus of haiku. Norma Guttiérez "'Aproximaciones': El exitoso adiós del José Emilio Pacheco," *El Informador*, December 2, 2009.

24. In his monograph on the poet, Ronald Friis mentions the value of Pacheco's translations but stops short of analyzing them. See Ronald Friis, *José Emilio Pacheco and the Poets of the Shadows* (Lewisburg, PA: Bucknell University Press, 2001), 59–60, 105.

25. Whereas the first two editions of his collected poems, *Tarde o temprano* (1980, 1986), end with his *Aproximaciones (1958–1978)*, the third and fourth editions (2000, 2009) exclude the translations. Although the 2000 edition promised another volume just of translations, this collection has not yet come to fruition. I do not know what motivated the separation of Pacheco's approximations from his poetry: author request, editorial choices, publisher's mandates, copyright issues, etc. This editorial choice impacts scholarship: the edited collection of essays *Pasión por la palabra: Homenaje a José Emilio Pacheco* does not include any analysis of his translations, and all citations are from the third or fourth editions of *Tarde o temprano* (2000, 2009), which exclude his approximations. Edith Negrín and Álvaro Ruiz Abreu, eds., *Pasión por la palabra: Homenaje a José Emilio Pacheco* (Mexico City: Universidad Autónoma Metropolitana, 2013).

26. Gordon Brotherston, *Book of the Fourth World* (Cambridge: Cambridge University Press, 1992), 343.

27. "The defense of the Indigenous people and the recovery of their cultural origins within a national state constructed and sustained by a *criollo/mestizo* ideology after the Mexican Revolution allowed the use of the Pre-Columbian

imaginary in the different discourses that have sustained the revolutionary regime's ideology. . . . A large intellectual tradition of recovery of the Pre-Columbian past as icon of the agendas of the revolutionary regime has led to a reading of León-Portilla's work as one of the bases for the constitution of a national ideology." Ignacio M. Sánchez Prado, "The Pre-Columbian Past as a Project: Miguel León-Portilla and Hispanism," in *Ideologies of Hispanism*, ed. Mabel Moraña (Nashville: Vanderbilt University Press, 2005), 49.

28. Pacheco, *Aproximaciones*, 8.

29. Pacheco, *Aproximaciones*, 189.

30. Bierhorst is not the only US poet to work on translations of Indigenous works as a poet and not an anthropologist. Others such as Jerome Rothenberg represent a supplemental and literary approach to the work by US ethnographers such as Dennis Tedlock, who translated the Popol Vuh into English.

31. Pacheco, *Aproximaciones*, 136–37.

32. John Bierhorst, ed., *In the Trail of the Wind: American Indian Poems and Ritual Orations* (New York: Farrar, Straus and Giroux, 1971), 84.

33. Bierhorst, *In the Trail of the Wind*, 140.

34. "Many winters ago, our wise ancestors predicted: the white-eyed-monster will come from the East. As it advances it will consume the earth. This monster is the white race. The prophecy is about to be fulfilled." Pacheco, *Aproximaciones*, 137.

35. Dictionaries include also the formulation *estar apache* as a verb, "to be Apache-like": "Se dice del indio nómada de las llanuras de Nuevo México, caracterizado por su gran belicosidad." (What one calls the nomadic Indigenous person from the plains of New Mexico, characterized by their aggressiveness). *Real Academia Española*, 2014.

36. The word "current" also evokes an electric metaphor from Walt Whitman; Paz uses *Corriente alterna* as the title of one of his essay collections.

37. Pacheco, *Aproximaciones*, 135.

38. "The Indian poet does not consider himself the originator of his material but merely the conveyor. Either he has heard it from an elder or he has received it from a supernatural power. Describing more or less the same processes, the self-conscious European or Euro-American poet speaks of reworking traditional materials or, fancifully, of drawing inspiration from a muse. But the Indian, being relatively unself-conscious, does not see it this way. Indian poetry, then, is usually attributed not to an individual but to his culture." Bierhorst, *In the Trail of the Wind*, n.p.

39. Pacheco, *Aproximaciones*, 187.

40. "*Bugraria* in Brazilian Portuguese is the territory inhabited by *bugres*, the racist term against the 'uncouth or docile' Indigenous person. As an adjective, *bugre* designates 'a savage individual: coarse, perfidious, suspicious.' It would be the Brazilian equivalent of the sinister Mexican term 'naco.' According to Francisco J. Santamaría, 'naco' initially meant 'Indian in white pants.' A quarter of a century after his *Dictionary of Mexicanisms* collected these and other infamies, the word now designates the rural person who tries to adapt himself to the city. It is well proven that exploitation can only be based on a theory of racial superiority." Pacheco, *Aproximaciones*, 121.

41. Pacheco, *Aproximaciones*, 128–29.

42. Pacheco, *Aproximaciones*, 130.

43. Pacheco, *Aproximaciones*, 131.

44. Pacheco, *Aproximaciones*, 131.

45. Elsewhere in *Bugraria*, especially in "Rimbaud en Abisinia," Pacheco as heteronym Oliveira Azevedo further explores this critique of poetry as antidemocratic performance of elitist language. Pacheco, *Aproximaciones*, 121–22.

46. See José Emilio Pacheco, trans., *Cuatro cuartetos* (Traducción de José Emilio Pacheco), by T. S. Eliot (Mexico City: Fondo de Cultura Económica, 1989); José Emilio Pacheco, trans., "The Dry Salvages: Versión y notas de José Emilio Pacheco," by T. S. Eliot, *Letras Libres* 154 (October 2011): 20–32; and José Emilio Pacheco, trans., "East Coker: Aproximación y notas de José Emilio Pacheco," by T. S. Eliot, *Letras Libres* 181 (January 2014): 20–29.

47. Helen Vendler interprets the last books of poets as a retreading of ground covered through their poetic career, as in the Irish folk tradition of taking one "last look" around your property when death is nigh. See Helen Vendler, *Last Looks, Last Books: Stevens, Plath, Lowell, Bishop, Merrill* (Princeton, NJ: Princeton University Press, 2010), 1–25.

48. Eliot himself began this controversy, dismissing his annotations in "The Frontiers of Criticism" (1957), where he laments them as "bogus scholarship" added at the last minute because "the poem was inconveniently short" but they have subsequently "led critics into temptation." T. S. Eliot, *The Waste Land*, ed. Michael North (New York: W. W. Norton, 2001), 112–13. Michael North rejects this explanation, as the poet's correspondence shows he was considering the notes long before the publication he claims required them. See Eliot, *The Waste Land*, 21fn1.

49. Eliot decided to add it after his friend John Hayward did not understand that "The Dry Salvages" referred to a place. Helen Gardner, *The Composition of "Four Quartets"* (New York: Oxford University Press, 1978), 120–21.

50. T. S. Eliot, *Collected Poems 1909–1962* (New York: Harcourt, 1991), 191.

51. Gardner, *Composition*, 120.

52. José Emilio Pacheco, trans., "The Dry Salvages: Versión y notas de José Emilio Pacheco," by T. S. Eliot, *Letras Libres* 154 (October 2011): 27.

53. Eliot, *Collected Poems*, 191.

54. Pacheco, "The Dry Salvages: Versión y notas," 20. The word choices of Pacheco's 1989 approximation are largely the same, but in that earlier publication he maintains the lineation of the source, only adding one break between "rages, destroyer." This second approximation splits five of these nine opening lines in two.

55. Pacheco, "The Dry Salvages: Versión y notas," 27.

56. Gardner writes that the drafts of his *Four Quartets* demonstrate Eliot's gradual connection between the two spaces of his childhood, St. Louis and New England, through the Mississippi River and the rocks he knew as "The Dry Salvages." These "two symbols from his childhood came together as symbols of the permanence of past agonies: the Mississippi and the reef of the Dry Salvages off Cape Ann." Gardner, *Composition*, 49–50.

57. Sara Melzer traces French early modern distinctions between "barbarian" and *sauvage* (savage): the former was from the Greek, an onomatopoetic term for babbling sound that refers to someone "not Greek, outside of language," which had attached to the French themselves; the latter was the preferred label for a non-French other who was wild but could potentially be assimilated. See Sara E. Melzer, *Colonizer or Colonized: The Hidden Stories of Early Modern French Culture* (Philadelphia: University of Pennsylvania Press, 2012), 67–72. The "wild West" in Eliot's poem is depicted from the perspective of those who imagined taming that "empty" or "wild" space; in Pacheco's annotated approximation, by contrast, there is a humanity given to those who are invisible in Eliot's poem.

58. As with many of the translation projects in this book, the translations in *O anticrítico* tend to fall through the cracks in favor of analysis of Augusto's anticritical porous prose. Adam Shellhorse focuses on the critical genealogy of the porous-prose poem "américa latina: a contra-boom da poesia" rather than the accompanying translations of Vicente Huidobro or Oliveiro Girondo. Shellhorse, *Anti-Literature*, 74–76. Daniel Lacerda identifies in both Augusto and John Cage a form of *proseia colagística* or "collage-like prosetry," again focusing on the porous-prose criticism rather than the works of translation. "Alguma coisa sobre o nada: A anticrítica," in *Sobre Augusto de Campos*, eds. Flora Süssekind and Júlio Castañon Guimarães (Rio de Janeiro: Edições Casa de Rui Barbosa / 7 Letras, 2004), 243. Gonzalo Aguilar leaves the volume aside while discussing Augusto's translations as "metamorphosis of heterogeneous discourses." Gonzalo Moisés Aguilar, *Poesía concreta brasileña: Las vanguardias en la encrucijada modernista* (Rosario, Argentina: Beatriz Viterbo, 2003), 317–32.

59. From *Transblanco* by Octavio Paz (studied in chapter 2) to Goethe's *Faust*, Homer's Iliad, or the Hebrew Bible, Haroldo tended toward larger selections or complete major works.

60. "Haroldo wrote through *serial expansion* while Augusto de Campos sought *minimalist synthesis*, unity in the spatial visualization of the poem. Augusto's poems are constructed not by accumulation and dispersion—like in *Galáxias*—but rather by limitation and condensation." Aguilar, *Poesía concreta brasileña*, 271.

61. "'Ventilated prose' is the expression of Buckminster Fuller, who had put something similar into practice in his short treatise on industrialization titled *Untitled Epic Poem on the History of Industrialization*." Augusto, "Antes do anti," 9.

62. Augusto, "Antes do anti," 9.

63. Augusto, "Antes do anti," 9.

64. Augusto, *O anticrítico*, 16.

65. See Gómez, "Anti-surrealism?," 376–79.

66. Augusto, *O anticrítico*, 78–79.

67. Augusto, "Doublets," in *O anticrítico*, 140.

68. Like many of the pieces in this anthology, Augusto included this work in an earlier volume, where it was labeled along with others an "Intradução" and anthologized in *Viva vaia* (1949–79).

69. Augusto, *O anticrítico*, 97.

70. Decades later, conceptual poet Caroline Bergvall would expand this poetic gesture anticipated by Augusto de Campos in "VIA (48 Dante Variations)" (2003). In this work, which appears as a printed poem and as a sound recording, Bergvall reads the first stanza of the *Inferno* in forty-seven English translations, along with the translator's name and publication year, in a haunting performance of this fourteenth-century poem's movement through the ever-changing English language and norms of English-language translation. Carlos Soto Román crafts a "traducción parcial" of Bergvall's poem into Spanish, repeating her conceptual procedure rather than translating any of the words. A Portuguese version by Adriano Scandolara titled "Via: 17 Variações de Dante" featured on the blog *escamandro* has attracted commenters adding additional versions. In short, the procedure is infinitely replicable. See Caroline Bergvall, "VIA (48 Dante Variations)," *Chain* 10 (Summer 2003): 55–59; Caroline Bergvall, "VIA (48 Dante translations) mix w fractals," *Soundcloud*, 2013; Carlos Soto Román, trans., "Via," by Caroline Bergvall, in "'A=A: Conceptualismo como traducción,' de Vanessa Place / 'Via,' de Caroline Bergvall" *Letras en línea*, July 29, 2013; and Adriano Scandolara, "Via: 17 Variações de Dante," in "Via, de Caroline Bergvall," *escamandro*, September 30, 2014.

71. Augusto, "dante: um corpo que cai," in *O anticrítico*, 15.

72. For a subtle reading of the fertile cross-pollination of political activist circles of Italian migrants to Brazil and the Pinheiro translation into Brazilian Portuguese, see Giulia Riccò, "Dante's *Purgatório Canto VI* in Nineteenth-Century Brazil: Translating the *Nazione/Nação*," *Mester* 45 (2016–17): 3–18.

73. Augusto, "dante: um corpo que cai," 16. My overly literal translation emphasizes word order to best display in English Augusto's observation that the other Portuguese versions end with "dead."

74. For further discussion of these transitions, see Perrone, *Seven Faces*, 17–24.

75. João Cabral de Melo Neto, "A Augusto de Campos," in *Agrestes: Poesia (1981–1985)* (Rio de Janeiro: Editora Nova Fronteira, 1985), 10.

76. The source text reads: "soube ler com acuidade / poetas revolucionados." Melo Neto, "A Augusto de Campos," 10.

77. See Augusto de Campos, "joão/agrestes," in *Despoeseia*, ed. Haroldo de Campos (São Paulo: Editora Perspetiva, 1996), 76–77.

78. As cited in the introduction, Haroldo traces a form of anthropophagous reason back through the Brazilian tradition to Gregório de Matos and specifically to his translation practice on the Spanish Baroque. To further specify the operation, he writes: "Gregório translated, with a highly personal, differential feature revealed in his ironic handling of the combination of literary topoi, two sonnets by Góngora ('Mientras por competir con tu cabello' ['While to Compete with Your Hair'] and 'Ilustre y hermosísima María' ['Illustrious and Most Lovely Maria']) to produce a third ('Discreta e formossísima Maria' ['Refined and Most Lovely Maria']) which took apart and made explicit the secrets of the Baroque sonnet-making machine." Haroldo, "Anthropophagous Reason," 165–6.

79. Augusto writes that in this poem "tentei mostrar, sob a forma do *blow up* de uma estrofe do 'Marinícolas,' a riqueza da tessitura lingística." Augusto, "Da

América que existe: Gregório de Matos," in *Poesia Antipoesia Antropofagia & Cia*, 116.

80. Augusto, "arte final para gregório," in *O anticrítico*, 86. The first two stanzas repeat the lines "pés de puas com topes de seda / cabelos de cabra com pós de marfim" (prickly feet covered up with silk / goat hair powdered with marble). Augusto gives them different typographical emphasis to elevate his Poundian reading of the *melopoéia*, or sound and rhythmic properties, and the *fanopoéia*, or the images or visual objects evoked. The final stanza reads "pés e puas de riso motivo / cabelos e topes motivo de rir" (feet and prickles causing laughter / hair and silk shoes reasons to laugh) and is labeled *logopoéia*, or the intellectual recapitulation of the first two.

81. Augusto, "arte final para gregório," 86.

82. Augusto, "arte final para gregório," 92.

83. Augusto, "Da América que existe," 115.

84. "*a poesia satírica* / (esta última geralmente / relegada à cozinha / longe das ante-salas / onde estão pendurados / os sonetos piedosos)." Augusto, "arte final para gregório," 88.

85. Augusto, "arte final para gregório," 89–90.

86. Augusto calls this work a "blow-up"; while it is possible he merely meant a typographical zoom-in, because of the film's international success, I am making the leap to connect the reference to the film and short story.

87. The genre-blending aesthetics, intertextuality, and political ambivalence of this violent, problematic, but nation-consolidating nonfiction treatise parallel to the Argentine *Facundo* have challenged and attracted translators, and the work has taken its place within inter-American literatures. Walnice Galvão begins her introduction by describing the love-hate relationship critics have with this frustrating, inexhaustible book. Walnice Nogueira Galvão, "Prólogo," in *Los sertones*, by Euclides da Cunha, ed. Galvão, trans. Estela dos Santos (Caracas: Biblioteca Ayacucho, 1980), ix. *Os sertões* was a valuable source text for Mario Vargas Llosa's novel *La guerra del fin del mundo* (1981). See Elizabeth Lowe and Earl E. Fitz, *Translation and the Rise of Inter-American Literature* (Gainesville: University Press of Florida, 2007). Elizabeth Lowe describes the challenges of style and genre that enhance her work as retranslator of *Os sertões* into English in 2010 after the 1944 translation by Samuel Putnam. See Elizabeth Lowe, "Revisiting Re-translation: Re-creation and Historical Re-vision," in *A Companion to Translation Studies*, ed. Sandra Bermann and Catherine Porter (Chichester, UK: Wiley-Blackwell, 2014), 413–24.

88. Jakobson outlines three "ways of interpreting a verbal sign": "intralingual translation or rewording," "interlingual translation or *translation proper*," and "intersemiotic translation" or "interpretation of verbal signs by means of signs of nonverbal sign systems." Jakobson, "On Linguistic Aspects of Translation," 139. Intralingual translation tends to be explored through fictional accounts of this practice, as in Borges's "Pierre Menard, Author of the Quixote" (1939) or in contemporary conceptual writing.

89. Augusto de Campos, "Transertões," in Augusto and Haroldo, *Os sertões dos Campos: Duas vezes Euclides* (Rio de Janeiro: Sette Letras, 1997), 32.

90. Haroldo often interpolates Brazilian classics into translations to draw attention to the two-way exchange of aesthetic information: Brazilian Portuguese taking from a source text and giving back a new third text to connect the source to the Brazilian tradition. The title *Deus e o diabo no "Fausto" de Goethe* (1977) famously interpolates the film directed by Cinema Novo director Glauber Rocha called *Deus e o diabo na Terra do Sol* (1964).

91. Haroldo, "Os Sertões dos Campos," in *Os sertões dos Campos*, 9.

92. Haroldo, "Os Sertões dos Campos," 9.

93. Krista Brune pairs the *sertão* of the Northeast with the Amazon setting of *Macunaíma* as "underrepresented" spaces in English translation but recurrent in and central to "Brazil's literary imaginary." She posits that since *Os sertões* (1902), "the Brazilian North-East has often been affiliated with the 'authentic' in the construction of national identity. Experiences of living in the harsh, dry interior inform the literary representation of the region as a critical component of the nation." Brune, "The Necessities and Dangers of Translation," 23.

94. "With the same freedom, Oswald cut up the writings of our first traveler-chroniclers in his poems of *Pau Brasil*." Augusto, "Transertões," 33. Augusto refers here to the series of four poems Oswald extracted, found-text style, from a 1500 letter by the Portuguese colonizer Pero Vaz de Caminha. This series titled "Pero Vaz Caminha" features in his collection *Pau-brasil*, originally published in 1925, and consisting of the poems "A descoberta," "Os selvagens," "Primeiro chá," and "As meninas da gare." See Oswald de Andrade, *Cadernos de poesia do aluno Oswald (Poesias reunidas)*, ed. Haroldo de Campos (São Paulo: Círculo do Livro, 1981): 71–72.

95. Augusto Meyer calls it "fine excess of poetry"; for Eugenio Gomes the work suffers from its "echo of too much parnasianism." Augusto, "Transertões," 15.

96. Augusto, "Transertões," 12.

97. Augusto, "Transertões," 33.

98. Augusto, "Transertões," 33.

99. Augusto, "Transertões," 33 .

100. In Damrosch's schema for producing world literature, in which a work is first read as literature and then circulated outside the source culture, Augusto answers the contested place of da Cunha's treatise in the Brazilian canon by performatively reading it *primarily* as literature and reading its literary qualities as its most effective and valuable ones.

101. Augusto, "Soldado," in *Os sertões dos Campos*, 35.

102. Augusto, "Rodeio," in *Os sertões dos Campos*, 37.

103. "I took the most liberties with the reconstruction of 'The Prisoner' (596), but even there I made no textual modification. Only the typographical placement is new, and I dispensed with punctuation." Augusto, "Transertões," 33.

104. Augusto, "O prisioneiro," in *Os sertões dos Campos*, 49.

105. Euclides da Cunha, *Os sertões*, ed. Walnice Nogueira Galvão (São Paulo: Brasiliense, 1985), 457. My translation maintains all the commas from the source text, as transformed into line breaks in Augusto's untranslation. For

comparison, a published English version renders this moment perhaps more efficiently, but with fewer emotional pauses: "One of them was barely conscious and had to be supported under the armpits by a soldier on either side. He had a deep scar on his chest from a saber wound." Euclides da Cunha, *Backlands: The Canudos Campaign*, ed. Ilan Stavans, trans. Elizabeth Lowe (New York: Penguin Books, 2010), 429.

CONCLUSION

1. Citing from the paratextual biographical material, the work introduces Haroldo, who "translated Homer's *Iliad*, texts by Goethe, fragments of the Bible, Nahuatl poetry, among others . . . at the time of his death he was still learning Arabic and translating 'Paradise' from the *Divine Comedy*." Haroldo de Campos, *El ángel izquierdo de la poesía: Poética y política. Antología bilingüe*, ed. Gonzalo Aguilar, trans. Arturo Carrera, Roberto Echavarren, Daniel García Helder, Reynaldo Jiménez, and Andrés Sánchez Robayna (Lima: Sarita Cartonera, 2005), n.p.

2. Haroldo, *El ángel izquierdo*, 119–26.

3. Craig Epplin, *Late Book Culture in Argentina* (New York: Bloomsbury Academic, 2014), 60.

4. The poem "o anjo esquerdo da história" would later appear in Haroldo's collection *Crisantempo*. Haroldo de Campos, *Crisantempo (No espaço curvo nasce um)* (São Paulo: Editora Perspectiva, 1998), 67–72.

5. Shellhorse, *Anti-Literature*, 170.

6. For further discussion of this *cartonera* volume, see Gómez, "A Laboratory of Texts," 367–70.

7. Augusto began to use Flash videos to rewrite some of his poems into brief "poem-clips" (2003) viewable on his website; his "(in)traduções" project continues with several born-digital examples, and his recent publication *Outro* (2015) includes a print book and an online compendium of video-poems. Adam Shellhorse defines Augusto's "post-concrete phase" as an "anthropophagic opening to poetry's other, to nonpoetry, to the dialogue with other arts and poets, and to the mass media." Adam Shellhorse, "Augusto de Campos," in *Twenty-First Century Brazilian Writers* (Farmington Hills, MI: Gale Cengage, 2019), 77–79.

8. Although all the works, titles, and descriptions are authored by Augusto, his granddaughter and her husband manage the account on his behalf. Conversation with the author, June 13, 2019.

9. For more analysis of Augusto de Campos's poetic and translation work featured on Instagram, see Isabel C. Gómez, "*Bizarre Poets on the Internet*: Extranslations and Counterpoems by @poetamenos," in "Augusto de Campos aos 90," special issue, *Santa Barbara Portuguese Studies*, 2nd ser., 8 (2021): 167–89.

10. The text reads, all in capital letters, "CONSTITUICÃO FEDERAL / ARTIGO 5° / LVII / NINGUÉM SERÁ CONSIDERADO / CULPADO / ATÉ O TRANSITO EM JULGADO / DE SENTENCA PENAL / CONDENATÓRIA." Augusto de Campos (@poetamenos), Instagram image, April 2, 2018.

11. Ernesto Londoño and Letícia Casado, "Ex-President 'Lula' Is Freed from Prison in Brazil after Supreme Court Ruling," *New York Times*, November 8, 2019.

12. Supporters of Lula celebrated his liberation on November 7, 2019, while he awaited further appeals; charges against him were annulled on March 8, 2021, setting him up for his successful 2022 presidential run. Ernesto Londoño and Letícia Casado, "Brazil's Ex-President 'Lula' May Run for Office Again as Court Cases Are Tossed," *New York Times*, March 8, 2021.

13. Augusto de Campos (@poetamenos), Instagram image, October 2019.

14. Cummings, "of all the blessings which to man," in *Complete Poems*, 544.

Bibliography

Aching, Gerard. "The 'Right to Opacity' and World Literature." *1616: Anuario de Literatura Comparada* 2 (2012): 33–47.

Adame, Ángel Gilberto, ed. *Octavio Paz en 1968: El año axial. Cartas y escritos sobre los movimientos estudiantiles*. Mexico City: Taurus, 2018.

Aguilar, Gonzalo Moisés. *Poesía concreta brasileña: Las vanguardias en la encrucijada modernista*. Rosario, Argentina: Beatriz Viterbo, 2003.

Ahern, Maureen, ed. *A Rosario Castellanos Reader: An Anthology of Her Poetry, Short Fiction, Essays, and Drama*. Austin: University of Texas Press, 1988.

Albuquerque, Severino J. "Reading Translation Queerly: Lispector's Translation of *The Picture of Dorian Gray*." *Bulletin of Hispanic Studies* 76, no. 5 (1999): 691–702.

Amaral, Aracy, ed. *Arte y arquitectura del modernismo brasileño (1917–1930)*. Caracas: Biblioteca Ayacucho, 1978.

Andrade, Mário de. "Em cartas." In *Macunaíma* by Mário de Andrade, edited by Telê Porto Ancona Lopez, 249–85. Rio de Janeiro: Livros Técnicos e Científicos, 1978.

———. *Macunaíma*. Translated by E. A. Goodland. New York: Random House, 1984.

———. *Macunaíma. (El héroe sin ningún carácter)*. Preface by Haroldo de Campos. Transcreation and Posfacio by Héctor Olea. Barcelona: Seix Barral, 1977.

———. *Macunaíma. The Hero with No Character*. Introduction by John Keene. Translated by Katrina Dodson. New York: New Directions, 2023.

———. *Macunaíma: O herói sem nenhum caráter*. Edited by Telê Porto Ancona Lopez. Rio de Janeiro: Livros Técnicos e Científicos, 1978.

———. *Obra escogida: Novela, cuento, ensayo, epistolario.* Edited by Gilda de Mello e Souza. Translated by Santiago Kovadloff, Héctor Olea, and Márgara Russotto. Caracas: Biblioteca Ayacucho, 1979.

Andrade, Oswald de. *Cadernos de poesia do aluno Oswald (Poesias reunidas).* Edited by Haroldo de Campos. São Paulo: Círculo do Livro, 1981.

———. "Cannibalist Manifesto." Translated by Leslie Bary. *Latin American Literary Review* 19, no. 38 (July–December 1991): 38–47.

———. "Manifesto antropófago." *Revista de Antropofagia* 1, no. 1 (May 1928): 3–7.

———. *Obra escogida.* Edited by Haroldo de Campos and K. David Jackson. Translated by Santiago Kovadloff, Héctor Olea, and Márgara Russotto. Caracas: Biblioteca Ayacucho, 1981.

Aparicio, Frances R. *Versiones, interpretaciones y creaciones: Instancias de la traducción literaria en Hispanoamérica en el siglo veinte.* Gaithersburg, MD: Ediciones Hispamérica, 1991.

Appiah, Kwame Anthony. "Thick Translation." In Venuti, *The Translation Studies Reader*, 389–401.

Apter, Emily. *Against World Literature: On the Politics of Untranslatability.* London: Verso, 2013.

———. *The Translation Zone: A New Comparative Literature.* Princeton, NJ: Princeton University Press, 2006.

Arenas, Fernando. "Being Here with Vergílio Ferreira and Clarice Lispector: At the Limits of Language and Subjectivity." *Portuguese Studies* 14 (1998): 181–94.

Balderston, Daniel, and Marcy E. Schwartz, eds. *Voice-Overs: Translation and Latin American Literature.* Albany: State University of New York Press, 2002.

Barnhisel, Greg. *Cold War Modernists: Art, Literature, and American Cultural Diplomacy.* New York: Columbia University Press, 2015.

———. "*Perspectives USA* and the Cultural Cold War: Modernism in Service of the State." *Modernism/Modernity* 14, no. 4 (2007): 729–54.

Bassnett, Susan, and André Lefevere. *Constructing Cultures: Essays on Literary Translation.* Clevedon, PA: Multilingual Matters, 1998.

Bassnett, Susan, and Harish Trivedi. "Of Colonies, Cannibals, and Vernaculars." In *Post-colonial Translation Theory*, edited by Bassnett and Trivedi, 1–18. London: Routledge, 1998.

Baudelaire, Charles, trans. *Histoires extraordinaires.* By Edgar Allan Poe. Paris: A Quantin, 1884.

Benjamin, Walter. "The Critic's Technique in Thirteen Theses." In *One-Way Street and Other Writings*, translated by Edmund Jephcott and Kingsley Shorter, 66–67. London: NLB, 1979.

———. "The Task of the Translator: An Introduction to the Translation of Baudelaire's *Tableaux Parisiens*." Translated by Harry Zohn. In Venuti, *The Translation Studies Reader*, 75–85.

Bergvall, Caroline. "VIA (48 Dante translations) mix w fractals." *Soundcloud*, 2013. https://soundcloud.com/carolinebergvall/via-48-dante-translations-mix.

Bergvall, Caroline, and Dante. "VIA (48 Dante Variations)." *Chain* 10 (Summer 2003): 55–59.

Bermann, Sandra. "Performing Translation." In *A Companion to Translation Studies*, edited by Bermann and Catherine Porter, 285–96. Chichester, UK: Wiley-Blackwell, 2014.

———. "World Literature and Comparative Literature." In D'haen, Damrosch, and Kadir, *The Routledge Companion to World Literature*, 169–79. London: Routledge, 2011.

Bernardo, Ana Maria. "Poetry Anthologies as *Weltliteratur* Projects." In *Translation in Anthologies and Collections (19th and 20th Centuries)*, edited by Teresa Seruya, Lieven D'hulst, Alexandra Assis Rosa, and Maria Lin Moniz, 107–21. Amsterdam: John Benjamins, 2013.

Bierhorst, John, ed. *In the Trail of the Wind: American Indian Poems and Ritual Orations*. New York: Farrar, Straus and Giroux, 1971.

Blixen, Carina, and Alvaro Barros-Lémez. *Cronología y bibliografía de Ángel Rama*. Montevideo: Fundación Ángel Rama, 1986.

Boll, Tom. *Octavio Paz and T. S. Eliot: Modern Poetry and the Translation of Influence*. London: Legenda Modern Humanities Research Association and Maney Publishing, 2012.

Borowski, Gabriel. "Beyond Cannibalism: Reviewing the Metaphor of Anthropophagy in Contemporary Translation Studies." Paper presented at "Poetry, Criticism, Translation: Haroldo de Campos" conference, Yale University, New Haven, CT, December 13–14, 2019.

Bottmann, Denise. "Alguns aspectos da presença de Edgar Allan Poe no Brasil." *Tradução em Revista* 8, no. 1 (2010): 1–19.

Bradu, Fabienne. *Los puentes de la traducción: Octavio Paz y la poesía francesa*. Mexico City: Universidad Nacional Autónoma de México, 2004.

Braz, Albert. "Traducing the Author: Textual (In)fidelity in E. A. Goodland's Translation of *Macunaíma*." *Graphos* 9, no. 1 (2007): 189–94.

Brewster, Claire. *Responding to Crisis in Contemporary Mexico: The Political Writings of Paz, Fuentes, Monsiváis, and Poniatowska*. Tucson: University of Arizona Press, 2005.

———. "The Student Movement of 1968 and the Mexican Press: The Cases of *Excélsior* and *Siempre!*" *Bulletin of Latin American Research* 22, no. 2 (2002): 171–90.

Brotherston, Gordon. *Book of the Fourth World*. Cambridge: Cambridge University Press, 1992.

Brune, Krista. "The Necessities and Dangers of Translation: Brazilian Literature on a Global Stage." *Comparative Critical Studies* 15, no. 1 (2018): 5–24.

Campos, Augusto de, trans. *10 poemas*. By E. E. Cummings. Rio de Janeiro: Ministério de Educação e Cultura, 1960.

———, trans. *40 poem(a)s*. By E. E. Cummings. São Paulo: Editora Brasiliense, 1984.

———, trans. *40 poem(a)s*. By E. E. Cummings. Expanded ed. São Paulo: Editora Brasiliense, 1986.

———. *O anticrítico*. São Paulo: Companhia das Letras, 1986.

———. *Despoesia*. Coleção Signos. Edited by Haroldo de Campos. São Paulo: Editora Perspetiva, 1996.

———. *e. e. cummings poem(a)s*. Campinas, Brazil: Editora Unicamp, 2012.

———. *Poesia Antipoesia Antropofagia & Cia*. São Paulo: Companhia das Letras, 2015.

———. *Verso, reverso, controverso*. São Paulo: Editora Perspectiva, 1978.

———. *Viva Vaia: Poesia, 1949–1979*. São Paulo: Livraria Duas Cidades, 1979.

Campos, Augusto de, and Haroldo de Campos. *Os sertões dos Campos: Duas vezes Euclides*. Rio de Janeiro: Sette Letras, 1997.

———, eds. "Poesía concreta: Configuración / textos." Translated by Antonio Alatorre. Special issue, *Plural* 8 (May 1972): 21–28.

———. *Traduzir & trovar (poetas dos séculos XII a XVII)*. São Paulo: Edicões Papyrus, 1968.

Campos, Haroldo de. *El ángel izquierdo de la poesía: Poética y política. Antología bilingüe*. Edited by Gonzalo Aguilar. Translations by Arturo Carrera, Roberto Echavarren, Daniel García Helder, Reynaldo Jiménez, and Andrés Sánchez Robayna. Lima: Sarita Cartonera, 2005.

———. *Crisantempo: No espaço curvo nasce um*. São Paulo: Editora Perspectiva, 1998.

———. *Da transcriação: Poética e semiótica da operação tradutora*. Edited by Sônia Queiroz. Belo Horizonte, Brazil: Viva Voz, 2011.

———. Selections from *Galaxias*. Translation by Héctor Olea. *Vuelta* 25, no. 3 (December 1978): 15.

———. *Novas: Selected Writings of Haroldo de Campos*. Edited by Antonio Sergio Bessa and Odile Cisneros. Foreword by Roland Greene. Evanston, IL: Northwestern University Press, 2007.

———. "La poesía concreta según Haroldo de Campos." Interview by Danubio Torres Fierro. *Vuelta* 25, no. 3 (December 1978): 16–22.

———. "Prefacio: *Macunaíma: La fantasía estructural*." In *Macunaíma* by Mário de Andrade, translated by Héctor Olea, 7–21. Barcelona: Seix Barral, 1977.

———. "The Rule of Anthropophagy: Europe under the Sign of Devoration." Translated by María Tai Wolff. *Latin American Literary Review* 14, no. 27 (1986): 42–60.

———. *O sequestro do barroco na formação da literatura brasileira: O caso Gregório de Mattos*. Salvador da Bahia, Brazil: Fundação Casa de Jorge Amado, 1989.

———. "Tradition, Translation, Transculturation: The Ex-Centric's Viewpoint." Translated by Stella E. O. Tagnin. *TradTerm* 4, no. 2 (1997): 11–18.

———. *Transcriação*. Edited by Marcelo Tápia and Thelma Médici Nóbrega. São Paulo: Editora Perspectiva, 2013.

———. "Uma poética da radicalidade." In *Obras Completas: Poesias reunidas* by Oswald de Andrade, 9–59. Rio de Janeiro: Civilização Brasileira, 1971.

Candido, Antonio. "Literature and Underdevelopment." In *Latin America in Its Literature*. Edited by César Fernández Moreno, Julio Ortega, and Ivan A. Shulman. Translated by Mary G. Berg. New York: Holmes & Meier, 1980. 263–82.

Carpenter, Victoria. "The Echo of Tlatelolco in Contemporary Mexican Protest Poetry." *Bulletin of Latin American Research* 24, no. 4 (2005): 496–512.

Carroll, Lewis. *Doublets: A Word-Puzzle.* London: Macmillan, 1879.

Casanova, Pascale. *The World Republic of Letters.* Translated by M. B. DeBevoise. Cambridge, MA: Harvard University Press, 2007.

Cassin, Barbara, ed. *Dictionary of Untranslatables: A Philosophical Lexicon.* Translated by Emily Apter, Jacques Lezra, and Michael Wood. Princeton, NJ: Princeton University Press, 2014.

Castellanos, Rosario. *Juicios sumarios: Ensayos.* Xalapa, Mexico: Universidad Veracruzana, 1966.

———. *Materia memorable.* Mexico City: Universidad Nacional Autónoma de México, 1969.

———. *Mujer de palabras: Artículos rescatados de Rosario Castellanos.* Vols. 1–3. Edited by Andrea Reyes. Mexico City: Conaculta, 2004, 2006, 2007.

———. *Mujer que sabe latín.* 1973. Repr., Mexico City: Fondo de Cultura Económica, 1995.

———. *Obras II: Poesía, teatro y ensayo.* Edited by Eduardo Mejia. Mexico City: Fondo de Cultura Económica, 1998.

———. *Poesía no eres tú: Obra poética: 1948–1971.* Mexico City: Fondo de Cultura Económica, 1972.

———. *El uso de la palabra.* Edited by José Emilio Pacheco. Mexico City: Ediciones de Excélsior, 1975.

Castro, Eduardo Viveiros de. *Cannibal Metaphysics: For a Post-Structural Anthropology.* Translated and edited by Peter Skafish. Minneapolis: Univocal, 2016.

Castro-Klarén, Sara. "A Genealogy for the 'Manifesto antropófago,' or The Struggle between Socrates and the Caraïbe." *Nepantla: Views from the South* 1, no. 2 (2000): 295–322.

Cesar, Ana Cristina. "Bastidores de la traducción." In *El método documental,* 179–91. Edited and translated by Teresa Arijón and Bárbara Belloc. Buenos Aires: Manantial, 2013.

Chamberlain, Lori. "Gender and the Metaphorics of Translation." In Venuti, *The Translation Studies Reader,* 306–21.

Cheah, Pheng. *What Is a World? On Postcolonial Literature as World Literature.* Durham, NC: Duke University Press, 2016.

Cho, Sumi, Kimberlé Crenshaw, and Leslie McCall. "Intersectionality: Theorizing Power, Empowering Theory." *Signs* 38, no. 4 (Summer 2013): 785–810.

Cisneros, Odile. "From Isomorphism to Cannibalism: The Evolution of Haroldo de Campos's Translation Concepts." *TTR: Traduction, terminologie, rédaction* 25, no. 2 (2012): 15–44.

———. "Traducción y poéticas radicales: El caso de Octavio Paz y el grupo *Noigandres.*" In *Estudios hispánicos en el siglo XXI,* edited by Jelena Filipović et al., 213–27. Belgrade: University of Belgrade, 2014.

Cleary, Heather. *The Translator's Visibility: Scenes from Contemporary Latin American Fiction.* New York: Bloomsbury Academic, 2021.

Cohn, Deborah. *The Latin American Literary Boom and U.S. Nationalism during the Cold War.* Nashville: Vanderbilt University Press, 2012.

Corbett, John, and Ting Huang, eds. *The Translation and Transmission of Concrete Poetry*. London: Routledge, 2019.

Crenshaw, Kimberlé. "Demarginalizing the Intersection of Race and Sex: A Black Feminist Critique of Antidiscrimination Doctrine, Feminist Theory, and Antiracist Policies." *University of Chicago Legal Forum* 1, no. 8 (1989): 139–67.

Croce, Marcela. "Ángel Rama: La utopía americana destellando en un momento de peligro." In *Latinoamericanismo: Canon, crítica y géneros discursivos*, edited by Marcela Croce, 127–62. Buenos Aires: Corregidor, 2013.

Cummings, E. E. *Complete Poems 1904–1962*. Edited by George J. Firmage. New York: Liveright, 1991.

———. *Poems 1923–1954*. New York: Harcourt, Brace & Company, 1954.

Cunha, Euclides da. *Backlands: The Canudos Campaign*. Edited by Ilan Stavans. Translated by Elizabeth Lowe. New York: Penguin Books, 2010.

———. *Os sertões*. Edited by Walnice Nogueira Galvão. São Paulo: Brasiliense, 1985.

Daghlian, Carlos. "A recepção de Poe na literatura brasileira." *Fragmentos* 25 (2003): 45–54.

Damrosch, David. *What Is World Literature?* Princeton, NJ: Princeton University Press, 2003.

Damrosch, David, and David L. Pike, eds. *The Longman Anthology of World Literature*. New York: Pearson/Longman, 2008.

Delgado Moya, Sergio. *Delirious Consumption: Aesthetics and Consumer Capitalism in Mexico and Brazil*. Austin: University of Texas Press, 2017.

D'haen, Theo. "Anthologizing World Literature in Translation: Global/Local/Glocal." *Forum for World Literature Studies* 9, no. 4 (2017): 539–57.

D'haen, Theo, David Damrosch, and Djelal Kadir, eds. *The Routledge Companion to World Literature*. London: Routledge, 2011.

Dias, Jamille Pinheiro, Marília Librandi, and Tom Winterbottom, eds. *Transpoetic Exchange: Haroldo de Campos, Octavio Paz, and Other Multiversal Dialogues*. Lewisburg, PA: Bucknell University Press, 2020.

Dickinson, Emily. *The Poems of Emily Dickinson: Reading Edition*. Edited by Ralph W. Franklin. Cambridge, MA: Belknap Press of Harvard University Press, 1999.

Di Leo, Jeffrey R. "Analyzing Anthologies." In *On Anthologies: Politics and Pedagogy*, edited by Di Leo, 1–27. Lincoln: University of Nebraska Press, 2004.

Docter, Mary. "José Emilio Pacheco: A Poetics of Reciprocity." *Hispanic Review* 70, no. 3 (2002): 373–92.

Dodson, Katrina, trans. *Macunaíma. The Hero with No Character.* By Mário de Andrade, introduction by John Keene. New York: New Directions, 2023.

Draper, Susana. *1968 Mexico: Constellations of Freedom and Democracy*. Durham, NC: Duke University Press, 2018.

Dupont, Vladir. *A outra voz*. São Paulo: Siciliano, 1993.

Durán, Manuel. "In Memoriam: Jaime Torres Bodet, Salvador Novo, Rosario Castellanos." *Revista Iberoamericana* 41, no. 90 (January–March 1975): 79–83.

Edwards, Magdalena. "Benjamin Moser and the Smallest Woman in the World." *Los Angeles Review of Books*, August 16, 2019. https://lareviewofbooks.org/article/benjamin-moser-and-the-smallest-woman-in-the-world/.

———. "The Translator's Colors: Elizabeth Bishop in Brazil and Elsewhere." PhD diss., University of California Los Angeles, 2007.

Eliot, T. S. *Collected Poems 1909–1962*. New York: Harcourt, 1991.

———. *The Waste Land*. Edited by Michael North. New York: W. W. Norton, 2001.

Emmerich, Karen. *Literary Translation and the Making of Originals*. New York: Bloomsbury Academic, 2017.

Epple, Juan Armando. "Las voces de Elena Poniatowska: Una entrevista." *Confluencia* 5, no. 2 (1990): 127–29.

Epplin, Craig. *Late Book Culture in Argentina*. New York: Bloomsbury Academic, 2014.

Ergun, Emek, Denise Kripper, Siobhan Meï, Sandra Joy Russell, Sara Rutkowski, Carolyn Shread, and Ida Hove Solberg. "Women (Re)Writing Authority: A Roundtable Discussion on Feminist Translation." In *The Routledge Handbook of Translation, Feminism, and Gender*, edited by Luise von Flotow and Hala Kamal, 5–14. London: Routledge, 2020.

Esplin, Emron. *Borges's Poe: The Influence and Reinvention of Edgar Allan Poe in Spanish America*. Athens: University of Georgia Press, 2016.

Fan, Jiayang. "Han Kang and the Complexity of Translation." *New Yorker*, January 15, 2018. www.newyorker.com/magazine/2018/01/15/han-kang-and-the-complexity-of-translation.

Feinsod, Harris. *The Poetry of the Americas: From Good Neighbors to Countercultures*. New York: Oxford University Press, 2017.

Fernández, Nora, and Facundo Gómez. "Biblioteca Ayacucho: La utopía de América." In *Latinoamericanismo: Canon, crítica y géneros discursivos*, edited by Marcela Croce, 41–78. Buenos Aires: Corregidor, 2013.

Fernández, Shirley, ed. *Biblioteca Ayacucho: Catálogo General 1974–2007*. Caracas: Fundación Biblioteca Ayacucho, 2007.

Ferreira, Élida Paulina, and Karin Hallana Santos Silva. "Edgar Allan Poe em português: Os limites entre tradução e adaptação." *Domínios de lingu@gem: Revista Eletrônica de Linguística* 5, no. 3 (2011): 20–37.

Friis, Ronald. *José Emilio Pacheco and the Poets of the Shadows*. Lewisburg, PA: Bucknell University Press, 2001.

Galvão, Walnice Nogueira. "Prólogo." In *Los sertones*, by Euclides da Cunha, edited by Galvão, translated by Estela dos Santos, ix–xxv. Caracas: Biblioteca Ayacucho, 1980.

Gardner, Helen. *The Composition of "Four Quartets."* New York: Oxford University Press, 1978.

Gaspar, Martín. *La condición traductora*. Rosario, Argentina: Beatriz Viterbo, 2014.

———. "Minor Translations and the World Literature of the Masses in Latin America." In *Translation and World Literature*, edited by Susan Bassnett, 107–27. London: Routledge, 2019.

Gavronsky, Serge. "The Translator: From Piety to Cannibalism." *SubStance* 6–7, no. 16 (Summer 1977): 53–62.

Gentzler, Edwin. "Macro- and Micro-turns in Translation Studies." *Translation and Interpreting Studies* 6, no. 1 (2011): 121–41.

———. *Translation and Identity in the Americas*. London: Routledge, 2008.

Gómez, Isabel C. "Anti-surrealism? Augusto de Campos 'Untranslates' Spanish American Poetry." *Mutatis Mutandis* 11, no. 2 (2018): 376–99.

———. "*Bizarre Poets on the Internet*: Extranslations and Counterpoems by @poetamenos." In "Augusto de Campos aos 90," special issue, *Santa Barbara Portuguese Studies*, 2nd ser., 8 (2021): 167–89.

———. "Brazilian Transcreation and World Literature: *Macunaíma* Journeys from São Paulo to Caracas." *Journal of World Literature* 1, no. 3 (2016): 316–41.

———. "José Emilio Pacheco and Reciprocity between Literary Cultures: Gift Theory as Translation Studies Methodology." *Transfer* 14, nos. 1–2 (2019): 73–99.

———. "A Laboratory of Texts: The Multilingual Translation Legacies of Haroldo de Campos." In *Routledge Handbook of Latin American Literary Translation Studies*, edited by Denise Kripper and Delfina Cabrera, 364–82. London: Routledge, 2023.

Gonçalves, Fabiano Bruno. "Tradução, interpretação e recepção literária: Manifestações de Edgar Allan Poe no Brasil." PhD diss., Universidade Federal do Rio Grande do Sul, 2006.

González de León, Ulalume, trans. "Los Totum Revolutum." By Edward Lear. *Plural* 15 (December 1972): 9.

Goodland, E. A., trans. *Macunaíma*. By Mário de Andrade. New York: Random House, 1984.

Gordon-Burroughs, Jessica. "Monuments and Ephemera: The Biblioteca Ayacucho." *A Contracorriente* 11, no. 3 (2014): 90–118.

Grossman, D. Jon, trans. *En traduction*. By E. E. Cummings. Paris: Pierre Seghers, 1960.

Guldin, Rainer. "Devouring the Other: Cannibalism, Translation and the Construction of Cultural Identity." In *Translating Selves: Experience and Identity between Languages and Literatures*, edited by Nikolau Paschalis and Maria-Venetia Kyritsi, 109–22. London: Continuum, 2008.

Gunew, Sneja. "Excess of Affect: In Translation." *Hecate* 42, no. 2 (2016): 7–22.

Gutiérrez, Norma. "'Aproximaciones': El exitoso adiós del José Emilio Pacheco." *El Informador*, December 2, 2009. https://www.informador.mx/Cultura/Aproximaciones-el-exitoso-adios-de-Jose-Emilio-Pacheco-20091202-0005.html.

Guzmán, María Constanza. *Gregory Rabassa's Latin American Literature: A Translator's Visible Legacy*. Lewisburg, PA: Bucknell University Press, 2010.

———. "Translation North and South: Composing the Translator's Archive." *TTR: Traduction, terminologie, rédaction* 26, no. 2 (2013): 171–91.

Hayot, Eric. *On Literary Worlds*. New York: Oxford University Press, 2012.

Hedrick, Tace. "'Mãe é para isso': Gender, Writing, and English Language Translation in Clarice Lispector." *Luso-Brazilian Review* 41, no. 2 (2004): 56–83.

Hesse, Eva, trans. *Gedichte.* By E. E. Cummings. Munich: Langeweische-Brandt, 1958.

Hind, Emily. Femm*enism and the Mexican Woman Intellectual from Sor Juana to Poniatowska: Boob Lit.* New York: Palgrave, 2010.

Honig, Edwin. "Conversations with Translators, II: Octavio Paz and Richard Wilbur." *MLN* 91 (1976): 1073–98.

Hulme, Peter. "Introduction: The Cannibal Scene." In *Cannibalism and the Colonial World*, edited by Francis Barker, Peter Hulme, and Margaret Iversen, 1–38. Cambridge: Cambridge University Press, 1998.

Jakobson, Roman. "On Linguistic Aspects of Translation." In Venuti, *The Translation Studies Reader*, 138–43.

Jáuregui, Carlos A. *Canibalia: Canibalismo, calibanismo, antropofagia cultural y consumo en América Latina.* Madrid: Iberoamericana, 2008.

Johnson, David E. *Kant's Dog: On Borges, Philosophy, and the Time of Translation.* Albany: State University of New York Press, 2012.

Johnson, Randal. "The Dynamics of the Brazilian Literary Field, 1930–1945." *Luso-Brazilian Review* 31, no. 2 (1994): 5–22.

———. "Tupy or Not Tupy: Cannibalism and Nationalism in Contemporary Brazilian Literature and Culture." In *Modern Latin American Fiction*, edited by John King, 41–60. London: Faber and Faber, 1987.

Jones, Ellen. *Literature in Motion: Translating Multilingualism Across the Americas.* New York: Columbia University Press, 2022.

King, John. *The Role of Mexico's* Plural *in Latin American Literary and Political Culture: From Tlatelolco to the "Philanthropic Ogre."* New York: Palgrave, 2007.

Kristal, Efraín. "'Considerando en frío . . .': Una respuesta a Franco Moretti." In *América Latina en la "literatura mundial,"* edited by Ignacio M. Sánchez Prado, 101–16. Pittsburgh: Instituto Internacional de Literatura Iberoamericana, 2006.

———. *Invisible Work: Borges and Translation.* Nashville: Vanderbilt University Press, 2002.

———. "Jorge Luis Borges y Octavio Paz: Poéticas de la traducción y traducción poética." *Studi Ispanici* 5 (2002): 261–70.

———. "Philosophical/Theoretical Approaches to Translation." In *A Companion to Translation Studies*, edited by Sandra Bermann and Catherine Porter, 28–40. Chichester, UK: Wiley-Blackwell, 2014.

Lacerda, Daniel. "Alguma coisa sobre o nada: A anticrítica." In *Sobre Augusto de Campos*, edited by Flora Süssekind and Júlio Castañon Guimarães, 229–43. Rio de Janeiro: Edições Casa de Rui Barbosa / 7 Letras, 2004.

Levine, Suzanne Jill. *The Subversive Scribe: Translating Latin American Fiction.* Champaign, IL: Dalkey Archive, 2009.

Lévi-Strauss, Claude. *Tristes tropiques.* Translated by John Russell. New York: Criterion, 1961.

Lima, Thayse Leal. "Translation and World Literature: The Perspective of the 'Ex-Centric.'" *Journal of Latin American Cultural Studies* 26, no. 3 (2017): 461–81.

Lispector, Clarice, *Água Viva*. Edited and with an Introduction by Benjamin Moser. Translated by Stefan Tobler. New York: New Directions, 2012.

———. *A Breath of Life*. Edited by Benjamin Moser. Preface by Pedro Almodóvar and Benjamin Moser. Translated by Johnny Lorenz. New York: New Directions, 2012.

———. *The Complete Stories of Clarice Lispector*. Edited and with an Introduction by Benjamin Moser. Translated by Katrina Dodson. New York: New Directions, 2015.

———, trans. *Historias extraordinárias de Allan Poe: Textos selecionados e reescritos por Clarice Lispector*, by Edgar Allan Poe. 15th ed. Rio de Janeiro: Ediouro Publicações, 1998.

———. *The Hour of the Star*. Introduction by Colm Tóibín. Translated by Benjamin Moser. New York: New Directions, 2011.

———. *Near to the Wild Heart*. Edited and with an Introduction by Benjamin Moser. Translated by Alison Entrekin. New York: New Directions, 2012.

———. *The Passion According to G. H.* Edited by Benjamin Moser. Introduction by Caetano Veloso. Translated by Idra Novey. New York: New Directions, 2012.

Londoño, Ernesto, and Letícia Casado. "Brazil's Ex-President 'Lula' May Run for Office Again as Court Cases Are Tossed." *New York Times*, March 8, 2021. https://www.nytimes.com/2021/03/08/world/americas/brazil-lula-supreme-court.html.

———. "Ex-President 'Lula' Is Freed from Prison in Brazil after Supreme Court Ruling." *New York Times*, November 8, 2019. https://www.nytimes.com/2019/11/08/world/americas/lula-brazil-supreme-court.html.

López, Kimberle. "*Modernismo* and the Ambivalence of the Postcolonial Experience: Cannibalism, Primitivism, and Exoticism in Mário de Andrade's *Macunaíma*." *Luso-Brazilian Review* 35, no. 1 (1998): 25–38.

Lopez, Têle Porto Anacona. "Traduções de *Macunaíma*." In *Macunaíma* by Mário de Andrade, edited by Telê Porto Ancona Lopez, 407–15. Rio de Janeiro: Livros Técnicos e Científicos, 1978.

Lowe, Elizabeth. "Revisiting Re-translation: Re-creation and Historical Revision." In *A Companion to Translation Studies*, edited by Sandra Bermann and Catherine Porter, 413–24. Chichester, UK: Wiley-Blackwell, 2014.

Lowe, Elizabeth, and Earl E. Fitz. *Translation and the Rise of Inter-American Literature*. Gainesville: University Press of Florida, 2007.

Maciel, Maria Esther. "América Latina Reinventada: Octavio Paz e Haroldo de Campos." *Revista Iberoamericana* 64, nos. 182–83 (1998): 219–28.

Madureira, Luís. *Cannibal Modernities: Postcoloniality and the Avant-Garde in Caribbean and Brazilian Literature*. Charlottesville: University of Virginia Press, 2005.

Magalhães, Couto de. *O selvagem: Trabalho preparatorio para aproveitamento do selvagem e do solo por elle ocupado no Brazil. Tomo II. Origens, cos-*

tumes, Região Selvagem. Methodo a empregar para amansal-os por intermedio das colonias militares e do interprete militar. Rio de Janeiro: Typographia da Reforma, 1876.

Mello e Souza, Gilda de. "Prólogo: El tupí y el laúd" and "Notas a *Macunaíma*." In Mário de Andrade, *Obra escogida*, edited by Gilda de Mello e Souza, ix–lvi, 113–49. Caracas: Biblioteca Ayacucho, 1979.

Melo, Alfredo Cesar. "*Macunaíma*: Entre a crítica e o elogio à transculturação." *Hispanic Review* 78, no. 2 (2010): 205–27.

Melo Neto, João Cabral de. *Agrestes: Poesia (1981–1985)*. Rio de Janeiro: Editora Nova Fronteira, 1985.

Melzer, Sara E. *Colonizer or Colonized: The Hidden Stories of Early Modern French Culture.* Philadelphia: University of Pennsylvania Press, 2012.

Meyer-Minnemann, Klaus. "Octavio Paz-Haroldo de Campos *Transblanco*: Punto de intersección de dos escrituras poéticas de la Modernidad." *Poligrafías: Revista de Literatura Comparada* 3 (1998–2000): 102–16.

Mignolo, Walter, and Freya Schiwy. "Transculturation and the Colonial Difference: Double Translation." In *Translation and Ethnography: The Anthropological Challenge of Intercultural Understanding*, edited by Tullio Maranhão and Bernhard Streck, 3–29. Tucson: University of Arizona Press, 2003.

Miller, Martha LaFollette. "The Ambivalence of Power: Self-Disparagement in the Newspaper Editorials of Rosario Castellanos." In *Reinterpreting the Spanish American Essay: Women Writers of the 19th and 20th Centuries*, edited by Doris Meyer, 167–76. Austin: University of Texas Press, 1995.

Milton, Heloisa Costa. "*Macunaíma* no reino hispânico (A propósito de tradução)." *Revista de Letras* 33 (1993): 55–70.

Milton, John. "Literary Translation Theory in Brazil." *Meta: Journal des traducteurs / Meta: Translators' Journal* 41, no. 2 (1996): 196–207.

Milton, John, and Paul Bandia, eds. *Agents of Translation.* Amsterdam: John Benjamins, 2009.

Moreira, Paulo. *Literary and Cultural Relations between Brazil and Mexico: Deep Undercurrents.* New York: Palgrave, 2013.

Moretti, Franco. "Conjectures on World Literature." *New Left Review* 1 (January 2000): 54–68.

Moser, Benjamin. *Why This World: A Biography of Clarice Lispector.* New York: Oxford University Press, 2009.

Moura da Silva, Márcia. "Análise da tradução de termos indígenas em Macunaíma de Mário de Andrade na tradução de Héctor Olea para o espanhol.". PhD diss., Universidade Federal de Santa Catarina, 2009.

Mufti, Aamir R. *Forget English! Orientalisms and World Literatures.* Cambridge, MA: Harvard University Press, 2016.

Nabokov, Vladimir. "Problems of Translation: 'Onegin' in English." In Venuti, *The Translation Studies Reader*, 115–27.

Negrín, Edith, and Álvaro Ruiz Abreu, eds. *Pasión por la palabra: Homenaje a José Emilio Pacheco.* Mexico City: Universidad Autónoma Metropolitana, 2013.

Neruda, Pablo. "Explico algunas cosas." In *Obras completas: Tercera edición aumentada*, 275–77. Buenos Aires: Editorial Losada, 1967.

Nettel, Guadalupe. *Octavio Paz: Las palabras en libertad*. Barcelona: Taurus, 2014.

Newcomb, Robert Patrick. *Nossa and Nuestra América: Inter-American Dialogues*. West Lafayette, IN: Purdue University Press, 2012.

Nóbrega, Thelma Médici, and John Milton. "The Role of Haroldo and Augusto de Campos in Bringing Translation to the Fore of Literary Activity in Brazil." In *Agents of Translation*, edited by John Milton and Paul Bandia, 257–79. Amsterdam: John Benjamins, 2009.

Nolasco, Edgar Cézar. "Clarice Lispector Tradutora." *Revista Cerrados* 16, no. 24 (2007): 263–72.

Nunes, Benedito. "Antropofagia ao alcance de todos." In *Obras completas de Oswald de Andrade: A utopía antropofágica*, 5–39. São Paulo: Secretaria de Estado da Cultura, 1990.

Nunes, Zita. *Cannibal Democracy: Race and Representation in the Literature of the Americas*. Minneapolis: University of Minnesota Press, 2008.

Ocampo, Silvina, trans. *Poemas*. By Emily Dickinson. Prologue by Jorge Luis Borges. Barcelona: Editorial Tusquets, 1985.

———, trans. *Poemas*. By Emily Dickinson. Barcelona: Editorial Tusquets, 2006.

O'Connell, Joanna. *Prospero's Daughter: The Prose of Rosario Castellanos*. Austin: University of Texas Press, 1995.

Olea, Héctor. "Posfacio." In *Macunaíma*, by Mário de Andrade, 237–66. Barcelona: Seix Barral, 1977.

Oliveira, Eduardo Jorge de, and Kenneth David Jackson, eds. *Poesia-Crítica-Tradução: Haroldo de Campos e a educação dos sentidos*. Berlin: Peter Lang, 2022.

Ortiz, Oscar Rodríguez, ed. *30 años de Biblioteca Ayacucho (1974–2004)*. Caracas: Biblioteca Ayacucho, 2004.

Oviedo, José Miguel. "José Emilio Pacheco: La poesía como 'Ready-Made.'" *Hispamérica* 5, no. 15 (1976): 39–55.

Pacheco, Carlos, and Marisela Guevara Sánchez. "Ángel Rama, la cultura venezolana y el epistolario de la Biblioteca Ayacucho." *Estudios: Revista de Investigaciones Literarias y Culturales* 22/23 (2003–4): 99–136.

Pacheco, José Emilio. *Aproximaciones*. Edited by Miguel Ángel Flores. Mexico City: Editorial Penélope, 1984.

———, trans. *Cuatro cuartetos (Traducción de José Emilio Pacheco)*. By T. S. Eliot. Mexico City: Fondo de Cultura Económica, 1989.

———, trans. "The Dry Salvages: Versión y notas de José Emilio Pacheco." By T. S. Eliot. *Letras Libres* 154 (October 2011): 20–32.

———, trans. "East Coker: Aproximación y notas de José Emilio Pacheco." By T. S. Eliot. *Letras Libres* 181 (January 2014): 20–29.

———. *No me preguntes cómo pasa el tiempo (Poemas 1964–1968)*. Mexico City: Joaquín Mortiz, 1969.

———. *Tarde o temprano*. Mexico City: Fondo de Cultura Económica, 1980.

———. *Tarde o temprano: Poemas 1958–2009*. 4th ed. Edited by Ana Clavel. Mexico City: Fondo de Cultura Económica, 2009.

Passos, José Luiz. *Ruínas de linhas puras: Quatro ensaios em torno a "Macunaíma."* São Paulo: Annablume, 1998.

Paz, Octavio. *The Collected Poems of Octavio Paz: 1957–1987*. Edited by Eliot Weinberger. Translated by Eliot Weinberger, Elizabeth Bishop, Paul Blackburn, Lysander Kemp, Denise Levertov, John Frederick Nims, and Charles Tomlinson. New York: New Directions, 1987.

———. *Corriente alterna*. Mexico City: Siglo XXI, 1967.

———. "e. e. cummings: Seis poemas y un recuerdo." In *Puertas al campo*, 86–96. Mexico City: Universidad Nacional Autónoma de México, 1966.

———. *Excursiones / Incursiones: Dominio extranjero*. Vol. 2 of *Obras completas*. Mexico City: Fondo de Cultura Económica, 1994.

———. *Fundación y disidencia: Dominio hispánico*. Vol. 3 of *Obras completas*. Mexico City: Fondo de Cultura Económica, 1994.

———. *El laberinto de la soledad*. Edited by Enrico Mario Santí. Madrid: Cátedra, 1993.

———. *Ladera este*. Mexico City: Joaquín Mortiz, 1969.

———. *Libertad bajo palabra: Obra poética, 1935–1957*. Mexico City: Fondo de Cultura Económica, 1960.

———. *Miscelánea I: Primeros escritos*. Vol. 13 of *Obras completas*. Mexico City: Fondo de Cultura Económica, 1999.

———. "Los nuevos acólitos." In *Obras completas*, vol. 3: *Fundación y disidencia: Dominio hispánico*, 360–62. Mexico City: Fondo de Cultura Económica, 1994.

———. *Obras completas*. Edited by Octavio Paz. 2nd ed. 15 vols. Mexico City: Fondo de Cultura Económica, 1994–2004.

———. *Obra poética I (1935–1970)*. Vol. 11 of *Obras completas*. Mexico City: Fondo de Cultura Económica, 1997.

———. *Obra poética II (1969–1998)*. Vol. 12 of *Obras completas*. Mexico City: Fondo de Cultura Económica, 2004.

———. "Poesía de soledad y poesía de comunión." In *Obras completas*, vol. 13, *Miscelánea I: Primeros escritos*, 234–45. Mexico City: Fondo de Cultura Económica, 1999.

———. "¿Poesía latinoamericana?" In *Obras completas*, vol. 3, *Fundación y disidencia: Dominio hispánico*, 69–79. Mexico City: Fondo de Cultura Económica, 1994.

———. "Siete poemas y un recuerdo." In *Obras completas*, vol. 2, *Excursiones / Incursiones: Dominio extranjero*, 304–12. Mexico City: Fondo de Cultura Económica, 1994.

———. *Topoemas*. Mexico City: Imprenta Madero, 1968.

———. "Topoemas." *Revista de la Universidad de México* 22, no. 10 (June 1968): 1.

———. *Traducción: Literatura y literalidad*. Barcelona: Tusquets, 1971.

———. "Translation: Literature and Letters." Translated by Irene del Corral. In *Theories of Translation: An Anthology of Essays from Dryden to Derrida*, edited by Rainer Schulte and John Biguenet, 152–62. Chicago: University of Chicago Press, 1992.

———. *Versiones y diversiones*. Mexico City: Joaquín Mortiz, 1974.

———. *Versiones y diversiones*. 2nd ed. Mexico City: Joaquín Mortiz, 1978.

Paz, Octavio, and Haroldo de Campos. *Constelação: Pequena antologia*. Introduction and translation by Haroldo de Campos. Rio de Janeiro: AGGS Industrias Gráficas, 1972.

———. *Transblanco (em torno a "Blanco" de Octavio Paz)*. Rio de Janeiro: Editora Guanabara, 1986.

Peña, Karen. *Poetry and the Realm of the Public Intellectual: The Alternative Destinies of Gabriela Mistral, Cecília Meireles, and Rosario Castellanos*. Leeds, UK: LEGENDA / Modern Humanities Research Association / Maney Publishing, 2007.

Perloff, Marjorie. "Refiguring the Poundian Ideogram: From Octavio Paz's *Blanco/Branco* to Haroldo de Campos's *Galáxias*." *Modernist Cultures* 7, no. 1 (2012): 40–55.

———. *Unoriginal Genius: Poetry by Other Means in the New Century*. Chicago: University of Chicago Press, 2012.

Perrone, Charles A. *Seven Faces: Brazilian Poetry since Modernism*. Durham, NC: Duke University Press, 1996.

Perrone, Charles A., and Christopher Dunn, eds. *Brazilian Popular Music and Globalization*. London: Routledge, 2001.

Pignatari, Décio, Haroldo de Campos, and Augusto de Campos, eds. *Antologia do verso à poesia concreta 1949–1962: Noigandres 5*. São Paulo: Massão Ohno, 1962.

Pires Vieira, Else Ribeiro. "Liberating Calibans: Readings of *Antropofagia* and Haroldo de Campos' Poetics of Transcreation." In *Post-colonial Translation Theory*, edited by Susan Bassnett and Harish Trivedi, 95–113. London: Routledge, 1998.

———. "A Postmodern Translational Aesthetics in Brazil." In *Translation Studies: An Interdiscipline*, edited by Mary Snell-Hornby, Franz Pöchhacker, and Klaus Kaindl, 65–72. Amsterdam: John Benjamins, 1994.

Plural. "Encuestas de *Plural*." *Plural* 16 (January 1973): 45–46.

———. "Mocosuena." *Plural* 13 (October 1972): 40.

Poe, Edgar Allan. *The Complete Stories*. Edited by John Seelye. New York: Knopf, 1992.

Prado, Paulo. "Poesía Pau Brasil." In Oswald de Andrade, *Poesias reunidas*, vol. 4 of *Obras completas*, ed. Haroldo de Campos. São Paulo: Civilização Brasileira, 1974.

Pratt, Mary Louise. "'No me interrumpas': Las mujeres y el ensayo latinoamericano." Translated by Gabriela Cano. *Debate Feminista* 21 (2000): 70–88.

Quine, Willard Van Orman. *Word and Object*. Cambridge, MA: MIT Press, 1960.

Rabassa, Gregory. *If This Be Treason: Translation and Its Dyscontents: A Memoir*. New York: New Directions, 2006.

Rama, Ángel. "La Biblioteca Ayacucho como instrumento de integración cultural latinoamericana." In *30 años de Biblioteca Ayacucho (1974–2004)*, edited by Oscar Rodríguez Ortiz, 63–93. Caracas: Biblioteca Ayacucho, 2004.

———. *Diario: 1974–1983*. Edited by Rosario Peyrou. Montevideo: Trilce, 2001.

Retamar, Roberto Fernández. "Caliban: Notes towards a Discussion of Culture in Our America." In *Caliban and Other Essays*, translated by Edward Baker, 3–45. Minneapolis: University of Minnesota Press, 1989.

Ribeiro, Darcy, ed. *La fundación de Brasil: testimonios 1500–1700*. Caracas: Biblioteca Ayacucho, 1992.

Ribeiro Coelho, Haydée. "A vida em movimento: A correspondência entre Ángel Rama, Berta, e Darcy Ribeiro." In *Diálogos latino-americanos*, edited by Haydée Ribeiro Coelho and Pablo Rocca, 19–38. São Paulo: Editora Global, 2014.

———. "O Brasil na 'Biblioteca Ayacucho': Vertente literária e cultural." *O eixo e a roda* 18, no. 2 (2009): 85–103.

Ribeiro Coelho, Haydée, and Pablo Rocca, eds. *Diálogos latino-americanos: Correspondência entre Ángel Rama, Berta e Darcy Ribeiro*. São Paulo: Editora Global, 2014.

Riccò, Giulia. "Dante's *Purgatório Canto VI* in Nineteenth-Century Brazil: Translating the *Nazione/Nação*." *Mester* 45 (2016–17): 3–18.

Rice, Alan. "Who's Eating Whom? The Discourse of Cannibalism in the Literature of the Black Atlantic from Equiano's *Travels* to Toni Morrison's *Beloved*." *Research in African Literatures* 29, no. 4 (1998): 106–21.

Ricoeur, Paul. *On Translation*. Translated by Eileen Brennan. London: Routledge, 2006.

Rocca, Pablo, ed. *Un proyecto latinoamericano: Antonio Candido y Ángel Rama, Correspondencia*. Montevideo: Editora Estuario, 2016.

Rónai, Paulo. *Escola de tradutores*. Rio de Janeiro: Livraria São José, 1956.

Sá, Lúcia. *Rain Forest Literatures: Amazonian Texts and Latin American Culture*. Minneapolis: University of Minnesota Press, 2004.

Sakai, Naoki. "Dislocation in Translation." *TTR: Traduction, terminologie, rédaction* 22, no. 1 (2009): 167–87.

Sánchez Prado, Ignacio M., ed. *América Latina en la "literatura mundial."* Pittsburgh: Instituto Internacional de Literatura Iberoamericana, 2006.

———. "The Persistence of the Transcultural: A Latin American Theory of the Novel from the National-Popular to the Global." *New Literary History* 51 (2020): 347–74.

———. "The Pre-Columbian Past as a Project: Miguel León-Portilla and Hispanism." In *Ideologies of Hispanism*, edited by Mabel Moraña, 40–61. Nashville: Vanderbilt University Press, 2005.

Santí, Enrico Mario, ed. *Archivo Blanco*. By Octavio Paz et al. Madrid: Ediciones Turner, 1995.

Sawyer-Lauçanno, Christopher. *E. E. Cummings: A Biography*. Naperville, IL: Sourcebooks, 2004.

Scandolara, Adriano. "Via: 17 Variações de Dante." In "Via, de Caroline Bergvall." *escamandro*. September 30, 2014. https://escamandro.wordpress.com/2014/09/30/via-de-caroline-bergvall/.

Seruya, Teresa, et al. "Introduction: Translation Anthologies and Collections. An Overview and Some Prospects." In *Translation in Anthologies and Col-*

lections (19th and 20th Centuries), edited by Teresa Seruya, Lieven D'hulst, Alexandra Assis Rosa, and Maria Lin Moniz, 1–13. Amsterdam: John Benjamins, 2013.

Sheller, Mimi. *Consuming the Caribbean: From Arawaks to Zombies*. London: Routledge, 2003.

Shellhorse, Adam. *Anti-Literature: The Politics and Limits of Representation in Modern Brazil and Argentina*. Pittsburgh: University of Pittsburgh Press, 2017.

———. "Augusto de Campos." In *Twenty-First-Century Brazilian Writers*, edited by Monica Rector and Robert N. Andreson, 69–80. Farmington Hills, MI: Gale Cengage, 2019.

———. "The Verbivocovisual Revolution: Anti-Literature, Affect, Politics, and World Literature in Augusto de Campos." *CR: The New Centennial Review* 20, no. 1 (Spring 2020): 147–84.

Sheridan, Guillermo. *Habitación con retratos: Ensayos sobre la vida de Octavio Paz*. Vol. 2. Mexico City: Ediciones Era, 2015.

———. *Poeta con paisaje: Ensayos sobre la vida de Octavio Paz*. Vol. 1. Mexico City: Ediciones Era, 2004.

Simeoni, Daniel. "Translation and Society: The Emergence of a Conceptual Relationship." In *In Translation: Reflections, Refractions, Transformations*. Edited by Paul St-Pierre and P. C. Kar. Amsterdam: John Benjamins, 2007, 13–26.

Simon, Sherry. *Gender in Translation: Cultural Identity and the Politics of Transmission*. London: Routledge, 1996.

Siskind, Mariano. *Cosmopolitan Desires: Global Modernity and World Literature in Latin America*. Evanston, IL: Northwestern University Press, 2014.

———. "The Genres of World Literature: The Case of Magical Realism." In D'haen, Damrosch, and Kadir, *The Routledge Companion to World Literature*, 345–55.

Sloterdijk, Peter. *Rage and Time: A Psychopolitical Investigation*. Translated by Mario Wenning. New York: Columbia University Press, 2010.

Solt, Mary Ellen, and Willis Barnstone, eds. *Concrete Poetry: A World View*. Bloomington: Indiana University Press, 1968.

Soto Román, Carlos, trans. "Via." By Caroline Bergvall. In "'A=A: Conceptualismo como traducción,' de Vanessa Place / 'Via,' de Caroline Bergvall" *Letras en línea*, July 29, 2013. https://letrasenlinea.uahurtado.cl/aa-conceptualismo-como-traduccion-de-vanessa-place-via-de-caroline-bergvall/.

Spivak, Gayatri. *Death of a Discipline*. New York: Columbia University Press, 2003.

Stam, Robert, and Ella Shohat. *Race in Translation: Culture Wars around the Postcolonial Atlantic*. New York: New York University Press, 2012.

Steele, Cynthia. "Entrevista." Interview with Elena Poniatowska. *Hispamérica* 18, nos. 53–54 (1989): 89–105.

———. "Power, Gender, and Canon Formation in Mexico." *Studies in 20th Century Literature* 20, no. 1 (1996): 65–100.

Steinberg, Samuel. *Photopoetics at Tlatelolco: Afterimages of Mexico, 1968*. Austin: University of Texas Press, 2016.

Strand, Mark, trans. "The Shame of the Olympics" by Octavio Paz. *New York Review of Books*, November 7, 1968.

Strasser, Melanie. "Tradução canibal? Sobre a poética da tradução de Haroldo de Campos." In *Poesia-Crítica-Tradução: Haroldo de Campos e a educação dos sentidos*, edited by Eduardo Jorge de Oliveira and Kenneth David Jackson, 319–331. Berlin: Peter Lang, 2022.

Süssekind, Flora, and Júlio Castañon Guimarães, eds. *Sobre Augusto de Campos*. Rio de Janeiro: Edições Casa de Rui Barbosa / 7 Letras, 2004.

Tápia, Marcelo. "O eco antropofágico: Reflexões sobre a transcriação e a metáfora sanguíneo-canibalesca." In *Transcriação*, by Haroldo de Campos, edited by Marcelo Tápia and Thelma Médici Nóbrega, 215–32. São Paulo: Editora Perspectiva, 2013.

Tomlinson, Charles. "Textos y poemas." Translated by Ulalume González de León and Octavio Paz. *Plural* 22 (July 1973): 3–5.

Trilling, Lionel, ed. *Perspectives USA* 2 (Winter 1952).

Trilling, Lionel, and Edouard Roditi, eds. *Profils* 2 (1953).

Tymoczko, Maria. "Cultural Hegemony and the Erosion of Translation Communities." In *A Companion to Translation Studies*, edited by Sandra Bermann and Catherine Porter, 165–78. Chichester, UK: Wiley-Blackwell, 2014.

Vendler, Helen. *Last Looks, Last Books: Stevens, Plath, Lowell, Bishop, Merrill.* Princeton, NJ: Princeton University Press, 2010.

Venuti, Lawrence. "The Poet's Version; or, An Ethics of Translation." *Translation Studies* 4, no. 2 (2011): 230–47.

———, ed. *The Translation Studies Reader*. 2nd ed. New York: Routledge, 2004.

———. "World Literature and Translation Studies." In D'haen, Damrosch, and Kadir, *The Routledge Companion to World Literature*, 180–93.

Verani, Hugo J. "José Emilio Pacheco: La voz complementaria." *Revista de Crítica Literaria Latinoamericana* 24, no. 47 (1998): 281–92.

Von Flotow, Luise. "Contested Gender in Translation: Intersectionality and Metramorphics." *Palimpsestes* 22 (2009): 245–55.

Von Flotow, Luise, and Hala Kamal, eds. *The Routledge Handbook of Translation, Feminism, and Gender*. London: Routledge, 2020.

Waisman, Sergio. *Borges and Translation: The Irreverence of the Periphery*. Lewisburg, PA: Bucknell University Press, 2005.

Walkowitz, Rebecca. *Born Translated: The Contemporary Novel in an Age of World Literature*. New York: Columbia University Press, 2015.

———. "Translating the Untranslatable: An Interview with Barbara Cassin." *Public Books*, June 15, 2014. https://www.publicbooks.org/translating-the-untranslatable-an-interview-with-barbara-cassin/.

Weinberger, Eliot, trans. "Interruptions from the West (3) (Mexico City: The 1968 Olympiad)." In "Paz in Fury, 1968." *Los Angeles Times*, October 14, 1990. https://www.latimes.com/archives/la-xpm-1990-10-14-op-3367-story.html.

Williams, Emmet, ed. *An Anthology of Concrete Poetry*. New York: Something Else Press, 1967.

Williams, William Carlos. *By Word of Mouth: Poems from the Spanish, 1916–1959*. Edited by Jonathan Cohen. New York: New Directions, 2011.

———. *Veinte poemas*. Translated by Octavio Paz. Mexico City: Ediciones Era, 1973.

Woodard, Vincent. *The Delectable Negro: Human Consumption and Homoeroticism within U.S. Slave Culture*. Edited by Justin A. Joyce and Dwight A. McBride. New York: New York University Press, 2014.

Wrobel, Jasmin. "Signos em rotação: Desde *Transblanco* até *Un tal Lucas*; Três exemplos dos frutíferos diálogos inter-americanos de Haroldo de Campos." *Cadernos de Literatura Comparada* 32 (2015): 205–26.

Young, Robert J. C. "Philosophy in Translation." In *A Companion to Translation Studies*, edited by Sandra Bermann and Catherine Porter, 41–53. Chichester, UK: Wiley-Blackwell, 2014.

Yun, Charse. "How the Bestseller 'The Vegetarian,' Translated from Han Kang's Original, Caused an Uproar in South Korea." *Los Angeles Times*, September 22, 2017. www.latimes.com/books/jacketcopy/la-ca-jc-korean-translation-20170922-story.html.

Zaid, Gabriel. "Poetas ejemplares." *Plural* 36 (September 1974): 91–93.

Index

Note: Page numbers in italics indicate figures.

Credits

#335 "'Tis not that Dying hurts us so." *The Poems of Emily Dickinson: Reading Edition*, edited by Ralph W. Franklin (Cambridge, MA: Belknap Press of Harvard University Press). Copyright © 1998, 1999 by the President and Fellows of Harvard College. Copyright © 1951, 1955 by the President and Fellows of Harvard College. Copyright © renewed 1979, 1983 by the President and Fellows of Harvard College. Copyright © 1914, 1918, 1919, 1924, 1929, 1930, 1932, 1935, 1937, 1942 by Martha Dickinson Bianchi. Copyright © 1952, 1957, 1958, 1963, 1965 by Mary L. Hampson. Used by permission. All rights reserved.

Excerpt from "Love Song of a Young Man." from *In the Trail of the Wind: American Indian Poems and Ritual Orations*, edited by John Bierhorst. Copyright © 1971, renewed 2000 by John Bierhorst. Reprinted by permission of Farrar, Straus and Giroux Books for Young Readers. All rights reserved.

"La flecha," from *Tarde o temprano.* © José Emilio Pacheco, 2009 y Herederos de José Emilio Pacheco

"Canción de amor de los Kwakiuti," "Cantos a las corrientes de la tierra," and excerpt from "Western," from *Aproximaciones.* © José Emilio Pacheco, 1984 y Herederos de José Emilio Pacheco.

Excerpt from "The Dry Salvages: Versión y notas de José Emilio Pacheco," by T. S. Eliot. © José Emilio Pacheco, 2011 y Herederos de José Emilio Pacheco

Translated by Maureen Ahern from Rosario Castellanos, *A Rosario Castellanos Reader*, edited by Maureen Ahern, translated by Maureen Ahern and others. Copyright © 1988. Courtesy of Fondo de Cultura Economica and the University of Texas Press.

"Dos veces antes se cerró mi vida," excerpt from "Meditación en el umbral," "Yo conocí una paloma," "Morir no hiere tanto," and excerpt from "Nota roja," from *Poesía no eres tú: Obra poética 1948–1971*, by Rosario Castellanos, D. R. © 1972, Fondo de Cultura Económica, Carretera Picacho Ajusco 227, 14738 Ciudad de México, https://elfondoenlinea.com/detalle.aspx?ctit=013922L.

Excerpt from "The Dry Salvages" from T. S. Eliot, *Four Quartets*. Copyright © 1941 by T. S. Eliot, renewed 1969 by Esme Valerie Eliot. Reprinted by permission of Mariner Books, an imprint of HarperCollins Publishers LLC. All rights reserved.

Excerpt from "The Dry Salvages" from T. S. Eliot, *Collected Poems, 1909–1962* (New York: Harcourt, 1991), 191. Reprinted by permission of Faber & Faber Ltd.

FLASHPOINTS

1. *On Pain of Speech: Fantasies of the First Order and the Literary Rant*, Dina Al-Kassim
2. *Moses and Multiculturalism*, Barbara Johnson, with a foreword by Barbara Rietveld
3. *The Cosmic Time of Empire: Modern Britain and World Literature*, Adam Barrows
4. *Poetry in Pieces: César Vallejo and Lyric Modernity*, Michelle Clayton
5. *Disarming Words: Empire and the Seductions of Translation in Egypt*, Shaden M. Tageldin
6. *Wings for Our Courage: Gender, Erudition, and Republican Thought*, Stephanie H. Jed
7. *The Cultural Return*, Susan Hegeman
8. *English Heart, Hindi Heartland: The Political Life of Literature in India*, Rashmi Sadana
9. *The Cylinder: Kinematics of the Nineteenth Century*, Helmut Müller-Sievers
10. *Polymorphous Domesticities: Pets, Bodies, and Desire in Four Modern Writers*, Juliana Schiesari
11. *Flesh and Fish Blood: Postcolonialism, Translation, and the Vernacular*, S. Shankar
12. *The Fear of French Negroes: Transcolonial Collaboration in the Revolutionary Americas*, Sara E. Johnson
13. *Figurative Inquisitions: Conversion, Torture, and Truth in the Luso-Hispanic Atlantic*, Erin Graff Zivin
14. *Cosmopolitan Desires: Global Modernity and World Literature in Latin America*, Mariano Siskind
15. *Fiction Beyond Secularism*, Justin Neuman
16. *Periodizing Jameson: Dialectics, the University, and the Desire for Narrative*, Phillip E. Wegner
17. *The Practical Past*, Hayden White
18. *The Powers of the False: Reading, Writing, Thinking Beyond Truth and Fiction*, Doro Wiese
19. *The Object of the Atlantic: Concrete Aesthetics in Cuba, Brazil, and Spain, 1868–1968*, Rachel Price
20. *Epic and Exile: Novels of the German Popular Front 1933–1945*, Hunter Bivens
21. *An Innocent Abroad: Lectures in China*, J. Hillis Miller
22. *Form and Instability: East Europe, Literature, Postimperial Difference*, Anita Starosta
23. *Bombay Modern: Arun Kolatkar and Bilingual Literary Culture*, Anjali Nerlekar
24. *Intimate Relations: Social Reform and the Late Nineteenth-Century South Asian Novel*, Krupa Shandilya
25. *Media Laboratories: Late Modernist Authorship in South America*, Sarah Ann Wells
26. *Acoustic Properties: Radio, Narrative, and the New Neighborhood of the Americas*, Tom McEnaney

27. *The New Woman: Literary Modernism, Queer Theory, and the Trans Feminine Allegory*, Emma Heaney
28. *Civilizing War: Imperial Politics and the Poetics of National Rupture*, Nasser Mufti
29. *Late Colonial Sublime: Neo-Epics and the End of Romanticism*, G. S. Sahota
30. *Globalizing Race: Anti-Semitism, Empire, and the Politics of Scale in Modern French and European Culture*, Dorian Bell
31. *Domestications: American Empire, Literary Culture, and the Postcolonial Lens*, Hosam Mohamed Aboul-Ela
32. *Behold an Animal: Four Exorbitant Readings*, Thangam Ravindranathan
33. *Capital Letters: Hugo, Baudelaire, Camus, and the Death Penalty*, Ève Morisi
34. *Immaterial Archives: An African Diaspora Poetics of Loss*, Jenny Sharpe
35. *Figures of the World: The Naturalist Novel and Transnational Form*, Christopher Laing Hill
36. *Imperfect Solidarities: Tagore, Gandhi, Du Bois, and the Forging of the Global Anglophone*, Madhumita Lahiri
37. *Fictional Environments: Mimesis, Deforestation, and Development in Latin America*, Victoria Saramago
38. *How to Read a Moment: The American Novel and the Crisis of the Present*, Mathias Nilges
39. *Secondhand China: Spain, the East, and the Politics of Translation*, Carles Prado-Fonts
40. *New World Maker: Radical Poetics, Black Internationalism, and the Translations of Langston Hughes*, Ryan James Kernan
41. *The Idea of Indian Literature: Gender, Genre, and Comparative Method*, Preetha Mani
42. *Concepts of the World*, Effie Rentzou
43. *Traces of the Unseen*, Carolina Sá Carvalho